Queenship and Power

Series Editors
Charles Beem
University of North Carolina, Pembroke
Pembroke, NC, USA

Carole Levin
University of Nebraska-Lincoln
Lincoln, NE, USA

This series focuses on works specializing in gender analysis, women's studies, literary interpretation, and cultural, political, constitutional, and diplomatic history. It aims to broaden our understanding of the strategies that queens—both consorts and regnants, as well as female regents—pursued in order to wield political power within the structures of male-dominant societies. The works describe queenship in Europe as well as many other parts of the world, including East Asia, Sub-Saharan Africa, and Islamic civilization.

More information about this series at
http://www.palgrave.com/gp/series/14523

Gillian B. Fleming

# Juana I

## Legitimacy and Conflict in Sixteenth-Century Castile

palgrave
macmillan

Gillian B. Fleming
Brighton, UK

Queenship and Power
ISBN 978-3-319-74346-2 ISBN 978-3-319-74347-9 (eBook)
https://doi.org/10.1007/978-3-319-74347-9

Library of Congress Control Number: 2017964575



Cover credit: World History Archive/Alamy Stock Photo

Printed on acid-free paper

This Palgrave Macmillan imprint is published by Springer Nature
The registered company is Springer International Publishing AG
The registered company address is: Gewerbestrasse 11, 6330 Cham, Switzerland

This statue of Juana I, by the Zamoran sculptor Hipólito Pérez Calvo, stands on the site of the royal palace of Tordesillas (Valladolid). Here she is shown with the church of San Antolín in the background (*Source* Alberto Paredes / Alamy Stock Photo)

*To the memory of Peggy and Lynda*

# Preface

In December 2003, in his column in *El Mundo*, a well-known Spanish writer, journalist and polemicist, who had recently seen and enjoyed Vicente Aranda's film *Juana la Loca*, was moved to declare that the "whole of Spain is Juana la Loca." Francisco Umbral argued that great and lucid *locos* have tried, and invariably failed, to rule or influence a land that remains, stubbornly and ungovernably, in the grip of a disparate multitude of regionalisms and particularisms. He used Juana as a metaphor for a madness and failure that is, in some sense, both heroic and inevitable.

Although the "beautiful madness" of Umbral's Juana is not the subject of this book, it does accept that failure, heroic and inevitable or not, is at least as important a subject as success. The focus here is on Juana as a political figure; on the strategies she pursued; and on the long crisis of legitimacy that arose out of her political marginalisation. In other words, it focuses on Juana I rather than Juana 'the Mad.' Popular as that latter figure became, reflected back to us by 'historical' painters of the nineteenth century such as Pradilla Ortíz, Rosales and Vallés, these convey far less about the reality of the situation than, say, Velázquez' *Black Servant*, or *Kitchen Maid with Christ at Emmaüs*—a painting which, as Norman Bryson writes in his magnificent book of essays, *Looking at the Overlooked* (1990), expresses, perhaps more eloquently than any other, "the suppression and confinement of those outside the charmed circle of history or greatness." Like Velázquez' black servant, Juana was eventually confined to her "woman's things," to the rhyparos of everyday life, so that she could not fully grasp—though perhaps overheard—the subjects of great import being discussed in the other room. Nonetheless, she belongs within the charmed circle of history to the extent that she, and her use and representation of power, mattered to her kingdoms a great deal. The purpose of this monograph is to explore how and why.

The natural constraints imposed by the choice of a relatively narrow focus on a multi-dimensional subject have obliged me to deal only summarily with much that a traditional biography would include, such as Juana's early childhood experiences and education; the personal and cultural aspects of her life; the different milieux in which her six children were raised; her queenly patronage; the successive households built around her, but with which she had little contact; the impact of her marriage and motherhood on the world beyond Castile, and so forth. As the title indicates, the focus here is on the realms of Castile, not those of Aragon, nor the lands that Juana knew in her capacity as countess of Flanders, duchess of Burgundy and archduchess of Austria; nor yet the lands across the 'Ocean Sea,' from which, in her fleeting period in government, she drew financial support. Evidently, in the realms and crown territories of Aragon and elsewhere there was also great conflict, and I am well aware of the continuing need for an in-depth examination of the impact, whether direct or indirect, of Juana's life on such areas.

Given that her political role remains widely unknown, I have adopted a chronological and narrative structure on which to base an analysis of her use and experience of power at a time of tremendous dynastic and political crisis. The unevenness of pace and time span in the narrative reflects the uneven pace of Juana's own life. Some chapters are densely packed with significant events that tumble together within a brief period; others cover years in which Juana was imprisoned and isolated from events and the 1540s remain largely a blank. Very few letters emerge from the palace of Tordesillas during that decade and very little directly affecting her was reported. One exception is the royal family's concern with the queen's irregular and unsatisfactory spiritual practices, and the two last chapters explore further the effects on Juana of her imprisonment and its connection to the concepts of 'melancholy,' 'possession' and 'penitence.'

As regards the use of sources, I would echo the former director of the Archivo General de Simancas, José Luis Rodríguez de Diego, when asking how it is possible, with respect to Juana, to "follow the vital trail of a person isolated and marginalised, on whom silence and confinement were imposed." Important letters of Juana's were sometimes deliberately destroyed, and the problem of her documentary footprint was compounded by her sense of the traps and fictions that beset her, and her refusal to sign acts of government while a prisoner. The sixteenth-century Aragonese historian, Zurita, who manipulated a vast mass of archival documents, nonetheless refers to the bafflement of those who "knew that the Queen wrote letters with such facility and ease that few of the kings of Castile and Aragon, her antecedents, could write better." Precious material then available to him and stored in the Diputación Provincial de Zaragoza perished in flames in 1809; only a small fraction of Zurita's original 'Alacena' remains. An inventory of Juana's possessions in 1545 indicates the existence of chests and letter cases full of writings (*escrituras*). Of these only a few are specifically mentioned, such as "a royal order (*cédula*) that the queen our lady sent to the bishop of León"; a navigation map; a "brief that the cardinal of Santa Cruz sent to her highness"; a "memorial that her highness wrote for the testament of the king her father about certain things that she had to send," and so on. References like this one, from Ferrandis, suggest that Juana, at least for part of her life, was a more active correspondent than we know.

While material may yet come to light, not least from private archives currently unavailable to researchers, the paucity of letters to and from Juana inevitably shifts attention to other, less direct sources, including Royal Council provisions; private correspondence; key Cortes and Junta proceedings; histories, chronicles and despatches. But diplomats were only extremely rarely granted access to Juana, whereas they enjoyed constant access to her husband, father or son, and relied greatly on hearsay. Nonetheless, some of the information conveyed by envoys and ambassadors is invaluable, not least when it is the only source for a particular event or expression of opinion.

This monograph uses a variety of documents in their source languages (Spanish, Italian, English, French and German), fleshing out the bones of a doctoral thesis awarded by the London School of Economics and Political Science in 2012. Some sources are inevitably familiar. Others have been widely overlooked in previously published studies. They include a series of recently restored and transcribed letters from Simancas, addressed to Juana as archduchess (for which all credit is due to Rodríguez de Diego); John Stile's despatches and other English contemporary accounts; formerly unpublished material from Diego de Guevara's despatches and Pedro Fernández de Velasco's memorial about his uncle, the constable of Castile. I have also consulted a manuscript in the British Library, which differs, if only slightly, in wording and spelling from the *Relación del discurso de las Comunidades*, edited and published by Ana Díaz Medina, and which includes a number of interesting letters. I would also mention the royal provisions from the time of Juana's personal rule; the marquis of Priego's appeal of 1509; and the crucial letter from Luis Ferrer to Fernando of 10 August 1511. The despatches of the Venetian ambassador, Francesco Corner, relatively little known, but of much interest for the transitional period between 1508 and 1509 are, like those of his counterpart, Vincenzo Querini, held in the archives of the Biblioteca Nazionale Marciana in Venice. Where Querini is concerned, we also have Constantin von Höfler's published transcriptions and Rawdon Brown's unpublished translations into English over a wider timescale, and housed at the National Archive in Kew (London).

The sheer brevity of Juana's effective reign did not allow for the appointment of chroniclers of her own, who could rely on her favours. The royal chroniclers accepted *a priori* Juana's inability to rule; to do anything else would have been tantamount to sedition, since those who governed for her did so on grounds of her continuing incapacity. Kagan, in *Clio and the Crown* (2009), his study of the official histories of Spanish monarchs between medieval times and the mid-eighteenth century, has highlighted the particular importance of chroniclers to Spanish monarchs. He notes that, as monarchs who attached great importance to the writing of history and left little to chance, Isabel and Fernando oversaw, coordinated and dismissed their chroniclers, who were expected to act as temporal evangelists, immortalising the *fama* of their employers and sharing their goals. In the circumstances, and given that Juana was, throughout her reign, the prisoner of kings and emperors who exercised power in her stead, it is hardly surprising that contemporary writers paid her so little serious attention. Even so, they offer glimpses of the queen and are essential for an understanding of the period.

I am grateful to many people for their help in the course of preparing this book—firstly, and most especially, for the invaluable advice, erudition, generosity and patience over time of Maria-José Rodríguez-Salgado, professor of international history at the London School of Economics and Political Science. I have also benefited greatly from the advice, kindness and encouragement of Dr. John Edwards of Oxford

University. Dame Janet Nelson, emerita professor of King's College, London, gave generously of her time and expertise in looking at early chapters and Dr. Jenny Stratford, senior research fellow at the Institute of Historical Research, London, helped open up the mysteries of paleography and the wonderful world of illuminated manuscripts. I am indebted to Dr. Raymond Fagel of Leiden University, and owe much to Isabel Aguirre Landa, *jefe de sala* of the Archivo General de Simancas. I am also beholden to Miguel-Ángel Zalama, professor of art history at the University of Valladolid, and to his work and conferences on Juana. The stimulating series of symposia on different aspects of the comunero uprising that Dr. Istvan Konrad Szászi León-Borja and María Jesús Galende Ruíz have spent so much time and labour organising at Villalar de los Comuneros in conjunction with the Ayuntamiento of Villalar and the Fundación Villalar, have been a magnet for historians throughout Spain and beyond, myself included. I have received much help and courtesy from archives and libraries in Spain, Venice, France and the UK, and, among a number of others, most particularly from the Archivo General de Simancas (Valladolid); the Archivo de la Diputación Provincial de Zaragoza; the Real Academía de la Historia and Biblioteca Nacional (Madrid); the Biblioteca Nazionale Marciana (Venice); the Archives du Département du Nord (Lille) and British Library (London). I am most grateful to the editors and production team at Palgrave Macmillan for their unfailing help and guidance. Last, but by no means least, I owe much moral support and encouragement to Ann Walker.

The dates of editions given in the bibliographical references are those of the editions I have consulted and not always the dates of first publication. All translations are my own, unless otherwise indicated. Decisions on nomenclature are seldom easy or satisfactorily consistent. Where individuals are concerned, I have generally adopted the baptismal name. But Philip is probably more familiar than Phelippe or even Philippe. Katherine, queen of England, is evidently more familiar outside Spain than Catalina. Juana's younger son is called Ferdinand (although baptised Fernando), not only to distinguish him from the king of Aragon but because, torn out of his native land at an early age, he became eventually, and universally, known as Ferdinand I. Juana's parents were more than simply the 'Catholic Kings,' for they were the monarchs of non-Catholics too. At the same time, the term expresses, better than any other, certain important things about them. Use of the word 'Spain' for this period is not always entirely anachronistic. While Juana's long list of titles shows that she was nominally queen and mistress of numerous realms and lands within the two crowns of Castile and Aragon, and 'Spain' was not yet a juridical concept, it has sometimes been used here to refer to both these kingdoms at once, and often at the time expressed an idea and aspiration. When referring to his annexation of the kingdom in Navarre in 1512, Fernando, for example, referred to its importance for completing the Spanish project ("*lo que el reino de Navarra importa para cerrar la idea de España*").

Brighton, UK Gillian B. Fleming
2017

# Contents

# Abbreviations[1]

| | |
|---|---|
| ADN | Archives du Département du Nord (Lille) |
| AGS | Archivo General de Simancas |
| C | Cédulas |
| CC | Comunidades de Castilla (subsection of PR) |
| CSR | Casas y Sitios Reales |
| PR | Patronato Real |
| RGS | Registro General del Sello |
| AHN | Archivo Histórico Nacional (Nobleza) (Toledo) |
| APD.Z | Archivo de la Diputación Provincial de Zaragoza |
| BL | British Library (London) |
| BN | Biblioteca Nacional (Madrid) |
| BNMVe | Biblioteca Nazionale Marciana (Venice) |
| CODOIN | Colección de Documentos Inéditos para la Historia de España |
| CSP. Sp. | Calendar of State Papers (Spanish) |
| RAH, Salazar | Real Academía de la Historia, Colección Salazar y Castro (Madrid) |
| RB | Real Biblioteca (Madrid) |
| TNA | The National Archive, Kew (London) |

[1]Cited in Notes and Reference lists.

# List of Figures

CHAPTER 1

# In the Footsteps of Juana I

The castle of Benavente (Zamora), in northwest Spain, was once celebrated for its gardens. Separated from the castle by a bridge spanning a tributary of the Órbiga river, they formed a series of walled parks where copses and avenues of black poplars offered shelter from the sun. There were orchards, fountains, hunting lodges, pleasure domes and ponds containing trout and barbells. The bosquet was packed with game and, in the menagerie, in 1494, the German humanist scholar Hieronymus Münzer was startled to see two lions eating with a wolf and being stroked by, and in turn caressing, a black servant.[1]

On the evening of 28 June 1506, the gardens formed the backdrop to a less tranquil scene when Alonso Pimentel, count of Benavente, played host to the new monarchs of Castile. Isabel I had died almost two years earlier, leaving her twenty-four-year-old daughter, Juana, heir to a dazzling inheritance: the realms of Castile, León, Granada, Seville, Córdoba, Murcia, Jaén, the Algarves, Algeciras, Gibraltar, the Canary Islands and the "Indies and terra firma of the Ocean Sea." She was also "lady of Vizcaya and Molina." As proprietary monarch, she, and she alone, embodied the kingdoms of Castile and only she could dispose of them. But Juana was living in Brussels when Isabel died, and her father, Fernando II of Aragon, governed Castile in her name.

In January 1506, Juana and her husband, Philip, count of Flanders, duke of Burgundy and archduke of Austria, set out to receive the oaths of allegiance of the Cortes (the Castilian parliament), and to swear, in return, to uphold Castilian rights and privileges. They travelled together,



G. B. Fleming, *Juana I*, Queenship and Power,
https://doi.org/10.1007/978-3-319-74347-9_1

but with diametrically opposed intentions. Juana was tenaciously loyal to her father. Philip was determined to oust him from Castile and marginalise Juana, through whom he claimed his legitimacy as king, and whom he treated not only as his wife but as his hostage.

That day, Philip broke catastrophic news to Juana—from her point of view. Philip and Fernando had signed a treaty ceding Castile to Philip and excluding her from power. Feigning indifference, Juana expressed a wish to visit the famous gardens. But, as she turned back to the castle, she suddenly galloped off across the park and down the hill, leaving her escorts dumbfounded. The alarm was raised. Philip's German soldiers gave chase. Juana took refuge in a bakery or flourmill. There she spent the rest of the day, the night and the following day, surrounded by hundreds of infantry under the command of Oberster Hauptmann Wolfgang zu Fürstenberg. Philip tried to persuade her to leave the place, but "I do not know," wrote Venetian ambassador, Vincenzo Querini, "how he will do it."[2]

This incident was one of several to mark the crisis of legitimacy with which this study is concerned, and was variously interpreted. Philip argued that it demonstrated her unfitness to assume the mantle of a ruling queen and asked the deputies to the Cortes to agree to her imprisonment. Others saw it as a desperate bid to escape captivity by foreign forces, poised to seize charge of kingdoms that were hers by right.

As in the case of her youngest sister, Katherine, it is against the background of her marriage that Juana has mainly been defined. Of the five children of Isabel and Fernando, she and Katherine were caught in events of immense historical significance: in the first case, through a turbulent marriage and problematic legacy that brought about a highly troubled dynastic transition, with all that this entailed for Spain and the Western world; in the second, through a no less turbulent divorce that brought about the establishment in England of a national church separated from Rome.

Juana's life and position were far from simple. She was a Trastámara queen and the last monarch of her dynasty, but she was also the mother of Charles V and thus of the Spanish Habsburg line. From 1504, she was a sovereign queen, but also a wife subjected to the ambitions of a husband of inferior status, a wily father who had ruled Castile before her and was determined to do so again, and a son who thirsted after his Spanish inheritance and controversially proclaimed himself king after Fernando's death. Juana dwelt always on and between frontiers: the shifting frontiers of the territories through which she travelled as a child; the frontiers between the Low Countries and Spain; between contractual government and creeping royal absolutism; sovereign queenship and female submission; freedom and captivity; 'sanity' and 'madness.' Beyond these considerations, and at the core of Juana's story, is a crisis that culminated in what was arguably the first modern revolutionary uprising of its kind in Europe.

To place Juana at the heart of such a crisis is to grant her an importance that has generally been denied to her by a historiographical confinement—over and above the terrible years of her real imprisonment—to the madwoman's attic or black servant's kitchen (see preface). Until relatively recently, Juana was invariably referred to as 'the Mad.' But madness, or *locura*, was a term used, in her lifetime, to cover a wide range of behaviour, from idiocy to political transgression, and applied to Juana far less frequently than the word 'indisposition.' The subsequent focus on her 'madness,' her 'insanity,' her 'dementia,' her 'crazed' this-and-that, has obscured the political dimension of her thoughts and actions and significance for Castile. Historians have brushed examples of political agency aside by recourse to the convenient device of 'moments of lucidity.' An a priori acceptance of her madness has created a tendency to see it everywhere as the mainspring of her conduct, with the very moniker '*Juana La Loca*' rendering such remarks irresistible, where elsewhere they might seem gratuitous. In his study of Henry VII (1999), Chrimes rightly comments on the lack of a critical approach to the "very successful propaganda put out by her ruthless and unscrupulous father and son." He believes it "probable that Henry VII knew or suspected the truth, which oddly appears largely to have evaded the serious consideration of modern historians."[3]

A second consequence of this approach has been a curious periodisation. Use of the word 'reign' in relation to Juana still raises eyebrows. General histories often skip from the Catholic monarchs (1474–1516) to Charles V, without any reference to the proprietary queen of Castile and Aragon and, as a specialist in fiscal history has pointed out, "in the first two decades of the sixteenth century every historian has used a different chronology."[4] Thus, the 'first regency' of Fernando (1504–1506) preceded the 'reign' of Philip of Burgundy (1506); the 'regency' of archbishop Cisneros (1506–1507) preceded the 'second regency' of Fernando (1507–1516), which was followed by the 'second regency' of Cisneros (1516–1517), eating into the 'reign' of Charles V (1516–1558).

Alternatively, many historians and history textbooks extend the dual monarchy of Isabel and Fernando to the latter's death in 1516, although he ceased to be king of Castile on Isabel's death in 1504. This allows historians to refer to Charles as the heir not of his mother, but of his grandparents. However, the confusion does not stop there. Since Charles was absent from the Spanish kingdoms for most of his life, he had to leave them in the hands of a string of 'regents.' The traditional failure to recognise a *reign* of Juana I, who remained the legitimate proprietary monarch until her death, muddies the waters of history and prevents us from being able to fully interpret the reason things happened as they did.

Over time, Juana's story shifted to suit successive preoccupations. In the Fronde years of seventeenth-century France, Juana surfaced in a *mazarinade* called *La Chronologie des Reynes Malheureuses*—a dire warning about the dangers of jealous passions in queens.[5] In the eighteenth century, the Augustinian monk Flórez asserted that Juana's nickname was based on her extravagantly grief-stricken response to Philip's death. This enduring notion, emptied by time of the political concerns that motivated and troubled Juana I, was crystallised in the popular, early twentieth-century pasodoble that many Spaniards can still cite or sing by heart:

*¿Reina Juana por qué lloras*
*si es tu pena la mejor?*
*porque no fue un mal cariño*
*que fue locura de amor.*

This verse has its visual counterparts in a series of nineteenth-century romantic paintings and sketches that pathologise widowed grief; and in nineteenth and twentieth-century poems, novels and operas—to which Juana's story naturally lends itself—Juana is the doomed hero ine of tragic personal unfulfillment or the macabre black widow of an interminable funeral cortege. Attempts to modernise her figure have largely succeeded only in perpetuating a broadly apolitical view. Vicente Aranda's film *Juana La Loca* (2001) aims to show her as a sexually liberated woman beyond her time, flouting regal propriety to flaunt herself before a shocked Philip as "your wife, your woman, your whore." Her animal nature is reinforced by a scene in which, giving birth to the future emperor in a privy, she tears off the umbilical cord with her teeth. The result is the "creation of a Juana whose sexuality and 'natural' instincts seem to be all that constitutes her persona to the exclusion of her' 'cultural' and political image as a Queen." By ironic contrast, a film that appeared in 1948—Juan de Orduña's *Locura de amor*—set out, despite the title and portrayal of Juana as a domesticated wife, to emphasise her also as a public figure and political heroine, albeit one driven by the nationalist ideals dear to Franco.[6] By the 1980s, Juana's figure had changed again. Joaquín Sabina's song, *Juana la loca*, about the family man who decides to throw a life's lies and conventions to the wind, converts her into a gay or transgendered icon:

> *y te fuiste a la calle*
> *Con tacones y bolso y Fernando el Hermoso por el talle.*
> *Desde que te pintas la boca*
> *En vez de Don Juan te llamamos Juana la loca …*

More recently, Juana re-appeared in the Spanish TV series *Isabel* and in its cinematic sequel of 2016, *La Corona Partida*, with Irene Escobar as a spirited young queen, abused both by husband and father, who eventually appears to resign herself to a life of confinement. In the same year, Spanish actress Concha Velasco toured Spain performing a monologue set by Ernesto Caballero in the last day of the queen's life. Caballero's script returns to a transgressive, religiously sceptical, intensely sexual Juana, punished for her rebelliousness and for her flouting of convention.

Any political study of Juana must penetrate the romantic aura that historians have themselves helped to generate. Commenting on the films directed by Aranda and Orduña, Martin Pérez refers to an on-going debate that oscillates between two "compelling" questions: "Was Juana really mad?" and "How much political power did she exercise?"[7] A third question is the extent to which Juana's marginalisation from power—as well as her use of and subjection to power—fomented, prolonged and accentuated the series of political crises in the first part of the sixteenth century.

The polemical modern historiography on Juana began with an excited message from east Prussian historian Bergenroth, who had been working heroically, and in the face of much official suspicion, in the General Archive of Simancas (Valladolid). He told Lord Romilly, Master of the Rolls: "No respectable historian has ever admitted a doubt about

[Juana's] insanity … Now, I find in the papers which formerly were not accessible to me, that she was never mad … that the stories of her madness were invented by her mother, her father, her husband, and at a later period, by her son, to serve their own purposes …".[8] A few months later, in 1868, Bergenroth published several volumes of state papers on Anglo-Spanish relations from Simancas, including a supplementary volume on Juana and Katherine. In this he expanded on earlier comments: "the madness of Queen Juana was, as it were, the foundation stone of the political edifice of Ferdinand and of Charles, which would have immediately crumbled to pieces if she had been permitted to exercise her hereditary right." Her life he described as "a succession of attempts at rebellion which, however, collapsed as soon as she was called upon to vindicate her independence by active measures." He concluded that a "disbelief in Roman orthodoxy" explained her marginalisation and imprisonment.[9]

Tragically, Bergenroth died before he could develop his projects further. While defending Bergenroth's scholarship, French-born, Belgium-based historian and archivist Gachard (1800–1885) maintained that Juana's extravagant conduct after Philip's death was the result, rather, of mental aberration.[10] Spanish historian Rodríguez Villa (1843–1912) denied that Juana was mad in any technical sense but gave a romantic turn to the debate when taking seriously Juana's *locura de amor*.[11] In 1885, German historian Höfler, who edited the despatches of the Venetian ambassador, Vincenzo Querini, wrote a short biography of a tragic but passive Juana, concerned only with embarrassing her husband.[12] In 1892, Rodríguez Villa returned to the subject with a major, richly documented study that remains a fundamental source on the matter.[13]

In the twentieth century, new psychiatric terms were applied. In 1930, Pfandl identified Juana as a schizophrenic who inherited and passed on her condition.[14] Other twentieth-century preoccupations, such as nationalism and Marxism, are reflected in a contrasting view by Ukrainian historian Prawdin, who takes Juana seriously as a political figure and tragic heroine.[15] Brouwer, a Dutch Hispanist, first published his study of Juana three years or so before his execution by the Nazis. He described her as an essentially enigmatic figure with an unceasing capacity to surprise, and who thus needed to be treated with caution. Actions that appeared one moment to show evidence of clouded mental powers could be seen the next as sober-minded deliberation.[16]

The second half of the twentieth century saw a turn in attitudes to madness. Notably, Foucault argued that mental illness should be understood as a cultural construct and that the history of madness should properly deal with questions of freedom and control, knowledge and power. Given the radical splits emerging within psychiatry about the nature of madness, it is unsurprising that, in the twenty-first century, Juana 'the Mad' began to disappear from scholarly studies. Even where biographers still used the term, their studies reflect reservations. Fernández Álvarez's best-selling biography, first published in 2000, has Juana suffering from depression, although he also refers to a mad obsession with Philip and an invincible repugnance to affairs of State.[17] In his depiction are valuable insights but also yawning gaps.

Aram, whose influential biography was first published in Spanish in 2001, and in English in 2005, provided a much-needed challenge to the 'psychotic' school of thought. She follows Prawdin in recovering Juana as a political figure, adding much documentary detail, but concludes that, although she had earlier shown an unwillingness to let others rule on her behalf and had herself tried to govern, Juana's ultimate political significance lay in her defence of the Habsburg dynasty. Aram adapts Kantorowicz's theory of the king's two bodies—the body politic and body natural—to the argument that, in the transition from Trastámara to Habsburg rule, Juana helped sanction "the facto disjunction between her titular rights and actual authority" by a partially compliant separation from power in order to protect Charles' interests and confirm Habsburg "corporate interests." Thus, when discussing Juana's long confinement at Tordesillas, Aram resists the notion of a bleak captivity, opting instead for a pious and ascetic retirement on the part of a queen who, although conflicted, sought to dedicate herself to a life of spiritual contemplation. Her Juana remains an ambivalent figure whose inaccessibility is both "voluntary and enforced," and who shows an "inability or unwillingness to rule."[18] These, however, are very different things, raising further fundamental questions.

In a second, revised edition of his examination of Juana at Tordesillas, published in 2002, Zalama remains convinced that Juana was unable to govern and had no interest either in political or religious life. He argues that Aram "*se traiciona a sí misma*" by insisting on a theory about Juana's "*recogimiento*" that contradicts Aram's own extensive data.[19] Zalama, an art historian, contributes invaluably to the hitherto neglected subject of Juana's long life at Tordesillas. But since he accepts from the outset that she was schizophrenic, and effectively mindless, he offers no new insights into Juana as queen. Indeed, in a subsequent work, he argues that since Juana never governed, any biography or study of her *as queen*, focusing on the events in which, to a greater or lesser degree, she was the protagonist, is a nonsense, and can be done only "in the negative."[20]

Certainly, the histories of both Trastámara and Habsburg dynasties provide plentiful examples of temperamental instability. But, in his intellectual history of Juana's great-grandson, Rudolf II, Evans is rightly sceptical about the argument (made in this instance by Luxemberger) that schizophrenia was proven in the cases of Juana I and Prince Carlos, and presumed in Charles V, Philip II, and Philip III, and that—for good measure—Rudolf's mother, the Empress María, and Rudolf's brother, Albert, were "schizoid psychopaths." All this, as Evans remarks, is "suspect territory for the historian."[21] Juana's disposition was certainly aggravated by the effects of long-term imprisonment, and by social and political isolation. But, to borrow from Evans' observation of Rudolf, it remains doubtful that Juana was mad in any serious technical sense, while much hinges on the meaning of words like 'melancholy' and 'possession.'

In recent years various Spanish medieval historians have been willing to accept a political role for Juana. Valdeón Baruque has described her as a woman of "undoubted character," whose figure was not nearly as negative as traditionally believed. Del Val Valdivieso has observed that Juana showed a wish to govern, or co-govern. A brief study by Lorenzo Arribas describes a queen whose more extreme patterns of conduct were principally determined by deprivation of freedom of movement.[22] Nonetheless, the overall neglect of Juana by those who have taken an advance position on her incapacity, even suggesting dementia, has made it almost inevitable that the successive conflicts between 1504–1522 have been seen as struggles between kings, or between kings and their subjects, marginalising the queen from any role in events. The struggle for power between 1506, for example, is almost invariably seen as a duel between Fernando and Philip. This means that any attempt to admit the 'mad' Juana's involvement in events verges on the surreal. Rawdon Brown, who translated the despatches of Vincenzo Querini into English, writes, for instance, that: "... on more than one occasion, the victor in this political duel [Philip] was very nearly outwitted by his demented consort, who single-handedly did her utmost to thwart him on every occasion."[23] This does not prevent Brown from continuing to describe the struggle as a "duel." At the same time, the events of the period are often seen as pre-determined. For Blockmans, the death of Fernando and the incapability of Juana meant that Charles was "obliged to take possession of the considerable heritage of the Spanish kingdoms and south of Italy."[24] This sense of inevitability not only throws a smokescreen over the real drama of the period, but means that little serious attention has been paid to the second of the questions mentioned by Martín Pérez: how much political power did Juana exercise?

This raises, in turn, the question of the meaning, or meanings, of power. Juana's enduring attraction for popular culture owes much to her historical obscurity and to the fact that she seemed to wield 'power' so little. As the Spanish ambassador, Pedro de Ayala, once cynically remarked of Henry VII's wife, Elizabeth of York, she was beloved because she was powerless.[25] However, in her study of medieval queenship in Europe, Earenfight argues that a queen's indirect or passive power could be as powerful as any other.[26] With reference to the Emma, queen consort of England, Denmark and Norway, Stafford similarly looks to a wider definition of power than that traditionally focused on coercion and force. It can, for instance, be seen as "the ability or chance to realise our own will, if necessary against the resistance of others. It is efficacy, that is the ability to act effectively, to produce effects, with some definitions concerning coercion, threat and force." As she remarks, some feminist anthropologists, concerned with an overemphasis on coercion, "prefer to stress that power is the ability to have and follow a strategy, to be a social actor, to have long- and short-term aims and to be able to follow them—with the emphasis on strategy and pursuit rather than primarily on successful outcome." She calls this "power as process."[27]

In his study of power, Lukes has argued that 'negative' actions, or failures to act, "can sometimes properly be seen as actions with consequences" and that *positive* actions have no special significance; there are times when to act can, in reality, be a sign of weakness.[28] Clark has pointed out that the German language has at least three words for power: *Gewalt* (the ability to compel people to do what they do not necessarily wish to do); *Herrschaft* (the dominion of a lord, monarch or executive); and *Macht* (the ability to make decisions or achieve outcomes).[29] Elsewhere, Butler, whose work has been influenced by her reading of Kafka, has examined *The Pyschic Life of Power* in terms of subjection to power as a force in human formation. Kafka struggled throughout his life with the overbearing power of his father and, when considering the sheer ungraspable nature of power that his novels, *The Trial* and *The Castle,* evoke, Clark memorably refers to a "line of flight" from father back to father, a "long corridor plunged in deepening shadow, at the end of which there could be no definite reckoning with power."[30]

In this study, power is seen in various guises. It is force and coercion and also the extraordinary use of deception and illusion. It is process and strategy and 'negative' as well as 'positive' strength. Juana sometimes used power, in the abovementioned sense of *Macht*, to great effect, though rarely in her own best interests. At the same time, Juana became gradually aware of an insidious force working within herself—a subjection to her parents' terrifying psychic power.

Juana I was, by any standards, a failed queen regnant. As I argue here, this does not mean that her period of personal rule between 1506 and 1507 was of less than fundamental importance to Castile, or that it did not point strongly to her willingness, ability and desire to govern. But it was far too brief to allow for the drawing of definite conclusions about the kind of ruler she might have become. It is more fruitful to focus on Juana as a key player at the heart of a deep and lengthy crisis of legitimacy, and to demonstrate the way in which her changing attitudes and strategies, and use of, as well as subjection to, power influenced a crucial period of transition for Spain and Europe.

Juana was the unique embodiment of royal legitimacy and her tragedy was also her kingdoms' tragedy. As the mother of Charles V, she successfully defended her eldest son as the heir to Castile and Aragon. But this should not obscure the fact that she showed no wish to abandon a political life and that she saw Castile, in essence, as the realm of her childhood and as a primarily Trastámaran domain. During her effective reign and the months she spent with the Junta and General Cortes of 1520, as well as during her long years as a political prisoner, she struggled to give meaning to her life, proprietary status and royal authority, and to uphold the values with which she was familiar. These were Isabelline and Castilian rather than Caroline and imperial.

The crisis of legitimacy to which the title refers began with the death of Juana's brother in 1497 and reached a climax with the revolutionary war of the Comunidades. Accumulating resentment and conflict over the question of lawful right drove a tremendous political storm belt across the Spanish kingdoms and buffeted other parts of Europe in the first decades of the sixteenth century. Legitimacy, in this context, is linked not only to the legal and hereditary right of royal succession but to the notion of the honour and integrity of land and pueblo and the values of 'community' or *Comunidad*. Juana acted, or tried to act, in defence of the royal patrimony and of her realms, while her political adversaries, for whom she was fundamentally and dangerously irresponsible, or simply useless, couched their opposition to her right to exercise power in alternative legitimating terms of justice and the 'common good.' Even after the defeat of the Comunidades, and even though a prisoner, Juana continued to embody the Spanish and Trastámara patrimony and any attempt to dispose of her kingdoms remained dubious in law. Thus, the problem of legitimacy did not truly end until her death in 1555.

Given the concern of this monograph with conflict and legitimacy, it is inevitable that it should focus, to the exclusion of much else, on a description and analysis of the queen as a political figure, including her relations with the nobility and cities, and the way in which she was perceived. It differs from the major studies mentioned above in its depiction of Juana as a queen who not only played a political role but clung to her Trastámara inheritance and identity and whose bitter and lifelong struggle against marginalisation and captivity formed her main *raison d'être*. There are, of course, many other Juanas—as many, perhaps, as there are histories, essays, novels, films, theatrical dramas, poems, songs, operas, flamenco shows and ballets. There will never be a definitive Juana, for, as Brouwer noted, anyone seeking to grapple with a figure as elusive as the last Trastámara monarch is obliged to construct, with the remaining fragments, a narrative that cannot hope to be more than flawed and partial. As Brouwer also knew, those same shards of evidence warn against the discovery of a single truth. In Arnold's words, the idea of a *single* true story is "tremendously attractive, and hence tremendously dangerous."[31] But despite the fact that the vast bulk of the historiography has "disappeared" Juana, except as madwoman in the attic or maid in history's kitchen, marginal to the great events happening nearby, these fragments tell us that another story is possible. That story is about Juana as a central figure at the heart of the first troubled decades of sixteenth-century Castile and about the impact of her life on her realms and beyond.

## Notes

1. Münzer (Firth, ed. 2014).
2. Querini (Höfler, ed. 1884), 118, 29 June 1506.
3. Chrimes (1999), 292, 292n.
4. Alonso García (2007), 349.

5. BL, Collection Giuliano Mazzarini (Paris, 1649).
6. Martin Pérez (Marsh/Nair, eds. 2004), 71–85.
7. Martin Pérez, 83.
8. Cartwright (1870), 171.
9. Bergenroth (1868), x, xxv, xxxi, lxvii.
10. Gachard (1869a, b).
11. Rodríguez Villa (1874).
12. Höfler (1885).
13. Rodríguez Villa (1892).
14. Pfandl (1930).
15. Prawdin (1938).
16. Brouwer (1949).
17. Fernández Álvarez (2002).
18. Aram (2005), 164, 165, 169.
19. Zalama (2003), 12.
20. Zalama (2010), 11.
21. Evans (1997), 48–49.
22. Valdeón Baruque (2006); Del Val Valdivieso (2005); Lorenzo Arribas (2004).
23. Brown, ed. TNA, PRO 31/14.1, f. 8 (introduction).
24. Blockmans (2002).
25. For Elizabeth of York see Okerlund (2009).
26. Earenfight (2013).
27. Stafford (Duggan, ed. 2002), 11.
28. Lukes (2005), 77.
29. Clark (Rublack, ed. 2011).
30. Butler (1997); Clark, 153–154.
31. Arnold (2000), 118.

## References

Alonso García, David. 2007. *El Erario del Reino: Fiscalidad en Castilla a principios de la Edad Moderna, 1504–1525*. Valladolid: Junta de Castilla y León.

Aram, Bethany. 2005. *Juana the Mad: Sovereignty and Dynasty in Renaissance Europe*. Baltimore and London: John Hopkins University Press.

Arnold, John. 2000. *History: A Very Short Introduction*. Oxford: Oxford University Press.

Bergenroth, G.A. (ed.). 1868. *Calendar of State Papers, Spanish, Supplement to Vol. 1 and Vol. 2 of Letters, Despatches and State Papers Relating to the Negociations Between England and Spain, Preserved in the Archives of Simancas and Elsewhere*. London: Longmans, Green, Reader and Dyer.

Blockmans, Wim. 2002. *Emperor Charles V, 1500–1558*. London and New York: Arnold.

Brouwer, J. 1949. *Johanna de Waanzinnige. Een tragisch leven in een bewogen tijd*. Amsterdam: J.M. Meulenhoff.

Brown, Rawdon (ed.). 1872. *Transcripts and Translations from the Despatches and Reports of Vincenzo Querini, 1505–1506* (TNA).

Butler, Judith. 1997. *The Psychic Life of Power: Theories in Subjection*. Stanford: Stanford University Press.

Cartwright, William Cornwallis. 1870. *Gustave Bergenroth: A Memorial Sketch*. Edinburgh: Edmonston and Douglas.

Chrimes, S.B. 1999. *Henry VII*. New Haven and London: Yale University Press.

Clark, Christopher. 2011. Power. In *A Concise Companion to History*, ed. Ulinka Rublack, 130–154. Oxford: Oxford University Press.

Del Val Valdivieso, María Isabel. 2005. *Isabel la Católica y su Tiempo*. Granada: Universidad de Granada.

Earenfight, Theresa. 2013. *Queenship in Medieval Europe*. London and New York: Palgrave Macmillan.

Evans, R.J.W. 1997. *Rudolf II and His World*. London: Thames and Hudson.

Fernández Álvarez, Manuel. 2002. *Juana La Loca: La Cautiva de Tordesillas*. Madrid: Espasa.

Gachard, Louis-Prosper. 1869a. Sur Jeanne La Folle et les documents concernant cette princesse qui ont été publiés récemment. In *Bulletins de l'Académie Royale des Sciences, des Lettres et des Beaux-Arts de Belgique (BARB)*, 2ème série, 27. Brussels: M. Hayez.

———. 1869b. *Sur Jeanne La Folle et la publication de M. Bergenroth*. BARB, 2ème série, 28. Brussels: M. Hayez.

Höfler, C.R. (ed.). 1884. *Depeschen des Venetianischen Botschafters Dr Vincenzo Querino, 1505–1506*. Vienna: Österreichische Akademie der Wissenschaften, Archiv für Kunde österreischer Gechichts-Quellen, Band 66–67.

———. 1885. *Donna Juana, Königin von Leon, Castilien und Granada*. Vienna: Denkschriften der Kaiserlichen Akademie der Wissenschaften.

Lorenzo Arribas, Josemi. 2004. *Juana I de Castilla y Aragón (1479–1555)*. Madrid: Ediciones del Orto.

Lukes, Steven. 2005. *Power: A Radical View*. Basingstoke and New York: Palgrave Macmillan.

Martin Pérez, Celia. 2004. Madness, Queenship and Womanhood in Orduña's *Locura de amor* (1948) and Aranda's *Juana la loca* (2001). In *Gender and Spanish Cinema*, ed. Steven Marsh and Parvati Nair. Oxford and New York: Berg Publishers.

Münzer, Hieronymus. 2014. *Dr Hieronymus Münzer's Itinerary and the Discovery of Guinea*, ed. James Firth. London: Firth.

Okerlund, Arlene Naylor. 2009. *Elizabeth of York*. London and New York: Palgrave Macmillan.

Pfandl, Ludwig. 1930. *Johanna die Wahnsinnige*. Freiburg im Bresgau: Herder.

Prawdin, Michael. 1938. *Johanna die Waansinnige: Habsburgs Weg zum Weltreich*. Vienna: Otto Lorenz Verlag.

Rodríguez Villa, Antonio. 1874. *Bosquejo biográfico de la reina Doña Juana*. Madrid: Aribau.

———. 1892. *La Reina Doña Juana La Loca: Estudio histórico*. Madrid: Murillo.

Stafford, Pauline. 2002. Emma: The Powers of the Queen in the Eleventh Century. In *Queens and Queenship in Medieval Europe*, ed. Anne Duggan. Woodbridge: Boydell Press.

Valdeón Baruque, Julio. 2006. La Reina y sus Planteamientos Políticos. In *Doña Juana, Reina de Castilla*. Madrid and Barcelona: Fundación Rafael del Pino/ Real Academía de la Historia/Marcial Pons.

Zalama, Míguel-Ángel. 2003. *Vida cotidiana y Arte en el Palacio de la Reina Juana I en Tordesillas*. Valladolid: Universidad de Valladolid.

———. 2010. *Juana I. Arte, Poder y Cultura en torno a una reina que no gobernó*. Madrid: Centro de Estudios Europa Hispánica.

CHAPTER 2

# 'Señora Archiduquesa' (1496–1497)

## 2.1 Voyage into the Unknown

At midnight on 22 August 1496, a fleet of some 130 ships set sail from Laredo (Cantabria) under the command of Fadrique Enríquez, admiral of Castile. Bound for the Low Countries, the fleet had at its core an armada of two huge carracks from Genoa, fifteen naos, five caravels and twenty swift pinnaces. In its protective shadow, a number of merchant vessels, linked to the wool trade, were expected to offer auxiliary firepower if needed. The voyage, as Isabel I told Henry VII, "is very dangerous on account of the many French ships now at sea."[1]

Isabel was referring not only to hostilities with France and to the unpredictability of Atlantic swell waves, winds and currents, but to the mission's extreme political and dynastic sensitivity: to send one bride to the Low Countries and bring another to Castile. Much of the matrimonial architecture and destiny of two of Europe's greatest dynasties depended on the success of this exchange.

The bride who set sail on that shining night was the third child and second daughter of the Catholic Kings.[2] Born in Toledo on 6 November 1479, Juana had been known since childhood as the '*señora archiduquesa*' on account of her betrothal to Philip of Burgundy, son of Mary of Burgundy and Maximilian I, king of the Romans, and subsequently Holy Roman Emperor. France's growing power threatened the interests of much of Europe and, at the end of 1488, Maximilian had sent Baudouin of Lille ('Bastard of Burgundy') and Juan de Salazar


G. B. Fleming, *Juana I*, Queenship and Power,
https://doi.org/10.1007/978-3-319-74347-9_2

('Salazar the Small') to negotiate marriage alliances with the Spanish monarchs. These resulted in the betrothals of Juana to Philip, and of Juan to Philip's sister, Margaret.

The double union had assumed special urgency after August 1494, when Charles VIII of France invaded Italy, as a first step towards the liberation of Constantinople and Jerusalem from the Turks—a dream shared by many of Christendom's rulers. The ease with which Charles' forces cut through Pavia, Pisa and Florence and won Naples horrified his European neighbours—not least Juana's father, Fernando II of Aragon, who saw the kingdom of Naples as his by right. On 31 March, the League of Venice, or Holy League, was formed against Charles, bringing the Spanish kingdoms and Holy Roman Empire together with the papacy, duchies of Milan and Mantua and republics of Venice and Florence. The marriage contracts, signed at Antwerp (Brabant) on 20 January 1495, declared the double union to be a "triple knot," tying the Spanish kingdoms to the Holy Roman Empire and Low Countries in defence of the Catholic faith, peace, prosperity and the common good. These, the agreement specified, depended on the need to maintain the balance of power, particularly in Italy. Instead of a dower, Juana and Margaret would each receive an annual payment of 20,000 gold ecus from their country of destination within two months of union.

On 5 November, the double marriage was celebrated by proxy at the church of St Petrus en Pauluskerk in Malines/Mechelen. On 10 December, a ceremonial exchange of nuptial rings took place in Brussels and Philip wrote to his "tenderly cherished bride," regretting the continuing separation between them and expressing hopes for a fine progeny. On 3 January 1496, Juana ratified the union. Her brother took part in a similar ceremony on 25 January. During the last stage of a complex procedure, at Brussels on 11 April, Philip and Margaret promised to respect all the terms of the agreement.[3]

It has been said that Juana was the only daughter of the Catholic Kings (the title conferred by the pope in 1494) to marry beneath her.[4] However, it might equally be said that she was the only daughter likely to become an empress. From the viewpoint of strategic importance and cultural splendour, Philip's maternal inheritance was greater than most and, while the imperial legacy was uncertain, given the theoretically elective nature of the imperial title, he was a likely successor to the throne of Charlemagne. Yet the lack of a regal title had long irked the dukes of Burgundy and may explain a "sort of political megalomania" which, according to Calmette, "seemed to lie behind the House of Burgundy's obsessional determination to outshine in splendour every other dynasty in Christendom, to reach the front rank of sovereign states."[5] Maximilian, for his part, had no doubt about the glory a regal title bestowed, reminding his son that the house of Austria "*est la primière* [sic] *noble et ancienne maison selon l'ancienneté de toutes les maisons et royaumes du monde.*"[6]

The assembly of the fleet casts its own light on dynastic policy and self-presentation towards the end of the reign of the Catholic Kings, as well as on the relative wealth and maritime expertise of Castile, with its flourishing wool trade; its major international trading centres in Seville and Burgos; its great international fairs at Villalón, Medina del Campo and Medina de Rioseco; and its iron foundries and shipyards in the Basque Country. The contribution of the smaller kingdom of Aragon was, perhaps, most evident in Juana's magnificent trousseau: in her Italian silks, carpets and cushions, trunks and cutlery; in the clavi-organ from Zaragoza—a formidable instrument that must have deeply impressed her when she first saw it, or the similar one that had been presented to her brother—and in the Valencian perfumes and sweetmeats for which, in earlier years, Fernando would send his Aragonese officials "a thousand blessings" on the children's behalf.[7]

With Fernando in Roussillon, where a new front had opened against France, the overall task of supervision was Isabel's and demonstrates the organisational skills and almost obsessive grasp of detail of a queen who had acquired a reputation for the quality of her military field hospitals during the Granadan campaigns of 1482–1492.[8] The fleet was intended to deter, but also to impress. The loyalty to the monarchy of important noble houses, such as those of Enríquez and Manrique, secured or reinforced by the Granadan campaigns, was reflected in their cooperation in the assembly of the vessels, in the infanta's personal household and in her wider accompaniment. Beyond a nucleus of over ninety-six household members, up to 200 persons surrounded her. The total number of men who sailed, over and beyond the 4,500 crew and military, was possibly as many as 15,000.

Isabel gave strict orders with respect to Juana's on-board health, comfort and safety. Heavy artillery was placed on the carracks and several Basque pilots travelled on the infanta's. All flames, except those in lanterns, had to be extinguished by nightfall. Juana, her three dueñas, her eight ladies and other high-ranking women were to eat white bread baked with flour from Tierra de Campos. Her drinking water was to be filtered and supplied in ceramic containers. Chroniclers and poets recorded the valedictory tears shed by the queen and her children, including Catalina, the later 'Katherine of Aragon,' whose destiny was to follow Juana across northern waters. The queen, wrote Milanese humanist chronicler and epistler, Pietro Martire de Anghiera, was "tormented not to know whether she has escaped the Charybdian whirlpools of the Britannic sea, or whether she has yet crossed the sandbanks of Flanders in the Arctic Ocean." Isabel continually interrogated Columbus and other mariners experienced in tidal seas.[9]

A contemporary poet shows Isabel dogging her daughter's footsteps, weighed down with sorrow at the thought of separation from someone she "loved more than herself."[10] Nonetheless, the fact that Juana's departure was, in all probability, definitive, points up the sacrificial nature of the dynastic imperative. The great humanist scholar, Desiderius Erasmus, who knew Philip, and probably Juana, describes the particularly "heartless" effect of exogamic marriages on girls "sent away into remote places, to men who have no similarity of language, appearance, character or habits, just as if they were being abandoned to exile."[11] Political and dynastic considerations overrode all such reservations. Ruling dominance by a particular family or bloodline—in this case the house of Trastámara—enshrined the notion of a sacred mission, and not merely the temporary embodiment of collective rights to lands and titles. The notion of dynasty, as Rodríguez-Salgado remarks, shared "the time span of the angels (*aevum*); only God occupied the third level (*aeternitas*)." A dynasty's members were bound by an unbreakable bond. Each owed obedience to the head and each was at the disposal of the head for the "greater glory of the whole."[12]

Demands on that obedience and disposability were particularly striking in the case of daughters and wives. Countless mirrors of princes, or conduct books, of the time stress the importance of subjection to parents and husbands, from the *Siete Partidas*, the major compendium of law put together in the reign of Alfonso X of Castile, to the *Llibre de les dones* (Book of Women) by Oxford-educated Catalan Franciscan, Francesc Eiximenis (c. 1327–1409). Isabel had commissioned a Castilian translation of this work, *Carro de las Donas*, and Juana had her own copy.[13] The scope of Eiximenis's highly influential writing cannot be covered here. For Eiximenis, however, the fact that there was no greater wickedness than a woman's made the education of royal and noble girls, and the need to train them—in effect, to break them in—of the utmost importance.[14] Womanly obedience is also a theme in popular works of literature such as Diego de San Pedro's *Cárcel de Amor* (1492) , along with the all-consuming importance of honour and the preservation of *fama*, reputation. In this complex novel, references to which will recur in this study, the anxiety about *fama* of the heir to the throne, Princess Laureola, and the extent of her filial obedience—even after her father imprisons and sentences her to death as the consequence of a suspected affair with a noble vassal—are truly striking, if arguably thought excessive by the book's author and narrator.

Unlike Laureola, Juana was not her father's heir at the time. But she resembled the fictional princess in her pride, sensitivity and acute consciousness of status and rank. She was remarkably well-educated. Her tutors seem to have included Isabel's confessor, Fernando de Talavera, and the remarkable Beatríz de Galinda ('La Latina'), described in Baeza's court accounts as a *criada*.[15] She was also clever, and her Dominican tutor, Andrés Miranda, who travelled with her in 1496, boasted of her learning and courtly and linguistic skills to German physician and traveller, Dr. Hieronymus Münzer, during a visit the latter made to court in 1494: "The second daughter, called Joanna, is (for a girl) good and fluent in speaking and singing. She is 14; she greatly enjoys literature."[16] Her abilities were later remarked upon, among others, by Martire (in general no admirer); the anonymous author of an updated edition of Eiximenis' work, who described her as "very judicious and well-read" (at least before her widowhood); and by Zurita (see preface).[17]

Juana, with her fondness for literature, may herself have read *Cárcel de Amor*, which Isabel had in her library and which, in its preface, refers specifically to Juana's friend, Marina Manuel de la Cerda. This high-ranking lady of the court, great granddaughter of the famous author of the *Libro del conde Lucanor*, and the woman to whom San Pedro had dedicated his earlier *Sermón*, married Baudouin of Lille in 1489, in a possibly deliberate preparation for Juana's marriage. But, whatever Juana thought of the teachings of Eiximenis and of other 'mirrors of princes'—and, indeed, of the lessons to be drawn from San Pedro's bestseller—her mixed emotions as she prepared to embark for the Low Countries were evident at least to the closest members of her entourage. Juana later referred to her homesickness and anguish, in particular over her separation from Isabel.[18]

Zalama cites an order of Isabel's of November 1495, forbidding entry to Juana's rooms and communication with her female staff, as evidence of the "first symptoms of the strange conduct that Juana's actions would soon make patent."[19] But, notwithstanding the roller-coasting emotions of an infanta poised to leave family, friends and homeland forever, the notion that her parents would have risked honour and reputation by committing to so costly and prestigious an enterprise a daughter who bore signs of mental illness seems wildly improbable. It is unclear to just what degree Isabel and Fernando were aware of the political differences between the emperor and his son, but Isabel's biographer, Azcona, rightly refers to the great expectations that Isabel had of the marriage.[20]

Still, Juana's departure was more challenging in its way than any yet experienced by her close relatives. Juana was bred to grace a foreign court and, as Duindam observes, it was dynastic practice for 'princesses' to travel long distances to join the courts of their ruling husbands.[21] However, long journeys were not always frequent ones. The last Castilian infanta to marry into a northern European dynasty had been Constanza, daughter of Pedro I, who had married John of Gaunt in 1372, and whose own daughter (Juana's maternal great grandmother), Catherine of Lancaster, had later married Enrique III of Castile. The only members of Juana's immediate family yet to travel abroad to marry were her elder sister, Isabel, and her maternal grandmother, Isabel de Avís, secluded at Arévalo (Ávila). Juana's elder sister would twice cross the Portuguese frontier as a bride—in 1490 and 1497—but these were relatively modest journeys and the country of destination known to her from childhood. Isabel herself, as queen regnant, and formerly as princess (a title that, in the Spanish realms, was conferred exclusively on heirs to the throne), had none of the personal experience of exogamy that queens consort habitually imparted to their daughters.[22] Thus, it is no exaggeration to describe Juana's journey as a voyage into the unknown. But momentous as it was, no-one could have seen it at the time as a departure marking what has been called the "most transcendental event in the relationship of Spain with Europe in the whole of the modern era."[23]

## 2.2 Welcome, Janne, and Protect Us!

By the end of August, the fleet had come within sight of Zeeland but was beaten back to Portland (Dorset) on the English coast. It finally made landfall at Arnemuiden in early September. Before negotiating the sandbanks of Walcheren, Juana transferred from her cumbersome carrack, the *Lomollina*, to a slighter nao.[24] It was a sensible precaution;

the other carrack foundered, resulting in the loss of much of that painstakingly gathered trousseau.

In his later idealised autobiography, *Der Weiß Kunig*, Maximilian shows Philip and his retinue greeting Juana as she disembarks. The archduke leans eagerly forward in fine brocade. He wears a collar of the Golden Fleece and a ducal hat, or perhaps an anticipatory crown. But the scene is an imaginative, and perhaps compensatory, re-creation. That April, Philip had set out for Germany and the Tyrol for a summit with Maximilian that would be stormy, and despite the impression given in earlier letters to Juana and her parents, Philip did not show much urgency to get home.[25] In his place, members of his *Conseil privé* had been instructed to receive Juana at Bruges, but winds and currents decided otherwise and in Zeeland only a small party awaited her. Significantly, these were all keen supporters of the Spanish marriage and included her friend, Marina Manuel, and Marina's sister-in-law, Anne of Burgundy, wealthy and powerful widow of Adolphe of Cleves-Ravenstein.[26] Juana also met various members of the Berghes family, and within days became godmother to the child of Jean III de Berghes. Jean was Philip's first chamberlain and the brother of Henri, bishop of Cambray, who counted Erasmus among his secretaries and was the president of Philip's council.

Difficulties in communication cannot alone explain the anticlimactic nature of Juana's arrival. Although Maximilian had eagerly promoted a Spanish marital alliance and had the support of the Berghes and their close ally, Margaret of York—the dowager duchess of Burgundy, fondly known as 'Madame la Grande'—it remained controversial with other key advisers, including Philip's former tutor, François de Busleyden, bishop of Besançon. Maximilian's will had driven the marriage forward, but had not secured Philip's agreement to the anti-French alliance on which the marriage was based.

Clues to its political sensitivity emerge from the moment of Juana's arrival. Zeelanders looked upon the armada with alarm and resentment, rather than with the admiration expected, and there were outbreaks of violence between Zeelanders and the Spanish "bluecaps" or *blauwe kaproenen*. Owing to Philip's delayed return and to lack of diligence thereafter, preparations for Margaret's departure had not yet been finalised. Thousands of seamen and soldiers, set on an immediate return to Spain, were trapped for months in port with inadequate food and clothing. When the fleet eventually departed, in February

1497, with Margaret of Austria, it left in Zeeland, and in Southampton too, an astonishing body count. Padilla's estimate of 9,000 fatalities (from hypothermia, starvation and illness—possibly a dangerous form of influenza) may be an exaggeration, but the numbers inspired a secretary of Henry VII to remark that the Spanish who were expected to come to England with Katherine would die of over-eating and not of starvation.[27]

Juana entered Antwerp on the evening of 19 September. One of the greatest art and trading centres in Europe, Antwerp had strong Spanish links and its international merchant community joined the margrave and college and town officials to 'reverence' the daughter of the conquerors of Granada. The chronicler, Molinet, reports that Juana, surrounded by ladies, carried herself with beauty and grace, riding bareheaded on a mule "*à la mode d'Espaigne*" and was dressed in cloth of gold and jewels of incalculable value. The crowds shouted "*Vive la princesse d'Espagne! Vive la princesse Jeanne*!"[28]

Yet there must have been a somewhat poignant and stoic air about a bridal procession that, as it wended its way inland, and down the days and weeks, had yet to meet the bridegroom. Buglers did what they could to "*resveiller les bons courages.*" Juana acknowledged the cries and, when the burgomaster made her a speech, responded in Latin in a clear voice. In his book, *De institutione feminae christianae*, first published in 1524, Vives notes surprised admiration at Juana's ability to extemporise in Latin during her joyous entries. But the strains of the journey took their toll. At the monastery of Saint-Michel, Juana fell feverishly ill, perhaps from the same fever that had begun to cut swathes through the fleet. Luis Osorio, bishop of Jaén, who had travelled with her to officiate at the marriage, fell ill and died at the same time.

Juana finally met Philip at Lierre (Brabant). Lack of detail about the first meeting has fed the legend of an instant passion. Films, novels, operas and television dramas stress the air of anticipation, rushed footsteps, lingering first glances, impatience to consummate an overwhelming sexual desire that would become, from this perspective, Juana's all-consuming obsession. Much the same story belongs, however, to at least three of Juana's siblings. The younger Isabel's first Portuguese wedding took place in a monastery where the princes of Portugal reportedly consummated their marriage at once, to the scandal of the monks.[29] Similar comments, linked to the widespread belief in women's *furor uterinus*, were made about

Margaret, and Katherine did not escape the charge of excessive libidinous desire with respect to both of her husbands.

On 18 or 19 October, Juana's chief chaplain, Diego Ramírez de Villaescusa, conferred the nuptial blessing. This was followed on 20 October, at the church of St Gommaire/Sint Gummaruskerk by the full religious ceremony, presided by Henri de Berghes. After a few days of festivity in Lierre, Juana and her entourage returned with Philip and Margaret to Antwerp. From there the siblings continued to Zeeland, but strong winds prevented Margaret's departure until the following year.

Juana's lone entry into Brussels on 9 December is documented in the first known manuscript to illustrate a joyous entry in Europe. It comprises sixty-three watercolours on paper and is accompanied by short Latin commentaries, probably meant for Juana's perusal.[30] The manuscript depicts a long procession of religious and civic representatives, followed by Juana riding bareheaded and in cloth of gold among members of the elite guild of archers. All hold flaming torches as they pass the hôtel de ville, itself ablaze with light. There are a series of six comic *esbattements* and another of *tableaux vivants*, including one of Isabel receiving the sword of justice from the last of the Nasrid kings of Granada, Mohamed XII (better known in Europe as 'Boabdil'). Isabel finds herself in the company of the *Neuf Preuses*—women of valour whose heroic feats were a stock in trade of fifteenth-century cultural reference and mirrors of princes, and included the biblical tyrannicide, Judith; the conqueror of Thebes, Delphide and Tomyris, who defended her people from Persian invasion and beheaded the Persian leader, Cyrus. The message was clear: Juana, Jeanne, Janne, Tsanne must show the same values of courage and combativeness in defence of her new lands and people as the heroines of antiquity and, indeed, as her own mother. She must, as the Ghentenaars cried out the following March, when Philip and Juana travelled there together, "protect us well" ("*schat noch gout*").[31]

Only with hindsight does this appear unduly optimistic. The couple were of the same age, and glamorous and good-looking.[32] Both loved music and dance. Although Juana is unlikely to have engaged in anything but the most superficial expression of courtly love at Isabel's court, she would certainly have known enough to be able to 'read', during the great festivities at Barcelona in 1492, the string of coloured bonnets with which her later master of the horse would serenade his future wife in a courtly kind of semaphore.[33] She seemed to fulfill many of the hopes and expectations of the rhetoricians, the members of the chambers of rhetoric, or *rederijkerkamers* who played so important a part in Netherlandish culture, and who presented their theatrical spectacles to her in 1496 and 1497. She enchanted Maximilian, who first saw the pregnant archduchess at an abbey outside Brussels in November 1498. After several hours with Juana and Margaret of York, Gómez de Fuensalida describes the emperor as barely able to contain his delight: "What a good matchmaker God is," he exclaimed to the ambassador, "to have given such a wife to such a husband and such a husband to such a wife!"[34]

Philip showed genuine affection for his "*compaigne.*" He "loved the Queen very much," writes Padilla after he and Juana succeeded as princes of Castile—a factor that may not have been altogether disassociated from his love.[35] But, if this was linked, in Philip, to political ambition and in Juana (as in Katherine and their sisters) to her belief in the God-given nature of her marriage, reinforced by the husband's radiant centrality to all aspects of court life, the sexual chemistry between them was both powerful and dynastically successful; their six children would all reach adulthood to become emperors, kings and queens. Their first child, named Eleanor after Philip's paternal, Portuguese grandmother, Leonor, was born in November 1498; the second, Charles, named after Charles the Bold, was born in February 1500 to demonstrations of spectacular pyrotechnic joy.

Perhaps the early relationship between Juana and Philip can best be described through the interweaving of their personal mottoes. Philip, who delighted in chivalric display, had adopted as his devise the taunting challenge of the *pas d'armes* from the jousting ground: "*Qui vouldra?*" ("Who wants it?" or "Who dares?"). In Philip's case, his marriage to Juana would transform that defiant feat of arms into an expression of love, symbolised by the green crest, sparkling with filigree, that he wore in the joust held to celebrate Eleanor's birth, and in the green lined with yellow, or *jaune*, sported by his attendants in a chivalric play on the French version of Juana's name: Jeanne or Jehane. Juana adopted, as a response, the phrase "*Je le veux*" ("*I* want it" or "*I* do"), which also appeared as "*Moi tout[e] seul[e].*" She was, in other words, the only significant challenger to Philip in the lists of love, the one successful claimant on his heart.[36] Only in later years, as they became increasingly alienated from one another, and as Juana adopted a strategy of lonely resistance, does "I want it" begin to sound more like obstinacy or determination, and "I alone" to acquire an adversarial ring.

## 2.3 Seeds of Future Conflict

Despite the fact that Juana and Philip seemed well suited, differing outlooks with respect to female rule drove the struggle that broke out between the couple after Juana inherited her mother's kingdoms in 1500.

Highly unusually, both spouses had sovereign rulers for mothers. Juana was bred in the court of a female king, whose international reputation was reflected back upon her from the streets of Antwerp, Brussels, Bruges and Ghent. Isabel herself had carefully fostered that reputation during the war of the Castilian succession of 1475–1479, when she had challenged the right of that other Juana, the daughter and heir of her predecessor, Enrique IV, to rule Castile, countering allegations of usurpation with a brilliant propaganda campaign, and going to great lengths to emphasise a legitimacy expressed in redemptive and teleological terms. The letters convoking the Cortes of Madrigal of 1476 provided a catastrophic vision of the old regime of her half-brother, Enrique IV, which she and Fernando undertook to sweep away with a wide-ranging programme of remedy, reform and regeneration.[37]

The last years of the Granadan wars, reinforcing the providential image of the joint monarchy, had dominated Juana's childhood. As a child, she had engaged with some of its most significant events. The three messengers sent with letters by the ten-year-old infanta to the encampment of Baza in 1489, and recorded in the accounts of Isabel's treasurer, Gonzalo de Baeza, suggest her active interest in that long and difficult siege.[38] On 18 June 1491, she was by her mother's side at Zubia for the last great clash between Muslim and Christian forces in the *vega* of Granada and was again with Isabel at Santa Fé, when a candle, blowing in the wind, burned the encampment down. On 6 January 1492, she rode behind her parents as they made their ceremonial entrance into Granada. That August, the symbol of the split pomegranate, which plays with the place name and with the Castilian word for the fruit, and had formerly been Enrique's personal badge (together with the words "to rule is bittersweet"), was incorporated into the royal coat of arms. The city and the symbol represented for Juana, as for Katherine, a fundamental part of the identity she took with her to northern Europe. The heraldic name of her king-of-arms, Miguel Franco, who accompanied her to the Low Countries, was 'Granada.'

Juana, born at a moment of great optimism for the new regime, had daily lived the experience that women could rule—at least within the context of a sympathetically shared dual enterprise. Isabel's real power was reflected in the chess her children played, in which the queen had gradually replaced the role of vizier, and, from being narrowly restricted in her movements ("aslant only," as one medieval treatise had put it, "because women are so greedy that they will take nothing except by rapine and injustice") could, by Isabel's time, roam freely, as shown in the influential treatise that Luis de Lucena dedicated to Prince Juan, *Repetición de amores y arte del ajedrez*.[39]

Isabel's lands, from old León to new Granada, covered about two-thirds of the total area of the Iberian peninsular and were three times the size of Fernando's, with a larger population of between four million and five million inhabitants. Her court, less austere than often assumed, reflected that larger size, numbering about 500 persons by the time of her death and reflecting, too, the number of ladies and pages not only around the queen but her children.[40] Under her *mayordomo mayor*, Gonzalo Chacón, and other eminent officials such as Gutierre de Cárdenas, a plethora of offices included a dental hygienist; several cirgers who ensured the clarity and purity of the wax used at court, and whose *mozos de la cera* bestowed kisses upon the candlebra as they lit them in reference to the sacred origins of the act of bringing light to the palace. There was a night watch of *monteros de Espinosa*, who, armed with swords and lances, scoured the rooms, poised to kill intruders. Perfumers included a keeper of civet cats. Bound in chains, these African captives, to which Juana made a striking, explicit reference shortly before her death, were milked for their yellow musk and known for their cunning, hot temper and ferocity.[41]

In 1489, the Portuguese diplomat, Roger Machado, who led an English delegation to Medina del Campo, wrote a vivid description of the monarchs' reception, paying particular attention to Isabel's appearance. Surrounded by thirty-seven ladies, she wore a girdle of white leather "made in the style that men usually wear." Machado insisted on the unique equality between the monarchs: "… because some may blame me that I speak of 'kings', and some people may be astonished, and say 'How! Are there two kings in Castile?' No [I say], but I write 'kings' because the king is king on account of the queen, by right of marriage, and because they call themselves 'Kings' and superscribe their letters 'By the King and Queen,' for she is the heiress [proprietor]." In 1502, a member of Philip's entourage would also feel the need to explain

Isabel's relatively curious elevated position: "*l'on ne fait jamais ung commandement de par le Roy que la Royne ne fut nommée, pour ce qu'il est Roy de par la Royne.*"[42]

The successes and failings of the joint monarchy have been the subject of constant debate (see Chapter 4). The visibility and mobility of their courts was important to notions of contractual governance and it was, perhaps, for being constantly in the saddle that the monarchs were most fondly remembered—"*andando, andando,*" as a contemporary poet puts it, "*y nunca parando.*" They rapidly traversed the well-beaten system of earth tracks that were the legacy of *Reconquista*. Ahead went the royal purveyors (*aposentadores*) who scouted out lodgings and supplies. The monarchs and their children rode mules or travelled in litters covered with satin and often of exquisite workmanship. Juana, whose inventories reflect a fondness for Moorish design, had riding outfits that included *aljaremes*, wide white or yellow Moorish-style turbans and Moorish-style *borceguies*, soft leather knee-length boots of bright leather.[43] In his *Cancionero*, with its fifty-eight coloured miniatures, on which he worked between 1482 and 1502, Aragonese official Pedro Marcuello touches upon the restless transhumance and personal devotion to care and duty of monarchs who rode ceaselessly and in snow, wind and rain, on affairs of state. Admiral Fadrique Enríquez, who led Juana's fleet to Flanders, later recalled that era when, in a deluge of advice and admonition, he expressed to Charles V his belief in a "familiar" monarchy, rather than in a wider imperial ideal. They were "the kings of these kingdoms alone; they were of our language, born and bred among us, they knew us all, they raised their children among us … those who died in their service believed that in them they left parents to their children, they knew whom to reward and who merited reward … they travelled their kingdoms, and were known by great and small, available to all … there was not the estrangement of now, or the armed troops devouring the pueblos."[44] Enríquez' viewpoint would not be lost on Juana. The bond between mother and children was close, even if problematic in the case of the increasingly rebellious daughter that Juana became. Despite the tight, complex knot in their later relationship, Isabel would always remain her daughter's compass point.

In the Burgundian Netherlands, as in Castile, women could rule in the absence of a male heir. But, in contrast with Juana, Philip had little personal recollection of his mother. The only heir of Charles the Bold, Mary became ruler in January 1477, at the age of twenty, when Charles was killed in battle at Nancy. France's new monarch, Louis XI, who governed a country where the Salic law prevailed, contested Mary's right of succession, claiming it for himself. He took advantage of a momentary power vacuum, moving swiftly to seize the duchy of Burgundy and subsidiary lands of Artois and Picardy, reintegrating them into the French crown.

Mary was thus almost immediately deprived of her spiritual and dynastic heartland, with its capital at Dijon. Her lands were disparate and far-flung, from Franche-Comté in the south to an agglomeration of northern states. Fearing further depredations, Mary married Maximilian. Thenceforth the king of the Romans and later emperor—a man of extraordinary dynamism and intellectual energy and a warrior who revelled in the devotion of his soldiers—saw the Burgundian inheritance as part of the Reich. But, despite his victory at Guinegatte-Thérouanne in 1479, which brought a halt to French advances, he never recovered the duchy of Burgundy itself. Its loss haunted Mary's successors for decades and would remain a major factor in the later wars with France. Mary's brief reign was further complicated by rebellion in the economically powerful Flemish towns, whose *échevins*, smarting from the loss of old privileges and freedoms under Philip the Good and Charles the Bold, obliged her to reinstate them in the Grand Privilège, or great charter, of 1477. Despite courageous and passionate appeals, she proved unable to prevent the execution of two of her most important advisers.

An obsessive falconer, Mary died as the consequence of a riding accident in 1482 and the states of Flanders and Brabant, hostile to a Maximilian regency, placed Philip under the guardianship of Ghent. Power lay with the States General until Philip came of age in 1494. His education was confided to noblemen closely linked to Franco-Burgundian traditions, like Olivier de la Marche and the younger François de Busleyden, a second father who helped attach Philip to his Valois roots. His models of rulership, exclusively male, may account, at least partially, for the position he adopted vis-à-vis his wife. He saw Juana as his *compaigne* but never as his political equal.

Philip's contemporaries stress his charm, liberality, affability, impressionability, philandering, and his insatiable appetite for junketing. In his end-of-mission report to the Venetian Senate, Querini remarks that Philip, though intelligent, lacked resolution and relied in everything on the opinion of his *Conseil privé*.[45] Philip's political strategy at the time of his marriage was to compromise between two opposing forces and, in a sense, between two fathers. Philip had acquiesced to Maximilian's double marriage plans while assuring his pro-French advisers that he would never allow the Spanish alliance to compromise friendship with France. His marriage was internationally prestigious, allowing for a cautious and partial emergence from France's shadow, and brought the prospect of an inflow of funds to the country's ever-draining coffers, and rich pensions to the ruling elite. But there was a streak of steel in his make-up and it seems likely that the Catholic Kings had seriously underestimated the determination with which he strove to safeguard the terms of the treaty of Senlis of May 1493. This had confirmed continuing French possession of the duchy of Burgundy and Picardy while accepting that the free counties of Burgundy and the Low Countries belonged to Philip. The young archduke's efforts to protect an independent political identity exasperated both his father and his parents-in-law. Unresolved foreign policy arguments between Maximilian and Philip's team of advisers at the summit in the Tyrol are likely to have been a major factor in Philip's delay in meeting his bride.

Such considerations not only help to account for the reserve with which the Spanish fleet was greeted in September 1496, but for Juana's subsequent difficulties in exerting authority over her household and her children's households. Unlike Margaret, Juana would never receive the annual payment of 20,000 gold ecus settled on her by the marriage agreement, and years later was still frustrated about the massive sums that were owed to her.[46] Juana, and successive envoys from the Spanish monarchs, failed to persuade Philip to honour the agreement and when monies were collected from the towns of Valenciennes and Ath, they did not reach the intended recipient. Unlike former duchesses, such as Isabel of Portugal and Margaret of York, Juana was also disadvantaged by the fact that she had no fiefs or manors (*châtellenies*) or lordly domains from which she could draw income and to which, like both Isabel and Margaret, she could head for refuge at times of political turbulence.[47]

At the end of 1496, or the beginning of 1497, Juana bade farewell to most of those who had accompanied her to the Low Countries. This was anticipated. But she also suffered a haemorrhage of staff who she might have hoped to retain. In part, this may have been Juana's fault. In 1498, one of her dueñas, Teresa de Távora, countess of Camiña, wrote to her from Zaragoza that she had left the Low Countries because Juana "was not content with my service."[48] Over a year earlier, in March 1497, Philip issued the first of a series of ordinances that re-arranged Juana's household along Burgundian lines, effectively enshrining the subordination of his consort's household to his own. Aram estimates that, by March 1497, only sixteen men out of an original ninety-eight remained with her, while seventy new Burgundian attendants took up positions in her household.[49]

At the head of Juana's female staff Philip placed Jeanne Comynes-Halewijn, who had served his mother. A modern Belgian historian describes Jeanne d'Halewijn as a sensible, courageous and loyal supporter of the house of Valois, and one whose great vivacity of spirit was expressed in a "Flemish bluntness (*verdeur*) of language."[50] Zurita thought her to be a "great favourite" of Juana's.[51] A hard core of Spanish staff remained. These included her chief chaplain, Diego Ramírez de Villaescusa; her dueña, Ana de Beaumont; her treasurer, Martín de Mújica (or Móxica); her secretary, Sebastián de Olano; her chief chamberlain, Diego de Ribera, and several ladies whom the Flemings called *Espaignottes*.

Although Isabel and Fernando were unhappy about it, the replacement of a foreign consort's original staff was a long-established international practice and reasonable from Philip's view. The bulk of the Portuguese and English retinues of Juana's above-mentioned predecessors had also returned home. So did most of Margaret of Austria's retinue. Once in England, Katherine, like Juana, was left with a relatively small group of Spaniards and with little power and influence over her household. In 1500, Henry even told the Spanish ambassador, Gutierre Gómez de Fuensalida, that he saw Philip's household management as a model for Arthur's.[52]

In essence, Juana's problem with regard to her ability to defend and promote Spanish interests was her lack of a regular, independent income and the protective envelope of territorial endowment. She and her depleted Spanish staff were thus dependent on Philip's good will and generosity. This was a strategy driven forward by the powerful pro-French elements of Philip's *Conseil privé*, and it became a burning issue when, in 1500, Juana became princess of Asturias and Gerona and heir to her parents' kingdoms.

## Notes

1. CSP. Sp. (ed. Bergenroth), 1, 147, Isabel to Henry VII; 149, Isabel to Dr. Puebla, 17 August 1496. The most comprehensive history of the fleet, from which many of these details derive, may be found in Ladero Quesada (2003).
2. Isabel was born in 1470; Juan in 1478; María in 1483 and Catalina (the later Katherine 'of Aragon') in 1485.

3. Hulst (1958).
4. Aram (2005) and Ladero Quesada (2003).
5. Calmette (2001), 222.
6. Chmel (ed. 1845). Mémoire à Guillaume Pingon (before 1502), 225–227.
7. Ladero Quesada (2003).
8. In his *Cancionero* a contemporary, Pedro Marcuello, describes these field hospitals with their pure water, herbs and spices, violet juleps, rosewaters and other medical brews (Blecua, ed. 1987), f. 84v.
9. Martire (López de Toro, ed. 1953), 9, 172, 10 December 1496.
10. BN, Mss/12935/36, *Coplas fechas sobre el casamiento de la hija del Rey d'España con el hijo del Emperador.*
11. Erasmus (Jardine, ed. 1997). When Juana was just one Isabel and Fernando had contemplated sending her to Portugal as a guarantee (*en tercerías*) to the keeping of the peace treaty of Alcáçovas.
12. Rodríguez-Salgado (Soly, ed. 1999), 26–111.
13. Ferrandis (1943).
14. Eiximenis (Naccarato, ed. 1981). For an engrossing overview of his work and influence on Iberian court culture see Silleras-Fernández, *Chariots of Ladies* (Cornell 2015).
15. Martire, 10, 179, 15 July 1497. '... *la Princesa Juana, educada por ti no menos que por sus padres, ha caido muy bien entre los flamencos* ...'; Baeza (De la Torre/De la Torre, eds. 1955), I, 1487, 1488).
16. Münzer (Firth, ed. 2014), 127–128. See also illustrated Spanish-language editions of 1991 and 2002, prefaced by Ramón Alba (Polifemo, Madrid).
17. Martire, 10, 351, 5 July 1507; Clausell Nácher (ed. 2005), I, 435.
18. See Chapter 3.
19. Zalama (2010), 24–25.
20. Azcona (2002), 530. See also Fleming (2010).
21. Duindam (2016).
22. Carmi Parsons (1994).
23. Ochoa Brun (2003), IV, 184.
24. Juana's carrack may have been the same ship that sank during a tornado in 1516, while undergoing repairs at Villefranche-sur-Mer in the duchy of Savoy.
25. Cauchies (2003), 49.
26. Padilla (ed. 1846), CODOIN, 8.
27. CSP. Sp. 294, 1501.
28. Molinet (ed. 1935), II, 429.
29. Pérez (2002).
30. Kupferstichkabinett, Ms. 78 D5, Staatliche Museen Preussicher Kulturbesitz, Berlin.

31. The couple's entries into Ghent and Bruges in 1497 are the subject of poems in *Blijde Inkomst: Vier Vlaams-Bougondische gedichten* (G. Degroote, ed. 1950).
32. Rodríguez-Salgado (1999).
33. Fernández de Oviedo, I (1983–2002); Münzer (2014), 127–128.
34. Fuensalida (Berwick y Alba, ed. 1907), 11 November 1498, 106–107.
35. Padilla, 149.
36. Domínguez Casas (1993).
37. Carrasco Manchado (2006).
38. Baeza, I (1955), I, 301.
39. Willis, 'Chess', *Intelligent Life*, July/August 2015; Córdova Miralles (2002).
40. González Marrero (2005).
41. Münzer, 23.
42. Gairdner (ed. 1858); Chmel (ed. 1845), 1, 597.
43. Baeza, I, 426.
44. BL, Egerton 2081, f. 104, 'Carta del Almirante de Castilla para el Emperador sobre el gobierno destos Reynos'.
45. Albèri (ed. 1840).
46. See Chapter 9.
47. Sommé (1998).
48. AGS, CSR 402. 2, 11 October [1498], to the archduchess, on the occasion of her pregnancy, in Rodríguez de Diego (ed. Zalama 2010).
49. Aram (2005).
50. Dumont (1982), 76.
51. Zurita (Canellas López, ed. 1992), 3, 215.
52. Fuensalida, 132.

## References

Albèri, Eugenio (ed.). 1840. *Relazioni degli Ambasciatori Veneti al Senato*, Serie 3, vol. I. Florence: Clio.

Aram, Bethany. 2005. *Juana the Mad: Sovereignty and Dynasty in Renaissance Europe*. Baltimore and London: John Hopkins University Press.

Azcona, Tarsicio de. 2002. *Isabel La Católica. Vida y Reinado*. Madrid: La Esfera de los Libros.

Baeza, Gonzalo de. 1955. *Cuentas de Gonzalo de Baeza, Tesorero de Isabel la Católica*, ed. Antonio de la Torre and E.A. de la Torre. Madrid: CSIC.

Berwick y Alba (ed.). 1907. *Correspondencia de Gutierre Gómez de Fuensalida, embajador en Alemania, Flandes y Inglaterra (1496–1509)*. Madrid: Alemana.

Blecua, José Manuel (ed.). 1987. *Pedro Marcuello: Cancionero*. Zaragoza: Institución Fernando el Católico.

Calmette, Joseph. 2001. *The Golden Age of Burgundy*. London: Phoenix.

Carrasco Manchado, Ana Isabel. 2006. *Isabel I de Castilla y la sombra de la ilegitimidad*. Madrid: Sílex.

Cauchies, Jean-Marie. 2003. *Philippe le Beau: Le dernier duc de Bourgogne*. Turnhout: Brepols.

Córdova Miralles, Álvaro Fernández de. 2002. *La Corte de Isabel I. Ritos y ceremonias de una reina (1474–1504)*. Madrid: Dykinson.

Chmel, Joseph (ed.). 1845. *Urkunden, Briefe und Aktenstücke zur Geschichte Maximilian I und seiner Zeit*, vol. IX. Stuttgart: Bibliothek des literarischen Vereins.

Clausell Nácher, Carmen. 2005. Carro de las donas. Valladolid 1542. Doctoral Thesis, Universidad Autónoma de Barcelona, Barcelona.

Degroote, G. (ed.). 1950. *Blijde inkomst: vier Vlaams-Bourgondische gedichten (1496–1497)*. Amsterdam: De Nederlandsche Boekhandel.

Domínguez Casas, Rafael. 1993. *Arte y Etiqueta de los Reyes Católicos: artistas, residencias, jardines y bosques*. Madrid: Alpuerto.

Doutrepont, Georges, and Omer Jodogne (eds.). 1935. *Chroniques de Jean Molinet*. Brussels: Académie Royale de Belgique.

Duindam, Jeroen. 2016. *Dynasties: A Global History of Power, 1300–1800*. Cambridge: Cambridge University Press.

Dumont, Georges-Henri. 1982. *Marie de Bourgogne*. Paris: Fayard.

Fernández de Oviedo, Gonzalo. 1983. *Batallas y Quinquagenas*, ed. Pérez de Tudela. Madrid: Real Academía de la Historia.

Ferrandis, José (ed.). 1943. *Datos documentales para la Historia del Arte*, vol. III. Madrid: CSIC.

Fleming, Gillian Beatrice. 2010. La Visita a Inglaterra de Juana I (enero-abril de 1506). In *Juana I en Tordesillas: su mundo, su entorno*, ed. Miguel-Ángel Zalama. Valladolid: Grupo Página.

Gairdner, James (ed.). 1858. Journal of Roger Machado: Embassy to Spain and Portugal. In *Historia Regis Henrici Septimi a Bernardo Andrea Tholosate*. London: Rolls Series.

González Marrero, María del Cristo. 2005. *La Casa de Isabel la Católica: Espacios domésticos y vida cotidiana*. Ávila: Diputación de Ávila.

Hulst, Henri d'. 1958. *Le Mariage de Philippe le Beau avec Jeanne de Castille*. Antwerp: Lloyd Anversois.

Jardine, Lisa (ed.). 1997. *Erasmus: The Education of a Christian Prince*. Cambridge: Cambridge University Press.

Ladero Quesada, Miguel-Ángel. 2003. *La armada de Flandes: Un episodio en la política naval de los Reyes Católicos (1496–1497)*. Madrid: Real Academía de la Historia.

López de Toro, José (ed.). 1953–1957. *Petrus Martyr Anglerius: Epistolario*. CODOIN, 9–12. Madrid: Imprenta Góngora.

Münzer, Hieronymus. 2014. *Dr. Hieronymus Münzer's Itinerary and the Discovery of Guinea*, ed. James Firth. London: James Firth.

Naccarato, Frank (ed.). 1981. *Lo llibre de les dones d'Eiximenis*. Barcelona: Curial.

Ochoa Brun, Miguel-Ángel. 2003. *Historia de la Diplomacia Española*, vol. IV. Madrid: Ministerio de Asuntos Exteriores.

Padilla, Lorenzo de. 1846. CODOIN, 8. In *Crónica de Felipe I llamado el Hermoso*, ed. Miguel Salvá and Pedro Sainza de Baranda. Madrid: Imprenta de la viuda de Calero.

Parsons, John Carmi. 1994. Mothers, Daughters, Marriage, Power: Some Plantagenet Evidence, 1150–1500. In *Medieval Queenship*, ed. Parsons. Stroud: Sutton.

Pérez, Joseph. 2002. Los Hijos de la Reina: La Política de Alianzas. In *Isabel la Católica, Reina de Castilla*, ed. Pedro Navascués Palacio. Barcelona and Madrid: Iberlibro.

Rodríguez-Salgado, María José. 1999. Charles V and the Dynasty. In *Charles V: 1500–1558*, ed. H. Soly. Antwerp: Fonds Mercator.

Silleras-Fernández, Nuria. 2015. *Chariots of Ladies: Francesc Eiximenis and the Court Culture of Medieval and Early Modern Iberia*. Ithaca and London: Cornell University Press.

Sommé, Monique. 1998. *Isabelle de Portugal, duchesse de Bourgogne: Une femme au pouvoir au Xvè. Siècle*. Paris: Septen-Trion.

Zalama, Miguel Ángel. 2010. *Juana I. Arte, Poder y Cultura en torno a una reina que no gobernó*. Madrid: Centro de Estudios Europea Hispánica.

Zurita, Jerónimo. 1992. *Historia del Rey Don Hernando el Católico: De las Empresas y Ligas de Italia*, vol. 3, ed. Ángel Canellas López, Magdalena Canellas, and Antonio J. López. Zaragoza: Gobierno de Aragón.

CHAPTER 3

# A Troubled Transition (1497–1504)

## 3.1 Princes by God's Grace

Juana had been in the Low Countries for little more than a year when her brother's death transformed the Spanish political landscape. The fabulous yet toxic legacy that became hers in 1500 would greatly complicate her life as she tried to reconcile her role as consort, wife and mother with her new role as princess of Asturias and Gerona, and as a future proprietary monarch whose royal status surpassed her husband's. This chapter re-examines the events that brought her the succession while placing it again in doubt.

Once, when expressing relief at the birth of a male heir, Louis VII of France had remarked that he had been "terrified by a multitude of daughters."[1] While the elaboration of the Salic law in France and traditions surrounding the election of Holy Roman Emperors ruled female sovereigns out of contention, kingdoms like Castile, Portugal and England did not explicitly bar women from inheriting the throne in the absence of male heirs in the direct line. Nonetheless, it was one thing for queens to transmit their rights to their male descendants and another to rule in person. Sovereign queenship was seen as a 'virile' anomaly and, where it existed, was tainted by the dynastic and political crises that had given rise to it in the first place. As Duindam notes of the two queens regnant of later sixteenth-century England and the cluster of *tsaritsas* who ruled eighteenth-century Russia, they reflect "persistent dynastic crisis rather than wholehearted acceptance of female power."[2]



G. B. Fleming, *Juana I*, Queenship and Power,
https://doi.org/10.1007/978-3-319-74347-9_3

Queens regnant, as opposed to female regents or lieutenants-general, faced a seemingly insoluble conundrum. The first duty of a princess or 'proprietary' queen (who embodied, and alone disposed of, the royal patrimony) was to find a suitable husband, and through marriage and the birth of an heir, protect and stabilise the realm. But, in the absence of the concept of male consorts, what exactly did suitability mean? A foreign prince who became king-by-marriage exposed the queen and her patrimony to the perils and uncertainties of outside interests and dynastic change. Yet a queen whose husband was chosen from among her native lords risked arousing jealous internecine strife. Such problems emerged in the reign of England's first queen regnant, Mary I, while the extraordinary circumstances in which Mary's grandmother, Isabel I, came to power, and partially circumvented the marriage dilemma, are briefly outlined in Chapters 4 and 5 of this study.

While lacking a specific legal concept of *salicité*, the realms of Aragon had, down the years, successfully fought off challenges to exclusive male sovereignty. When Martín I left no surviving heirs, the conclave that met at Caspe in 1412 chose to elect a Castilian infante, Fernando's grandfather, Fernando *de Antequera*, rather than submit to the claims of Violante, daughter of Martín's predecessor, Juan I. Fernando and Isabel subsequently placed their hopes for the union of Castile and Aragon in their only son, whose birth was bathed in a providential light. Given a thorough apprenticeship in governance, he presided his own court at Almazán (Soria), symbolically located on the borders of Castile and Aragon. His death in October 1497 thus caused an immense shock on both political and religious levels: "*Triste España sin ventura*," begins a famous ballad of the time, "*todos te deven llorar …*". A Burgundian chronicler described the forty decreed days of mourning as "*si merveilleux dueil que nul ne le sçaurait croire …*". A poet from Messina asked: "What does it mean, this horrible din day and night? And why do so many torches blaze from piled funeral monuments as night stars in the clear skies?" Years later a member of the prince's staff described the sorrowful gait and loss of appetite of Juan's beloved companion, his lurcher, Bruto, as a metaphor for the grief of entire kingdoms.[3]

Juan's death marked the turn of the dynastic tide, triggering a half-century of political storms and disquiet and shaking confidence in a sacrosanct monarchy. No-one reflects this bewilderment better than Juana's chief chaplain and adviser, Ramírez de Villaescusa, who happened to be in Castile in 1498 and who, in a treatise later translated from Latin into

Spanish as *Cuatro diálogos sobre la malhadada muerte del Príncipe de las Españas*, depicts the queen's stunned incomprehension. When encountering the figure of Death in a corridor she tries at first to have him arrested.[4]

Villaescusa hoped, as will be seen, that Juan's death would encourage the monarchs to address serious failings in justice and governance. Instead, a sense of divine admonition raised questions as to whether the Christian community had fallen short with respect to religious reform and defence against heresy. Converted Jews (*conversos*) and the proponents of a relatively tolerant approach to religious conversion, such as Talavera, Isabel's confessor and first archbishop of Granada, were among the propitiatory victims of the prince's death. As Rawlings has pointed out, Talavera's methods no longer matched the "increasingly intransigent religious policy of the crown."[5] Talavera, of whom Villaescusa was a protégé, had kept alive the spirit of *convivencia*—the hybrid fruit of the *dhimma*, or pact, by which Muslims, Christians and Jews had lived under earlier Muslim rule—and had sought to adapt Christianity to Moorish customs and needs. But in 1499, Francisco Jiménez Cisneros, a Franciscan friar elevated to the primacy of Toledo in 1495, and a key figure in the Observant movement of religious reform, replaced Talavera in the mission to convert its Muslim community to Christianity. Cisneros' conversion strategy, implacably pursued, included bonfires of Arab and Muslim writings and led to a series of uprisings that spread to the Alpujarras and to Ronda and the sierras on the western borders of Granada. These were crushed with difficulty in the period between 1499 and 1502, following atrocities on both sides. A royal pragmatic law (*pragmática*) of 2 February 1502 adopted the measures taken earlier against Jews and required Muslims unwilling to convert to Christianity to leave Castile within a year.

While Isabel lost much of her political drive, the problems of an insecure succession, and his own ambitions, prompted Fernando to build an 'Aragonese' party within Castile's administration, ousting Isabel's most devoted supporters from their places—among them Isabel's *converso* royal secretary, Álvarez de Toledo.[6] Gaspar de Gricio, Miguel Pérez de Almazán and his nephew, Lope de Conchillos, were among the Aragonese officials who replaced them.

The heirs to Castile and Aragon continued, meanwhile, to die. Prince Juan's wife, Margaret, whom he had married only that March, gave birth to a stillborn child. The younger Isabel, who had recently married Manoel I of Portugal, hurried home for the *juramento* of the Cortes of Castile and Corts of Aragon. But when she and Manoel entered a sultry

Zaragoza on 1 June 1498, they found the procurators unprepared to swear allegiance. The problem momentarily resolved itself when, on 24 August, the princess died after giving birth to a son. Miguel de la Paz was sworn-in at the Corts of Zaragoza in 1498 and Cortes of Ocaña in 1499. But his health was fragile.

As Juana and Philip moved closer to the succession, they came under increasingly critical scrutiny. In 1498, Juana refused to join Philip in paying public homage to Louis XII, successor to Charles VIII, for the counties of Flanders and Artois, but her lack of political clout at the Burgundian court, combined with reports that she tolerated lax religious practices, worried the monarchs. Her tutor, Miranda, had fled the Low Countries in a state of cultural shock. He warned Juana against confessing "to those sort of friars who live in Paris" and giving them money, like the thirty florins she gave to one "so that he could enjoy himself."[7]

The monarchs warned Villaescusa that messengers were arriving without letters from either Juana or Philip.[8] Sancho de Londoño and Dominican monk Tomás de Matienzo, who had been trying to persuade Henry VII to act more rigorously against refugees from the Spanish Inquisition, were sent to probe into affairs in Brussels. Matienzo's letters to Isabel describe a series of increasingly uncomfortable interviews with the archduchess. She "showed a certain agitation" which, he suspected, was linked to rumours that he "came as her confessor."[9] There may have been other reasons too. Villaescusa, whom Juana could not have regarded more highly, and whose departure for Astorga (León) as bishop-elect coincided with Matienzo's arrival in Brussels, indirectly acknowledged the distrust that existed between the Spanish and Burgundian courts when referring, in a later report, to Isabel's suspicions that he had been too zealous in Juana's service, and, by extension, in Philip's. Although Villaescusa's (temporary) return to Castile in 1498 was connected to an ecclesiastical promotion and appears to demonstrate the monarchs' favour, he, and probably Juana, suspected that it was also a means of detaching him from her side.[10]

Matienzo questioned Juana about her irregular confessional habits, while later reassuring the monarchs that: "there is as much religion in her household as in a strictly observant convent and in this she is very vigilant and deserves much praise." He also quizzed her about her failure to protect her Spanish household. Her defensiveness and extreme reserve led the Dominican to burst out that she had a "hard and pitiless heart" and was "devoid of piety [compassion]."[11]

Juana did write letters. But her silences were unsettling. In December 1496, her former *aya*, Teresa Manrique, who had been her daily companion and instructor, wrote from Burgos: "I am amazed, knowing the distress and anxiety of the king and queen … when they do not receive letters from your highness with all the messages that come here … About myself I do not know what to say except that, since I can no longer see your highness, I realise that I do not live; although I have recovered somewhat from my illnesses, the troubles of my heart … for that the best remedy would be to have news of you …".[12] Juana was also taken to task in a chaotic letter from María Manrique Chacón: "Your highness does not remember her very dear friend doña María, and the toasted chick-peas she gave me that made me ill, the friend she loves so much …".[13] Miranda too reproved her: "although I have written very often, you have never sent me a word or written to me … I ask pardon that I am so bold with you, whom I love so much, and serve by day and night before God … If your highness does not answer me, I shall never write again, and this shall be my last letter."[14]

In general, Juana's failure to keep in regular touch with family and friends seems to owe less to indifference than to extreme sensitivity to criticism and to her reputation. She admitted that she had longed for home and had felt "so dispirited and depressed that every time she remembered how far away she was from [Isabel] she could not stop weeping to be forever so separated from her."[15] Her treasurer, Mújica, subsequently informed the monarchs that: "when some days go by without hearing from your highnesses she is the most distressed woman in the world."[16] As Parsons has noted, royal daughters, unlike their brethren, had to "negotiate loyalties to natal and affinal families in often forbiddingly politicised contexts …".[17] Juana was torn between demanding parents and a husband whose advisers resented their interference. Juana had apparently good relations with powerful, highly esteemed ladies of the Burgundian milieu like Margaret of York and Jeanne d'Halewijn, and later with the widowed Margaret of Austria, all of whom were sometimes judged harshly and suspiciously by Spanish correspondents. And cultural difference led to mockery. We can imagine the ambivalence with which she read the letter from her 'mad' friend María, who, apart from telling her about her new little dog, Zaragoçita, describes a hilarious visit from Juana's treasurer, Mújica: "We cannot eat at table on account of all the crazy things he says about your highness being married over there." Juana, María adds, should send her a little box to put her "madnesses" in because "I can't contain them, they're spilling everywhere; [but] I shan't write any more so as not to annoy you …".

A sense of humour is one of the most difficult things for historians to capture across the centuries, but Juana clearly had one, and the fact that she kept her 'mad' friend's letter suggests it meant something to her. The tug of love was beginning, however, to tax her loyalty and resourcefulness. It is not implausible that the *turbación* to which Matienzo refers had arisen from that cruel and radical separation at Laredo in 1496, as well as from resentment at overly high expectations; a suspicion that words and deeds of hers were being and would be misinterpreted; an awareness that she was ceaselessly watched and scrutinised and expected to reconcile apparently irreconcilable differences of outlook.[18]

Certainly, there is a danger in reading too much from hindsight into Juana's early silences. Villaescusa's comment that, after receiving a letter from her *aya*, her "conduct has improved somewhat," indicates that there was further contact with Teresa Manrique.[19] Subsequent actions show that Juana did not forget Miranda, even if, as he believed, his flight from her side had angered her. Juana tried to foster Spanish interests and had some diplomatic success in paving the way for Katherine's marriage to Prince Arthur.[20] She was also active as consort and mother, lavishly entertaining Margaret of Austria in Bruges in 1501, bestowing religious patronage and accompanying her children as she travelled between Brussels, Ghent and Bruges.[21] One entry in the account books shows her hiring a little boat at Ghent to "*jouer sur l'eaue.*"[22] On another occasion Mújica told the monarchs that "The greatest pastime that [Juana] has here is Madame Leonor [Eleanor] …".[23]

Perhaps in that closeness to her children lurked the presentiment of imminent and indefinite separation. For the death of Prince Miguel at Granada on 20 July 1500, five months after the birth of Charles, at Ghent, would convert Juana into heir apparent, and her lost homeland into her future and destination. But while the conversion of the archdukes into princes greatly enhanced their international standing, it also set their marriage on a downward spiral.

The massive change in their status is celebrated in the side panels of a triptych painted by the Master of the Life of St Joseph. Differences in the posture, attire and location of Philip and Juana are undoubtedly designed to show Philip (not Juana) as future ruler of the Spanish kingdoms. Philip stands in front of the city walls, an open crown over his helmet, and in his right hand he holds the sword of justice and sovereignty. Juana is shown in the park of the Warande, a part of the Coudenberg palace complex. Her expression is melancholy and distant. Although she wears heraldic arms and a crown, it is virtually indistinguishable from the vegetation behind her and she has no sword.

The monarchs reinforced diplomatic representation at Brussels. Fuensalida's first task was to assess the quality of Juana's advisers and help her find a voice among the members of Philip's council. He thought she looked radiant.[24] His despatches between the summer of 1500 and end of 1501 portray an intelligent, realistic, pragmatic, well-informed princess whose antechamber was busy; they do not underestimate the tasks that faced her, and show her moving cautiously, if with fortitude, through difficult terrain. What they fail to illuminate is Juana's attitude to her sudden elevation in status. Padilla comments that the news of Miguel's death pleased the archdukes, "as was only natural."[25] But, while there is no question that Philip was immensely attracted by the thought of a royal title and fabulous legacy—a subject on which, for once, he saw eye to eye with Maximilian—he hesitated before the commitment it involved. Juana, for her part, must have relished the thought of a family reunion, but subsequent actions and statements suggest that she accepted her new status with some ambivalence.

As Evans has noted with respect to Rudolf, the burden of such eminence and responsibility is a difficult subject for study.[26] Juana was highly jealous and defensive of her royal prerogatives but the emotional impact upon her of the conflict in her roles would become gradually apparent. A remark made to Fuensalida when he asked whether Matienzo and Villaescusa should be withdrawn from her service suggests the mixture of reluctance and modesty, but also perhaps of exhilaration, with which she reflected upon her future role as queen. If, she said, it was her fate to rule ("*si las cosas avian de venir a su governación*") she would need Villaescusa beside her, for there was no one who advised her so well.[27] Excessive importance should not be attached to a single remark, but this does seem to reflect both acceptance of her legacy and an awareness of the tragic circumstances in which dynastic transitions so often occurred. Miguel's death had forced her parents to reach beyond the Iberian 'family' to a more radically foreign house, with territories sprawled inconveniently across Europe. Baffled by providence, their remark to the princes that they had God alone to thank for their elevation could be understood in different ways.[28]

Juana tried to coax Philip into responding favourably to her parents' pleas that they should perform their contractual obligations as a matter of urgency. She told Fuensalida that she had Philip's good will when alone with him because "she knows that he loves her." But his position often shifted after council meetings and, owing to his indiscretion, she felt unable to "tell him things that it seems to her reasonable to tell him and do."[29] With Fuensalida and Villaescusa she often discussed the tactics to adopt with Philip and the council and tried to speed up preparations for the journey by opposing as unnecessary a preparatory mission to Spain, led by Busleyden. Not surprisingly, she had reservations about a connected plan to marry Charles to the daughter of Louis XII and Anne of Brittany. One night, angry and sulky over her refusal to authorise Busleyden's mission, Philip told her: "if he doesn't go I can't go either, and I certainly won't go because I don't know how to go; I don't know the customs of the land, or the people, or the issues … and if the Archbishop doesn't go, I shan't send anyone else; and so I shan't go to Spain …".

The ambassador was as impressed by Juana as Philip's subservience to Busleyden dismayed him: "Since I lack the capacity to praise such a princess as she deserves. I will say only how satisfied I feel that she is the daughter of your highnesses in all things, and for her age has no equal in the world," he told the monarchs that November. Later he added: "If she did not possess such virtues she would be unable to suffer what she sees; but I do not think I have ever seen such wisdom (*cordura*) in one so young."[30]

## 3.2 The Princes' Journey

Busleyden went on his mission and returned to Brussels in June 1501 with Spanish and French consent to the betrothal of Charles with Claude. A marriage contract was signed on 10 August. The procedure for milking the États-généraux of funds for the journey was lengthy and complex and Juana was again pregnant. On 15 July 1501, she gave birth, in Brussels, to her third child, Isabeau (later queen of Denmark). A new Spanish envoy, Juan Rodríguez de Fonseca, bishop of Córdoba, reported that Juana seemed eager to serve her parents and was widely thought to be "very sensible (*cuerda*) and very level-headed (*asentada*)." Opinion was divided as to whether she should do more to promote Spanish interests.[31]

The children were placed with Margaret of York and Anne of Burgundy in Mechelen and Philip signed new household ordinances for the journey. At the core of Juana's household were the Spanish women who had accompanied her to the Low Countries in 1496, but the majority of her household were Burgundian and Flemish and less than half the size of Philip's household, which comprised 400.[32]

There are several vivid accounts of the journey.[33] The princes left Brussels on 4 November 1501, travelling until Mons with Margaret of York and down through France to Blois. Philip delighted in detours, but Juana, more aloof and withdrawn, preferred the straighter route. Spanish-language chroniclers interpret the emphasis placed by Juana on her Spanish identity as a challenge to assumptions of French and Burgundian superiority. At Blois, she is reported to have vexed Anne of Brittany by refusing to make an offering with money that Anne sent her, and famously performed a Spanish dance alone before the court. But if pride and sensitivity about status created friction between them, both women seem to have worked to smooth it over: "it seems to me," wrote a chronicler here called the *Reise* author, "that the Queen and madame the archduchess love one another like two sisters …".[34]

The author notes a happy encounter at Guitres (Aquitaine) between Juana and a group of Spanish trumpeters fresh from England, who told her about Katherine's reception there. Juana's subsequent adventures in the Gironde—she and her entourage, stuck in the mud churned up by Philip's retinue, were forced to shelter for the night in a hamlet and beg for eggs—inevitably broke protocol down and amused the prince, who, from the snugness of the castle of Cadillac, sent out a search party. While Philip hunted rabbits, Juana chatted to the jolly châtelaine and later dined with a group of French officials round the same table. But at the frontier, where Spanish mules replaced Burgundian carriages, she re-adapted to reserved Spanish customs.

They took the high pass of San Adriano, toiling through heavy snow toward Salvatierra/Agurain, where crowds of Basques surrounded them. The *Reise* author describes the princes's hands going red from all the *besamanos*. Throughout the journey French-language chroniclers emphasise Philip's primacy. The Spanish monarchs tried, however, to protect Juana's status, issuing instructions to various cities to ensure that the princes "come together" under the canopy.[35] At the monastery of Santa María la Real de las Huelgas, outside Burgos, where they attended mass and kissed relics, two 'equal' seats awaited them at the high altar. Bernardino Fernández de Velasco, constable of Castile, greeted them a half-league from the city, whose gates were closed ritually against them until they swore to uphold its privileges. When, at nightfall, they processed to the cathedral, they did so together, under a golden pallium. A single sword, symbol of sovereign justice, was held before Juana and another before Philip.[36]

At Olías, north of Toledo, Philip came down with measles. This must, nonetheless, have been one of the happiest moments of Juana's life. Late one April afternoon, she watched from a gallery as, among an incoming party of riders, she glimpsed a familiar and "very pleasant, laughing face." As Juana struggled to get through the crush, Fernando stepped forward, sweeping off his headgear, and kissed her twice "for joy." Seizing his hand, she led him to an inner chamber where she acted as interpreter between father and husband.[37] An enthusiastic Philip told his chancellor, Maigny, that Fernando had been "*très humain et bégnin … autant ou plus que s'il feust esté mon propre père.*"[38]

The ritual struggles, or *mystères*, as Molinet calls them, between displays of precedence on one hand and modesty and respect on the other, were strikingly apparent during the entry into Toledo on 7 May. Lalaing continues to stress Philip's pre-eminence. The *Reise* author also focuses attention on Philip and Fernando.[39] Aram argues that Fernando "collaborated to marginalize Juana and to undermine the principle of female inheritance that both sanctioned and threatened their authority in Castile."[40] However, to publicly slight the proprietary heir would have breached the orders that the monarchs themselves had issued to ensure that the princes "come together" under the pallium, and other versions seem more plausible. Molinet has Fernando riding between them to the gates of Toledo, after which he alone took precedence because of the lack of space beneath the canopy. Philip relates that he and Fernando embarked upon a ceremonial struggle, during which Fernando drew both Juana and himself beneath the pallium, while Philip tried to fall to the rear, but "*ne cessoit icelluy nous retirer et approchier de luy.*"[41] Philip's dynamic description argues for a view of historical events of greater fluidity than the frozen shots often provided by chronicles and histories.

As they approached the cathedral, Toledo thundered and shook with bells, trumpets and artillery. After "humbling themselves" before the cross at the cathedral's Puerta del Perdón, the princes prayed before the great altar in the presence of Cisneros.[42] Isabel, surrounded by ladies, awaited them in a great hall hung with a tapestry depicting Hercules, mythical founding hero of the Spanish monarchy. As Fernando and the princes entered, Isabel and her ladies stood and the crowd was forced back to allow Isabel to step forward in a gesture of respect. Philip bowed thrice, so low that the queen also had to bow to raise him from his knees. Philip persisted in seeking her hand, watching for a moment to snatch it to his lips. His efforts to do so, even "when she was no longer thinking about it," caused "*une grande risée*" among the Castilians, breaking the tension.[43] Then Isabel turned to Juana, her face shining with "tears of joy."[44]

On 22 May, seated below the monarchs in the cathedral, Juana and Philip were sworn-in as the heirs to Castile, León and Granada. At the ceremony, both sacred and contractual, which opened the Cortes of Toledo of 1502, Juana received allegiance first, followed by Philip as "legitimate husband." Juana's pride in her status is reflected in her commissioning of six stunning tapestries, bought for her pleasure, on 10 August 1502. The "golden tapestries," worked predominantly in gold and silver thread by Philip's *valet de chambre* and *tapissier*, Pierre van Aelst (or Pieter van Edinghen), with whom Juana had a close working association, and dedicated to the Virgin Mary, remain among the greatest treasures of the Spanish state. Art historians have noted the link they draw between central episodes of the Virgin's life and events from the Trastámara–Habsburg marriages. The lower left secondary panel of the *Coronation of the Virgin* depicts a golden-haired woman crowning a younger woman, also golden-haired, with a sword-engirdled, dark-haired man in a red bonnet standing beside her.[45]

Marcuello's *Cancionero* contains two images from the time of the *juramentos* of Toledo and Zaragoza, which offer a sly cultural and political comparison between Burgundy and Spain. One shows Marcuello presenting his book to Philip at a Burgundian-style ceremony, with a dog dozing quietly in the foreground. The other offers a less ornate Spanish version, with 'AMOR REGINA' inscribed on the wall at the back and two playful, barking dogs. In the Burgundian version, Philip holds an orb, symbol of royal justice. The king-of-arms beside him holds a sword, and Philip is clearly the book's recipient. In the Spanish version, the orb, which was not part of Trastámara regalia, is missing, and Juana's hand seems to flutter over the book, if rather absent-mindedly (Fig. 3.1).

Although his illustrator awards iconographic pre-eminence to Philip, it is to Juana—"infanta, worthy of kingdoms/whom I ask to be my lady"—that Marcuello dedicates his book.[46] He wanted to secure a place for Isabel, his daughter, in Juana's household, while Juana's wider mission, as he saw it, was to follow in the steps of the "great shining" queen

**Fig. 3.1** The Burgundian version of the presentation to Juana and Philip of the *Cancionero* by Pedro Marcuello, c. 1502. Now in the Museo Condé, Chantilly, this was formerly in the possession of the Cartuja de Aula Dei, Zaragoza (*Source* PRISMA ARCHIVO/Alamy Stock Photo)

and pursue and extend the war against the infidel, granted new urgency after the Moorish rebellions in the Alpujarras and Sierra Bermeja, east of Ronda, between 1500 and 1502.

The chronicles, so rich in detail prior to the oath-taking at Toledo, are ominously silent about Philip's response to it. There is no doubt that his manner darkened. He shunned the ancient seat of the Visigothic kings for the riverbank estates or *cigarrales* and open spaces of the Guadarrama, among foreigners then and since to share Molinet's view that Toledo was a sewer.[47] Divergences within his council boiled over after Fernando left to prepare the princes' reception in Zaragoza.[48] These, connected to foreign policy, seem to involve the whole question of Philip's political independence vis-à-vis his parents-in-law and wife. In a show of spectacular defiance, Philip sent home the major architects of the Spanish marriage within his council, including its president, Henri de Berghes, and refused to accept the combined pleas of Isabel and Juana to reconsider his decision.

The plague may have started to stalk the city. Several courtiers died at this time. Busleyden replaced Berghes but fell sick and, on 23 August, he too died. When the princes left for Zaragoza on 29 August, the political honeymoon was well and truly over. Philip's "feet itch, his blood boils … and he can settle nowhere," writes Martire.[49] The princes entered Zaragoza on 26 October for the ceremony of oath taking before the Corts. Philip was accepted as future king, but only in Juana's lifetime. Juana herself became the first female heir to Aragon, and, in the event, its first and last proprietary queen. Nonetheless, this was a pact conditional upon Fernando failing to produce a new son.

Despite the reservations against female rule, the large numbers attending the ceremonies in Toledo and Zaragoza suggest enthusiasm for the princes. But, following the partition of Naples, the eruption of fresh hostilities between Fernando and Louis, culminating in the latter's expulsion from Naples, made Philip highly anxious. Fernando rushed to Madrid, where Isabel was in poor health, before preparing for a fresh military campaign. Alerted to Philip's desire to return home, the monarchs summoned him for talks. Juana was left to preside at the Corts for almost three weeks before she too was recalled. Later Aragonese testimony describes her then much as Fuensalida and Rodríguez de Fonseca had reported: "very sensible (*discreta*), prudent (*cuerda*) and with excellent natural gifts."[50] After conducting "some affairs" she left Zaragoza on 24 November.[51]

Philip's refusal to stay longer shocked monarchs and procurators alike. Castilian procurators warned that, if he crossed France in wartime, he would be seen as a traitor, exposing himself to the mercy of his enemies while endangering Juana's life: "God save her highness for the lives of pregnant women can be endangered by very small causes." This undermined not only the monarchs but the interests and honour of "all Spain," and would cause "very great agitation."[52] Aragonese procurators appealed to Philip in similar terms.[53] But, although the monarchs persuaded Juana to remain for the birth of their fourth child, Philip left Madrid on 19 December.

Martire was vituperative about Juana, who showed not a shred of "royalty or courage."[54] Burton, perhaps familiar with Martire's letters, later summarised the situation in his opus on melancholy. Juana was "so impatient and melancholy upon [Philip's] departure, that she would scarce eat her meat, or converse with any man; and though she were with child, the season of the year very bad, the wind against her, in all haste would to sea after him."[55] Historians too have attributed this distressing episode to Juana's personal obsession with Philip, underestimating the wider political dimension. Like all royal women, Juana had been born into an intensely political environment. Though not temperamentally power-hungry, honour and reputation mattered to her. She was affected not only by separation from her husband but by the way in which his conduct had reflected upon her. Thus, Juana, who wore violet for her reunion with Isabel in May, donned "*grandt deuil*" when bidding Philip farewell that December.[56]

Almost certainly, this signalled more than personal grief. When writing about Juana's niece and daughter-in-law, Isabel of Portugal, in the absence of Charles, Rodríguez-Salgado notes that, according to contemporary norms, princely wives separated from their husbands were expected to live relatively secluded lives. Although this would not affect Isabel's ability to govern, the many long absences of Charles V were "invariably interpreted as a signal of the husband's diminished appreciation of the woman's personal and political worth."[57] Evidently, in Juana's case, the situation was far more dramatic. She was heir to the many realms of Castile and Aragon and, beyond personal grief and dishonour, her mourning signalled a political calamity. The perception that Philip had run from his commitments as soon as the oath-taking was over sowed serious doubt over the succession, bringing sharply into focus the extreme improbability that the Spanish kingdoms could be personally and jointly governed by princes who were also archdukes of Austria and dukes of Burgundy. This left Juana with a bitter choice, although not necessarily a definitive one: to abandon her husband and children by staying to face an uncertain future in Castile; or (should Isabel die) to let Fernando continue to govern until Charles came of age.

Given the extent of hostile comment about Juana's conduct, it is worth recalling that, into the spring, she continued to fulfill royal duties. She made various acts of religious patronage, including visits that January to the Clarisan monastery of Rejas.[58] Further evidence of her religious patronage of the Franciscan order emerges in a note from fray Francisco Segarra, whom the monarchs had appointed inspector for the reform of monasteries in Aragon in 1493. Segarra thanks Juana for an (unspecified) act of charity and for her letters, in which she had urged him not to hesitate to approach her for further help, and he hopes to be able to visit her soon.[59] On 10 April, she brought much solace to her parents with the birth, at Alcalá de Henares, of a second son, Ferdinand, whom she agreed to leave in Castile. Sandoval describes Juana's pleasure at the birth and the (flattering) sermon about her that Villaescusa preached at the baptism.[60] Zurita refers to the "great respect that the princess always had for the queen."[61] Edwards and Aram remind us that she worked hard to please her parents and uphold Spanish interests.[62] Torn, nonetheless, between mother and husband, old frustrations and resentments erupted. She feared that Isabel planned, in Padilla's word, to *descasar* ('unmarry') her.[63] She would have been seriously worried by news that Philip, always vulnerable to fever, had fallen dangerously ill at Lyon.[64] It can be no mere coincidence that, just as Louis' doctors were despairing of Philip's recovery, Isabel's doctors were concluding that relations between mother and daughter had become so bad that they had to be separated.[65] Even if Juana did not fully realise the seriousness of Philip's illness, her instinct would have been to rush to his side, and she may have reminded Isabel of the monarchs' remark of 1500: "do not think that you are coming here never to return. Rather, you can come and go as you wish after being sworn-in."[66] But the seas were beginning to build and Juana could not travel through France while hostilities endured. Above all, Isabel's own health was deteriorating. She tried to conceal Philip's eventual arrival home from Juana "because, in truth, she did not want her daughter to return to Flanders, since she felt very unwell with the illness from which she died."[67]

Philip, once recovered, kept up the pressure for Juana's return, sending a series of messengers and letters. In August, Juana assured him that preparations for her departure were under way; that she and Isabel were heading for Burgos and that Ferdinand was well.[68] In the event, Isabel stayed at Segovia while Juana, proceeding north, stayed in the stronghold of La Mota at Medina del Campo.

Her residence in the fortress remains something of a mystery. Rearing from its hill, the red brick castle with its massive quadrilinear keep and bartizan towers, was Castile's arsenal as well as archive and occasional lodging place and prison, and it still has a colossal, almost live, presence. The most likely explanation for Juana's stay is that, with trust failing on both sides, Isabel had decided that she could be better guarded at La Mota than at the royal palace. On 6 September, a ship's captain told Fernando that he had received an order from Juana to await her at Bilbao.[69] A dismayed Isabel wrote: "I do not think, or expect, and so cannot believe you are leaving, for although there are many necessary reasons for your departure, greater problems may follow if you leave like this."[70] Juana complied. But by late November, she was coming under renewed pressure from Philip, who used the four-year-old Charles to send her an emotional appeal.[71] Juana's last reserves of self-control broke down.

Martire describes her prowling the outer precincts of the castle like "an African lion."[72] In Isabel's description of these events, her distress as a mother and a queen is almost palpable. Juana planned to "walk through the streets and mud to the posada where the horses were kept …". When she realised that Isabel had ordered that the gates be shut she "remained in the outer precinct of the house all evening and all night and all the next day until the second hour in the humidity and night dew and without either hat or coat, during one of the coldest nights of the year so far, and not for a moment would she return to her room." The international fair was in full swing, with the saddle and leather workers conducting trade close to the castle walls. Concerned that Juana's departure would cost her authority and reputation, Isabel sent a series of high-ranking emissaries, including Cisneros, in vain attempts to persuade her to return inside. In the end, Isabel had to come in person "with more effort and haste and making longer days of it than I knew was good for my health." But Juana "spoke to me so heatedly and with words so disrespectful and so far beyond what a daughter should say to a mother that had I not seen the state she was in I would not have tolerated it for a moment."[73]

We do not have Juana's account. Did she, when arguing with her mother, venture into the darker territory of Isabel's past? Might she even have referred to Isabel's role in the *descasamiento* of Afonso V of Portugal and Juana ('la Beltraneja') of Castile when the war of the Castilian succession of 1475–1479 ended in their defeat?[74] In 1503, the daughter and heir of Enrique IV, still languished in monastic confinement in Portugal but would never renounce her claim on the throne of Castile.

Writing from Medina on 2 December 1503, Lope de Conchillos told his uncle, Fernando's secretary, Miguel Pérez de Almazán, that Isabel was well but "very afflicted and tired" of the princess.[75] In March 1504, Juana was finally allowed to depart. Diego Ramírez de Guzmán, bishop of Catania, was sent with her to reinforce the Spanish diplomatic presence in Brussels. Crucially, Diego Ramírez de Villaescusa, bishop of Málaga, did not accompany her. Juana's journey, from beginning to end, was a reversal of the first. There were no tears when she left Laredo, but Philip eagerly awaited her at Blankenburg. While Isabel wondered bitterly if she would remain as "discontented, as she was while here, with everything to do with here," she was the toast of the Low Countries.[76]

Juana's decision to abandon Castile would go on to have immense repercussions for her future and for that of her kingdoms. Prawdin thought she had made an emotional, political, even religious rupture with "all Spain."[77] For Aram too, "It was clear that Juana was willing to use her health and compromise her status to obtain what she wanted and that was not to reign over Castile."[78] Others have seen her conduct as a symptom of madness. Zurita thought the incident at La Mota "revealed the indisposition and dementia (*demencia*) of the Princess, which was not formerly public knowledge."[79] Ladero Quesada too has Juana "passing the threshold of dementia: while for Suárez Fernández: "since that stormy night of November 1503 … her parents … had not the slightest doubt that [Juana] suffered from a mental disturbance so great that it could prevent her from assuming her functions."[80]

None of this seems exact. The problem with the notion of rupture is that it does not convey the messy complexity of the challenges, and torment of indecision, with which Juana struggled. She took her marriage vows seriously but had also made sacred vows to her future kingdoms before the altars of Toledo and Zaragoza, and her subsequent insistence on protecting Castilian interests, as she saw them, would wreck relations with the husband she had longed to rejoin. As for the argument that Juana was stricken by incapacitating mental illness, this ignores one salient fact. Isabel had fought hard to persuade her daughter to stay beside her in the hope that she could ensure, with Fernando's help, a successful transition. Isabel's struggle for Juana was, in other words, a struggle for the very future of her kingdoms. As such, it is unnecessary to argue that she thought Juana intrinsically incapable of governing.

## 3.3 Conflict in Brussels

Erasmus' Epiphany speech of 1504, made to Philip on the Coudenberg, was characteristically flattering both to Philip and to Juana. The princess was as chaste as Penelope; as pious as Claudia; as noble as Cornelia, mother of the Gracchi. Yet Erasmus had a pointed message: Spain was a temptation that Philip (and, by extension, Juana) had to resist. Speaking in the voice of the Low Countries he declared: "Spain crowned you, but I bore you. I admit I owe everything to you, but in return you owe yourself to me. That is a bold thing to say, but it is the truth. For I know I address my true prince, and not a tyrant."[81]

Jan Smeken, leading poet, or *facteur*, of Brussels' chamber of rhetoric, De Lelie (Lily), feted Juana's return in similar vein as essential to the peace, prosperity and impregnability of the Low Countries. He compared her to the Trojan Palladium, divine image of Pallas Athene, which had put Troy beyond the reach of Greece.[82] But neither Erasmus nor Smeken had counted on Philip's new favourite, Juan Manuel, lord of Belmonte de Campos, brother of the late Marina Manuel, and an ambitious and able diplomat. Manuel had helped prepare Juana's first voyage to the Low Countries, commissioning the two Genoese carracks. Although loyal to Isabel, he had a passionate antipathy for Fernando and was determined to whet Philip's appetite for Castile. Fuensalida felt sidelined: "Don Juan … speaks in such obscure terms that I cannot understand the meaning, although I understand the words … They only speak to me in general terms; they do not call me to their meetings. I understand that these are about matters very different to those your highnesses would like to hear about, indeed, they are the contrary of them…".[83] After Manuel's arrival, Juana's relations with the three Spanish ambassadors, whose joint despatches resound with Manuel's voice, deteriorated sharply.

Juana's reunion with Philip and the children was joyful.[84] But soon afterwards she suspected, or discovered, an affair between Philip and a noblewoman in her entourage: "they say," writes Martire, "that, her heart full of rage, her face vomiting flames, her teeth clenched, she rained blows on one of her ladies, whom she suspected of being the lover, and ordered that they cut her blond hair, so pleasing to Philip …". Philip's response was equally furious. He had "thrown himself" on his wife and insulted her in public. Sensitive and obstinate, "Juana is heartbroken … and unwell …". Isabel "suffers much, astonished by the northener's violence."[85]

Maximilian's biographer, Wiesflecker, describes Juana's response as the symptom of a pathological, passionate, if not unfounded, *Haßliebe*, fomenting continual strife.[86] But again, this is to overlook the political dimension. Juana would have known for years about Philip's visits to the *baigneries* and his more ephemeral relations with women. But this affair seemed a direct challenge to her standing and dignity. Juana knew her own faults and had tried to limit them. In 1500, after becoming princess, she had asked Isabel to send her an honest and prudent Spanish lady who "knows how to advise her, and where she sees something out of order ('*deshordenado*') in her conduct could say so as servant and adviser but not as an equal, because, even if the advice were good, if expressed in a disrespectful way it would create more anger in she to whom it was said than it would allow for correction."[87]

These words reveal an awareness of her difficulty in controlling a quick temper and her hypersensitivity about perceived threats to her status from some high-ranking women. But they also reflect Isabel's attitude. Ladero Quesada notes that, as queen regnant, Isabel "needed to construct a human entourage … formed by women who would not obstruct but support her political actions." They were "like an extension of the queen, in their feminine condition and in their capacity to govern their households, together with their husbands, as Isabel governed hers. In this respect, deviations were particularly damaging."[88] Isabel had dismissed the women she suspected of liaisons with Fernando. Juana had no comparable means of doing so. Instead, having begun her journey home as a Spanish princess and ended it as a Burgundian 'widow,' she now re-asserted her Spanish identity. But, by refusing to accept the women whom Philip continued to impose upon her, she was obliged to cut herself off from court life.

Philip's subsequent actions may be seen in the context of a strategy, encouraged by Manuel, to legitimate his claim to Castile through his wife but at her expense. He exploited the bitter circumstances of Juana's departure from Castile to try to re-spin his reputation to her detriment.

He had a record of her extravagances sent to the monarchs through Mújica, who now worked as Philip's agent rather than as Juana's loyal servant. When, after Isabel's death, Philip's Burgundian envoy and specialist in Spanish affairs, Philibert ('*La Mouche*') de Veyré, reproached Philip for this action—it was "not well done"—Philip protested angrily that he had been forced to "defend my right," adding: "Whether the Queen is mad or not I shall have what belongs to her and me and will govern or lose my life in the attempt …".[89]

Apart from signing and sending this dossier, Philip withheld crucial information from Juana. On 26 September, Fernando informed them of an irreversible decline in Isabel's health, urging them, on her behalf, to return to Castile.[90] Philip, fearing that Juana's presence there would cause him "many difficulties," weakening his authority, ordered the ambassadors not to show her the letter. The ambassadors' compliance infuriated Fernando. Did he have to remind them, he demanded, that Juana was the "heir," "the everything"?[91] He recalled Guzmán, but was unable to recall Manuel.[92]

Uninformed and misinformed, Juana tried to keep track of Isabel's health, as a letter she wrote to Katherine makes clear.[93] Between July and November 1504, Philip discovered a plan of Juana's to slip out of Brussels by night, take refuge in a monastery, and from there continue to a seaport and re-embark for Spain. His dismissal of several of Juana's Spanish servants, and the dismissal or retirement of Jeanne d'Halewijn, took place at this time, although it is unclear to what extent such dismissals related to the escape plan, or to rumours of a plot to abduct Charles.[94] Philip responded to these plans, or rumours of plans, and to Juana's fierce resistance to the dismissal of her slaves, or former slaves, by locking her in her rooms. These were above Philip's and connected by a spiral staircase. All night she banged on the floor with a 'stone' or 'stick' and tried to tear up the floorboards with a knife. The next day she told him she would die rather than do anything he wanted. The ambassadors reported that: "Given that the Princess did not want any other company than her slaves, owing to her frequent bathing and hair-washing [which], according to the doctors, caused her much harm, the Prince agreed to dismiss them." The ambassadors added that Juana had reportedly struck one slave and "taken it into her head to mark their faces."[95]

Philip himself bathed frequently and the palace was well equipped with baths and sauna. But watery imagery was often used to reflect female transgression and instability, from Dürer's pen drawing of

*The Women's Bath* to the highly popular story of the shape-shifting water spirit, Melusina—a beautifully illustrated version of which Philip kept in his library.[96] On his journeys to and from Spain, Philip had visited sites associated with Melusina, whose secret and magical ablutions had eventually led to her expulsion from court, and from the mortal world, and when homeward bound, he had stopped to visit the place where "Remondin lies, husband of Mellusine ... as in the greatest desert in the world."[97] Standing beside Remondin's grave, did Philip reflect on his own problematic marriage? Certainly, by drawing attention to Juana's secret ablutions under the influence of her "indecent," "dishonourable" and probably *morisca* slaves, he implied that Juana's conduct had become irrational and dangerous, a destabilising factor at court and a source of dishonour to them both.

As Isabel lay dying, a new injection of sarcasm and insolence—almost certainly Manuel's—is detectable in the joint despatches from Brussels. According to one of these, Juana was entirely to blame for her own isolation: "Her Highness is her own doorkeeper ...". They could hardly bribe their way in and if they tried to break down the door, they would risk being injured. Much as they wanted to see her, "since it would give us authority," she refused point blank to see *them*; she was, she said, "*mala de la cabeça*."[98]

This indicates something more serious than a headache but does not tally with Philip's own remarks about Juana's desire to return to Spain and the influence he feared she would exert there. Nor does it tally with her willingness to see the ambassadors as long as they limited their discussions to Spanish affairs.[99] In any event, Juana's isolation and Philip's determination to "defend my right" worked to the detriment of both. As Fuensalida remarked to Almazán, echoing St Paul's letter to Timothy: "matters between the Prince and Princess are such that unless God miraculously deprives her of her caprices (*fantasía*) and does not bestow on him a different temperament, it will be impossible for them ever to agree. If a house is in such disorder as theirs is now, how can so many and such great realms as those to which they are to succeed ever work in harmony?"[100]

## Notes

1. Lambert (Duggan, ed. 2002).
2. Duindam (2016), 94.
3. Fernández de Oviedo (ed. 1870).
4. Villasecusa (González Olmedo, ed. 1944).
5. Rawlings (2002).

6. Albaladejo (1992).
7. AGS, Estado 1-2, f. 366, Miranda to Juana, 1 September 1498.
8. RB II/2205.1, Real Cédula, Alcalá de Henares, 18 March 1498; RB II/2205.2, Real Cédula, Alcalá de Henares, 10 March 1498.
9. CSP (Queen Juana), Bergenroth, ed. Matienzo to monarchs, 16 August 1498.
10. '... *desde el primero día que començé a seruir a la R[eina] n[uestro] s[eñora] su madre fuí affectionadissimo y muy fiel a su seruicio, y ... por esto la R. doña ysabel ... me tuuo por sospechoso a su seruicio, y aficionado al estado de su padre ...*' '*Instrucción*', González Olmedo (ed. 1944).
11. AGS, PR 52, f. 116, Matienzo to monarchs, 15 January 1499.
12. Teresa [Manrique?] to Juana, 20 [?] December [1496], in Rodríguez de Diego (Zalama, ed. 2010), 41–42.
13. María Manrique Chacón de Acuña Fajardo to Juana [1498?], in Rodríguez de Diego, 42–43.
14. AGS, Estado 1, f. 366, Miranda to Juana, 1 September 1498.
15. AGS, PR 52, f. 116, Matienzo to monarchs, 15 January 1499.
16. Mújica to monarchs, 16 May 1501, in Rodríguez de Diego, 43.
17. Carmi Parsons (Duggan, ed. 1997).
18. In 1498, Juana was not yet princess. But the similarity of her situation, in certain striking respects, to that of San Pedro's Laureola, is a theme of this study. See, for instance, E. Michael Gerli (2008).
19. CSP. Sp. 219, Villaescusa to monarchs, 17 August 1498.
20. Fleming (Zalama, ed. 2010).
21. ADN B3459, États journaliers de la dépense de l'hôtel de Jeanne, 3 May 1501; ADN B3459, hôtel de Jeanne, 1501; AGS, CSR, 420.2, 16 May 1501.
22. ADN B3459, 15 February 1501.
23. AGS, CRS 402.2, Rodríguez de Diego (Zalama, ed. 2010).
24. Fuensalida (Berwick y de Alba, ed. 1907), 4 August 1500, 138.
25. Padilla (CODOIN, 8), 68.
26. Evans (1997).
27. Fuensalida, 6 August 1500, 141.
28. Fuensalida, 5 November 1500, 158.
29. Ibidem.
30. Fuensalida, 22 March 1501, 175–182.
31. RAH, Salazar, A-9, f. 132, Fonseca to Almazán, 12 August 1501.
32. Domínguez Casas (1993), Aram (2005), Zalama (2010).
33. Lalaing (Gachard, ed.), I; *Reise* (Chmel, ed. 1840), I.
34. *Reise*, 572.
35. Córdova Miralles (2002), 313.
36. Porras Gil (Zalama, ed. 2010).
37. *Reise*, 644; Lalaing, 173.

38. Molinet (Doutrepont and Jodogne, eds. 1935–1937), II, 514–515; Philip to governors of Low Countries (Gachard, ed. ), 378–384.
39. Lalaing, 174–176; *Reise*, 651.
40. Aram (2005), 62.
41. Philip to governors of Low Countries (Gachard, ed.), I, 11 May 1502, 379.
42. Vallejo (de la Torre, ed. 1913), 54–55.
43. *Reise*, 652; Molinet, II, 515.
44. '*Et larmoioit la Royne de joye, de voir sa fille* ...' (*Reise*, 652).
45. Yarza Luaces; Herrero Carretero (2001).
46. Marcuello (Blecua, ed. 1987), f. 84v.
47. Molinet, II, 381–382. '*Nous sommes, Dieu merchy, deslogiez de Thoulette.*' Philip to Nassau, *lieutenant-général*, and Maigny, *chancelier* [undated].
48. Padilla, 88.
49. Martire (López de Toro, ed. 1955) 10, 250, 20 September 1502.
50. Argensola (Lanaia, ed. 1630), 39–40.
51. Lalaing, 240–242.
52. RAH, Salazar, A-11, f. 354 [Undated copy; 1502].
53. Zurita, 3 (Canellas López, ed. 1992).
54. Martire, 10, 253, 4 January 1502 [1503]; 255, 10 March 1503.
55. Burton (Jackson, ed. 2001), 282.
56. Lalaing, 245.
57. Rodríguez-Salgado (Soly, ed. 1999), 69.
58. ADN, B. 3461, hôtel de Jeanne.
59. AGS, CSR, 420.2, fray Francisco Segarra to Juana, 24 April 1502–1504, Rodríguez de Diego (Zalama, ed. 2010), 44.
60. Sandoval (ed. 1955).
61. Zurita, 3, 215.
62. Edwards (2004); Aram (2005).
63. Padilla, 115.
64. Padilla, 92; Lalaing, 290–293.
65. RAH, Salazar, A-11, f. 380v.381, Doctors de Soto, Julián and de la Reyna to Fernando, 20 June 1503.
66. Fuensalida, 5 November 1500, 158.
67. Padilla, 114.
68. Philip to Nassau and Maigny (Gachard, ed.), I, 15 August 1503, 383.
69. RAH, Salazar, A-9, f. 227, Hugo de Urries to Fernando, 6 September [1503].
70. BL, Additional Ms. 28572, f. 43, Isabel to Juana, 12 September [1503].
71. Martire, X, 268, 29 December 1503.
72. Martire, X, 268.
73. Fuensalida (Isabel) [1504], 195–197.
74. The marriage, though given papal dispensation, was probably dissolved when both Afonso and Juana promised to enter monasteries. In

*Mary I* (2011), John Edwards suggests that Katherine's later vehement rejection of Henry VIII's proposal that she retire to a monastery might have been influenced by memories of Juana of Castile's enclosure in a convent. See Azcona (2007).

75. RAH, A-9, f. 219, Conchillos to Almazán, 2 December [undated; 1503].
76. Fuensalida (monarchs), 10 May 1504, 238.
77. Prawdin (1938), 93.
78. Aram (Nieto Soria, ed. 2008), 34.
79. Zurita, III, 215.
80. Ladero Quesada (2012), 137; Suárez (2006), 55.
81. Erasmus (Riber, ed. 1964); Jardine, ed. (1997), 122.
82. Mareel (Wijsman, ed. 2010), 213–230. The title of Smeken's play, *Spel op hertoge Karle ons keyser nu es* ('Play about Duke Charles, now our Emperor'), was applied later.
83. Fuensalida, 10 April 1504, 223.
84. Fuensalida (joint despatch), 4 June 1504, 248.
85. Martire, 10, 272, 26 June 1504.
86. Wiesflecker (1971–1986), III, 270.
87. Fuensalida, 6 August, 1500, 142.
88. Ladero Quesada (Valdeón Baruque, ed. 2004), 20.
89. Fuensalida, 15 May 1505, 356.
90. Fuensalida (Fernando), 26 September 1504, 286–287.
91. Fuensalida (joint despatch), 6 October 1504; Fuensalida (Fernando), 11 November 1504, 307.
92. Fuensalida, 11 November 1504, 307.
93. Katherine refers to Juana's letter in one of her own to Isabel of CSP. Sp. 1, 413, 26 November 1504.
94. ADN B. 2186.73342, 3 July 1504; ADN B. 2189.73659; ADN B. 2186.73343, 3 November 1504; Fuensalida, 10 November 1504, 304–305; ADN B. 2188.73487; B. 2190.73846, 3 July 1504; B. 2192.73934, 8 January 1505.
95. Fuensalida (joint despatch), 1 November 1504, 297–301. Cortés López (1989) is, however, surely right to dismiss as 'gratuitous' the assertion by Pfandl that Juana tortured her slaves for fun.
96. Wijsman (2010). The Melusina manuscript is now in the British Library (BL, Harley 4418).
97. Lalaing, 144, 253.
98. Fuensalida (joint despatch), 3 December 1504, 312.
99. Fuensalida (joint dispatch), 1 November 1504.
100. Fuensalida, 1 November 1504.

## References


Aram, Bethany. 2005. *Juana the Mad: Sovereignty and Dynasty in Renaissance Europe*. Baltimore and London: John Hopkins University Press.

———. 2008. La Reina Juana entre Trastámaras y Austrias. In *Gobernar en tiempo de crisis: Las quiebras dinásticas en el ámbito hispánico (1250–1808)*, ed. J.M. Nieto Soria and M.V. López-Cordón Cortezo. Madrid: Sílex.

Argensola, Bartolomé Leonardo de. 1630. *Primera Parte de los Anales de Aragón que prosigue los del Secretario Gerónimo Çurita*, ed. I. Lanaia. Zaragoza: I. Lanaia.

Azcona, Tarsicio de. 2007. *Juana de Castilla, mal llamada La Beltraneja*. Madrid: La Esfera de los Libros.

Berwick y de Alba (ed.). 1907. *Correspondencia de Gutierre Gómez de Fuensalida, embajador en Alemania, Flandes y Inglaterra (1496–1509)*. Madrid: Alemana.

Blecua, José Manuel (ed.). 1987. *Pedro Marcuello: Cancionero*. Zaragoza: Institución Fernando el Católico.

Burton, Robert. 2001. *The Anatomy of Melancholy*, ed. H. Jackson. New York: New York Review of Books.

Carmi Parsons, John. 1997. The Burials and Posthumous Commemorations of English Queens to 1500. In *Queens and Queenship in Medieval Europe*, ed. Anne Duggan. Woodbridge: Boydell Press.

Chmel, Joseph (ed.). 1840. Reise des Erzherzogs Philipp nach Spanien. In *Die Handschriften der K. K. Hofbibliothek in Wien*, vol. 1: Verlag Carl Gerold.

Córdova Miralles, Álvaro Fernández de. 2002. *La Corte de Isabel I: Ritos y ceremonias de una reina (1474–1504)*. Madrid: Dykinson.

Cortés López, José Luis. 1989. *La Esclavitud Negra en la España Peninsular del Siglo XVI*. Salamanca: Universidad de Salamanca.

Domínguez Casas, Rafael. 1993. *Arte y etiqueta de los Reyes Católicos: Artistas, residencias, jardines y bosques*. Madrid: Alpuerto.

Doutrepont, Georges, and Omer Jodogne (eds.). 1935–1937. *Chroniques de Jean Molinet*. Brussels: Académie Royale de Belgique.

Duindam, Jeroen. 2016. *Dynasties: A Global History of Power, 1300–1800*. Cambridge: Cambridge University Press.

Edwards, John. 2004. *Isabel la Católica: poder y fama*. Madrid: Marcial Pons.

———. 2011. *Mary I: England's Catholic Queen*. New Haven and London: Yale University Press.

Evans, R.J.W. 1997. *Rudolf II and His World*. London: Thames and Hudson.

Fernández Albaladejo, Pablo. 1992. *Fragmentos de monarquía*. Madrid: Alianza Universidad.

Fernández de Oviedo, Gonzalo. 1870 (ed.). *Libro de la cámara real del Príncipe Juan e oficios de su casa e serviçio ordinario*. Madrid: Sociedad de Bibliófilos Españoles.

Fleming, Gillian Beatrice. 2010. La visita a Inglaterra de Juana I (enero-abril de 1506). In *Juana I en Tordesillas: su mundo, su entorno*, ed. M.-A. Zalama. Valladolid: Ayuntamiento de Tordesillas/Grupo Página.

Gerli, Michael E. 2008. Conflictive Subjectivity and the Politics of Truth and Justice in *Cárcel de Amor*. In *Queen Isabel I of Castile: Power, Patronage, Persona*, ed. Barbara F. Weissberger. Woodbridge: Tamesis.

Herrero Carretero, Concha. 2001. Tesoro de devoción de la corona de España. In *A La Manera de Flandes: Tapices Ricos de la Corona de España* (cat.). Madrid: Patrimonio Nacional.

Jardine, Lisa (ed.). 1997. Panegyric for Archduke Philip of Austria. In *Erasmus: The Education of a Christian Prince*. Cambridge: Cambridge University Press.

Ladero Quesada, Miguel Ángel. 2004. La Reina en las crónicas de Fernando de Pulgar y Andrés Bernáldez. In *Visión del Reinado de Isabel la Católica*, ed. Julio Valdeón Baruque. Valladolid: Instituto Universitario de Historia Simancas/Ámbito Ediciones.

———. 2012. *Isabel I de Castilla: Siete ensayos sobre la reina, su entorno y sus empresas*. Madrid: Dykinson.

Lalaing, Antoine de. 1876. Voyage de Philippe le Beau en Espagne en 1501. In *Collection des Voyages des Souverains des Pays-Bas*, vol. 1, ed. Louis-Prosper Gachard. Brussels: Commission Royale d'Histoire.

Lambert, Sarah. 2002. Queen or Consort: Rulership and Politics in the Latin East, 1118–1228. In *Queens and Queenship in Medieval Europe*, ed. Anne Duggan. Woodbridge: Boydell Press.

López de Toro, José (ed.). 1955–1957. *Petrus Martyr Anglerius: Epistolario.* CODOIN, 9–12. Madrid: Imprenta Góngora.

Mareel, Samuel. 2010. Theatre and Politics in Brussels in the Time of Philip the Fair: The Leemans Collection. In *Books in Transition at the Time of Philip the Fair*, ed. Hanno Wijsman. Turnhout: Brepols.

Padilla, Lorenzo de. 1846. CODOIN, 8. In *Crónica de Felipe I llamado el Hermoso*, ed. Miguel Salvá and Pedro Sainz de Baranda. Madrid: Imprenta de la viuda de Calero.

Prawdin, Michael. 1938. *Johanna die Wahnsinnige: Habsburgs Weg zum Weltreich*. Vienna: Otto Lorenza Verlag.

Porras Gil, María Concepción. 2010. El arte de recibir: fiestas y faustos por una princesa. In *Juana I en Tordesillas: su mundo, su entorno*, ed. M.-A. Zalama. Valladolid: Tordesillas/Grupo Página.

González Olmedo, S.I., Félix. 1944. *Diego Ramírez de Villaescusa (1449–1537), fundador del Colegio de Cuenca y autor de los Cuatro Diálogos sobre la Muerte del Príncipe Don Juan*. Madrid: Editora Nacional.

Rawlings, Helen. 2002. *Church, Religion and Society in Early Modern Spain.* Basingstoke and New York: Palgrave Macmillan.

Riber, Lorenzo (ed.). 1964. *Erasmo: Obras escogidas*. Madrid: Aguilar.

Rodríguez de Diego, José Luis. 2010. La huella documental de una reina sin gobierno. In *Juana I en Tordesillas: su mundo, su entorno*, ed. M.-A. Zalama. Valladolid: Ayuntamiento de Tordesillas/Grupo Página.

Rodríguez-Salgado, María José. 1999. Charles V and the Dynasty. In *Charles V: 1500–1558*, ed. H. Soly. Antwerp: Mercatorfonds.

Sandoval, Prudencio de. (ed.) 1955–1956. *Historia de la vida y hechos del Emperador Carlos V.* Madrid: Biblioteca de Autores Españoles.

Súarez Fernández, Luis. 2006. Coyuntura Europea en el Reinado de Juana. In *Doña Juana, Reina de Castilla*. Madrid and Barcelona: Fundación Rafael del Pino/Real Academía de la Historia/Marcial Pons.

Vallejo, Juan de. 1913. *Memorial de la Vida de Fray Francisco Jiménez de Cisneros*, ed. De la Torre y del Cerro. Madrid: Centro de Estudios Históricos.

Wiesflecker, Hermann. 1971–1986. *Kaiser Maximilian I. Das Reich, Österreich und Europa an der Wende zur Neuzeit.* Vienna: Verlag für Geschichte und Politik.

Wijsman, Hanno. 2010. Philippe le Beau dans les livres. In *Books in Transition at the Time of Philip the Fair*, ed. Hanno Wijsman. Turnhout: Brepols.

Yarza Luaces, Joaquín. 2001. Reinas promotoras, colecciones dispersas. In *A La Manera de Flandes: Tapices Ricos de la Corona de España* (cat.). Madrid: Patrimonio Nacional.

Zalama, Miguel-Ángel. 2010. *Juana I. Arte, Poder y Cultura en torno a una reina que no gobernó.* Madrid: Centro de Estudios Europa Hispánica.

Zurita, Jerónimo. 1992. *Historia del Rey Don Hernando el Católico. De las empresas y ligas de Italia*, vol. 3, ed. Ángel Canellas López, Magdalena Canellas and Antonio J. Rodríguez. Zaragoza: Gobierno de Aragón.

CHAPTER 4

# Fernando's House (1504–1505)

## 4.1 Able and Willing

While Philip locked Juana's doors, Isabel had a new door and windows cut into her room in the palace of Medina del Campo to let in air and light. Around her were tapestries illustrating the Book of Revelations, then thought to be the work of her patron saint, St John the Evangelist, whom she described in her will as her "special advocate in this present life" and whom she hoped would stand by her at that "very terrible and stringent judgment, most terrible against the powerful." With her too was a tapestry of the Mass of St Gregory, in which a vision of Christ appears on the altar during the miracle of the transubstantiation.[1] This, probably Juana's gift, was returned to Juana after Isabel's death.[2]

The queen's will of 12 October 1504 is a remarkable political and religious manifesto, but only its succession clause concerns us here. Isabel confirmed Juana as "universal heir of all my realms and lands and lordly domains and all my landed property." Her subjects were to receive Juana as "true queen and native-born sovereign lady." But Isabel hedged this about with conditions. If Juana were not in her kingdoms, "or having come to them, has at some point to leave them again and remain abroad, or being in them, does not wish or is not able to govern them" ("*no quiera o no pueda entender en la governaçión dellos …*"), Fernando should govern on her behalf. If these conditions still applied after Fernando's death, Charles should rule as governor (not king) in Juana's lifetime. But if Juana *were* willing and able, she and Philip should "always be very



G. B. Fleming, *Juana I*, Queenship and Power,
https://doi.org/10.1007/978-3-319-74347-9_4

obedient and subject to the king [of Aragon]… and follow his orders and advice … in such a way that, in everything that touches upon his lordship, *it were as if I were still alive*" [my emphasis].[3] Subsequently, Isabel signed a codicil and letter patent, appointing Fernando governor-general under the same conditions.[4] These references to the imperative of obedience recall the will of Blanca I of Navarre, first wife of Fernando's father, Juan of Navarre and Aragon, who had urged her son and heir, Charles of Viana, to assume his Navarrese inheritance only with his father's blessing.

A Fernando-led governorship of Castile during the minority of Prince Juan had been foreseen from the moment of Juan's recognition as heir at the Cortes of Toledo of 1480. But, by 1499, when Miguel was hurriedly sworn-in at the Cortes of Ocaña, poor attendance meant that Isabel had been obliged to secure compliance to a possible future governorship, or regency, through dozens of individual warrants (*cédulas*).[5] These did not mention Fernando by name but the general assumption was that he, and not Miguel's father, or a regency council, would govern.

In view of her difficulties at Ocaña, Isabel would have known of Fernando's unpopularity among Castilian nobles and prelates, resentful of growing Aragonese power within the administration. Her decision to make Fernando a conditional grant of the governorship was taken late in the day—if, at least, one is to believe her vigorous response to a complaint of Philip's in July 1504. Denying she had made the nobles and procurators of Castile swear to accept Fernando as governor after her death, she declared that this was "a great and malicious falsehood on the part of whoever wrote it; this was never done … and not only was it not done, but … [although] many begged that the oath be sworn as it had been done for Prince Juan, the King and I refused to consent – quite the contrary, in no way would we hear of it – and the Prince and Princess our children were sworn-in unconditionally, as freely and entirely and fully as any prince was ever sworn in …".[6]

On the other hand, Isabel's will mentions confidential discussions between the monarchs and procurators at Toledo, and subsequently at Madrid and Alcalá de Henares, about arrangements to ensure the future governance of Castile. It declares that, after further consultation with some nobles and prelates, it had been agreed to ensure governance as outlined in the succession clause. But if the key words "*no puede*" were indeed hers, Isabel did not clarify what she meant by them. The ambiguity, as Zalama notes, would open Pandora's box.[7]

In his study of the "succession crisis," Carretero Zamora focuses on the "*incapacidad política manifiesta*" of the future queen.[8] The anonymous son of a witness to the Cortes, and author of an account of the rise of the Comunidades similarly notes that: "Of the Queen [Juana] there is no point in talking, because she always was as she is now … the truth is, she was mentally unstable ("*la verdad es que ello era falta de juicio*"), because I heard my father, who was at Alcalá de Henares in 1502, say that she was already ill ("*mala*"), and that the queen her mother asked Dr. Soto, one of her doctors, how the princess could be cured of her illness ("*enfermedad*") and the doctor said: 'The only remedy is a good beating' and this angered the Queen, who said: 'You don't speak that way about royal persons.'" If, however, such comments are judged alongside Fuensalida's high praise for Juana in 1500–1501; the opinions harvested by Fonseca in Brussels; Villaescusa's (admittedly hagiographic) sermon at Ferdinand's baptism; the views of Juana at the Corts of Zaragoza, mentioned by Argensola; the emotions and arguments that inspired subsequent events and the bafflement shown by at least some of the procurators at the Cortes of Toro of 1505 about the wording of the succession clause, it seems fair to conclude that the question of Juana's 'political incapacity' remained at the very least controversial, and was connected as much to her attachment to her husband as to her natural abilities.

This was crucial. According to the abovementioned author of the *Relación de las Comunidades*, whether from ignorance of the language or the customs of the Spanish kingdoms, or from natural indisposition, Philip "seemed to have no aptitude for governing."[9] Highly doubtful about his commitment to Spain, Isabel banned foreigners, ignorant of the "laws and *fueros* and rights and usages and customs of my realms," from taking any civil and ecclesiastical posts. She warns that "the prince my son is of another nation and language," and if he and Juana did not govern by these laws and rights and customs "they will not be obeyed and served as they should, and from this some outrage could result, and they would not be loved as I wish them to be."

Despite Isabel's emphatic denial of plans to marginalise Philip, his conduct when in Spain and thereafter, combined with Juana's depression and *descontamiento*, had spurred the monarchs on to explore possible alternatives to the succession. Only this explains a somewhat desperate plan, put to Philip by Fernando while Juana was still in Castile, to secure possession of Charles in exchange for Ferdinand. According to this plan—not dissimilar from one earlier advanced by Fuensalida—once the exchange had taken place, Philip, with the agreement of both Spanish and French monarchs, would govern the entirety of the kingdom of Naples for Charles and Claude (alongside Spanish officials) until the betrothed couple came of age. Naples, Fernando added, was "all gold."[10] Not unnaturally, Philip refused to part with his elder son. Instead, in September 1504, he signed a new agreement with Louis. Under the treaty of Blois, the marriage of Charles and Claude was confirmed, with Naples as dowry, but it was agreed that Louis, not Philip, should be interim governor.[11]

At the same time, the dossier delivered by Mújica (see Chapter 3), and the joint despatches from Brussels, bombarded Medina del Campo with news about an imploding marriage. Fernando later told Philip that he had only himself to blame for the wording of Isabel's will: "wanting to justify your desire to place the queen, her daughter, in a fortress, you sent [Isabel] a long document signed by your hand, which contained so much detail about [Juana's] illness that this, above all, beyond what she herself had seen and known, moved the queen … to order in her will what she did."[12]

Yet, as noted earlier, Isabel was loath to give up on her daughter. Only this can explain Fernando's urgent request that the princes return to Castile before she died, by comparison to the hope he nursed, after her death, that they might indefinitely postpone their journey. Her will and codicil carefully placed various courses of action before them as monarchs, and she asked that Juana be received and respected as true queen and sovereign with full rights to govern. That Juana's *desire*, rather than inability, to govern was Isabel's foremost worry is suggested by a subsequent alteration in the original manuscript, each clause of which was signed and endorsed by Gaspar de Gricio. As Zalama notes, the key words "*o no pueda*" ("or is unable") and again—this time in the conditional—"*o no podiere*" were missing from the original manuscript, and subsequently, and exceptionally, inserted above the line and between the phrases "*no quiere*" ("does not wish") or "*no quisiere*" ("should not wish") and "*entender en la governación*" ("govern").[13] Perhaps these insertions were the result of a purely accidental clerical omission made at the time. Perhaps they were the subject of subsequent discussion with Isabel or added later by Fernando and Gricio. Fernando denied accusations that he had put any pressure on Isabel.[14] Whatever the case, the fact that they were originally omitted does suggest that Isabel was concerned less about Juana's innate inability to govern than about the very real possibility that her daughter would allow, or be unable to prevent, a government led by Philip.

## 4.2 Problems and Ambitions of the King of Aragon

Isabel's physical and mental decline from 1497, and the consequent 'Aragonisation' of Castile, had aggravated malaise in the cities. Now Fernando faced the prospect that the nobles would again flex their muscles. His prestige crumbled "radically."[15] Poor harvests in 1501 led to hiked food prices, and from late 1504 heavy rains spoiled the wheat. Plague erupted. Castilian resources were being drained to fund military ventures seen as fundamentally Aragonese.[16] With its large *morisco* and *converso* population, the south remained a hotbed of political and religious unrest. In December 1500, Fernando had spurred Córdoba's inquisitor, Rodríguez Lucero, to yet greater zeal against heretics.[17] Between 1501 and 1504, hundreds of suspected Juaizers, or their effigies, were burned and hundreds more imprisoned by the Inquisition, including nobles and clerics. In 1507, the soldier, chronicler and *veinticuatro* of Córdoba and later comunero, Gonzalo de Ayala, reminded Fernando's chief secretary, Almazán, how, years before, he had warned that the misery of the south was "such that any neighbouring prince" (let alone Philip) could have ousted Fernando. Ayora urged greater distribution of wealth and fiscal and inquisitional reform.[18]

As Fernando's reputation fell, Isabel's posthumous fame rose, assuming almost mythical proportions. The Florentine historian and envoy, Francesco Guicciardini, lauds her vision, magnanimity and prudence while remarking that her reign was not without blood and war.[19] In his *Book of the Courtier*, Baldassare Castiglione, who came to Castile as apostolic nuncio, places in the mouth of Giovanni de Medici some of the most celebrated words to have been written about her. Medici describes her recovery of Castile from the grandees; her conquest of Granada; her fine judgment and rigorous standards of justice, balanced by clemency and generosity. Popular reverence for the queen was based both on love and fear: the people "appear to believe that she is watching them still from heaven," and thus her authority endures, like a wheel that, having been spun, "continues to turn a space by itself." Even today, the sense of a mutually protective presence lingers, perhaps especially on the Castilian meseta. A modern guidebook to Sepúlveda (Segovia)—a town that had once come to the aid of Isabel and Fernando against Enrique IV—goes out of its way to stress Sepúlveda's unconditional loyalty to Isabel.[20] A modern road sign at Arévalo, listing the stages of her funeral cortege through the province of Ávila as if it were only yesterday, reads like a stark litany of love and loss: "*Medina del Campo, El Bohodón, Gotarrendura, Cardeñosa, Ávila, Cerebreros …*".

The triumphs of the dual monarchy have been widely recognised. With support from a half-subdued nobility, and from cities keen to throw off seigneurial abuse, it had laid the groundwork for a stronger and potentially unified state and royal administration, its coffers filling with the proceeds from treasury reforms and efficient revenue collection. Long-term projects, like the incorporation of the Canary Islands and conquest of Granada and Naples, were completed. Its victory over the Nasrid emirate enabled it to shine on the European stage, while the huge significance of the American adventure was as yet only partially glimpsed. Well before the Reformation swept Europe, the mighty archbishopric of Toledo cooperated actively in the monarchical programme of monastic reform, and the establishment of the Inquisition on a permanent basis, and under government control, made it into an effective political weapon.

All these achievements were the consequence of a unique political experiment. When asking why a "tough-minded, strong-willed man with a reputation for ruthlessness" like Fernando would willingly help construct a form of monarchy that limited his powers, Earenfight finds one answer in the Aragonese institution of the lieutenant-general, a position ably carried out by Fernando's mother, Juana Enríquez, at a time of great unrest in Catalonia. Juana Enríquez was, of course, a queen consort, not a sovereign ruler, but Fernando's first-hand experience of the possibilities that female partnership could bring to a monarchy helped prepare him to cooperate with a project admitting a "range of power-sharing options" and which "drew from a rich and complex history of corporate monarchy that permitted them a unique and formidable plurality of power."[21]

This partnership, based on the concordat of Segovia of 1475, which set out a template for joint rule, granted Isabel real as well as nominal recognition of her proprietary status. Only Isabel received the allegiance of royal fortress governors; appointed Castilian treasury officials and other offices; made grants in cash and rents; appointed officials to her Castilian household (a powerful means of bestowing favours); controlled the masterships (*maestrazgos*) of the military orders; nominated to senior church posts, and so forth. It should, however, be pointed out that parts of the concordat did not long survive their testing in the forge of war and even after signing it, Fernando referred to "the right I have to these my kingdoms [of Castile] and to succeed in and inherit them." This, as Carrasco Manchado notes in her detailed study of the means by which the monarchs had established their legitimacy, shows that Fernando did not see the concordat as setting his role in stone. She also points to "frictions" at the level of symbolic representation of the royal couple throughout their reign.[22]

The perceived successes of the dual monarchy masked a growing unease that would help fertilise the seeds of revolutionary war. Ever-increasing royal authority and the flow toward a strong state drained into a reservoir of accumulating grievances about the nature and degree of royal power and the meaning of freedom. The monarchs' much-lauded exercise of justice was partly vitiated by fear of alienating great magnates who had supported them during the war of succession and Granadan campaigns and who continued to grab land and extend their jurisdiction. Reflecting on Fernando Pulgar's depiction, in his *Crónica*, of the administration of royal justice, Gerli refers to the creation of a "climate of acute uncertainty and apprehension in the kingdom rather than one of peace and stability."[23] Justice might often take the form of those terrible executions to which critically refers in his *Cuatro diálogos sobre la malhadada muerte del Príncipe de las Españas*: garrottings; live burnings and flayings; whippings to death; even *acañaveados*, in which renegades were used as live targets for cane spears after the surrender of Málaga in 1487.[24] The institution of the *corregimiento*—the means by which royal 'correctors' were sent, for specific periods, into cities under royal jurisdiction to secure order and justice—provoked disquiet. Early and effective propagandists for the monarchs, such as Valera and Palencia, had, under the reign of Enrique, attacked the institution as contrary to the laws and liberties of Castile.[25] Although placed on a permanent, systematic footing at the Cortes of Toledo of 1480, *corregidores* faced challenges to their royal authority and fierce criticism about declining standards and corruption in city administration.[26] These criticisms had grown under Fernando, whose choice of 'correctors' was particularly controversial.

For those on the wrong side of the Marian cloak that Isabel had thrown over her Christian family, the price of unity continued to rise. *Convivencia* was systematically dismantled. Intended to uphold the integrity of the conversion to Christianity of former Jews, the Inquisition developed into an "insidious system that would end by poisoning Spain's public spirit, installing an authentic organised intolerance, based on the accusations of informers and the establishment of an evident ideological conformism."[27] From 1492, hundreds of thousands of Jews who chose not to convert were expelled. Academic, municipal and religious institutions and military orders increasingly adopted the blood purity statutes.[28] Years of war with

Granada were followed by mass baptisms, book-burnings, uprisings in the Alpujarras and the exodus of the Muslims of Granada in 1502.

Isabel had not suffered dissent gladly. As Edwards remarks: "The flow of satirical verses in Castilian, which had been a feature of the two previous reigns, seems largely to have dried up" under the dual monarchy.[29] Its cultural richness owed much to preceding decades and few dared openly dissent. In 1490, some satirical verses appeared at Jerez de la Frontera (Andalucia), criticising the subsidies demanded from Jerez for the Granadan campaigns. In a new play upon the famous *Coplas de Mingo Revulgo* that had satirised the predecessor of Isabel and Fernando, Enrique IV, as a bad shepherd to his flock, the shepherd is urged to listen, for once, to the clamour of his sheep, too often sheared and left to shiver and starve for their apparent good ("*por servicio de tu grey*") in a landscape of mountains flattened by the programme of wartime construction.[30] The pastoral response to this act of treason was to sentence the author, *veinticuatro* Fernando de Vera, to death and to confiscate his goods. Vera managed to flee, unlike his deputy, bachiller Trujillo, whose execution in the main plaza of Jerez exemplified the monarchs' determination not to brook dissent within urban administrations.[31]

Isabel's suspicions about Villaescusa, mentioned earlier, may have been linked in part to his critical attitude to overweening power, as well as to the relative ease with which he settled, studied and made friends in the Low Countries—a land whose customs she had looked upon with reserve. A brilliant theologian, Villaescusa had been a disciple, at Salamanca, of the prominent scholar and author of *Comentarios a la política*, Fernando López de Roa, who believed power should be subject to strict restraints.[32] When, in his *Cuatro diálogos*, Villaescusa transforms Fernando into a mouthpiece for temperate rule, he implies that the monarchy had much yet to do in laying the foundations for good government. In the third dialogue, between Fernando and Isabel, the former turns from conventionally theological arguments to an indictment of that "monstrous" form of tyranny that favours particular interests over the common good. Villaescusa's Fernando recommends that Isabel ask herself whether she really has judged with justice and equity, protected the innocent and defended wards and widows from the tyranny of the powerful, and whether she has remembered that she was born to face the same hardships and miseries as her subjects. Fernando counsels Isabel to refrain from acts of cruelty and tyranny and from fiscal measures that rewarded nobles and courtiers. She had, says Fernando, to be a mother, not a *step*mother, to her people.[33]

It is unclear that the actual Fernando knew Villaescusa's work, but much of his correspondence from this time sets out to show himself as the father of his kingdoms (kingdoms often left unspecified). He was determined to exert full control over every aspect of government and to fulfill the ambition of his own father whose memory he cherished and who would strike his fist upon the table in frustration at Fernando's perceived weakness vis-à-vis the daughter-in-law. This ambition was to gain absolute mastery of the larger kingdom, land of his dynastic roots and which, in his heart, had always belonged to him. Mastery of Castile would also provide the material means of Aragon's preservation. Naples, the jewel in Aragon's crown that Fernando flashed before Philip in 1504, had been won with Castilian revenues, slowly but steadily supplemented by the new flow of wealth from the Indies, and protected by Castilian military genius and manpower. In her will, Isabel had bequeathed Fernando the lucrative revenues from the three military orders of Castile—those of Santiago, Calatrava and Alcántara, which had been brought under royal control—and half the revenues from the Indies so far discovered. Isabel thus deprived her heirs of much of what had been at her own disposal, doubtless hoping to bind them to a financial dependence upon Fernando. As John Stile, Henry's resident ambassador in Spain, was to point out, these revenues provided "al hys reamys and hys estate."[34] But Fernando might yet have to fight to retain those precious funds.

Guicciardini observed in 1511 that nothing slipped Fernando's personal control. He was struck by the king's good fortune and by a certain legerdemain and tendency to cover his actions with the "*onesto zelo de la Religione e santa intenzione al bene comune*"[35] Fernando told him that Spain needed a strong man who knew how to keep order and discipline in kingdoms that tended naturally to internal discord.[36] This was not a purely political consideration, for Fernando was also motivated by the spiritual preoccupations of the age and, during the war of the Castilian succession, as during the later Granadan campaigns, had tried, like a latter-day Charlemagne, to "live out the millenarian expectations with which prophetic utterance endowed him – the 'promised prince' who would raise his banner in Jerusalem and rule the world until its appointed end …".[37]

The dangers of Fernando's boyhood had taught him to excel in guile and duplicity—never, literally, to have less than two strategies at his disposal. But, if the influence of his formidable mother had prepared him for cooperation in a unique political experiment, his deep and enduring reverence for his father, Juan II of Navarre and Aragon, assumed greater importance after Isabel's death. There is a remarkable parallel between Fernando's quest for power and treatment of his daughter at Toro and Juan II's treatment of his own elder children, Charles of Viana and Blanca of Navarre. After the death of his first wife in 1441, the king had refused to renounce his claim on her small but highly strategic Pyrenean realm, despite the fact that Charles was her heir. When Charles and Blanca defied the king, Juan had both declared "unfit (*inhábiles*), unworthy of the succession (*indignos de la sucesión*) and incapable (*incapaces*) …".[38] In 1504, under a semblance of self-abnegation and loyalty to Isabel, Fernando twisted the knife into Juana and Philip, much as his father had twisted it into Fernando's half-siblings. While arguing that Philip could only be recognised as king-by-marriage after returning to Castile to renew his allegiance to its laws, and bringing Juana with him so that she could demonstrate the falsity of the evidence that Philip had brought against her,[39] he embarked on Juana's political liquidation. For this, he had two main pieces of ammunition: the authority of Isabel's will, which he glossed to his advantage, and the dossier that Philip had sent to Spain in the hope that it would "defend my right."

## 4.3 The Cortes of Toro

When Isabel died, on 26 November 1504, Fernando stood at a political crossroads. His Aragonese advisers urged him to take "the royal road" and proclaim himself Isabel's legitimate successor.[40] But Fernando knew that he lacked sufficient backing to cling to the royal title in defiance of Isabel's will and took a more winding path toward perpetual power

On the day of Isabel's death he informed Castile's towns and cities and chanceries that she had granted him the governorship, and pre-prepared letters of convocation were sent to the eighteen cities with votes in the Cortes.[41] The letters were sent in Juana's name, although without her knowledge or signature. The tone of these letters of convocation seems curiously self-defeating for a newly-proclaimed sovereign. In them 'Juana' confirms that Isabel had appointed Fernando governor, but the absence of any reference to the key conditions on which his governorship was based, invested it with a solidity and permanence that Isabel had not necessarily intended. At the same time 'Juana' does mention the monarchs' confidential discussions with the procurators at the time of her *juramento* in 1502, despite their potentially negative implications for her right to govern. More importantly, 'Juana' omits inclusion of the American patrimony among her titles. Isabel's will confirmed that these belonged exclusively to the crown of Castile, but Fernando subsequently incorporated into them into the crown of Aragon.[42]

After issuing these letters, Fernando stepped onto a platform in a rainy grey plaza. Beside him, Fadrique de Toledo, duke of Alba, raised the royal standard for Juana—the same standard that had been Isabel's and "was there," observed Padilla, creating the impression that it was picked up almost as an afterthought[43]—and cried three times "*Castilla por la Reina Doña Juana nuestra señora*!" Philip was not mentioned. After a period of seclusion and consultation with archbishop Cisneros at the monastery of Mejorada, Fernando fired the first shot in his campaign to secure the governorship. The Cortes opened at Toro on 11 January 1505. Fernando's officials and supporters engineered a heavy bias towards him among procurators and Cortes officials, who included, as president, Garcilaso de la Vega; royal secretary Almazán; and Cortes secretary Bartolomé Ruiz de Castañeda. This bias made it relatively easy, as Martínez Millán has noted, for Fernando to obtain confirmation as administrator and governor.[44] Given the bafflement expressed by some about the succession clause, Fernando decided on a step that would have horrified Isabel. On 23 January 1505, he absented himself as the contents of Philip's dossier were revealed. In a preface, Fernando explained that, long before her death, Isabel had become aware of an "illness and passion" in Juana. But, for reasons of discretion (*comedimiento*), decency (*honestidad*) and the "great and deeply-rooted grief" it caused her, she could not bring herself to refer, in her will, to her daughter's unfitness (*impedimiento*), except by the general phrase "unable" ("*no poder*").[45] This was the phrase that had been added above the line in Isabel's will.

After further discussion, the procurators agreed to accept the interpretation of the phrase "unable" most favourable to Fernando—namely, that Juana was incapacitated by "illness and passion" rather than by physical absence or imprisonment. There was no reference to Juana's *willingness* or *wish* to rule, which, although it seems to have been Isabel's main concern, was possibly thought irrelevant in the circumstances. The procurators confirmed Juana as true, legitimate queen and natural and proprietary mistress of Castile, Granada and León, while Fernando was sworn-in as governor.[46]

On 15 April 1505, Fernando backed his authority by minting new silver coins for the 'Indias.' Strangely, these showed the arms and names of Isabel and Fernando and the heraldic symbols of the yoke and arrows, but bore no reference whatsoever to the new proprietary queen. Moreover, the general coinage minted after Isabel's death also continued to bear the image and names of Isabel and Fernando. The absence of Juana's name and image, notes an expert on the coinage of the time, is "odd to say the least, and even illegal."[47]

As the Cortes proceeded, Henry VII, who had retained control of Katherine after Arthur's death in 1502, sent envoys to probe his brother-in-law's strengths, weaknesses and intentions. Francis Marsin, James Braybrooke and John Stile found a smiling and "lusty," if rather solitary, king. They spoke mostly to Almázan, of whom they wrote: "we cannot hear, see or know that [Fernando] hath any man so near of his most secret counsel as is … his secretary."[48]

Almazán's interview with Henry's envoys puts one in mind of the remark of the wise fool in *King Lear*. A snail has a 'house' to put his head in, the fool tells the king, "not to give it away to his daughters, and leave his horns without a case." Fernando's determination to keep his house entire is reflected in Almazán's pugnaciousness about the drawbacks of shared monarchy—a statement with evident implications for the new proprietary monarch. Fernando could govern Castile better alone than ever had been possible beside Isabel: "after the decesse of the quyne, everiche of the grete lordes of this land thoughte in his herte for to rule and to be as a kynge," but Fernando "hathe so provided that he may destroye them all in a daye, and that they do welle knowe," for he could intervene more effectively in their *señoríos* "than ever was don in the life of the quyn."[49]

Almazán avoided references either to Juana's 'unfitness' or to the essentially conditional nature on which Isabel had based the governorship. Instead, he declared that Fernando was the lawful ruler of Castile, which he would govern, to its profit, in perpetuity:

> the Kyng my lord ys fully determined for to order and rewle thys reame of Castlle for the terme of hys life, and not for to menysshe nor lese therein of his onor and profite the valewe of a ben accordynge unto the quyne's laste wille and testment, for there be two thyngs that helpe hys highness

> that he shuld do so: oon ys the quyne's wille, and a nother, the lawe of thys land gevithe that every kynge after the decesse of the quyne by whom the land movithe haveynge childer by hire, the kynge shall governe the land for the terme of his life. And so wolle the kynge my lord do; and so hit ys most beneficiall unto thys reame that he shuld do so.

Henry's envoys discovered, as would Guicciardini, that everything passed through Fernando's hands. Although not king, he meant to rule and be obeyed as if he were. Moreover, he:

> resayvithe and persayvithe all the revenews and profits of the said reames of Castell and Lions and Granada unto his awne proper use and profite and ys at no composecion or at any apoyntemement with the archduke nor with the quyne his wife therefore; nor he intends not for to render or to gyve unto thym any account of the revenues and profettes of that land for duereynge the terme of his life, nor said kynge sufferithe nor wille not suffer any juge or other officer to be made nor putt within the said reames by the kynge archeduke.[50]

However, Henry's envoys noted that many of the lords who had flocked to Toledo in 1502 stayed away from Toro. Pedro Manrique de Lara, first duke of Nájera, and generally seen as leader of the magnates' opposition to Fernando, was eloquently absent. So too were the duke of Medina Sidonia, count of Benavente and marquis of Villena. Some nursed grievances about loss of lands, estates and titles, but others also believed Fernando to be a tyrant who had placed Isabel under intolerable pressure to change the dispositions of her will and exploit the report of Juana's 'impediment' to 'usurp' Castile.[51] The English ambassadors thought the duke of Nájera "a man of grete coraje" who made future allegiance to Fernando conditional upon Juana's presence and will, and "wille not come at the corte un to the tyme that she come." The duke had meanwhile declared that he would ignore the orders of *corregidores* and other justice officials unless they could demonstrate that the queen had authorised their measures.[52] Diego López de Pacheco, marquis of Villena, whose estates were centred on the Tagus basin, was also impatient for the young monarchs' arrival. During the war of succession, Villena's father, Juan Pacheco ('*el Grande*'), had supported Enrique IV's daughter against Isabel and Fernando, and when his son continued this support, the monarchs had confiscated his marquisate, which comprised nearly the whole of what is now Albacete and part of Murcia, Cuenca, Alicante and Valencia.

Throughout his long life, the marquis longed for its restoration. His relations with Juana were good and he placed hope in the advent of the new monarchs, for at "[Juana] laste beynge there she promsyed to hym that yef ever she were quyne of Castell that he schuld have hys land ayen; notwithstondeyne, he hath byn with the Kynge Don Fernando sithen the dethe of the quyne more for fere than for love."[53]

If Juana was the key figure for many nobles, she was just as crucial for the 'commons,' and support for Philip or Fernando was largely conditional upon the perception of their relations with Juana, the 'natural heir prince':

> some saied that the Quyn was grete with childe, wherfore she myghte not come, and that the kynge wold come with owte hire, wherewith the Spaynards be not plesid in case that he so will do, for they dissire more for to have the Quyn then the Kynge, for the common sayenge ys that in case that the Kynge and the Quyn bothe jointly come togethers, yet never shall Flemeynge nor Burgonyon have any office kepeynge of any towne or castell within the landes of Spayne.

Thus, Philip would only have the people's hearts if Juana came "jointly" with him, for "the estats and comons of thys land make more solemnyte and rekonynge of the qyne then of hir fader the Kynge." God might have given Fernando victories against the infidel. But his time was over:

> the said our kynge hathe byn ever sore and chargeabille unto us in causeynge us for to paye many taskes and talages in the life of the quyne our naturall lady … and wer fere that in case that the kynge schuld contenewally reyne on us, that he wold dayly putte us unto suche charges. Wherfore we be dessiros that the Quyne donya Joana and her husband the Kynge Archeduke shuld come, for as much as that all the land of Granada is conquered and this land is in rest and peas; so that we trust that hereafter we shall not nede for to be charged for to paye any more taske or talages, wherby this land ys made veray pore.[54]

Such views, together with later reports of Juana's support for Fernando, help us to understand why, behind Almazán's petrean front, Fernando trod shifting sands, and why, in 1505 and throughout the subsequent struggle for power, his portrayal of Juana veered back and forth, from an "unfit" and useless queen to one of "great capacity" for whose cause the king of Aragon would fight to the death.[55]

## Notes

1. Liss (2004).
2. Herrero Carretero (2001).
3. AGS, PR 30–2, ff. 5–5v. and f. 6, 'Testamento de Isabel la Católica.'
4. AGS, PR 56, f. 18, 'Carta patente', 23 November 1504.
5. Francisco Olmos (2002).
6. Fuensalida (Berwick y Alba, ed. 1907), letter from monarchs, 6 July 1504, 250.
7. Zalama (2010).
8. Carretero Zamora (2005).
9. Diaz Medina, ed. (2003), 53–54. A slightly different version of the same account exists in manuscript form in the British Library (BL, Ms. Egerton 309, 'Relación de las Comunidades', f. 9v.–10). Henceforth I refer to the latter.
10. In Fuensalida, 1 January 1504, 198–200.
11. Suárez (2006).
12. Fuensalida, 'Lo que dixo Mose de Vere,' [undated], 401–404.
13. Zalama (2006).
14. 'Lo que dixo Mose de Vere.'
15. Villacañas Berlanga (2008), 537.
16. Suárez (2004).
17. Edwards (1986).
18. RAH, Salazar, A-12, f. 153, to Almazán, 16 July 1507.
19. Guicciardini (ed. 1775–1776), II.
20. Lobo Iglesias (1989).
21. Earenfight (Weissberger, ed. 2008), 3–18.
22. Carrasco Manchado (2006), 'Carta de merced,' 10 May 1475, 126; 70.
23. Gerli (Weissberger, ed. 2008), 155.
24. Nicolle (1998).
25. Edwards (2000).
26. Lunenfeld (1987); Ladero Quesada (2003); Edwards (2000).
27. Rábade Obradó (1993), 25.
28. Rawlings (2002).
29. Edwards (2005), 37.
30. 'Open, open your ears/Listen, listen, shepherd/Why do you not hear/ The clamour of your sheep …' For a fuller version, see Ladero Quesada (2003), 177.
31. Liss (2004); Ferrer-Chivite (1997).
32. '*… en alguna ocasión desliza la idea de la consideración del reinado de Isabel y Fernando como una forma de tiranía, aunque sin mencionarlos expresamente.*' Nieto Soria (Nieto Soria/Foronda, eds. 2005), 87.

33. Villaescusa (González Olmedo, ed. 1944), 272–278. Olmedo translates this partially and fairly freely from Latin into Spanish. Two other translations have appeared since.
34. Brewer, ed. (1920), LP, 1, 162, 9 September 1509, 84.
35. Guicciardini, III, 283.
36. Villacañas Berlanga (2008), 542–544.
37. Fernández-Armesto (Carr, ed. 2000), 122–123.
38. Martín (2003), 113. See also Vicens Vives (2006) and, for the reign of Juan of Aragon, Vicens Vives (1953); Ryder (2007).
39. Zurita (Canellas López, ed. 1992), 3.
40. Zurita, 3, 332–333.
41. Carretero Zamora (González Alonso, ed. 2006).
42. Francisco Olmos.
43. AGS, PR 7, f. 248, 'De como Jaén alço pendones por la Reina Doña Juana'; Padilla (CODOIN, 1846), 121.
44. Martínez Millán (2000), 1, 67.
45. Zurita, 3, 354–356.
46. AGS, PR 69, f. 34, 'Resumen de algunos actos de las Cortes de Toro.'
47. Francisco Olmos.
48. The National Archive, Kew (TNA), E 36/192, 'Instructions to ambassadors to make enquiries concerning the king of Aragon, the governance of Aragon and Castile … with answers of the ambassadors to the articles' (1505), f. 44.
49. Vicens Vives (2006); TNA, E 36/192, f. 17–18.
50. TNA, E 36/192, f. 22.
51. Zurita, 3, 357; 402–403.
52. Zurita, 3.
53. TNA, E 36/192, f. 11–12.
54. TNA, E 36/192, f. 6–7.
55. Zurita, 3, 441.

## References

Berwick y Alba (ed.). 1907. *Correspondencia de Gutierre Gómez de Fuensalida, embajador en Alemania, Flandes y Inglaterra (1496–1509)*. Madrid: Alemana.

Brewer, John Sherren (ed.). 1920. *Letters and Papers, Foreign and Domestic, of the Reign of Henry VIII*. London: HMSO.

Carrasco Manchado, Ana Isabel. 2006. *Isabel I de Castilla y la sombra de la ilegitimidad: propaganda y representación en el conflicto sucesorio (1474–1482)*. Madrid: Sílex.

Carretero Zamora, Juan Manuel. 2005. Crisis sucesoria y problemas en el ejercicio del poder en Castilla (1504–1518). In *Coups d'État à la fin du Moyen*

*Age? Aux fondements du pouvoir politique en Europe occidentale*, ed. François Foronda, Jean-Philippe Genet and José Manuel Nieto Soria. Madrid: Casa de Velázquez.

———. 2006. Las Cortes de Toro de 1505. In *Las Cortes y las Leyes de Toro*, ed. Benjamin González Alonso. Salamanca: Cortes de Castilla y León.

Díaz Medina, Ana (ed.). 2003. *Relación del discurso de las Comunidades*. Valladolid: Junta de Castilla y León.

Earenfight, Theresa. 2008. Two Bodies, One Spirit: Isabel and Fernando's Construction of Monarchical Partnership. In *Queen Isabel I: Power, Patronage, Persona*, ed. Barbara F. Weissberger. Woodbridge: Tamesis.

Edwards, John. 1986. Trial of an Inquisitor: The dismissal of Diego Rodríguez Lucero, Inquisitor of Córdoba, in 1508. *Journal of Ecclesiastical History* 37 (2): 240–257.

———. 2000. *The Spain of the Catholic Monarchs, 1474–1520*. Oxford: Blackwell.

———. 2005. *Ferdinand and Isabella*. Harlow: Pearson Education.

Fernández-Armesto, Felipe. 2000. The Improbable Empire. In *Spain: A History*, ed. Raymond Carr. Oxford: Oxford University Press.

Ferrer-Chivite, Manuel. 1997. Sobre las coplas llamadas "del tabefe", su autor y sus avatares. *Scriptura* 13: 151–171.

Francisco Olmos, Jose María de. 2002. Estudio Documental de la Moneda Castellana de Juana La Loca fabricada en los Países Bajos (1505–1506). *Revista General de Información y Documentación* 12 (2): 291–321.

Gerli, Michael E. 2008. Conflictive Subjectivity and the Politics of Truth and Justice. In *Cárcel de Amor. Queen Isabel I of Castile: Power, Patronage, Persona*, ed. Barbara F. Weissberger. Woodbridge: Tamesis.

González Olmedo, Félix, S.I. 1944. *Diego Ramírez Villaescusa (1459–1537), fundador del Colegio de Cuenca y autor de los Cuatro Diálogos sobre la Muerte del Príncipe Don Juan*. Madrid: Editora Nacional.

Guicciardini, Francesco (ed.) 1775–1776. *Della Storia d'Italia*. Florence: Friburgo.

Herrero Carretero, Concha. 2001. Tesoro de devoción de la corona de España. In *A La Manera de Flandes. Tapices Ricos de la Corona de España* (cat.). Madrid: Patrimonio Nacional.

Ladero Quesada, Miguel Ángel. 2003. *La España de los Reyes Católicos*. Madrid: Alianza.

Liss, Peggy K. 2004. *Isabel the Queen: Life and Times*. Philadelphia: University of Pennsylvania Press.

Lobo Iglesias, Efrén. 1989. *Sepúlveda, ciudad medieval*. Madrid: J-M. Arquillos de la Torre.

Luis Suárez Fernández. 2004. *Fernando el Católico*. Barcelona: Ariel.

———. 2006. Coyuntura Europea en el Reinado de Juana. In *Doña Juana, Reina de Castilla*. Madrid and Barcelona: Fundación Rafael del Pino/Real Academía de la Historia/Marcial Pons.

Lunenfeld, Martin. 1987. *Keepers of the City: The Corregidores of Isabela I of Castile (1474–1504)*. Cambridge: Cambridge University Press.
Martín, José-Luis. 2003. *Enrique IV de Castilla, Rey de Navarra, Príncipe de Cataluña*. Hondarribia: Nerea.
Martínez Millán, José. 2000. *La Corte de Carlos V*. Madrid: Sociedad Estatal para la Conmemoración de los Centenarios de Felipe II y Carlos V.
Nicolle, David. 1998. *The Fall of Granada, 1481–1492*. Oxford: Osprey.
Nieto Soria, Jose Manuel. 2005. *Rex inutilis* y tiranía en el debate político de la Castilla bajomedieval. In *Coups d'État à la fin du Moyen Âge? Aux fondements du pouvoir politique den Europe occidentale*, ed. François Foronda, Jean-Philippe Genet and José Manuel Nieto Soria. Madrid. Casa de Velázquez.
Padilla, Lorenzo de. 1846. CODOIN, 8. In *Crónica de Felipe I llamado el Hermoso*, ed. Miguel Salvá and Pedro Sainz de Baranda. Madrid: Imprenta de la viuda de Calero.
Rábade Obradó, María del Pilar. 1993. *Una elite de poder en la Corte de los Reyes Católicos: Los judeoconversos*. Madrid: Sigilo.
Rawlings, Helen. 2002. *Church, Religion and Society in Early Modern Spain*. Basingstoke and New York: Palgrave Macmillan.
Ryder, Alan. 2007. *The Wreck of Catalonia: Civil War in the Fifteenth Century*. Oxford: Oxford University Press.
Vicens Vives, Jaime. 1953: *Juan II de Aragón (1398–1479): Monarquía y Revolución en la España del Siglo XV*. Barcelona: Editorial Teide.
———. 2006. *Historia Crítica de la Vida y Reinado de Fernando II de Aragón*. Zaragoza: Instituto Fernando el Católico.
Villacañas Berlanga, José Luis. 2008. *La Monarquía Hispánica (1284–1516)*. Madrid: Espasa Calpe.
Zalama, Miguel-Ángel. 2006. Recuperar la memoria. Juana I, el palacio real de Tordesillas y la Historia. In *Juana I de Castilla, 1504–1555: de su reclusión en Tordesillas al olvido de la Historia*, ed. Miguel-Ángel Zalama. Valladolid: Grupo Página.
———. 2010. *Juana I. Arte, Poder y Cultura en torno a una reina que no gobernó*. Madrid: Centro de Estudios Europa Hispánica.
Zurita, Jerónimo. 1992. *Historia del Rey Don Hernando el Católico. De las empresas y ligas de Italia*, vol. 3, ed. Ángel Canellas López, Magdalena Canellas and Antonio J. Rodríguez. Zaragoza: Gobierno de Aragón.

CHAPTER 5

# Castaway (1505–1506)

## 5.1 Two Queens of Castile

As Castilian cities raised Juana's standard from towers and battlements, shouting her name into the wind and rain, and as Isabel's funeral cortege fought its way through the elements to Granada, Juana remained her husband's prisoner. She would look upon Isabel's death as marking the emergence of a long-term strategy to marginalise her through ill-treatment, deceit and double-dealing.[1] Arguably, this began on 14 December 1504, when Fernando advised Philip to conceal from Juana the news of her mother's death because it might affect her pregnancy.[2] Fernando hoped in this way to gain time to reinforce his power in Castile. Indeed, both father and husband would argue that Juana's female 'illnesses'—linked to a hysteria associated with pregnancy, and thought to engender melancholia, listlessness and irrationality—disqualified her from exercising power in her own right.[3]

At some point after the arrival in Brussels of Fernando's envoys and supporters, Juan de Fonseca—now bishop of Palencia—and Lope Conchillos, Philip felt obliged to unlock Juana's doors. The new queen temporarily accepted a retinue of Flemish and Burgundian ladies in order to perform the mourning rites and receive the royal acclamation. On 14 January, she attended the church of St Gudula, during which Philip's king-of-arms, *Toison d'or*, approached him with sword unsheathed and, in ringing tones, declared: "Sire, this sword belongs to you to maintain justice, to defend your kingdoms and subjects."[4] As Juana gazed upon the



G. B. Fleming, *Juana I*, Queenship and Power,
https://doi.org/10.1007/978-3-319-74347-9_5

golden crown on the bier, symbolising Isabel's two bodies, and up at the six-storey tumulus—the first of its kind in the Burgundian Netherlands, soaring to a height of some fifty-two feet—we may imagine her reflecting, as she must often have done during the ritual six weeks of formal mourning, on the complexity of her relationship with her mother, with its mixture of love and resentment, and on the many crucial differences in their respective journeys.

Few women have become sovereign queens in circumstances as unfavourable as Juana's. To be sure, on her own path to queenship Isabel had faced years of conflict and all-out war. When Enrique IV died in December 1474, she had, however, struck with lightning speed to marginalise her rival and goddaughter, famously throwing off her white serge to walk through the wintry Segovian twilight behind an upturned, unsheathed sword of justice. By contrast, Juana acceded to the throne without even knowing it. Isabel's path had been difficult and bloody, but the death of her father and then her brother; the melancholic confinement of her mother; the political weakness of her half-brother, Enrique IV; and the youth, gender and contested legitimacy of her rival—the other Juana of Castile—had opened avenues of opportunity unavailable to her daughter. Isabel had chosen her own husband and advisers. Juana's life had been mapped out for her in advance and in a foreign land; she would later speak bitterly of the bonds of filial obedience that she had not known how to break.[5]

In 1505, as the mother of five healthy children, Juana was unquestionably a dynastic success. Yet that same success would only hasten the end of the house to which she herself belonged. Juana's decision to return to the Low Countries had allowed Fernando to seize the initiative at the expense of her reputation, while her refusal to embrace Philip's claim on Castile converted her into the hostage of a foreign court, without access to loyal advisers and at Philip's mercy. His imposition upon her of a Burgundian household might once have seemed reasonable, but his refusal to change tack after she became princess of Asturias and Gerona and proprietary queen showed an innate sense of male superiority as well as a vaulting ambition.

To follow to the throne a queen regnant of international renown was, inevitably, a mixed blessing. It was to bathe in Isabel's protective aura whilst simultaneously being pinned back by her towering shadow. The temperaments of the two queens were both similar and different. Juana had inherited Isabel's extraordinary iron will and tenacity, but lacked her ruthlessness, self-confidence and visionary drive. Unlike Isabel, she had not felt the need to seek legitimation. But, as the child of mighty parents, she would struggle to assert her own identity.

A modern statue of Juana I (see frontispiece) stands on the site of the palace of Tordesillas where she spent almost a half-century. It shows her with a crown in her hand and a globe at her feet. Seen from the front, she ignores both, gazing inscrutably downstream. But from another angle she seems to hold her crown as if wondering what to do with it. Juana's attitude toward her legacy seems to be both one of reluctance and hesitation, and of defensiveness and protectiveness and if power is seen as the possession and pursuit of a strategy that influences the direction and outcome of events, it would be mistaken to believe that she did not exercise it. Subsequent, repeated attempts to turn her against Fernando and to keep her aloof from her subjects would have made little sense had Juana not remained the proud and defiant font of political legitimacy and living embodiment of her kingdoms.

It is unlikely that she knew then of the conditions that Isabel had attached to Fernando's governorship. Fernando never mentioned them and the fact that the young monarchs had not seen the will—in 1506, Philip was still complaining that he had not received a copy[6]—allowed Fernando's envoys, Fonseca and Conchillos, to present his appointment as Isabel's absolute rather than conditional choice. As Guicciardini points out, Philip was right to argue that Isabel's will lacked the weight of law.[7] Nonetheless, it was a powerful legitimating tool and Juana would have seen it as law to all intents and purposes. Expressing a passionate reverence for her mother's memory and drinking from the waters of a myth already in full flow, Juana argued that Fernando, as "husband of the queen," had helped bring peace and justice to Castile and had earned his right to govern it. Her Basque secretary, Sebastián de Olano, heard her exclaim: "God forbid I should ever disobey my father and that ruffians should take his place!"[8] The Venetian ambassador, Querini, later commented that she "wishes her father to govern these realms, not her husband, who is so pliant and good-natured that he depends on his ministers rather than being their master."[9] This position converted her into his, and their, most feared political adversary.

For much of this period she lived in what may best be described as self-imposed seclusion within a wider state of captivity. As Fuensalida put it in November 1504: "When the Princess saw that the doors were shut, she shut herself in …".[10] Devoid of the sarcasm of Manuel, no longer ambassador, Fuensalida's despatches between February and June 1505 reveal sympathy for Juana's plight, although he frequently refers to the word "*falta*" ("lack") to describe her. This may have meant either lack of involvement in affairs (*falta de entendimiento*) or lack of sense, amounting to incapacitation (*falta de seso*). But, when telling an inquisitive Fernando that her "illness had hardened," he seems to place it within the context less of budding insanity than of intransigence, inflexibility and suspicion. Attempts were made to break down her loyalty to Fernando. In her seclusion, she sang often with Juan de Anchieta, her brother's former chapel-master, who had left Castile after Isabel's death to join the Burgundian court. Already conversant with northern musical traditions, the Basque had become one of Europe's most striking composers. Philip trusted him because he was as hostile to Fernando as if the king had "deprived him of the archbishopric of Toledo." Philip hoped some of that hostility would rub off on the queen.[11]

Conchillos told Querini that Juana was proud, spirited and principled:

> her husband treats her in the worst possible way; and so she always lives in seclusion, and never gives audience to anyone; yet she is an intelligent woman, of great spirit (*de gran core*) and very proud and has a melancholy and haughty nature. She is also jealous of her husband, and told me recently that she had made him a sacred oath that she would do the very reverse of what the king her husband ordered, and meant to keep it, not because she did not wish to obey him as wife, but because she knows it is not he but his advisers who govern and these are more wretched (*tristi*) than good.[12]

Juana's 'jealousy' has been generally seen as a pathological or morbid condition. Philip linked it to that strain of hysteric irrationality earlier mentioned. Thus, he brushed aside Juana's attempt to dismiss her treasurer, Mújica, after Juana had identified his role in making the dossier known. Juana's pregnancies "sometimes make her take offence without cause," Philip told him by way of apology.[13] But Conchillos' words, as Querini reports them, remind us that the political component in the word 'jealousy' should not be ignored.[14] As a sovereign, Juana was bound to react vigorously to any affront to her royal dignity. Juana's jealousy was linked to her conviction that those who, like her particular adversaries, Manuel and Charles de Poupet-Lachaulx, embroiled Philip in a struggle against Fernando and herself were not only misguided, but verging on the criminal.

Portrayals of the queen shifted according to the political weather. Following Fernando's exposure of the dossier at the Cortes of Toro—an act that dumbfounded Philip and about which Juana expressed shocked disbelief—Philip's advisers changed tack, denying that there had been "a single word in the whole report" about Juana's conduct to suggest that the queen was "mad as Fernando says."[15] Rather, she was "malicious." Fuensalida told Fernando that they "do not want to hear from anyone that the queen is incapacitated. Lachaulx told me not two days ago that no-one should believe reports about the queen's incapacitation." On the other hand, "nobody in the world had been born with so bad a disposition …".[16]

As we have seen, Fernando also veered between different perspectives on Juana. He had obtained agreement to his governorship by exploiting Philip's dossier, but the low turn-out of nobles at Toro meant that he still needed Juana's support and was as anxious as Philip to deny responsibility in the matter of the dossier. "God only knows," he exclaimed to Fuensalida, "what I felt in my heart and soul when I read [Philip's report] and never did I believe it, nor, please God, shall I … I shall work to the utmost to bring [Juana] to these kingdoms, even if I have to go there myself to fetch her …".[17]

## 5.2 Reign of Terror

Querini thought Philip was "lost in a great labyrinth."[18] The king-archduke's vexations were summarised by his adviser, Luxembourg-Ville: "Why should the King go to Spain, or why is he called King, since to be called King and not to act there as though he were King, would make of him, would it not, a mere child under the tutelage of others?"[19] But Philip also worried about the sheer logistical problems involved in ruling a sprawl of territories across Europe. This was a real predicament, later, and more famously, faced by his son, Charles: "I cannot be in Castile for ever," Philip told Fuensalida, "nor even for long, without having to leave to deal with the other affairs I have, which are weighty ones, here and in Germany."[20] At one moment, these considerations tempted him to seek a solution with Fernando. The next he was wondering how to oust him. Querini blamed certain '*maligni*' like Manuel and Lachaulx for Philip's failure to mend bridges with Fernando and, by extension, with Juana. Some, like the Luxembourg brothers and Philip's close Burgundian friend and master of horse, Claude de Bouton, favoured doing so. But

Querini thought Fuensalida and Conchillos ineffective: "If they were more diligent I think that they might easily persuade the king to do all they wish, but they are very lukewarm in their actions, whereas the others are very alert and experienced …".[21]

While isolating Juana from visitors, Philip began preparing for the second Spanish journey. A new treaty with France confirmed the future marriage of Charles and Claude, recognising France's interim governorship of Naples and Louis' rights to Milan in exchange for French support for Maximilian's coronation in Rome and Philip's claims on Castile. Louis also looked benevolently on a military campaign by Maximilian and Philip—who needed to leave his territories strongly defended before returning to Spain—against Charles Egmond II, duke of Guelders, keen to reclaim his ancestral duchy from Burgundian hands.

With Philip in Hagenau, Juana seized the opportunity to meet Conchillos. She marked her first act as queen by signing letters that endorsed Fernando's governorship, begging him to remain in Castile and not to abandon her. Höfler describes this first act as one of abdication.[22] But while she saw Fernando as Castile's rightful governor, by dint of merit and experience as well as Isabel's wishes, her hold on the crown and on her proprietary status gave her a latent power that caused fear, and that she never showed the slightest desire to relinquish.

Unfortunately for Fernando, Juana's messenger delivered these letters instead to Philip, who tore them up. Guards were placed around the queen's apartment and horses were brought into the palace yard while a meeting, held at dawn on 4 April, and attended by Juana's staff and by the magistrates and governors of Brussels, debated whether to imprison her in the fortress of Villeborde. Juana was seen at the door of her room in tears, exclaiming, "Am I such a bad woman, who are these guards they have imposed on me?" She then turned back, repeating "Oh, what a misfortune is this!" ("*O malaventurada de mí!*")[23]

It may have been argued that, since she was Castile's proprietary queen, she could hardly commit treason against herself. At any rate, she remained on the Coudenberg but under heavy guard. Ten to twelve archers with their crossbows were posted to her door. No Spaniard was allowed to visit her. The chaplain was ordered to keep silent after mass and her kitchen was moved to an adjacent room that normally served as chapel. Juana fought these measures, literally. After interrogating an altar boy, she summoned her *maître d'hôtel*, Charles de Croÿ, prince of Chimay, who, fearing the worst, arrived with a companion. An angry exchange followed, at the end of which Juana seized a poker, crying, "Get out, you old traitor, get out!" Chimay's companion took the force of the blow in his hands and a doorkeeper was reportedly knocked down. Juana was heard to say: "I swear by this cross that I'll kill you all!"[24]

The conversation between Querini and Conchillos, in which the latter mentions this or a similar vow, took place just hours before Philip made a hasty and brief return to Brussels. He had Conchillos arrested and taken by night to Villeborde. There he remained until the monarchs' departure for Spain at the beginning of 1506. He was tortured and, according to Padilla, "for several days went mad." Oviedo tells us that he was left with a chronic heart ailment.[25] Fuensalida, fearing that Conchillos would confess to everything and more, burned what papers he could find. Olano and Mújica, were arrested, interrogated and threatened with imprisonment if they refused to collaborate with Philip and report back on everything the queen said and did. The Spanish members of her chapel were also made to swear not to act as messengers. The royal children were nowhere to be seen. Fuensalida himself was isolated and kept under close surveillance. No-one, whether "Castilian or Frenchman," called on, or ate with him.[26]

Anxious that his fundamental disagreements with Juana should be concealed from the outside world, Philip exploited her pregnancy to discourage would-be visitors from seeking an audience. After arriving from the imperial court, Querini had logged repeated attempts to present her his credentials, "since," as he reminded Doge Loredano, "it was to her especially that your Serenity had appointed me your ambassador." He noted the efforts to which Philip's retinue went to refuse access to Juana and, increasingly mystified, approached a fellow Venetian, her doctor, Liberal de Treveris, who visited her daily. Liberal confirmed that her pregnancy was a difficult one, but an irascible Fuensalida, in the same position as Querini, exclaimed that "even if the Queen is at death's door her father's ambassador should not be denied the right to be able to speak to her."[27]

Juana remained under guard through the spring and cold rainy summer of 1505. Castilian nobles sent envoys to pay homage to the monarchs and secure and bolster their grants and privileges. As Bianchini notes in her work on Berenguela of Castile, it was vital for new monarchs to build consensus and support among the nobility by dispensing patronage and securing and rewarding bonds of personal loyalty on which lordship depended. But while these envoys might deal with

Philip, they were threatened with imprisonment if they tried to approach the proprietary sovereign—alone entitled to dispense such patronage. One messenger from the count of Ureña tried, in vain, to approach her by signalling from a chapel window but was threatened by guards.[28]

At the end of June, Fuensalida, in one of his last despatches from Brussels, penned a poignant description of the queen, pieced together from hearsay. Any order she gave was first relayed to those guarding her. Her confessor reported "no improvement" in her situation. Others maintained that she occupied herself with dresses, jewellery and music: "She is alone all the time; they say she sings a lot; there is no-one to serve her; she does everything for herself, whether dressing or undressing and everything else that requires the assistance of women and men: she pays attention neither to kingdoms nor to her children, nor to affairs [of state], nor is there anyone to speak to her or whom she wishes to hear. Two attendants, who enter with her dresses, report that what she says she says well. With those to whom she speaks she is always very sharp, very bitter, pathetic." He could not confirm it because he had not seen her. He called her Spanish servants "sons of Judas," intent only on currying favour with Philip. Only Olano, her Basque secretary, remained faithful. "It is," the ambassador concluded "very dangerous swimming in this sea. I swear by my faith I believe there is no man who would not tremble to hear what they say to me daily; there are few days when they do not condemn me to death …".[29]

## 5.3 The Treaty of Salamanca

Unable to obtain the queen's cooperation, Philip began forging her signature. In a letter of 3 May, ostensibly sent by Juana to Philip's envoy in Castile, '*la Mouche*' de Veyré, the writer expresses total support for Philip, while begging Fernando to dismiss the rumours about her mental disturbance. While admitting to faults provoked by jealous "passion," she asserts that false testimony has been brought against her and Fernando is criticised for publishing the famous dossier. 'Juana' adds that she would never deprive Philip of the government "as much from the love I bear him as from what I know of [Fernando]."[30] Apart from the mystery as to why she should write to *la Mouche* rather than to her father, the letter's contents are completely at variance with everything we know about Juana's support for Fernando during her first regnal year.

Understandably, Fernando disputed the authenticity of this letter. But what to do? Rumours circulated that he might try to lift himself out of a political morass by marrying Enrique IV's daughter, Juana of Castile, whom he and Isabel—denying her legitimacy—had fought and defeated in the war of the Castilian succession. The rumours were serious enough for Manoel I of Portugal to withdraw her from her convent and place her under heavy guard elsewhere, and to be noted in the pages of Zurita and Sandoval.[31] Whether Fernando ever considered such an alliance remains unclear. However, he looked to another old enemy, the king of France. While reinforcing the frontiers of Roussillon and Navarre, he sent inquisitor Juan de Engueva on a secret mission of friendship, calculating that Louis was unhappy at the thought of a former vassal sitting enthroned upon his borders and that the terms of Hagenau would not last long. Louis had, in fact, already secretly provided, in his will, that Claude should marry not Charles but the dauphin, François d'Angoulême, the future François I, and he proved receptive to Enguera's embassy. But he set the price of alliance high. Fernando had to marry into Louis' family and bequeath to any descendants the precious inheritance of Naples. The treaty of Tours was ratified on 28 July 1505. On 19 October, Fernando was married by proxy to Germaine de Foix, Louis's niece, and—as the granddaughter of Gaston de Foix and of Fernando's sister, Leonor—Fernando's great-niece.

Fernando's acquiescence was a measure of the desperation he felt at his inability to secure the material proof of his daughter's support. His marriage to Germaine jeopardised the fragile unity of the Spanish kingdoms and many Castilians saw it as an insult to Isabel's memory. But the risk bore fruit, reducing Philip's carefully cultivated relations with France to tatters, forcing him to negotiate a new agreement with Fernando and to prepare for a costly sea voyage. The Guelders campaign, though victorious, had drained resources and the second Spanish journey had serious long-term consequences for levels of debt in the Low Countries. Philip had to sell ducal domains and became heavily indebted to Henry VII, who granted him the immense sum of £108,000.[32]

That August, Juana and Philip met Maximilian. Juana had not been seen for months, Maximilian told the Venetian ambassador Francesco Cappello; he had to visit Brussels to 'comfort her.'[33] The emperor entered the city, in semi-secrecy, on 24 August and his presence drew Juana back into the public sphere. On 4 September, Querini met her for the first—and, most probably, last—time. He was:

> taken to a chamber where the most serene king of the Romans was keeping company with the queen his daughter-in-law, dressed in black velvet and with a fairly good complexion given the illness she has had. And it seemed to me, although it was night, that she was very beautiful, and she had the air of a wise and prudent lady. I made my reverence to her majesty in the name of your sublimity and spoke a few good words well adapted and appropriate to the time and place where we were … and these were amiably reciprocated by her majesty.

Afterwards, he joined Maximilian and Juana at a torch-lit joust in which Philip ran lances against his father, who was dressed incognito. This was followed by a sumptuous banquet and ball. Maximilian tried continually to draw Juana into the festivities and to "make her cheerful and happy, being aware that all her ailments proceeded from melancholy." The emperor believed that Philip could only succeed as king if he and Juana were "*una cosa medesima*."[34] But Juana refused to sign the series of letters in which Philip sought the support of Castilian nobles and prelates against the king of Aragon: "The more she was pressed to sign [these letters]," Zurita claims, "the more firmly she said she would do nothing to harm her father. And with much anger and vexation she let the letters drop from her hand." According to Querini, she "continues publicly to tell all who speak to her, that God forbid that she should thwart her mother's will (*voluntà*) or that, as long as her father lives, any but he should govern Castile."[35] Juana kept her thoughts about Germaine de Foix to herself but was publicly defiant about Fernando's marriage: "if he has taken a wife he has done well, in order to live as a Christian." But this did not prevent Juana from "being very certain that never did a father love a daughter so dearly as he loves her."[36]

On 15 September, feverish and in pain, the queen gave birth to a third daughter. Marie, the later Mary of Hungary, was baptised on 20 September at the church of Notre Dame de Sablon. Juana's seclusion and captivity had long deprived her of her children and, during those rare moments when Philip tried to use them to soften her stance towards him, she had found it unsettling. But she now sought to maximise her time with them. Early in November, Philip left Brussels for Mechelen and Antwerp on the first leg of the second Spanish journey. Juana set out separately, intending to travel through Ghent and Bruges, and, Querini noted, she "has had all the children brought from Malines [Mechelen] and takes them with her to enjoy their company …".[37] Suddenly, however, Juana changed direction and went instead by Waasmunster and Kalve, arriving at Middelburg on 14 November. Querini thought her choice of the shorter route reflected her impatience to leave the Low Countries. But, in Zurita's view, the change of direction stemmed from Philip's fear that the citizens of Ghent and Bruges (seeing her, perhaps, like Smeken, as their Trojan Palladium) might try to detain her.[38]

As the monarchs left Brussels, the last touches were being put to the treaty of Salamanca of 24 November. Contrary to assertions by some historians, this treaty did not grant Philip proprietary status, which remained Juana's alone. But Fernando was still governor and his rights to half the lucrative revenues from the Indies, the mastership of the military orders and other public monies were confirmed. If Juana's "indisposition and impediment" continued, Fernando and Philip would rule without her, one substituting the other where necessary. A complicated system was devised for appointment to public office. Fernando would draw up a list of candidates to the posts of *corregidor*, *contador mayor* and royal councillor, from which Philip would choose half and Fernando half. Fernando's name would come first on official documents, followed by Philip's, and lastly by that of the proprietary queen—"inasumuch as she wishes or is able to sign."[39]

The treaty was an impossible fudge and it seems likely that Juana was not even told about it. Philip's negotiators had agreed to it only as a means of avoiding armed conflict upon landfall in Castile, for not only did it sanction Fernando's governorship but left open the possibility that Juana and her supporters could dispute the "indisposition and impediment" on which the agreement was based.[40] More generally, it reflected the confusion that continued to plague Castilian political affairs for years to come.

## 5.4 Brief Encounter

Philip's fleet comprised about forty-three *voiles* and included up to 2000 soldiers, among whom were members of German infantry regiments (*Landsknechten*) and Swiss pikemen, under the command of one of Maximilian's military chiefs, Oberster Hauptmann Count Wolfgang zu Fürstenberg.[41] The monarchs boarded the *Julienne* on 8 January, after mass, but snow and wind caused further delays. On 10 January, at full moon, the fleet weighed anchor in the name of the Holy Ghost. But on 13 January, a mighty storm came roaring out of the south-west. The terrified passengers made many religious vows: "*ich kann dir nit scriben was jederman verhassen hat*," Fürstenberg told his wife, "*so vil haben zu verhassen*."[42] More than one fire broke out and after the *Julienne*'s mainsail blew overboard and the lee gunwhale went under, the ship seemed doomed. The storm scene in Maximilian's *Weiß Kunig* was probably based on a letter by a fellow passenger, the scholar and physician Ludovico Marliani, who told Maximilian that tears came to his eyes whenever he remembered the sight of the young monarchs embracing in the face of death.[43] But, after several heroic attempts, a mariner managed to retrieve the sail and right the vessel.

Accounts of the monarchs' reaction to the storm vary, but several mention the queen's intrepidity.[44] The comment attributed to her on board ship that she had never heard of a monarch drowning ("*nunca Rey murió ahogado*") was less likely to be an expression of belief in royal untouchability than an instance of dry humour, made in the knowledge that Philip had sworn to present twice his weight in silver to St James should he survive. It may also have been an attempt to instill courage in her entourage.[45] Conchillos had already mentioned her great spirit to Querini, while Oviedo remembered how, as a child and "red as a rose," she had bravely tried to calm her mule after they slipped into the Tagus and the current swept them downstream.[46]

The fleet was scattered along the south and south-west coast of England, and as far as Wales, but for nine days no-one heard from the *Julienne* as she rode out the storm at sea. Both Molinet, and a lordly Burgundian passenger called Boussut, tell the story of a little bird, captured before the beginning of the storm and taken to Philip, who released it. Now, at the storm's end, the bird reappeared and, to the amazement of all, sang with them as they knelt on deck for the *Te Deum*.[47] But if the *Julienne*'s passengers saw a good omen in the songbird, the English saw a different one in the eagles of St Paul's. "It was observed," writes Bacon, "that the great tempest which drove Philip into England blew down the golden eagle from the spire of St Paul's, and in the fall it fell upon a sign of the black eagle … and battered it and brake it down: which was a strange stooping of a hawk upon a fowl. This the people interpreted to be an ominous prognostic upon the imperial house, which was, by interpretation also, fulfilled upon Philip …".[48]

On 16 January, the *Julienne* drove into Melcome Regis (Dorset). The monarchs had to wade waist-high through huge waves to reach land.[49] The governor of Weymouth, Thomas Trenchard, sensing the strangers' importance, invited them to his home at Wolfeton, Charminster, but verbal communication became possible only after the arrival of a young merchant with fluent French.[50] Henry VII sent William Blount, earl of Arundel, in a blaze of torchlight, to invite them to Windsor. Much indebted to Henry, and fearing a trap, Philip had no wish to see his political differences with Juana exposed to the English court. Querini noted that he even contemplated going home "because he understands that as the queen is the real mistress it is she who will govern." He was instead persuaded to send Lachaulx to Castile to try to obtain Fernando's agreement to Juana's definitive marginalisation. This the Venetian believed to be motivated by the naked self-interest of Philip's ministers, who feared that, once in Spain, a vengeful Juana would draw strength from her native soil, inspiring insurrection among a 'bestial' people. These people, allied with the nobility, could rise up and proclaim her the "true *domina*." And if "the queen, who really hates [Philip's ministers] assumes authority in Spain she would not only try to deprive them of the favour and power the king grants them but they would lose their Castilian pensions …".[51] *La Mouche*, Lachaulx and Manuel were among those to whom Fernando had awarded privileges, rewards and pensions after the signing of the treaty of Salamanca.[52]

The monarchs left Wolfeton for Dorchester on 21 January but did not forget to thank Trenchard and his wife, Elizabeth Strangways, with portraits of themselves and children. On 28 January, they arrived at the home of Richard Fox, privy seal and bishop of Winchester, who had played a key role in the marriage of Arthur and Katherine.[53] Her youngest sister would have been much in Juana's thoughts. After Arthur's death in 1502, Katherine had been betrothed to his brother, Henry, but Isabel's death and Fernando's shaky future had reduced her desirability as a bride. The betrothal was broken off and her future uncertain. Katherine awaited Juana at court, while the fifteen-year-old prince of Wales marked his first appearance on the international stage when greeting the monarchs at Winchester.

Juana did not accompany Philip to Windsor. She was, reports the *Deuxième Voyage* chronicler, "*travaillée de la mer*."[54] This may be true. But she was a more experienced sailor than Philip, who was determined to keep Juana's stay at court to an absolute minimum. Nor did he want her to know about the documents he signed there. On 9 February, the day before her arrival, Philip ratified the treaty of Salamanca and, in a document relating to the treaty, he signalled yet another about-turn in his portrayal of the queen. He had recently denied emphatically that she was "mad." Now he again stressed her unfitness for office and unwillingness to participate in government "nor in anything." His promise to try to procure her signature was half-hearted.[55] He also signed a treaty of friendship and cooperation with Henry (the treaty of Windsor), in which the latter offered Philip military help in any future conflict with Fernando.[56]

Henry's terrifying reputation for extracting money from his subjects was matched by huge selective generosity, and he knew how to entertain and impress. The contrast between the exuberantly dressed and spangled assembly of Anglo-Welsh nobility and the sobriety of the small Burgundian entourage who met them at Clewer Green surprised an English merchant, William Makefyr, who hoped that Juana would provide a better display.[57] But the arrival of the queen, who travelled in the company of various English lords, including the earl of Arundel, and Thomas Butler, earl of Ormonde, was very low-key. She:

> entered by the Lytle Parke and so secretly came by the backseyd of the Castell unto the Kinges Newe Towere, wheare at the Stayrefoote the Kynge mett with her and kissed and embracede hir; howbeit that the Kinge of Casteele that ther was theare present with the Kynge, had duivers tymes before desired the kings highenes for to have Remained in his owne Lodginge, and not to have takene the paynes to have gone so farre. And after the kinge had welcomed hir, my Lady princes hir sistere and my Lady Mary the kynges daughtere, havinge many ladyes and gentlewomene attendinge upon them, welcomed hir; and so all together went uppe into the Kinge of Casteeles Logginge …[58]

Henry later told Fuensalida that Juana "made a very favourable impression on me and spoke with much dignity and grace and without losing an iota of her authority; and although her husband and those who came with her claimed she was mad I saw her only as sane; and so I believe she is now …".[59] But the next day, Philip asked Henry if they could dine alone. Katherine and Mary were sent to Richmond.

The truncated encounter between the sisters has led to much speculation, then and since. Martire surmised, from Valladolid, that Juana "rejects all blandishments, seeking the darkness …".[60] Santa Cruz referred to Katherine's vain attempts to console a sister who sought only solitude and obscurity.[61] Williams suspects, however, that Philip was the culprit, allowing Juana to meet Katherine for only a few hours under close supervision.[62] Starkey too concludes that Philip was behind Juana's speedy departure.[63] The *Deuxième Voyage* author corroborates this view: Philip "*la faisoit allé devant, espérant de la suyr à diligence.*"[64]

The brevity of Juana's stay angered Henry and, as Williams states, must have deeply upset both sisters. Katherine herself provides the best clue to what happened in an autograph letter to Juana of 25 October 1507:

> Most high and mighty Princess, Queen and Lady. Having kissed your highness' royal hands and humbly commended myself to you, I must express the joy that I felt when I saw you in this Kingdom, and the distress that filled my soul only a few hours afterwards because of the sudden and hasty departure you made from here. My lord the King of England was much affronted by your departure and if he had acted as he had personally wished he would have prevented it by all possible means, but as he is a very hot-tempered King, his Council thought it advisable to warn him not to intervene between husband and wife; on which account, and for other secret reasons (*mysterios*) of which I was well aware, he concealed the feelings provoked by Your Highness' departure, although it certainly weighed upon his heart ...[65]

Katherine's remarks about the differences between Juana and Philip and Juana's "sudden and hasty departure" lead to one overriding conclusion: at Windsor, a row between the monarchs of Castile threatened to spark a grave diplomatic incident.[66]

After Katherine's departure from Windsor, Juana co-signed what appears to be an abbreviated and blandly worded form of the treaty of Windsor that bore no reference to a pact against Fernando.[67] On the Saturday, she headed southwest, in a litter that had belonged to Elizabeth of York, and spent the first night of journey at the great Benedictine abbey of Reading. But details remain obscure because the English chronicler of the monarchs' visit saw Juana as consort, not sovereign: "I leave the Queenes Jurneye to theme that sawe it," he writes, "and Returne to the kinge."[68] Presumably she took the same route as Philip did later, passing through Shaftesbury, Sherbourne and Honiton, and waiting "*molti zorni*" for Philip at Exeter.[69]

After their arrival in Falmouth, relations between the couple soured again. Juana, who may have attended Windsor in the company of a single *dame d'honneur*, again refused to accept the Flemish or Burgundian ladies appointed to her by Philip. Aram indicates that the suspicious Juana "sought more sober company."[70] It is, however, important to recall that her opposition to Philip's female appointees was linked to her assertion of independence as proprietary queen. Isabel had chosen her own household; Juana wished to do likewise. She had, meanwhile, heard rumours about Fernando's unhappiness at the prospect of the monarchs' arrival in Castile, and hesitated to board ship. This might have suited Philip, had Lachaulx managed to win Fernando's approval to side-line Juana. But Fernando refused. His ambassador, Pedro de Ayala, was allowed a rare, brief audience to try to persuade her to embark:

> Don Juan Manuel, who accompanied him [to Juana's door] warned him that he would oblige the king by not lingering ... When he entered the chamber the queen was extremely amiable; she did not allow him to kiss hands and insisted he sit down, and asked him many questions. In particular she asked him very tenderly how her father was, since it was six months since she had news of him; whether it was true that he wished her as much harm as she had been told, and whether, as a result of their fortunes, he had announced that she and her husband wanted to return to Flanders and not pursue their journey; and finally, she asked whether her journey to Spain displeased him so much. The ... ambassador replied that none of this was true, rather that the most serene king her father loved her and her husband as his own children, and had no greater desire than to see them, and [then] took his leave as quickly as he could ...[71]

On the evening of 22 April, the re-assembled fleet, to which Fernando had added four Basque ships, finally weighed anchor in the name of God, Mary and St James. Relief was mixed with apprehension. The monarchs' unscheduled visit to England had laid Philip's strategy bare to Henry's forensic gaze. Their reception in Castile was uncertain and at once became the subject of fierce argument.

## Notes

1. See Chapter 11.
2. Carretero Zamora (González Alonso, ed. 2006).
3. A study by Sánchez (1998) shows how the theme of hysteric illness was used both to exclude later royal Habsburg women from public power and as a tool to advance particular strategies.

4. Molinet (Doutrepont/Jodogne, eds. 1935–1937), II, 538–541.
5. See Chapter 9.
6. CSP (Queen Juana), Bergenroth, ed., 8 [undated: 1506].
7. Guiccciardini (ed. 1776), II.
8. Fuensalida (Berwick y de Alba, ed. 1907), 7 April 1505, 341–343.
9. Querini (Höfler, ed. 1884), 17, 22 April 1505.
10. Fuensalida, 1 November 1504, 300.
11. Fuensalida, 26 March 1505, 337–339.
12. Querini, 17, 22 April 1505.
13. Padilla (CODOIN, 8, 1846), Philip to Mújica, 30 July 1505, 314–315.
14. Boudet's *Les Mots de L'Histoire* (1998), 574, refers to a '*jalousie politique ... mère de toutes sortes de cabales ... d'intrigues de cour et de ministère ... l'un des fondements de la lutte de classe ... mais aussi de la lutte pour les trônes ...*'.
15. Fuensalida, 15 May 1505, 356–359. Juana, who was not told that the report bore Philip's signature, reportedly exclaimed to him: "Is there no one who will punish this, not the king my father, not you?".
16. Fuensalida, 26 March 1505, 339.
17. Fuensalida (Fernando), 16 May 1505, 368.
18. Querini, 57, 31 August 1505.
19. Fuensalida, 27 December 1504, 319.
20. Fuensalida, 15 May 1505, 357.
21. Querini, 28, 26 May 1505.
22. Höfler (1885).
23. Fuensalida, 7 April 1505, 341.
24. Fuensalida, 10 April 1505, 342–343.
25. Padilla, 127–129; Fernández de Oviedo (Tudela, ed. 1983), 209–210.
26. Fuensalida, 2 May 1505, 348–355.
27. Querini, 22, 13 May 1505; 36, 25 June 1505.
28. Bianchini (2012); Fuensalida, 5 July 1505, 391.
29. Fuensalida, 29 June 1505, 387–389.
30. Fernández Álvarez (2002), 132–133. Aram's study of Juana's signature (1998) convincingly disputes the letter's authenticity.
31. Azcona (2007).
32. Starkey (2003).
33. Cappello, Francesco, 'Lettere al Senato, 1504–1555' [unpublished], BNMVe (classe VII), f. 139r.
34. Querini, 59, 5 September 1505.
35. Zurita, 3 (Canellas López, ed. 1992), 417.
36. Querini, 69, 6 October 1506.
37. Querini, 75, 7 November 1505.

38. ADN, B3462, hôtel de Jeanne, 1505; Querini, 76, 12 November 1505; Zurita, III.
39. AGS, PR 56, f. 19, 'Cédula del Rey Fernando el Católico a los reyes Felipe y Juana, y acuerdo firmado por Filiberto de Veyré,' 24 November 1505.
40. Zurita, 4 (Canellas López, ed. 1994).
41. Fürstenberg (Schrenkenstein, ed. 1867–1869), I.
42. Fürstenberg, IV, 139.
43. Fleming (Zalama, ed. 2010).
44. Among these is Querini (89, 25 January 1506), who was on another ship, but gathered reports.
45. Rodríguez Villa (1892), 127. A similar remark was attributed to William II 'the Red' (see Vincent, *A Brief History of Britain, 1066–1485*, London, 2011). For a more detailed account of this episode and the three months in England, see Fleming (Zalama, ed. 2010), 407–420.
46. Fernández de Oviedo (ed. 1870), 96–98.
47. Boussut (Gachard, ed. 1876), 501–503; Molinet, II.
48. Bacon (Lockyer, ed. 1971), 221–222.
49. Sanuto (Fulin, ed. 1969–1970), VI, 295.
50. The story of John Russell, who became the earl of Bedford, is one of dramatic upward mobility and political survival.
51. Querini, 92, 30 March 1506, 197.
52. Cauchies (2003), 170.
53. ADN, B 3463.
54. Relation du Deuxième Voyage de Philippe le Beau (Gachard, ed. 1876), 422.
55. "en ninguna manera se quiere ocupar ny entender en nyngun negocio de regimiento di gobernación ni otra cosa." AGS, PR 56, f. 27. 2, 'Provisión del Rey Felipe I sobre la Concordia con el Rey Fernando el Católico acerca de la gobernación de los Reinos de España,' 9 February 1506.
56. TNA, E 30: 701, 9 February 1506.
57. Gairdner (ed. 1858), no. 1078, VI, 172–174.
58. Tighe and Davis (eds. 1858), 122.
59. Fuensalida, 5 July 1508, 457–465.
60. Martire (López de Toro, ed. 1955) 10, 300, 4 April 1406.
61. Santa Cruz (Mata Carriazo, ed. 1951), II, 39.
62. Williams (2013).
63. Starkey (2003).
64. *Deuxième Voyage*, 423–424.
65. AGS, PR 54, f. 33, "A la Reyna española Señora Doña Juana, De la Princesa de Gales su hermana (que agora es Reyna de Inglaterra)"; CSP. Sp (Queen Juana), 23, 25 October 1507. My translation differs here slightly from the Calendar's.

66. Fleming (2010).
67. TNA, E. 30: 1082, "Undertaking by Joan, Queen of Castile," 12 February 1506.
68. Tighe and Davis, 122.
69. Querini, 90, 17 March 1506.
70. Aram (2005), 82–83, and corresponding notes. The court accounts at Lille detail payments to various *dames d'honneur* and other women placed in Juana's service at this time.
71. Querini, 93, 4 April 1506.

## References

Aram, Bethany. 1998. Juana "the Mad's" Signature: The Problem of Invoking Royal Authority, 1505–1507. *Sixteenth-Century Journal* 29 (2), 331–358.

———. 2005. *Juana the Mad: Sovereignty and Dynasty in Renaissance Europe.* Baltimore and London: John Hopkins University Press.

Azcona, Tarscisio. 2007. *Juana de Castilla, mal llamada la Beltraneja.* Madrid: La Esfera de los Libros.

Bacon, Francis. 1971. *The History of the Reign of King Henry the Seventh*, ed. R. Lockyer. London: The Folio Society.

Bergenroth, G.A. (ed.). 1868. *Calendar of State Papers, Supplement to Vol. I and Vol. II of Letters, Despatches and State Papers Relating to Negotiations Between England and Spain, Preserved in the Archives of Simancas and Elsewhere.* London: Longmans, Green, Reader and Dyer.

Berwick y Alba (ed.). 1907. *Correspondencia de Gutierre Gómez de Fuensalida, embajador en Alemania, Flandes y Inglaterra (1496–1509).* Madrid: Alemana.

Bianchini, Janna. 2012. *The Queen's Hand: Power and Authority in the Reign of Berenguela of Castile.* Philadelphia: University of Pennsylvania Press.

Boudet, Jacques (ed.). 1998. *Les mots de l'histoire.* Paris: Larousse-Bordas.

Carretero Zamora, Juan Manuel. 2006. Las Cortes de Toro de 1505. In *Las Cortes de Toro y las Leyes de Toro*, ed. Benjamin González Alonso. Salamanca: Cortes de Castilla y León/Ayuntamiento de Tordesillas.

Cauchies, Jean-Marie. 2003. *Philippe le Beau: Le dernier duc de Bourgogne.* Turnhout: Brepols.

Doutrepont, Georges and Omer Jodogne (eds.). 1935. *Chroniques de Jean Molinet.* Brussels: Académie Royale de Belgique.

Fernández Álvarez, Manuel. 2002. *Juana La Loca. La Cautiva de Tordesillas.* Madrid: Espasa Calpe.

Fernández de Oviedo, Gonçalo. 1870. *Libro de la Cámara Real del Príncipe Juan.* Madrid: Sociedad de Bibliófilos Españoles.

———. 1983. *Batallas y Quinquagenas*, ed. Pérez de Tudela. Madrid: Real Academía de la Historia.

Fleming, Gillian Beatrice. 2010. La visita a Inglaterra de Juana I (enero-abril de 1506). In *Juana I en Tordesillas: su mundo, su entorno*, ed. M.-A. Zalama. Valladolid: Ayuntamiento de Tordesillas/Grupo Página.

Fulin, Rinaldo (ed.). 1969–1970. *I diarii de Marino Sanuto, 1466–1536.* Bologna: Forni Editore.

Gachard, Louis-Prosper (ed.). 1876. Relation du Deuxième Voyage de Philippe le Beau en 1506, par un Anonyme. In *Collection des Voyages des Souverains des Pays-Bas*, vol. I, 389–489. Brussels: Commission Royale d'Histoire.

———. 'Relation de la tempête qui assaillit la flotte de Philippe le Beau,' 27 January 1506 [Seigneur de Boussut]. In *Collection des Voyages des Souverains des Pays- Bas*, vol. I, 501–503. Brussels.

Gairdner, James (ed.). 1858. *Memorials of King Henry the Seventh (Rolls Series).* London: Longman, Brown, Longmans and Roberts.

Höfler, Constantin R. (ed.). 1884. *Depeschen des Venetianischen Botschafters Dr Vincenzo Querino, 1505–1506.* Vienna: Österreischische Akademie der Wissenschaften, Archiv für Kunde österreichische Geschichts-Quellen, Band 66–67.

———. 1885. *Donna Juana, Königin von Leon, Castilien und Granada.* Vienna: Denkschriften der Kaiserliche Akademie des Wissenschaften.

López de Toro, José, ed. 1955–1957. *Petrus Martyr Anglerius: Epistolario.* CODOIN, 9–12. Madrid: Imprenta Góngora.

Padilla, Lorenzo de. 1846. CODOIN, 8. *Crónica de Felipe I llamado el Hermoso*, ed. Miguel Salvá and Pedro Sainz de Baranda. Madrid: Imprenta de la viuda Calera.

Rodríguez Villa, Antonio. 1892. *La Reina Doña Juana: Estudio histórico.* Madrid: Murillo.

Roth von Schrenkenstein, K.H. (ed.). 1867–1869. Briefe des Grafen Wolfgang zu Fürstenberg zur Geschichte der Meerfahrt des Königs Philipp von Castilien (1506). In *Zeitschrift der Gesellschaft für Beforderung der Geschichts-, Altertums- und Volkskunde von Freiburg, dem Breisgau und den angrenzenden Landschaften*, vol. I.

Sánchez, Magdalena S. 1998. *The Empress, the Queen, and the Nun: Women and Power at the Court of Philip III of Spain.* Baltimore and London: John Hopkins University Press.

Santa Cruz, Alonso. 1951. *Crónica de los Reyes Católicos*, ed. Juan de Mata Carriazo. Seville: Escuela de Estudios Hispano-Americanos de Sevilla.

Starkey, David. 2003. *Six Wives: The Queens of Henry VIII.* London: Windus.

Tighe, Robert, and James Davis (eds.). 1858. *Annals of Windsor.* London: Longman, Brown, Longmans and Roberts.

Williams, Patrick. 2013. *Katharine of Aragon: The Tragic Story of Henry VIII's First Unfortunate Wife*. Stroud: Amberley.
Zurita, Jerónimo. 1992/1994. *Historia del Rey Don Hernando el Católico: De las empresas y ligas de Italia*, vols. 3 and 4, ed. A. Canellas López, Magdalena López and Antonio J. López. Zaragoza: Gobierno de Aragón.

CHAPTER 6

# Cortes (1506)

## 6.1 Divergent Paths

Fernando told Juana and Philip that he was so impatient to see them that every day seemed like a thousand years. He had even been travelling on a Sunday, which was not his habit.[1] Laredo had been the anticipated point of landfall. But the area was largely loyal to Fernando and Juana, but not to Philip, and Juana's refusal to buckle to pressure to support him raised the fear that, if Philip landed there, he could be in danger. Some felt they should head for Andalucia, where support was certain following a letter patent of Philip's of 30 September, expressing concern at the mass arrest of alleged heretics after Isabel's death, and ordering the suspension of inquisitorial activities pending further investigation.[2] In the event, the fleet blew into La Coruña (Galicia) on 26 April. The winds of fate, wrote Fürstenberg, saved Philip from betrayal, imprisonment, even murder.

The new monarchs were greeted by *feux de joie* and popular rejoicing. Sancha Cota recorded one song that would not have been to Juana's taste:

> Vosa è Castela,
> rey don Felipe,
> vosa è Castela,
> que no ay quien os la quite.
> E a nosa reyna
> Deos que la manteña;
> fazelde logar
> por do veña.[3]



G. B. Fleming, *Juana I*, Queenship and Power,
https://doi.org/10.1007/978-3-319-74347-9_6

There was, however, little need to make way for a queen who shunned public festivities and her refusal to confirm the city's rights and privileges angered and baffled those who feared she might favour the designs on La Coruña of Alonso Pimentel, count of Benavente. "The worst enemy of my lord of Castile, apart from the King of Aragon," Fürstenberg told Maximilian, "is the Queen, she is more malicious (*böser*) than I can describe …".[4]

For Querini, Juana's motives were more principled. He informed Venice that she sought harmony where the *maligni* sought only trouble and that she hoped to bring about an early reconciliation between Philip and Fernando by driving a wedge between her husband and his advisers. As "*la principal in Spagna*," he thought she might succeed.[5] According to a correspondent of Pedro Fernández de Córdoba, marquis of Priego and nephew of the Great Captain, Juana told Philip repeatedly that she could not support his political initiatives until she had met her father.[6] Philip's ambassador in Rome, Philibert Naturel, reported that the Great Captain was in a quandary after hearing that Juana was withholding cooperation from Philip until relations with Fernando—"*lequel elle tient Roy comme elle*"—were clarified. He had further been told that Philip had asked Fernando not to enter Galicia, but that Juana "*luy a mandé qu'il viengne*," while a group of Valencian merchants in Rome had informed the pope that Fernando and Juana were "*très-bien d'accord sans vous* [Philip]."[7] When the monarchs left for Santiago de Compostela toward the end of May, and when, after much persuasion, Juana attended mass at the cathedral, Querini noted the outpouring of affection for her as Isabel's daughter and heir. But he added that she had to make her voice heard.[8]

Among the nobles who descended on La Coruña and Santiago were the counts of Benavente and Lemos, marquis of Villena and duke of Nájera. But they were left to cool their heels in the corridors of houses and monasteries while Juana stayed in seclusion and Philip ate and hunted in private, hesitating between different positions. Divisions had broken out in his *Conseil privé*. Manuel encouraged Philip to take sole mastery of Castile. Others argued for a settlement along the lines of the treaty of Salamanca.[9]

As rumours filtered into Galicia that 3000 infantry under the command of the formidable Pedro Navarro, military engineer and veteran of the Italian wars, had returned from Naples to Andalucia and that Fernando was preparing to move artillery from the arsenal at Medina del Campo, Philip sent him a new envoy, Diego de Guevara, whom he had formally appointed Juana's *maître d'hôtel*. The Guevara family had long served the dukes of Burgundy, while Guevara himself is probably best known today as the first recorded owner of Van Eyck's Arnolfini portrait.[10] In early June of 1506, however, Guevara had other matters in mind than great works of art. He followed Fernando through León, Galicia and Zamora. In the Bierzo highlands, white with broom, the king interspersed amiable conversation on falconry with numerous questions about Juana—particularly about her female entourage.[11] Fernando was still hoping that he might assemble sufficient armed forces to use Philip's ill-treatment of the queen as a rallying cry and his impassioned draft letter to nobles and prelates exploited arguments very different from those presented at Toro. Instead of stressing Isabel's dismay with Juana, he described her dismay with Philip. Instead of focusing on the phrase '*no poder*' he focused on the word '*querer*': "by saying [Juana] has no wish [to govern] and that is her condition …[Philip thinks] he can keep Juana as close a captive in Castile as in Flanders in order to rule alone."[12]

Fernando hoped the Great Captain would bring him reinforcements, but Gonzalo Fernández de Córdoba was reluctant to leave Naples undefended and, still suspicious about the rift between Juana and Philip, he hesitated to act on Fernando's requests. In Andalucia, meanwhile, the infantry were demanding payment before committing themselves to a new conflict. Guevara thought Fernando's household unimpressive: a hundred *continos* travelled four leagues behind him, bearing only light arms, and by 12 June just a handful of magnates remained at his crestfallen little court.[13] After spending several days with him, sheltering from the heat in churches and monasteries and playing the card game known as flush, or *flusso*, a trickle of sympathy for Fernando is discernable in Guevara's despatches. He begged Philip to remember that he was also a prince of Aragon and Fernando's son-in-law.[14]

## 6.2 The Queen's 'Party'

Diego de Guevara soon discovered that there were not two but three parties to the conflict and, in the struggle for power, it was the queen who mattered: "Sire," Guevara told Philip, "do not deceive yourself … the great lords who are here will not come over to you unless you and the queen rule together (Fig. 6.1)."[15]

A key figure in this respect was the mighty constable of Castile, Bernardino Fernández de Velasco, and Fernando's son-in-law through his second marriage to the king's (illegitimate) daughter, Juana of Aragon. Velasco's nephew, Pedro, described him as a tall, attractive man with beautiful hands; a former hero of the Granadan wars who liked women and who, although not cruel to his vassals, did not heed them much.[16] Velasco's waspishness with Guevara was, perhaps, accentuated by inner turmoil. To whom, he asked rhetorically, did Castile belong? Guevara was careful to mention Juana first. Then why, retorted Velasco, did Philip mean to destroy Castile? Philip's difficulties with Juana made it all the more urgent to come to an understanding with Fernando.[17]

Yet, within days, Velasco had left Fernando, ostensibly on a visit to his daughter, but in reality in search of the queen.[18] As Bergenroth points out: "A third party was in the course of formation, with the Constable of Castile at its head."[19] Fadrique Enríquez, the admiral of Castile who had led Juana's fleet in 1496, looked warily on. As cunning a political operator as his first cousin, Fernando, passionate by temperament and capable of rashness, yet ever poised to catch the scent of the wind, he would figure prominently in the years of conflict to come. Enríquez later expressed the conviction that Juana and Philip must rule together if they ruled at all. But, on 14 June, he warned Guevara about Velasco's plans to block an agreement between the kings that excluded the queen and to muster support for her as "sovereign lady." The admiral wanted the constable to be stopped from speaking to her until he himself had been able to confer with Velasco and Philip. Writing at midnight from Rionegro, Guevara told Philip:

> Sire, j'ay parlé à l'almirante environ sept heures après midy. qu'il m'a dit pour autant qu'il désire vostre service et vostre bien, que vous ne laissiez en façon du monde parler le connectable à la Royne jusques a ce que l'almirante soit envers vous, pour luy dire devant vous que ce qu'il luy a dit en présence des gens de bien. C'est que le connétable luy a dit que luy et autres ne consentiront point que les deux roys s'accordent ensemble contre la royne car il disoit que elle est la souveraine dame, et qu'il ne fera autre chose fors ce qu'elle luy commandera et m'a dit le almirante que le dit connétable lui a requis de luy estre amy de ceste affaire, et puisque a luy qui n'est point son ami il a dit telles choses vous pouvez penser quelles choses il a dit à ceux qui sont amis. Le sr Roy beau père m'a pareillement dit le meme ...[20]

The constable was right to fear that Juana would be excluded from any forthcoming agreement. Fernando complained about Velasco's attempts to obstruct one and "in case this could not be done, to join together to adopt the cause of the queen against the king my son and against me." Fernando dreaded Velasco finding willing allies in Philip's camp.

He did not want a queen's 'party' in command of Castile any more than he wanted Philip in charge, and described Velasco's support for her as an affront to both kings.[21]

**Fig. 6.1** Diego de Guevara's letters reveal the formation of a juanista 'party' in the summer of 1506, and stress that Philip ignored Juana's significance at his peril. This fine portrait by Michael Sittow shows Guevara a decade later, c. 1515. His Spanish connections are visible in the emblem of the military order of Calatrava woven into his gold brocade doublet and his wide collar of Iberian lynx. Detail from diptych with Virgin and Child. Oil on wood. National Gallery of Washington (*Source* ACTIVE MUSEUM/Alamy Stock Photo)

What, then, motivated the 'juanistas'? Kingly failure to grant adequate favours or sufficient prominence provides the traditional explanation for aristocratic discontent and it has been widely argued that the queen's supporters were guided principally by resentment. As the count of Lemos later reminded Charles, Spaniards (like others) were accustomed to receiving rewards for their services.[22] Häbler's view is characteristic of many for whom the emergence of this grouping was less an expression of support for the "*wirklich geistig beschränke Königin*" than of rivalries and jealousies between clans.[23] Castilian nobles and knights lived at the time in fractured kingdoms, riven by differing poles of authority, all laying claim to the legitimate right to rule. In Iberia in 1506, there were even two Juanas of Castile with legitimate claims to proprietary status, and both—in *la Beltraneja* and *la Loca*—given insulting monikers by history. It was not, in such troubled times, a given that the first would languish forever in Portuguese confinement; the second, also confined, embodied realms still being governed by a guardian or father-king with a vestigial royal claim to those same realms, and whose authority was contested by another force, a 'king-archduke,' with all that this title implied. In such a climate, it was tempting and often fruitful for rival groupings to exploit the discourse of honour to their own advantage.

Yet, despite Häbler's description of the queen as mentally impaired, or limited, she was not widely, or predominantly, seen that way in the summer of 1506 and resentment with Philip or Fernando does not entirely explain the growth of a third 'party.' By alienating Philip, the nobles supporting Juana stood not only to lose political clout but forfeit their fortresses, estates, even lives. On the other hand, they could not be sure that a liberated queen would reward them by respecting their privileges and granting new ones, and the general tendency to focus on their ambitions and egoism means that key ingredients in their make-up have been downplayed.

Despite the evident fact that the discourse of honour, with its chivalric notions of loyalty, generosity and courage, was exploited by rival groupings, it was real, and had constantly to be guarded and re-asserted.[24] Alba's famous rebuke to Velasco ("I did not think you possessed honour until now when I see you losing it") demonstrates this eloquently enough.[25] Yet the constable's nephew claimed that Velasco faced death threats for supporting Juana.[26] Despite his warning to Guevara, Enríquez—whose youthful sense of honour and determination to exact revenge on a fellow courtier, had once led him down the road of imprisonment and exile—would later speak of dying, if necessary, in the queen's service. The count of Benavente, with close ties of kinship to both constable and admiral, used the language of honour to withdraw support for Philip's lone rule and express allegiance to Juana instead.[27] Alcocer, a member of the household of Toledan procurator López de Padilla, describes an emotional Padilla leaving an audience with the queen "ready to die for his loyalty."[28] The rhetoric of honour and fidelity also arose in a bitter dispute between Philip's envoys in Rome, Antonio de Acuña and Bernardino de Carvajal, cardinal of Santa Cruz, who had shifted his allegiance to Isabel's heirs but seems, by 1506, to have developed a poor opinion of Philip. Santa Cruz declared that he would serve his sovereign lady to the death, while the Great Captain spoke of defending Naples to the death "for doña Juana and her children."[29] In 1507, the procurator for Granada, Rodrigo Bazán, threatened to kill Maximilian's envoy, Andrea de Borgo, if Borgo dared attempt anything contrary to the queen's honour.[30]

Writing about Spanish kingdoms that had, by the mid-1550s, already changed much, Rodríguez-Salgado describes the enduring importance of honour in a culture that associated virtue and ability with arms.[31] This culture has elsewhere been described in terms of one of several ideological models on which royal power was based. According to the concept of *realeza caballeresca*, or chivalrous royalty, the knightly class enjoyed a privileged position beside monarchs and princes whose origins, accepted as sacred, transformed them into the *criadoras*, or nurturers, of those who showed courage and loyalty both to them and to the 'common good' (*bien común*) with which princes were identified.[32]

Velasco himself had illustrated this concept of *realeza caballaresca* only four years before with an ingenious entertainment laid on for the princes at Burgos in February 1502. After a sumptuous banquet, the tapestries around them had lifted towards the roof to reveal a garden of gold and silver-leaved trees and glittering vegetation, advancing upon the guests as if magically, on "*soubtilz ingiens.*" Bowing low before Juana and Philip, a knight in a long robe and white plumed hat, and carrying a flaming torch, had presented them with a letter begging for their help. Twelve knights, held chained and blinded in that enchanted garden, could only be freed, and their sight restored, through the favour and assistance of Juana and her ladies, who were asked, through dance, to gradually unfasten their shackles and blindfolds. As has been noted, this chivalric *leitmotiv* promoted, in stylised form, the "essence of a kingdom and its nobility."[33] At its core was a particular view of Juana as princess and heir, and who, like the Laureola of *Cárcel de Amor*, was seen as the "*criadora redentora*" or creator, nurturer and redeemer of the nobility around her. In casting Juana as saviour and redeemer of noble knights, the dance of liberation at the heart of the constable's ball was more than a courtly conceit; it highlighted the essence of the contract of mutual protection between them.

The catalyst for Velasco's rift with Fernando in the summer of 1506 may have been the moment he realised that the king of Aragon was poised to sacrifice Juana to a deal that would, in his view, damage the interests of Castile. Velasco was to show more than once impassioned opposition to a regime in which his sovereign mistress played no part. If, moreover, Fernando were expelled from Castile, Juana was the only hope for those determined to resist the implantation of an alien Habsburg government, operating in isolation from their lawful ruler. As an army of Germans approached the interior, with the true monarch a hostage in their midst, the duke of Alba's spat with the constable over a bowl of wild cherries provides a vivid illustration of the way in which conflicting demands on the honour and loyalty of the nobles were pulling them apart.

## 6.3 The Passions of the Queen

Philip's army avoided Fernando's small party by following one of the many pilgrim ways that interlace the terrain between Galicia, Leon and Zamora. The king of Aragon, deprived of a reunion with Juana that would reflect legitimacy upon him, found that the nobles through whose domains he travelled treated him like the enemy.[34] Having reached Villafranca del Bierzo (León), he withdrew along a southeasterly path toward the Tera valley. He sent Cisneros to negotiate with Philip in early June, with powers to marginalise Juana, if necessary, in any future settlement.[35]

The archbishop of Toledo was a complex figure in whom an exalted aspect and ascetic habits combined with huge political ambition and wealth and a capacity for intrigue. Zurita mentions his political appetites and obsession with holy war. His biographer, García Oro, refers to Cisneros's ultimate "crusading and missionary" objectives and dreams of a Christian Mediterranean wiped clean of Islam.[36] Castile could only achieve such objectives, in Cisneros's view, if its political regime was stable, its armies mobile and efficient, and its faith orthodox and effective.

Despite Cisneros' detestation of Aragonese influence in Castile's administration, he had worked with Fernando to neutralise Juana and Philip on the eve of the Cortes of Toro.[37] Now Fernando's influence was on the wane, while the impressionable Philip struck Cisneros as someone with whom he might do business, whom he might even remould. He met him often and Philip allowed him into Juana's presence.[38] Their meetings must have unsettled both. Cisneros had been among the emissaries sent by Isabel to La Mota in 1503 in an attempt to persuade the princess to abandon her reckless stance on the castle battlements, and the memory of those icy autumnal nights in the outer precinct of the fortress must have been as clear in his own mind as in Juana's. Like Fernando, Cisneros never underestimated the importance of the queen. But he differed from the constable in seeing her as the problem, not the solution.

Cisneros' biographers have sometimes struggled to explain the sheer determination with which he sought her political annihilation. But, to Cisneros, Juana was Isabel's antithesis. Having fled her political responsibilities in 1504, she represented all that, from the perspective of centuries of clerical thought, characterised the female sex: irrationality, mutability, instability, hysteria, malice and so on. Cisneros would have been at least partially familiar with the rich fund of thought on the nature of sovereignty and legitimacy, nourished by, among others, the works of John of Salisbury, Giovanni Bocaccio and Coluccio Salutati, and the fruit of the medieval conflicts between church and state. Such works had found fertile ground in the Spanish kingdoms, where the problem of tyranny and the *rex inutilis*—the 'useless' or shadow king, who loses legitimacy through the failure to rule well, or to rule at all—was a recurring theme of political literature. The seventy-year-old archbishop had seen for himself how Juana's grandfather, Juan II of Castile, and her uncle, Enrique IV of Castile, reviled in their time as failed kings, or tyrants—one twice imprisoned, the other fought and hunted—had been undermined by the warring 'infantes of Aragon' and by a series of bloody conflicts. Cisneros feared that Juana's female 'passions' could re-ignite them. At the same time, he saw popularity draining away from Philip because Juana lacked the "pomp and state that was necessary to such a queen, newly come to reign."[39] Juana's rumoured ill-treatment and mysterious invisibility combined lethally with drought and stirrings of plague and with the depredations of the German soldiers to make a tinderbox of Ourense, where he had joined the king-archduke. A *grandísimo alboroto* between these soldiers and the local inhabitants left several dead and wounded.[40]

Martire describes Philip's retinue struggling through fissures in almost impassable mountains. As drivers fled with their animals into the night, leaving carts unattended, and as violent altercations with the local population continued, Querini shook with anger. His were among 200 horses and mules to perish and all because the *maligni* feared a meeting with Fernando on the open road.[41] Eventually, between 18 and 19 June, they reached Puebla de Sanabria. The next day, at Remesal, Philip and Fernando finally met. Jacob van Laethem, an artist attached to Philip, shows Fernando's small, sober party facing the massed ranks of Philip's soldiers and pikemen. Philip sports a new white hat and violet silk. But the conqueror of Granada, sitting astride a chestnut pony, wears an old travelling bonnet and dusty gown of mulberry red and his small retinue is unarmed. His modest appearance and habitual air of bonhomie embarrassed some of those who had abandoned him, their figures swollen by cuirasses hidden beneath black silk. His reproachful query to an armed Garcilaso de la Vega, who had, not long before, presided the Cortes of Toro—"For me, García?"—may have deliberately recalled Casesar's supposed words to Brutus: "And *you*, my child?"[42]

The two kings spoke briefly and formally in the shade of a holm oak. Subsequently, Philip made for Benavente and Fernando withdrew to the salt marshes of Villafáfila. On 27–28 June, the treaty of Benavente-Villafáfila, substituting that of Salamanca, handed Philip sole effective possession of Castile. Although he seemed the victor, the agreement was costly. Fernando was awarded the lucrative masterships of the military orders and half the income from, and rights over, the islands of the Indies and Ocean Sea—rights he had already allocated himself at Toro.[43] But the most striking aspect of the treaty was its treatment of Juana. The main text, of which Cisneros was a principal architect, maintained the conditional basis on which Isabel's will had left Fernando the governorship. But in a move that would, once again, have horrified her, it made Philip sole ruler "for now and ever more," should Juana not wish to govern or fell "gravely ill" or died. Yet more shockingly, a secret coda, tacitly recognising the emergence of a force of juanistas, barred the queen from governing under any circumstances, owing to her illnesses and passions. In the unlikely event that she should herself seize the initiative, or be induced to do so by others, Philip and Fernando would join to prevent the "total destruction and perdition of these kingdoms."[44]

Copies of the treaty were sent to the eighteen cities with votes in the Cortes. It is unclear just how secret the secret coda was, but, either way, even Louis XII, who had met Juana at Blois, expressed astonishment at its treatment of the queen.[45] Aware of its preposterous nature, Fernando took immediate steps to cover himself. He summoned Thomas Malferit, president of the Chancery of Aragon, chief secretary Almazán and chamberlain Juan Cabrero (uncle of Marcuello) to witness his signature on a document that he held in reserve. In this, he vehemently repudiated the treaty as being "to the massive detriment" of the queen as well as to his own right as governor and administrator. He had signed it only because of intimidation.[46]

Juana was informed about these events in gradual stages. Querini describes her response to news that the meeting at Remesal had taken place without her as one of unbearable anguish ("*monstro haver tanto dolor non lo haver saputo che piu non se potria*"). Turning on her host, Benavente, and on the marquis of Villena, she demanded to know why they had not kept her informed, and threatened to punish them as traitors when she could. Later, she was heard shouting at length with Philip.[47] Such threats might remind modern readers of Alice's Queen of Hearts, who cries "Off with their heads!" at the slightest opportunity. Given, however, Juana's radical differences with Philip, whose status was inferior to hers, all acts of disloyalty and deceit by those who had sworn her fealty and proclaimed her queen, could indeed be construed as acts of lèse-majesté. The great compendium of Castilian law contained in the *Siete Partidas* contains several categories of *laese majestatis crimen*, or high treason—the "most vile and worst error that can befall the human heart." Among the gravest was not only to conspire to kill a king but to "cause him to lose the honour of his dignity" and to deceive him.[48] Yet the *ira regia* upon which Juana promised one day to act was a two-edged weapon, providing ammunition for the treaty's argument that her "illnesses and passions" made her dangerous and unfit. Querini noted that many who sided with Philip in 1506 did so precisely because they feared laying themselves open to the queen's vengeance.[49]

What happened next takes us back to the opening lines of this study, to Juana's visit to the "wood of the peacocks," to her race across the park and out of the castle. A good horsewoman, she might have hoped to throw off her pursuers, or, at the least, place Philip in such a position that he would have had to agree to a meeting between herself and Fernando. But Philip would not countenance the risk. Juana made another effort to contact her father through Villaescusa, her long-standing chief chaplain, adviser and envoy, whom she had called back to her side in Galicia. The letter she entrusted to him begged Fernando not to leave Castile until they met. But this too was discovered and destroyed. Versions of the incident differ. Querini reports that Philip, when alerted, threatened Villaescusa with imprisonment.[50] Villaescusa's own account, in his later

*Instrucción*, seems fudged, probably reflecting the caution with which he needed to approach Philip's son. It shows him trying to broach the matter with Philip first, then being dismissed from court, but does not explain why the king should punish him.[51] A third, more plausible version has Juana confiding the letter to Villaescusa on the road between Benavente and Valladolid and the bishop being searched when he refused to comply with an order to hand the letter over. It was found in his codpiece and he was thrown out of court. As he went, he was heard to mutter: "What a world is this, where no man of virtue can prosper at court but only villains!"[52]

## 6.4 "And sure, circa Regna tonat."[53]

Philip had ordered the suspension of the Cortes of Toro pending his and Juana's arrival in Castile. Guevara warned that the procurators, left in a state of disgruntled uncertainty, would cooperate with him only if they saw Juana. He advised Philip to order them to gather beyond the geographical reach of Fernando's influence or send them home until further notice.[54]

By 24 June, the procurators were assembling at Benavente. As was customary, two representatives had been sent from each of the cities with votes in the Cortes: Ávila; Burgos; Córdoba; Cuenca; Guadalajara; Granada; Jaén; León, Madrid; Murcia; Salamanca; Segovia; Seville; Soria; Toledo; Toro; Valladolid; and Zamora. A ceremony of *besamanos* took place amid a buzz of disquiet. Where was the queen? Querini noted that a Basque delegation refused to pay allegiance to Philip without first paying homage to Juana.[55]

Philip, who needed the procurators' support for the new treaty, tried to exploit Juana's conduct at Benavente to his advantage. Again he sent envoys to Fernando in the hope of persuading him to agree to her imprisonment. Fernando argued that, since he had not been allowed to meet Juana, he could not comment. At Mucientes, in the hills above Valladolid, Juana refused to move any further until she had seen her father. Philip called the procurators together. He had known for months, he told them, that Juana was unequal to the burden of government, but had kept the matter secret for the sake of her honour, and their children's, and in the hope that she would come to her senses. But, since the incident at Benavente, her unfitness was surely clear to everyone.

The spectacle of their native-born sovereign under the guard of German soldiers was, however, galling to many, who argued that, before any oaths of allegiance were taken, Juana must be free and able to address them. It was decided that the procurators should refer back to their city councils.[56] Leon and Burgos, where Flemish trading links were strong, sided with Philip, but the cities of the Castilian heartland—Toledo, Guadalajara, Madrid and Salamanca among them—took Juana's side. Granada was divided. Iñigo López de Mendoza, count of Tendilla and governor of the Alhambra, whose eldest son, Luis, was a procurator, concluded that, however regrettable, solitary rule by Philip should, if necessary, be supported. He backed this view by referring to orders formerly signed by Fernando alone during the days of the dual monarchy, particularly when Isabel had been ill.[57] But while Luis voted for Philip against Juana, his fellow procurator, Gómez de Santillán, refused.[58] Toledo city council meanwhile insisted that their representatives, Pedro López de Padilla and Miguel de Hita, recognise Juana as Isabel's true and legitimate successor. Only then could they acknowledge Philip as king-by-marriage.[59] When Seville's procurators, Pedro Ortíz de Sandoval and Fernando Santillán, argued that their city might profit by seizing control of the queen and "treating her in accordance with the requirements of her illness," the response was unequivocal. Not only must allegiance be sworn firstly to Juana, but it could be given to Philip only with Juana's consent. The firmness of these responses took Philip by surprise.[60]

His advisers suggested that he circulate a petition, threatening and cajoling the nobles and procurators into signing up to Juana's imprisonment. The count of Benavente later admitted that he had signed because "it was not ... safe to do the contrary."[61] But three of Castile's *grandes*, the constable, admiral and duke of Nájera—mindful of honour and doubtless affronted at the very thought of being asked to sign such a piece of paper—joined in Juana's defence. Putting aside long-standing feuds, the duke and constable declared publicly that nothing would induce them to betray the queen.[62] In a little-known manuscript, the constable's nephew described how Nájera warned Velasco of the danger and how the constable responded:

> Alerted to this [petition], the duke of Nájera went to Valladolid ... and contacted the constable, don Bernardino, who was on his estate, near Mucientes, called Cigales. And [the constable], accompanied only by don Iñigo de Velasco, his brother, and don Diego de Mendoza, count of

> Castro, went to Mucientes, and … found the king's guard of a thousand Germans assembled there, and he passed through their midst and entered the palace where the king was gathered with all the grandees above-mentioned … And [Philip] handed him the paper, saying that he could see how all the grandees had agreed to place the queen in a fortress, and asked him to sign it too. The constable begged the king not to order him to do so and [the king] snatched the paper angrily back and said: "How is it that you refuse to sign what all these other grandees have signed?" The constable replied that, unlike the rest, he had not had the opportunity to communicate with the queen. And the king went into his room and the constable returned to Cigales, and although he knew that a plan was afoot to arrest and kill him, he did not once retract his words, and thus the king was unable to place the queen in a fortress.[63]

This reads as though Juana's salvation depended entirely on Velasco, aided by Nájera. However, Enríquez's role was also significant. When he refused to sign the petition before seeing the queen, Philip reluctantly granted him an audience. According to Zurita, these talks, attended also by Benavente, lasted for ten hours, spaced over two days. We have Zurita's account of them and a fragment of evidence from Enríquez himself.

Juana sat in a dark room beside a window, in black and in *capirotes,* a headdress that partly obscured her face. She was, as always, under guard. At the door stood Cortes president Garcilaso de la Vega. Inside was Cisneros. Zurita observes that, when the admiral entered, she stood with a courtesy reminiscent of Isabel's, except that she further stressed her respect by remaining standing. They began by talking about Fernando, whom Enríquez had just met at Renedo de Esgueva. Juana exclaimed "*¡Dios le guardase!*" ("God protect him!"). How much, she said, she had longed to see him![64]

According to Enríquez, Juana spoke of the dangers for Castile of a Philip-led government, surrounded by a great influx of "Germans" (*alemanes*), and coloured by important cultural differences in language and discourse ("*en lengua y plática*"). Enríquez advised her to put concerns about Fernando aside. He was gone; "everything was hers." If she agreed to co-rule, acting upon Philip as a mitigating force, the admiral would support her. Afterwards, he told Philip that Juana had shown no sign of mental incapacity. Valladolid was very tense and if Philip did not enter the city with her—if he separated himself from her a finger's breadth—Castile would rise.[65]

Heading down to Valladolid, Enríquez crossed paths with a group of procurators, among whom he recognised Rodrigo Mexía of Jaén. He warned Mexía about the petition: "For God's sake, has the kingdom ever done anything so ugly?" Mexía asked if the procurators could depend on Enríquez' support should they refuse to sign it. The admiral gave his word of honour to save the queen or die in the attempt.[66]

One city deputy reportedly threatened with death was Toledan *regidor* and procurator López de Padilla, who had brought with him his young son, Juan, the future comunero leader. Alcocer watched with Juan as Cisneros and Manuel drew Padilla into the church belfry, but a Spanish servant warned him to move the boy away if he did not want him to see his father falling from the tower. In the end, Philip agreed to let Padilla see Juana. According to Alcocer, the queen spoke to him sensibly at first but, after they entered into detail, seemed confused. However, a tearful Padilla left the audience defiant in his loyalty to Juana.[67]

We have no details of this conversation but it is almost certain that Padilla assured the queen of Toledo's support, and that this, in turn, helped encourage her to order that the Cortes should be held there. In order to speak to the procurators she had to resort to guile. Querini describes her arguing at length with Philip on the crucial question of the order in which the *juramento* should be made. Juana insisted that she be sworn-in first, as Isabel had been, but eventually seemed to yield to Philip's arguments. Only then, was she admitted into the room where the procurators were gathered. At once, she summoned them and asked if they recognised her as "Juana, first and legitimate daughter and heir of the late queen Isabel." They assented. "Since you know me for who I am," she said, "I order you all to proceed to Toledo and await me there, because it is there that I intend to be solemnly sworn-in as queen of Castile and to observe all your laws and constitutions." The procurators stood with bowed heads: "No-one, great or small," Querini writes, "dared speak."[68]

Philip retreated in dudgeon to a monastery, while some procurators offered to try to obtain further clarification from the queen. They asked her four questions. Did she mean to govern Castile now Fernando was gone? Would she accept Philip as co-ruler? Would she agree to the company of Spanish ladies (the pre-requisite of a ruling Spanish queen)? Would she dress as a Spaniard? Juana answered that since it was neither honourable (*honesto*) nor appropriate (*conveniente*) for Castile to be governed by Flemings, and thus to be governed by a Fleming's wife, she had wanted Fernando to govern until her son came of age. As regards her female entourage, the procurators should hold their tongues. She would not have women (*donne*) in her household, given her husband's nature, but was happy to wear Spanish dress.[69]

On the face of it, these answers seem to contradict the position she had taken hours before, reinforcing preconceptions about her incapability.[70] But Querini's report, the only known source, is almost certainly a summary and requires context. On the question of a female entourage, the Venetian diarist Sanuto, who recorded extracts of Querini's despatches, understood Juana as referring to "*donzele*" (young, unmarried women) rather than "*donne*."[71] This would make sense in the context of Philip's philandering. But it would not have affected the fundamental problem posed by a felipista government intent on imposing a female entourage that was not of Juana's own choosing, and thus, in itself, a negation of her proprietary status. What then of her remark that since it was dishonourable for a Fleming to govern; it was not for a Fleming's wife to do so? Here, Juana seems to be reiterating the concerns she had voiced to Enríquez, and probably to Padilla, and which she had held consistently since the end of 1502. She had clung to one shred of hope: that she, Philip and Fernando might reach a lasting settlement of some kind. But Fernando's departure had obliged her to change position. If her responses to the procurators are combined with her lengthy arguments with Philip about pre-eminence, which Querini also notes; her public declaration at Mucientes; and the circumstances in which she later rode through Valladolid and insisted on examining the procurators' powers, Juana appears to be saying that, despite longstanding misgivings, she expected to be recognised as sovereign ruler and assume her responsibilities.

This interpretation tallies with Querini's further observation that Cisneros worked laboriously to persuade Juana to hand Philip power.[72] She appeared again to yield, but again this was a feint in the game of cat-and-mouse that she and Philip had begun to play. Philip's biographer, Cauchies, believes that, although mentally ill, Juana was "capable of moments of great lucidity" and had not abandoned "high politics."[73] Mounted on a white horse, or gray, trimmed with black velvet, she accompanied Philip into Valladolid on 10 July. But at the key moment of their entrance to the city, she ordered that Philip's standard be struck down and rode on behind her own and beneath the pallium, signalling her status as proprietary ruler of Castile. Philip's gracious smiles and waves contrasted strangely with Juana's severe appearance and demeanour, and with her unkindness in failing to respond to the welcome of the crowds. She was, writes Zurita, dressed in black, her face covered. Though the town was festively adorned and had staged entertainments along the route, she did not stop to watch them and the entry lacked the lustre of a Cortes but seemed like "something else not altogether understood."[74]

This was partly because Juana had not sanctioned Valladolid as the place for the Cortes. But the symbolism of her entry was, above all, an affirmation of her status and a tribute to Isabel.[75] Her gray represented sovereignty and the pre-eminence that Isabel had displayed when riding through Seville for the presentation of Prince Juan in 1478.[76] But Juana's mourning was also intended as a signal of her displeasure at an infamous treaty, at Fernando's expulsion from Castile and at the evils she felt would descend on Castile from Flemish rule. Her great-great grandfather, Juan I, had similarly ridden, dressed in black, to a Cortes in Valladolid to demonstrate grief at the misfortunes and failings of his reign.[77]

The monarchs continued to trick one another. Philip did not tell Juana that he had countermanded her order to suspend proceedings until they arrived in Toledo. At the monastery of San Benito, in the hours between their entry and the *juramento* of 12 July, debate raged over a last-ditch, and ultimately unsuccessful, attempt, led by Garcilaso de la Vega, to overcome the resistance of procurators and nobles and declare the queen unfit to govern. On 12 July, after dinner, Philip again led Juana into a room full of procurators. Gazing around in astonishment, she asked what they were doing there, and by whose orders, and angrily refused to allow the oath-taking. But, such were the pleas and exhortations of the procurators, combined with Philip's, that she "finally agreed to allow them to kiss hands and swear her in first as queen of Castile."[78] Placing their right hands on the cross and gospels, both monarchs swore to uphold the royal patrimony and laws, *fueros* and rights.

Regrettably, the debates in Mucientes and Valladolid were passed over in the official record.[79] The outcome, nonetheless, is clear. Juana was sworn in first, as "true queen and legitimate successor and natural proprietary mistress of these kingdoms and lordships of Castile, Leon and Granada" and in consequence had full powers to govern. The procurators then confirmed Philip as "true king and legitimate lord" in his capacity as Juana's husband. Charles was recognised as his mother's heir, and as king after her death.[80]

Referring to a different version of the *juramento*, archived at Lille, and granting Philip proprietary status, Aram suggests that Juana "may have decided to compromise with Philippe and relinquish the title of proprietary ruler in order to secure their son's subsequent rights to the throne."[81] However, these rights were not in question at the time and Juana's conduct at the Cortes strongly argues against a volte-face or compromise on her part. The fact that she remained the sole source of proprietary legitimacy within Castile is important for understanding the mounting frustration with Philip's disposal of a patrimony seen as exclusively hers, and with the Royal Council's actions when continuing to uphold those measures after his death. It is also important for understanding Juana's later motive in rescinding Philip's measures and changing the composition of the Royal Council (see Chapters 7 and 8). However, the limitations to Philip's mandate were not specifically laid down. This allowed him to act as if he were indeed the proprietary ruler and may explain Querini's assumption that Philip was recognised "*in ultimo loco*" as "*re et governator di questi regni.*"[82]

To conclude, Philip's continuing determination to act as though he were the sole source of power should not obscure Juana's triumph at the Cortes of Valladolid. Her risky strategy of resistance had borne fruit. Since her accession, treaties and agreements unfavourable to her had tumbled one after another. Castile's main representative institution, enfeebled by years of overweening monarchical rule, had shown it could still rise to events. Both cities and magnates had resisted immense pressure to protect the queen not only as the fount of political legitimacy but with full powers to govern. Philip might turn a deaf ear to the thunder round the throne. But the storms of summer were not yet over.

## Notes

1. BL, Egerton, Ms. 544, f. 345, April 1506.
2. Padilla (CODOIN, 8, 1846), Philip and Juana to Inquisitor General and Consejo de la Suprema, 30 September 1505, 337–342.
3. "Castile is yours/king don Felipe/Castile is yours,/let no-one take it from you./ And God protect/our queen/make way for her." Sancha Cota (Kenniston, ed. 1964).
4. Fürstenberg (Roth von Schrenkenstein, ed. 1867–1869), VII, 12 May 1506, 146.
5. Querini (Höfler, ed. 1884), 100, 2 May 1506; 104, 12 May 1506.

6. Undated letter [1506] in Paz y Mélia, A., ed. (1915–1922), I, 121–122.
7. ADN, B 18826. 24222, Naturel to Philip, 19 June 1506.
8. Querini, 110, 31 May 1506.
9. Querini, 106, 15 May 1506.
10. Hicks (2011).
11. ADN, B. 18825. 24186, 1 June 1506.
12. Zurita, 4 (Canellas López, ed. 1994), 15.
13. ADN, B. 18825. 24206/24207, 12 June 1506.
14. ADN, B. 18825. 24206/24207, 12 June 1506; ADN, B. 18826. 24211, 15 June 1506.
15. ADN, B. 18825. 24185, 1–2 June 1506. Padilla, in his *Crónica*, also notes growing support for Juana through the summer of 1506 (143).
16. BN, Ms. 3238, 'Origen de la Ylustrísima Casa de Velasco por D. Pedro Fernández de Velasco' (transcription).
17. ADN, B. 18825. 24186, 1 June 1506.
18. ADN, B. 18846. 29630, 10 June 1506.
19. CSP., ed. Bergenroth, (Queen Juana), xxxiv.
20. ADN, B. 18826. 24211, 14 June 1506. This partly unpublished letter was included in Fleming, *Juana I and the Struggle for Power* [thesis, 2011].
21. AGS, PR 56, f. 24, 'Despacho del Rey … a uno de sus embajadores sobre la oposición de algunos a su unión con los reyes … para gobernar los Reinos de España,' June 1506.
22. AGS, Estado 4, f. 66 [1517].
23. Häbler (1882).
24. Thomas (2009) describes "early modern" England, but his observation that aristocratic honour should not be dismissed as empty rhetoric (citing, inter alia, the examples of Elizabethans such as Essex, Raleigh and Grenville) is relevant to Spain (154–160).
25. Alcocer (Gamero, ed. 1872), 5.
26. BN, Ms. 3238, 'Origen'.
27. AHN, Osuna, C. 420, D. 1–4, 'Declaración,' 18 August 1506.
28. Alcocer, 14–15.
29. ADN, B. 18826. 24222, Naturel to Philip, 19 June 1506; and ADN, B. 18826. 24241, 28 June 1506.
30. RAH, Salazar, A-12, ff. 127–129 (postscript), Conchillos to Almazán.
31. Rodríguez-Salgado (1988).
32. Nieto Soria explores the concept of *realeza caballeresca* in Valdeón Baruque (ed. 2001).The 'common good' (*bien común*) here refers to the widespread idea that the common interests of the realm had to prevail over particular interests.
33. *Reise* (Chmel, ed. 1840), I, 618; Porras Gil (2010), 256.
34. Pérez (2014).
35. AGS, PR 7, f. 76, 2 June 1506, 'Cédula de Fernando el Católico al Arzobispo de Toledo'; CODOIN, 14: 307–308, 2 June 1506, 'Minuta

de poder que el Rey D. Fernando dió al Arzobispo de Toledo sobre cierto articulo que toca á excluir de la gobernación de los reinos á la Reina Doña Juana'.

36. Zurita, 4; García Oro (2005).
37. Pérez (2014).
38. Gómez de Castro (Oroz Reta. ed. 1984); Guevara to Philip, 6 June 1506, in Gachard (ed. 1876).
39. Zurita, 4, 23.
40. Vallejo (De la Torre y del Cerro, ed. 1913), 93.
41. Querini, 113, 17 June 1506.
42. Zurita, 4, 32–33.
43. AGS, PR 56, f. 28, 27 June 1506; PR 56, 28 June 1506.
44. "*la serenissima Reyna … en ninguna manera se quiere ocupar ny entender en ningun negocio de regimiento ni governación ni otra cosa y ahunque lo quisiese fazer seria total destruction y perdimiento destos Reynos según sus enfermedades y pasiones …*". AGS, PR 56, f. 21. 1, 27 June 1506; AGS, PR 56, f. 27. 2, 28 June 1506.
45. "*Louis s'émerveilla assés du traitié fait pour la reyne vostre compaigne.*" Philip's ambassador, Courteville, to Philip (Le Glay, ed. 1845), II, XLIII, 10 July 1506, 55.
46. AGS, PR 56, f. 30, 'Protesta del Rey Fernando de la capitulación ajustada con el Rey Felipe sobre el gobierno de los Reinos de España,' 27 June 1506.
47. Querini, 116, 25 June 1506.
48. *Las Siete Partidas*, VII, II, 1, distinguishes between treason, against the monarch, and treachery (*alevosia*), against others, or what might in English be termed high and petty treason. However, the distinction was not always rigidly maintained. See Iglesia Ferreiros (1971), 225–226n. See also Suárez Varela (Szászdi León-Borja y Galende Ruiz, eds. 2013).
49. Querini, 119, 4 July 1506.
50. Querini, 121, 11 July 1506.
51. 'Instrucción,' in González Olmedo (ed. 1944).
52. RAH, Jesuitas 9-16-3, f. 16, in González Olmedo, 81.
53. The quotation is from sixteenth-century poet Thomas Wyatt, based on a line from Seneca's *Phaedra* ("it thunders round the throne").
54. ADN, B. 1885. 24185, 1–2 June 1506.
55. Querini, 116, 25 June 1506.
56. Querini, 119, 4 July 1506.
57. Moreno Trujillo/Osorio Pérez (eds. 1996), Tendilla to Luis de Mendoza, 14 July 1506.
58. Alcocer; Carretero Zamora (1988).
59. AGS, Camara de Castilla (Pueblos) 20, f. 245, 'Carta del poder de la ciudad de Toledo' [1506].

60. Rodríguez Villa (1892); AGS, PR 60, f. 40, 4 July 1506, 'Carta de poder de la ciudad de Sevilla'; Querini, 121, 11 July 1506.
61. AHN, Osuna C. 420, D. 1–4, 'Declaración que hizo el señor Conde,' 18 August 1506.
62. Querini, 121, 11 July 1506.
63. BN Ms. 3238, 'Orígen,' 32–33.
64. Zurita, 4, 54–55.
65. Ibidem; BL, Egerton Ms. 309, ff. 153v.–155v. [1506], 'Carta del Almirante.'
66. Danvila (1897–1900), II, 547–548.
67. Alcocer, 14–15.
68. Querini, 121, 11 July 1506.
69. Ibidem.
70. According to Zalama (2003) "*No solo hace falta cordura sino intelligencia para dar semejante contestación ...*" (52). According to Calderón Ortega (2001): "*cualquier duda que hubieran podido tener* [los procuradores] *acerca de la incapacidad de la reina para gobernar quedó finalmente desechada*" (141).
71. Sanuto (Fulin, ed. 1969–1970), 6, 387.
72. Querini, 121, 11 July 1506.
73. Cauchies (Zalama/Vandenbroek, eds. 2006), 84.
74. Zurita, 4, 59.
75. Lorenzo Arribas (2004), 35.
76. Carrasco Manchado (2006), 337.
77. Palma (Escudero de la Peña, ed. 1879).
78. Querini, 122, 16 July 1506.
79. Carretero Zamora (1988).
80. AGS, PR 7, f. 74, 12 July 1506, "Juramento de los procuradores de Cortes a Doña Juana y Don Felipe". Juana is "*verdadera reina y legitima subçesora y señora natural proprietaria destos reynos e señoríos de Castilla, de León, de Granada.*"
81. Aram (2005), 87.
82. Querini, 122, 16 July 1506.

## References

Alcocer, Pedro. 1872. *Relaciones de algunas cosas que pasaron en estos reynos*, ed. A. Martin Gamero. Seville: Sociedad de Bibliófilos andaluces.
Aram, Bethany. 2005. *Juana the Mad: Sovereignty and Dynasty in Renaissance Europe*. Baltimore and London: John Hopkins University Press.
Calderón Ortega, José Manuel. 2001. *Felipe el Hermoso*. Madrid: Espasa Calpe.

Carrasco Manchado, Ana Isabel. 2006. *Isabel I de Castilla y la sombra de la ilegitimidad*. Madrid: Sílex.
Carretero Zamora, Juan Manuel. 1988. *Cortes, monarquía, ciudades: Las Cortes de Castilla a comienzos de la época moderna (1476–1515)*. Madrid: Siglo Veintiuno de España Editores.
Cauchies, Jean-Marie. 2006. Un príncipe para los Países Bajos, para España, para Europa. In *Felipe I el Hermoso: La Belleza y La Locura*, ed. Miguel-Ángel Zalama and Paul Vandenbroeck. Madrid: CEEH/Fundación Carlos de Amberes/Fundación Caja de Burgos.
Chmel, Joseph (ed.). 1840. Reise des Erzherzogs Philipp nach Spanien. In *Die Handschriften der K. K. Hofbibliotehek in Wien*, vol. I.
Danvila y Collado, Manuel (ed.). 1897–1900. *Historia crítica y documentada de las Comunidades de Castilla*. Madrid: Memoria Histórico Español.
Ferreiros, Aquilino Iglesia. 1971. *Historia de la Traición. La Traición Regia en Leon y Castilla*. Santiago de Compostela: Universidad de Santiago.
Fulin, Rinaldo (ed.). 1969–1970. *I diarii de Marino Sanuto, 1466–1536*. Bologna: Forni Editore.
Gachard, Louis-Prosper (ed.). 1876. Relation du Deuxième Voyage de Philippe le Beau en 1506, par un Anonyme. In *Collection des Voyages des Souverains des Pays-Bas*, vol. I. Brussels: Commission Royale d'Histoire.
García Oro, José. 2005. Cisneros. *Un cardenal reformista en el trono de España (1436–1517)*. Madrid: La Esfera de los Libros.
Gómez de Castro, Alvar. 1984. *De las hazañas de Francisco Jiménez de Cisneros*, ed. José Oroz Reta. Madrid: Fundación Universitaria Española.
González Olmedo, S.I., Félix. 1944. *Diego Ramírez Villaescusa (1449–1537), fundador del Colegio de Cuenca y autor de los Cuatro Diálogos sobre la Muerte del Príncipe Juan*. Madrid: Editora Nacional.
Häbler, Konrad, 1882. *Der Streit Ferdinand's des Katholischen und Philipp's I um die Regierung von Castilien, 1504–1506*. Inaugural Dissertation, Albanus'sche Buchdrukerei, Dresden.
Hicks, Carola. 2011. *Girl in a Green Gown: The History and Mystery of the Arnolfini Portrait*. London: Chatto & Windus.
Höfler, Constantin R. (ed.) 1884. *Depeschen des Venetianischen Botschafters Dr Vincenzo Querino, 1505–1506*. Vienna. Österreichische Akademie der Wissenschaften, Archiv für Kunde österreischer Geschichts-Quellen, Band 66–67.
Kenniston, Hayward (ed.). 1964. *Memorias de Sancho Cota*. Cambridge, MA: Harvard University Press.
Le Glay, André Joseph Ghislain (ed.). 1845. *Négociations diplomatiques entre la France et l'Autriche durant les trente premières années du XVIe. siècle*, vols I–II. Paris: Imprimerie Royale.
Lorenzo Arribas, Josemi. 2004. *Juana I de Castilla y Aragón (1479-1555)*. Madrid: Ediciones del Orto.

Moreno Trujillo, María Amparo, and Maria José Osorio Pérez (eds.). 1996. *Epistolario del Conde de Tendilla (1504–1506)*. Granada: Universidad de Granada.

Nieto Soria, José Manuel. 2001. Los fundamentos ideológicos del poder regio. In *Isabel la Católica y la Política*, ed. Julio Valdeón Baruque. Valladolid: Instituto Universitario de Historia Simancas/Ámbito Ediciones.

Padilla, Lorenzo de. 1846. CODOIN, 8. In *Crónica de Felipe I llamado el Hermoso*, ed. Miguel Salvá and Pedro Sainza de Baranda. Madrid: Imprenta de la viuda de Calero.

Palma, Bachiller. 1879. *Divina Retribución sobre la Caída de España en tiempo del noble rey Don Juan el Primero*, ed. J.M. Escudero de la Peña. Madrid: Sociedad de Bibliófilos Españoles.

Paz y Mélia, Antonio (ed.). 1915–1922. *Series de los más importantes documentos del archivo y biblioteca del exmo. señor duque de Medinacieli*, vol. I. Madrid: A Paz y Mélia.

Pérez, Joseph. 2014. *Cisneros, el cardenal de España*. Madrid: Santillana Ediciones.

Porras Gil, Maria Concepción. 2010. El arte de recibir: fiestas y faustas por una princesa. In *Juana I en Tordesillas: su mundo, su entorno*, ed. M-A. Zalama. Valladolid: Ayuntamiento de Tordesillas/Grupo Página.

Rodríguez-Salgado, María José. 1988. *The Changing Face of Empire: Charles V, Philip II and Habsburg Authority, 1551–1559*. Cambridge: Cambridge University Press.

Rodríguez Villa, Antonio. 1892. *La Reina Doña Juana. Estudio histórico*. Madrid: Murillo.

Schrenkenstein, Roth von (ed.). 1867–1869. Briefe des Grafen Wolfgang zu Fürstenberg zur Geschichte der Meerfahrt des Königs Philipp von Castilien (1506). In *Zeitschrift der Gesellschaft für Beforderung der Geschichts-, Altertums- und Volkskunde von Freiburg, dem Breisgau und den angrenzenden Landschaften*, vol. I.

Thomas, Keith. 2009. *The Ends of Life: Roads to Fulfilment in Early Modern England*. Oxford: Oxford University Press.

Vallejo, Juan de. 1913. *Memorial de la Vida de Fray Francisco Jiménez de Cisneros*, ed. Antonio de la Torre y del Cerro. Madrid: Bailly-Bailliere.

Varela, Antonio Suárez. 2013. La Mala Sedición. Un aproximación al discurso anticomunero. In *Imperio y Tiranía. La Dimensión Europea de las Comunidades de Castilla*, ed. István Szászdi León-Borja and María Jesús Galende Ruíz. Valladolid: Universidad de Valladolid.

Zalama, Miguel Ángel. 2003. *Vida cotidiana y Arte en el Palacio de la Reina Juana I en Tordesillas*. Valladolid: Universidad de Valladolid.

Zurita, Jerónimo. 1992/1994. *Historia del Rey Don Hernando el Católico: De las empresas y ligas de Italia*, ed. Ángel Canellas López, Magdalena Canellas, and Antonio J. López, vols. 3 and 4. Zaragoza: Gobierno de Aragón.

CHAPTER 7

# Queen and Archbishop (1506)

## 7.1 The Death of Philip

Maximilian's *Weiß Kunig* includes a portrayal of Philip being crowned at Valladolid by a group of bonneted Castilian nobles. Maximilian himself, or possibly Fernando, stands proudly to one side. This solitary *Kronung* was how Philip wished both his father and Louis XII to see it. But 'murmerings' grew off-stage. Martire notes that much of Juana's patrimony was disposed of without consultating her and Bernáldez refers to her agitation and anger.[1] The absence of her signature alongside Philip's on acts of government, either because it was not sought or because, as was widely recognised, Juana refused to accept Philip's authority, created a ready basis for disobedience and dissent. In at least one case, her name was deleted.[2] Where it did appear, the assumption grew that it was forged.[3] In late summer, several Andalucian nobles—the duke of Medina Sidonia; count of Ureña; marquis of Priego and count of Cabra—formed an alliance to demand that Juana be freed to "govern like the queen her mother."[4]

Philip's reaction to requests by the Cortes that only Castilians be granted government and ecclesiastical posts was to naturalise members of his Flemish and Burgundian entourage. He altered the composition of the Royal Council—the main organ of government and assistance in the elaboration of laws and responses to procurators' *peticiones*—and awarded control of the fortresses to allies. Manuel, already appointed *contador mayor*, was granted key fortresses like Segovia and Burgos.



G. B. Fleming, *Juana I*, Queenship and Power,
https://doi.org/10.1007/978-3-319-74347-9_7

Lachaulx was given Simancas. Between July and September, Philip launched a shake-up in the *corregimiento*, with over sixty new nominations. Villaescusa later commented that his practice of distributing posts to his supporters before they fell vacant made him unpopular throughout Castile.[5] Even the chronicler of the *Deuxième Voyage* mentions the bitterness caused by Philip's appointments of inexperienced and incompetent foreigners to key financial posts.[6]

The settlement with Fernando had left Philip short of funds. He had to rely partially on Cisneros' personal wealth to help honour debts, but these rose so fast that only his bowmen and musicians were still receiving regular pay. Louis XII offered support to the duke of Guelders against Philip and hostilities further drained Netherlandish resources.[7] Plague spread into Valladolid. Depressed and homesick, Philip longed to be out hunting chamois with his father in the Alps. Governing Castile was hard, he wrote, and "as with everything, the beginnings are the most difficult."[8]

In a letter to ambassador Rojas Fernando's secretary, Almazán, predicted civil war. He described Juana as "the most unfortunate woman who had ever been born, it would have been better for her to have been the wife of a labourer …". He added that "after we've gone, when they judge the time right, the grandees who now hold [Juana] captive will take up the cause against king Felipe on her behalf, and others will take up his, to force him to divide up the royal Crown, and if God does not miraculously provide otherwise, Castile will be hopelessly lost and destroyed …". This would fulfill the saying: "*el año siete, dexa España e vete.*"[9]

Years later, Enríquez told the comunero Junta of Tordesillas that his refusal to surrender fortresses to Philip as proof of loyalty to the king had converted him into a prime target of the new regime. When Manuel warned that Philip would destroy him, Enríquez sought the help of fellow lords in an attempt to muster forces to free the queen, "though I saw I was risking my life and estate."[10] His emphasis on his defence of Juana may have been linked to the identity of his interlocutors, but there can be little doubt of his courage or belief that an attack on the queen's sovereignty was also an attack on the native nobility and on Castile's laws, customs and institutions.

When Isabel's old allies, the marquis and marchioness of Moya, refused to yield the fortress of Segovia, Philip forced Juana to accompany him on a punitive expedition south with the twofold aim of exploiting her presence to enforce a surrender and of leaving her there on grounds of pregnancy.[11] Monterrey, Puebla de Sanabria, Benavente, Mucientes,

Portillo, the lonely keep of Íscar on its high ridge—each fortress on the road from Galicia onwards must have raised a terrible uncertainty in Juana's mind: was *this* where they would leave her? She refused to enter Cogeces de Íscar, riding back and forth through the fields all night, either because an "informer" warned her she would be imprisoned there or because of "some illness that overcame her."[12] This area of the meseta was largely uncultivated pasture, covered with ilex, walnut and pine. In July and August, the pines weep resin and the skies are thick with shooting stars. That summer, many chroniclers noted the appearance of a comet. One observed that those flocking to watch it at the field gate of Valladolid saw it as a portent of death.[13]

The Moyas' surrender allowed Philip's party to rest at Tudela de Duero before heading for Burgos. Juana was unwell. Philip, despondent and weary of the heat, travelled to and from Valladolid by cometic light.[14] Illness and death stalked the court. A haunting and strikingly beautiful epitaphion, taking the form of a dialogue with Music, tells us that Alexander Agricola, singer, musician and composer of Philip's chapel, whose voice reportedly astonished all who heard it, died of a "cruel fever" in the "fields of Valladolid" with the sun "in the zenith of Virgo." The motet, '*Musica, quid defles?*' ('Music, why do you weep?'), has been attributed to a collaboration between Anchieta and the (albeit disgraced) Villaescusa.[15] Whatever the case, it shimmers with the heat and tension of summer and, with its striking cadences and interrogative pauses, lingers in the air like another augury.

On 14 September, the monarchs attended mass at the Dominican monastery of San Pablo, home of Juana's former tutor, Miranda, to which the queen brought twelve of the heads of St Ursula's martyred virgins, granted her by the pope in October 1500. In her presence, Fray Pascual de Ampudia, eminent religious reformer, consecrated a chapel dedicated to the 11,000 virgins, and all present received full remission of sins ('*hubo jubileo*').[16] The monarchs stayed at the constable's palace, the Casa del Cordón, from which Philip evicted Velasco and the queen's half-sister, Juana of Aragon. Two days later, he rode through Burgos in triumph, feasted with Manuel at the fortress and played tennis. Later he complained of a pain in his side and became feverish.

As his condition deteriorated, Juana emerged from seclusion to nurse him. She was, comments the chronicler of the *Deuxième Voyage*, a "woman made to suffer and to see everything in this world, good or bad, immutable in her heart and courage." Lacking the "countenance of a woman," her manner was so assured it seemed nothing was amiss. She urged Philip to eat, drink and take medicine, taking it herself to encourage him.[17] Dr. Juan Parra, who had served Fernando and Prince Juan and who arrived in Burgos on 23 September, had nothing but praise for her: "In the five hours I was there," he told Fernando, "I saw the queen … continually ordering what was to be done and doing it and speaking to the king and to us and treating the king with the best manner and care and bearing and grace that I have ever seen in a woman of whatever estate."[18]

The pain in Philip's side became acute. He spat blood and erupted in small dark spots. He lapsed in and out of consciousness, alternating between cold sweats and high fevers. He died at one o'clock in the afternoon of 25 September. According to Santa Cruz, his body was seated, according to Burgundian custom, on an elevated throne "as if he were still alive."[19] But Molinet describes Philip as "*couchiet*" and surrounded by great flambeaux that burned until the following noon as people filed past, "*pleurans de pitié.*" Cisneros' page, Vallejo, who was there, describes him being placed on a finely embroidered brocade bed.[20] The body was then embalmed, wrapped in waxed linen and placed in a lead and wood-lined coffin. The heart was sent for burial beside Mary of Burgundy's remains at the Onze-Lieuve-Vrouekerk in Bruges.

In the last and fourth of the above-mentioned painted panels by van Laethem, the funeral procession is shown leaving the Cordón for the charterhouse of Miraflores. Torch smoke billows towards crowded walls and roofs as mourners process between a *chariot d'armes* covered with brocade. Looking on with an older woman, probably Juana of Aragon, the queen wears a red gown with white sleeves, decked in black mourning ribbon. If, as seems likely, Laethem witnessed the event, the contrast between Juana's attire and that of the other mourners may be significant. At the funeral in 1547 of François I of France, his son, Henri II, wore a great royal mourning cloak of purple—"a darkening, as it were, of the royal scarlet" that contrasted with the black garb around him and was seen as a response to 'the enigma of the *roi en deuil*'—the king who dies but never dies.[21] Philip's attendants had emphasised him as ruler by placing a sword and sceptre on either side of his body and Juana was probably well aware of the questions already being raised about Castile's future governance. If indeed her mourning dress contained that richness of colour, it would have brought attention to her continuing sovereignty and to the fact that she mourned Philip as lord and husband, but not as ruler.

In his will, drawn up at Bruges and Middelburg at the end of 1505, Philip had asked to be buried, should he die in Spain, beside Isabel. He requested 60,000 high and low masses, with two masses daily, and "desired and ordered" that Juana be given the huge sums owed by the marriage settlement.[22] Of this, however, there seemed no immediate prospect.

Mystery still surrounds Philip's death. He had always been susceptible to fevers and, only months before, his journey from Windsor to Falmouth had been delayed by illness at Reading. Parra reassured Fernando that no trace of poison was found, although one Dutch-language poem of uncertain date describes "young lady Tsanne" pouring poisoned wine from a gold cup.[23] A sliver of evidence that the iced water drunk by Philip was somehow contaminated is offered by the "strange" death two months later of Bernard d'Orley, whose task was to sample all drinks before serving Philip.[24] Parra referred to a possible chill. Marliani believed physical over-exertion had sensitised the king to the pestilential fever stalking Burgos. Other commentators, then and later, sought less direct explanations, such as depression brought on by an increasingly untenable political situation to which Juana had contributed. While praising Juana as good, beautiful, chaste, fertile and worthy of the love of the greatest men, the author of the *Deuxiéme Voyage* describes her "jealousy" as an inextinguishable "*rage d'amours*" that had led her to follow her husband through the fields in the (truly colossal and exclusive) company of between 10,000 and 20,000 men. Burton's *Anatomy of Melancholy* repeats the notion that her jealousy precipitated Philip's death.[25]

Others stress the grief of the queen. Speaking as Juana, the poet, Gratia Dey, places her in a trajectory of perpetual loss:

*A donde se hallaría,*
*quien fuese tan desdichada,*
*yo perdí la madre mia,*
*y un hermano quetenla*
*de mi padre, so olvidada …*[26]

Sancho Cota transforms her grief into an act of abdication, justifying Charles' coup of 1516. In the Spanish stateroom of the great ship of Europe, Juana stands in eternal lament over Philip's body, telling Death that if only the Turks had taken Philip instead she would gladly face the dangers of a Mediterranean voyage to pay his ransom in person. As it was, she had no use for her power.[27]

Historians have interpreted Juana's alleged catatonia—together, curiously enough, with her failure to weep in public—as a symptom of her mental illness. While Cisneros' first biographer, Gómez de Castro, mentions that Cisneros found Juana weeping within the Cordón, Martire suggests a link between tearlessness and incapacitation: "She shed not a single tear, whether because she is prey to profound grief or because she no longer knows what grief means."[28] More recently, Silleras-Fernández has described Philip's death as precipitating the "disastrous and debilitating melancholy that rendered Juana unfit to rule." This grief followed that of her elder sister, which seemed "to verge on the psychotic," and of their grandmother, Isabel de Avís.[29]

Juana's 'melancholy' is discussed later in this study. But the convention that she tipped into a grief-exacerbated 'madness' at the end of 1506 should be treated with caution. Extreme widowed grief was a reality but, like extreme passion in newlyweds, a contemporary topos too. In his *Cuatro diálogos* Villaescusa describes the widowed Margaret of Austria longing to become, like queen commander Artemisia I of Halicarnassus, a living tomb for her husband's ashes. Martire later indulged this literary convention when describing Juana's widowed daughter, Eleanor, as hovering on the "verge of madness," unable to detach herself from the tomb of Manoel of Portugal.

Despite a general belief that Philip's death dealt the coup de grâce to Juana's tottering reason, there is no serious evidence for a mental breakdown in 1506, as opposed to the breakdown she probably suffered in 1503–1504 and again in 1508, when deprived of her younger son, the infante, whom she clearly adored. It was normal practice for rulers to seclude themselves after a spouse's death, without necessarily retiring completely from view. Only days after Philip's death, she received a deputation from Cisneros and some of Philip's officials, who asked her to provide for the orderly implementation of his will. That, Juana replied, was their concern; hers was to "assume responsibility for interceding for her husband with God."[30] Whatever the prudence of this remark, it was not that of someone spiralling toward mental disintegration. She and Philip had received a plenary indulgence on 14 September. Nonetheless, as the abovementioned Burgundian ballad suggests, Juana felt she had important spiritual tasks to perform and called once again on Villaescusa to help her in the work of divine intercession, and, in general, to advise her

## 7.2 Shadow Queen

It is possible to see Philip's death as placing a fragile and temporary cap upon the outbreak of civil war. But, in the autumn of 1506, many shared Almazán's view that this was imminent, or that, as Bernáldez put it, the times of Enrique IV were back.

A king's death was invariably a moment to flag up grievances and settle scores, and, although technically only king-by-marriage, Philip's was no different. "There was no grandee," writes Alcocer, "who did not think of increasing his estate. In the cities the old *bandos* were resuscitated and people died."[31] But the situation was uniquely complicated by the proliferation of parallel administrations or by divisions within them. These, largely arising out of the rival ambitions of Juana's husband and father, and provisions of the treaty of Salamanca, nominally operated in the queen's name, but were in practice accountable to one or other of the kings, and the one's absence and the other's death did not prevent their rival appointees from continuing to seek and demand obedience. The Royal Council, itself a hotbed of conflicting loyalties, would have made it virtually impossible for the queen to initiate any laws of her own without significant support or force of arms. It was against this background that some of Philip's men tried to seize the infante.

Earlier that summer, Ferdinand had been moved from Arévalo to Valladolid so that Juana and Philip could see him. He was subsequently transferred to property of the admiral's at Simancas, south of Valladolid. On 25 September, Guevara led armed men there in an attempt to seize possession of a powerful asset for the Flemish 'party' in any future negotiations. In all likelihood, he and his companions intended to transfer the infante to the fortress of Simancas, which was held by Lachaulx. Forewarned, the governor of his household, Pedro Núñez de Guzmán, shut the town gates, posted guards on the walls, summoned help from the Royal Chancery and played for time by wining and dining Guevara in the three-year-old's presence. The bishop of Catania and some Royal Chancery jurists, galloping there from Valladolid, begged local officials not to allow any "scandalous person or tyrant or disloyal vassal of the queen our lady" to seize the infante. The officials pledged their loyalty to Juana, "to the point of losing their lives in the name of the queen." It was agreed that Ferdinand should be conveyed to Valladolid, deemed safe and loyal to Juana, who subsequently approved the action.[32] But so restive was Burgos that she felt unable to call her son to her side until months later, when well away from the city.

This abduction attempt lent greater urgency to the scramble to assemble an emergency government. On the eve of Philip's death, Cisneros' page, Vallejo, saw the archbishop's lodgings in Huerta del Rey steadily filling with lords and ambassadors. A second meeting took place on 26 September. In a highly charged atmosphere, full of threats and challenges, the three magnates most prominent in Juana's defence that summer nonetheless joined felipista leaders and the representatives of Maximilian and Charles, Borgo and Veyré, as arbiters of "all differences and dissensions" under Cisneros' leadership.[33] Existing militas were dissolved and new ones banned, while Cisneros recruited troops of his own to subdue a city whose mercantile elite favoured Flemish interests.

In public, Cisneros adopted a neutral stance to avoid alienating rival groups while secretly writing to Fernando, who had sailed for Naples, and begging him to return. He then called a further meeting to broker an interim agreement, which settled on a ninety-day period within which to convoke a Cortes. The agreement pledged its signatories to refrain meanwhile from hostile acts or to: "*carry out or plan any harmful action by the hand of her highness … or obtain from the queen our lady any letter or order detrimental to others unless their highnesses* [Juana and the infante] *are entirely in possession of their freedom and will …*" [my emphasis].[34] This was clearly designed to block any initiative by the queen and prevent any move to establish a government under Juana or on her behalf. As far as is known, not one noble rose to his feet or tossed down his bonnet in opposition to a measure so clearly detrimental to the queen, although Velasco soon regretted his part in approving the agreement.

Fernando's masterful propagandist, Martire, consistently, and influentially, depicts Juana's uselessness. She "drags out a wretched life, rejoicing in obscurity and withdrawal, with hand on chin, her mouth as tight shut as if dumb. She will not communicate with anyone, let alone women, whom she hates and keeps at a distance, as she did when her husband was alive, and she cannot be persuaded to write her signature or dictate a line in the interests of the government of the State."[35] In his analysis of the succession crisis and exercise of power in Castile between 1504 and 1518, Carretero Zamora argues that, confronted with a *rex inutilis* and a "monarchy that could not govern," Cisneros and the Royal Council sought a radically different source of legitimacy upon which to act. A new Cortes would, Cisneros hoped, finally sanction Juana's imprisonment. This was the only way out of a crisis caused, in Albaladejo's words, by the fact that, despite Juana's "total inaptitude for participating in tasks of government she could … not be parted from it."[36] Ladero Quesada cites Martire when agreeing that, after Philip's death, Juana showed no wish to rule, yet could freely have done so. At the same time, he notes the agreement to prevent Juana governing, or naming anyone to govern on her behalf.[37]

This apparent contradiction serves only to highlight the confusion and complexity of the situation. Juana was capable of sudden, and arguably reckless, moves. For many in 1506, her alleged unfitness was based not on any inability to think and act upon her thoughts (that is, on an intrinsic incapability) but on the contrasting possibility that she might spring into action at any moment, to the detriment both of those whose disloyalty she had sworn to punish and to the rights of Fernando, whose chances of reassuming the government could be jeopardised by the emergence of an able and willing female king.

Frustrated by indecision, alternately stalling and promising much, Juana encouraged uncertainty. During the ninety days in which independent initiatives by Juana were banned by the interim government, she refused to cooperate with Cisneros' illegal administration while promising future action. Gómez de Castro, recalling his talks with Cisneros' secretaries, expresses bafflement about a queen whose responses to the grandees were "very pertinent and prudent" but who refused to underwrite the documents presented to her: "Those who ventured most deeply into an analysis of this phenomenon said that women are naturally suspicious, but that the queen, tormented by a fit of madness, and utter irrationality, was driven more especially towards this propensity …". Although, he adds, "she possessed much imaginative power and a great memory, she lacked aptitude for the matters put to her, which require a healthy mind and one enlightened by experience."[38]

As far as can be established, the word 'tyranny' was never directly linked with Juana. But the treaty of Villafáfila, largely Cisneros' work, had described her as a queen whose disposition bordered on the tyrannical, in the sense that she had the potential to ruin her kingdoms. A recurring theme of Spanish political literature (and one of several definitions of tyranny in the *Siete Partidas*) is a failed monarch of this kind. In his *Doctrinal de príncipes*, which Diego de Valera had dedicated to Fernando as rightful lord of both Castile and Aragon, the cleric and chronicler describes two forms of tyranny: violent usurpation and lawful rule that goes wrong, to the detriment of peace, justice and the common good. Of these, the latter form was, in his view, worse.[39]

Valera's attempt to justify the ascent of the dual monarchy was written well before Juana's reign. But in Peters' study of the *rex inutilis* in medieval law and literature—the title of which, *The Shadow King*, was inspired by Marlowe's lines: "But what are kings when regiment is gone/But perfect shadows in a sunshine day?"—he lists Juana I among the ineffective, failed or shadow rulers whose mental capacities or political misjudgments spelt ruin to their kingdoms. Thus, he places her in the company of Richard II and Henry VI of England and Charles VI of France, while Henry VII and Fernando of Aragon are described as highly successful (too successful, "some men thought,") in the effective use of public power.[40]

If, however, any comparison between Juana and other monarchs is meaningful—and then only very partially—it lies with her uncle, Enrique IV, whose name, as Bernáldez reminds us, was constantly on people's lips in 1506. In the second half of his reign, Enrique had fallen victim to continual feuding and strife, while skilled propagandists undermined his reputation. An increasingly melancholic king had difficulty shaping and putting across his message, in which he was not helped by the seizure of his treasury, deliberate destruction of his chronicler's papers and lack of a team of advisers and collaborators to preserve his good name. Rival groupings and interests competed for influence. The nobility seized fortresses and reinforced their networks within the urban elites, while the cities struggled to preserve freedoms and privileges. One of the most enduring, and vindictive, portraits of Enrique was drawn by his contemporary, Palencia, who converts the king's Segovian heartland into a frozen world of mist, snow and ice within which, unnatural and perverse, and "*huyendo del trato civilizado*," the king denies nature's benefits to his cold and hungry vassals. This aspect of Enrique as fugitive tyrant and neglectful ruler was what Isabel's brother, Alfonso, had sought to hammer home when entering Segovia in 1467 and staging a hecatomb in which thousands of Enrique's beloved animals were slaughtered and his woods of mighty oaks, ilex and pines slashed down.[41] On 5 June, the king was symbolically deposed in a mock ceremony and replaced by Alfonso in a 'farce' that took the form of an auto-de-fé, legitimating tyrannicide.

Enrique's ghost had haunted the banquet of the dual monarchy and Isabel's projection of her regal qualities owed much to the half-brother she defined herself against. A number of those who forecast civil war in 1506 had personal memories of a reign that had become the acid test by which monarchical success or failure was judged. When reacting so quickly to the designs of Guevara and Lachaulx on the day of Philip's death, the Guzmáns showed their desire to avoid a second 'farce' of Ávila, in which Ferdinand unwittingly substituted for Alfonso in a mock deposition of the reigning monarch. The admiral's view of Juana, in the autumn of 1506, as a queen whose questionable capacity to govern called, if anything, for greater loyalty from her subjects, is reminiscent of cardinal Pedro González de Mendoza's argument at the time of the 'farce,' when urging that divinely appointed monarchs should be cured, not deposed.[42]

Evidently, unlike Enrique, Juana was a pregnant widow. But as a melancholic, reclusive and solitary monarch she bore him some resemblance. As Earenfight has argued, monarchy in medieval and early modern Spain was a "complementary dynamic" and depended largely on partnership of some kind.[43] That queens regnant needed the sympathetic help of husbands or sons was a point made by Fernando himself during his second and last meeting with Philip at Renedo de Esgueva on 5 July. At one of those rare moments in his life when Fernando had no direct personal interest to foster in Castile, he advised Philip to help cure Juana's "jealous" passions, just as he, Fernando, had helped Isabel cure hers, becoming "the queen that all the world remembers …".[44] The implication was that, with Philip's cooperation—with, that is, the mediation of male authority—Juana could become as able a queen as her mother had been.

But a lone queen was, for many, a politically disabled one. Many years later, Juana's son, Charles V, sent envoys to his aunt, Mary I of England, to impress upon her the need for marriage: "it will be necessary in order to be supported in the labour of governing and assisted in *matters that are not of ladies' capacity* [my emphasis], that she soon contract matrimony with the person who shall appear to her most fit from the above point of view."[45] The problem for Juana was that, even if she were amenable to a second marriage, it would undermine Fernando's re-awakened ambitions and endanger Charles' claim to the throne. Nor was there a precedent for rule by a widow. As in the later case of Maria Theresa, the only woman to govern the Holy Roman Empire, a ruling widow seemed an inherently contradictory entity, "combining governance and withdrawal, activity and reflection, and high status with humility and modesty." This "needed explanation …".[46] Juana's situation was further complicated by the fact that her absent eldest son was only six, and could not rule beside her, as Joseph did with Maria Theresa.

However, the most serious obstacle to Juana's exercise of power was Fernando himself, whose activities in Naples proved no hindrance to his continual intervention in Castilian affairs. He maintained a daily correspondence with Cisneros and the Royal Council; granted Cisneros authority to administer affairs jointly with the Council; set up staging-posts between Burgos and Naples to accelerate despatches, "suitable provisions" and news of Juana's health.[47] As always, he pursued a duplicitous strategy. On 6 October, he wrote to nobles, prelates and cities reaffirming his right to govern Castile. In a further letter of 6 November, he asked that Juana be obeyed, while reiterating his own right ("*mi derecho*"), and insisting that he was the sole means, after God, of preventing Castile's loss and destruction. Juana, he added, "does not involve herself with affairs of state …" and had repeatedly urged his return.[48] Unfettered by the old concordat of Segovia, he bought support from former felipistas and sought Maximilian's agreement to his governorship. He promised Cisneros big rewards for his assistance, later securing him a cardinal's hat (17 May 1507), appointing him inquisitor general of Castile (5 June 1507), and granting a church to his nephew, Fray Ruíz.[49] He wrote to Juana from Naples, asking her to refrain from making political decisions until his return.[50] On 12 November, his Aragonese ambassador, Luis Ferrer, told Murcian officials that Juana refused to involve herself in government affairs: "all is one, and serving the queen, gentlemen, you do what the king wishes, for the wishes of both are in such conformity that whoever serves one serves the other." Juana was "informed about everything by me. Her Highness does not wish to involve herself in affairs or involve herself in anything at all, while awaiting the king …".[51]

Sandoval claims that Juana had "very few" supporters. This is probably true to the extent that she had no specific territorial base or constituency within Castile on which she could rely as former queens had done and few believed she could rule alone. But, as the autumn wore on, Martire saw nobles turning to Juana and Maldonado notes the "great hopes that Juana could rival her mother as the most prudent mother of the country." Velasco and others spoke of "service to the Queen." Although Enríquez saw Fernando as "true doctor" of the Spanish kingdoms and distrusted Juana's discussions with the constable, he urged her to govern. Nájera looked to an anti-fernandino government, in which Juana might figure. Villena too urged Juana to govern but to also send for Charles.[52] These varying attitudes indicate both support for Juana and her vulnerability. She could dip into a reservoir of loyalty and goodwill but lacked a team of advisers and collaborators loyal exclusively, or primarily, to herself.

Cisneros was a powerful and extremely wealthy adversary with a court of his own and a private army. Zurita notes that Juana invited Cisneros to lodge at the Cordón, not because she wanted him to govern, but "for his company."[53] This may have been an attempt to win his loyalty, but the archbishop's attempts to control her dashed any such hope. While attempting to convoke a Cortes against her will, he asked—and expected—her to endorse the measures drawn up by his own, illegal administration. He invoked Fernando's authority when she refused to grant hers, ordering the royal accountants to release funds for various purposes, including payment of certain household members.[54] He tried to dismiss her *camarero mayor*, Diego de Ribera, whom he suspected of facilitating audiences with Fernando's opponents. He tried to get Juana to sign away her powers, citing the need to restore security, especially in the south. A furious queen finally threw Cisneros and his servants out of the palace, together with some of Fernando's servants. Although Velasco and his wife, Juana of Aragon, managed to placate her, she refused to accept the legality of Cisneros' administration, insisting on her sole right to obtain and allocate funds from the royal treasurers and that monies be released on her signed authority only.[55]

Cisneros knew that the "the queen abhorred him much and said he was mad, and he did not love her and feared her greatly."[56] The queen had witnessed his shifting allegiances. If he did not yet dare imprison her, she knew he wanted to do so. She was deeply irritated by his unshakeable sense that he was always in the right. Royal councillor Galíndez de Carvajal thought him a "high-minded man of great spirit, well-intentioned in public affairs." But these affairs could go astray when he "did not adopt the right means ("*no iba por medios derechos*"), indeed, once he settled upon something it had to be that way …".[57]

Juana, as Zurita rightly comments, "did not want to hear about anyone meddling [in government], or [to] entrust it to anyone in her name, even the king her father."[58] The admiral recorded a cautious dance with the queen early in December. While expressing her great desire to see Fernando, she would not commit herself to formally inviting him back. She told Enríquez that she did not want six-year-old Charles being drawn into the turmoil and that Maximilian had enough to deal with as Holy Roman Emperor and administrator of Philip's patrimony. Nor, she added, somewhat pointedly, would he know "how to govern my kingdoms, while, on the other hand, they are only too well known to my father," who had bequeathed them to her "at the cost of much labour and vigilance and in part [by] recovering what had been lost."[59]

Juana later reminded Ferrer, a constant presence beside her, of the influence he had exerted on Fernando's behalf. He knew as well as she that the grandees were "all minded to serve and obey her, and daily pressed her to govern and carry out affairs of state. But, out of respect for [Fernando] and as an obedient daughter, she had always intended to wait for [him] so that he could help her and her children and kingdoms."[60] This clearly implies that, after Philip's death, Juana saw Fernando not as sole ruler but as associate and auxiliary. Philip's death had removed the main obstacle to her rulership, but it had also left her and, by extension, Charles, exposed to Fernando's ambitions and, potentially, to those of Germaine de Foix. Juana, who had written Fernando desperate letters not long before, begging him not to leave Castile, now refused to write, repeating like a mantra that she dared not ask him to abandon his affairs to govern in "alien kingdoms" ("*reinos ajenos*"), where tumult and conflict could only be resolved with massive effort.[61]

What, then, was her plan?

## 7.3 Juana's Parallel Administration

The significance of the ban on any political initiatives by Juana has not been widely appreciated. Prawdin, an exception, describes it as an "oath meaning in practice that no-one would help Juana recover the government."[62] Her immediate response was to take steps to create the embryo of a royal household and administration of her own. The orders she started signing towards the end of 1506 and in 1507, although limited in scope, show, as Aram has noted, "an attempt to build a following of trustworthy persons rather than a refusal to govern."[63] Juana held court, often meeting *La Mouche* de Veyré, who represented Charles. She met an envoy of Louis XII, to whom she reaffirmed her support for Fernando's return to Castile, and on 4 December received a Portuguese envoy, Enrique, bishop of Ceuta, with whom she discussed questions of future governance.[64]

Her staff between 1506 and 1507 numbered about 100. Many, including a number of Flemish servants, were already in place.[65] But with respect to key positions, Juana showed a wish to begin building a model of Isabel's household by surrounding herself with Isabel's former servants, or those Isabel had formerly appointed to Juana's household. Significantly, she appointed as her *mayordomo mayor,* Diego de Cárdenas, son of Prince Juan's former chief of staff, Gutierre de Cárdenas. He was also military governor (*adelantado*) of Granada and controlled the main arsenal at Medina del Campo. He had received rewards from Philip but was seen as a fernandino and her choice dismayed the Flemish party.[66] She retained her secretary, Olano. Among other survivors were Matienzo, Anchieta and Ribera.

One of Juana's first actions after Philip's death was to invite women to join her. These, mostly widowed, were fernandinas. She had 'warmly' received Juana of Aragon, again provoking the consternation of former felipistas and of others whose access to the queen her half-sister tried to vet. When Villena complained to the queen that he had only been admitted when, hearing his voice, she had intervened in person to let him in, she said: "You know she's my sister, and it's natural for me to enjoy some relaxation with her in particular, and with the women who served the queen my lady [Isabel]; all the more so in that, as you know, I have no other company."[67]

Zurita describes María de Ulloa as a "great favourite" of Juana's.[68] Later she was formally appointed dueña, staying in post until about 1518. Ulloa's ultimate loyalty was, however, to Fernando, whose portrait, on a gold medal, she treasured.[69] Like Juana, she was recently widowed and in April 1506 had become legal guardian of her small son, third count of Salinas. Her father and father-in-law had been officials of Isabel's, and her mother-in-law, Marina de Villandrando, dowager countess of Salinas, was also at Burgos in 1506. Connected to them, and related to Juana, was Fernando's cousin Francisca Enríquez, daughter of Fernando's uncle and former *mayordomo*, Enrique Enríquez, and the wife of Bernardo de Sandoval y Rojas, marquis of Denia. María Fernández de Velasco, duchess of Roa, twice-widowed elder sister of the constable and Cárdenas' mother-in-law, may also have been at Burgos, for, according to Conchillos, the marchioness and duchess were "not to the taste of her highness."[70] Ferrer later describes the ferocity with which Juana, ever suspicious of the pretensions, ambitions and interference of certain high-ranking women, referred to the "late señora Doña María."[71]

Juana's desire to keep Philip's northern chapel was highly significant in terms of the strengthening of bonds between Flemish/Burgundian and Spanish musical traditions, perhaps first evident during the princes' visit in 1502. Juana's passion for music and care for her musicians' welfare have been seen as further symptoms of illness, as, again, in the case of Enrique IV. But, by prioritising payments to them with funds from the Casa de Contratación in Seville, Juana was simply continuing Philip's practice at the end of his life. What *is* remarkable is the amount she paid. Annual salaries were more than half again what the highest paid singers were receiving in Fernando's chapel.[72] They were also paid up to three months in advance. The pay lists she signed in 1506 and 1507 reflect her promotion to "first chaplain" of the remarkable composer Pierre de la Rue ('Pierrechon'), then probably at the height of his powers. De la Rue and that other fine composer, Anchieta, grace the top of the list with payments of over 20,000 maravedís each for the period between June and September 1507. The list of eighteen musicians includes other composers of polyphonic music, such as Guillem Reingot, Rogier Herben and Nicolas Champion, author of the four-voice motet, *De profundis clamavi*.[73]

This amount of pay and patronage may reflect Juana's emotional need to maintain the northern chapel under conditions undoubtedly trying for its members. Some had returned to the Low Countries but a significant proportion stayed on. These high payments may also reflect commissions for special work. It is difficult to pinpoint the dates at which compositions were written, but it would be surprising if no creative work emerged from this period, given the calibre of the chapel at Juana's disposal. Rue's motet, *Delicta juventutis*, an intense plea for Philip's soul, and the requiem mass, *Missa pro defunctis*, with its dense chromatic textures, probably dates from this mourning period.[74]

Juana's payments to her chapel, and other orders dating from October 1506, reveal her willingness to sign documents when she felt free to do so and had trusted servants beside her. Juana's orders bear the countersignature of royal secretary and accountant, Juan López de Lazárraga, whom Oviedo describes as a Basque noble of great integrity on whom, after Isabel's death, many important affairs depended. But Conchillos mocked him as Juana's one true supporter: "There is no-one, great or small, who does not say she is not ruined, and has not lost her mind, except for Joan [Juan] López, who says she is saner than her mother," he wrote scornfully when Juana left Burgos at the end of December. Conchillos blamed Lazárraga, along with her treasurer, Ochoa de Landa, for aiding Juana's departure.[75]

Her first documented public appearance, a visit to Miraflores, was made for the All Souls festival (1–2 November), tallying with the end of the customary six-week mourning period. She brought prior Romero money and pieces of brocade for Philip's sepulchre and, after a requiem mass, sung by northern and Spanish chapels together, stayed for lunch.[76]

Juana, who had dynastic ties with Miraflores, where her maternal grandparents and uncle, Alfonso, were buried, ordered that Philip's coffin be opened, possibly owing to rumours that his body had been spirited away to Flanders, but possibly, too, because such inspections were traditional (see Chapter 8). She looked on, then briefly touched the corpse, her expression inscrutable. Her visit caused a stir. At the gates and on the road to Miraflores, an "infinite" number of people flocked to see the queen and hand her petitions, some of which she accepted. Amid popular jubilation, those lords who had opposed her began to wonder whether they might, after all, have to take her into account.[77]

## 7.4 Bold Steps

The speed and insistence with which Juana was urged to summon a Cortes—the very day after Philip's death—are indicators of a prevailing sense of panic. Juana's refusal to do so, though widely interpreted as a sign of inability to govern, is perfectly understandable. By law, only the ruling monarch could convoke a Cortes and since Juana had expressed no wish to abdicate and had retained full powers, she told incoming procurators that a Cortes was not "necessary for now."[78] Supporters of a Cortes were therefore faced with three options: to continue to try to persuade her to agree to one; to open an inquiry into her fitness for office; or to override the law.

Royal Council secretary Bartolomé de Castañeda, when recording the royal councillors' attempts at the first option, describes an almost farcical scenario of successively closing and opening doors, windows and grilles. The bishop of Jaén, appointed president of the Council by Philip, arrived with several councillors. Juana herself opened the door, but closed it again, calling for her attendant, Espinosa, who told them to return that afternoon. They were then told she could not see them, upon which they resolutely entered the chamber. While Juana's action in opening the door was itself extraordinary, the attempt to breach it was a measure of the Council's desperation. Juana "then shut the other door of another chamber so that they could not see or speak …". The councillors next entered the chapel, where a grille communicated with her rooms. Through it, licentiate Polanco appealed to her "royal conscience," shouting that the "cities and towns were rising and there was no rule of law." Juana "paused to listen …". The president followed him to the grille to reiterate the urgent need for Juana to sign the letters. Her attendant assured them she had heard them, but would not receive them. Cisneros, reinforced by councillors, nobles and city officials, made a third unsuccessful assault on the Cordón.[79]

Castañeda's report ends here. On 6 October, urged on by Cisneros, the councillors adopted the third option: to bypass the law by themselves convoking the Cortes. They excused their action by arguing that Juana was indisposed and by the need to seek the common good. But procurators, arriving in November, found Burgos teeming with controversy. The duke of Alba argued that without Juana's support or Fernando's presence it would lack validity and could damage royal interests. Juan Rodríguez Portocarrero, Alba's emissary to a city the duke refused to enter, objected that the warlike atmosphere was inappropriate to a Cortes, which must be held "in the court of the Queen our lady."[80] Some argued that removing the queen would be scandalous and stir controversy rather than bring peace. The constable declared that a Cortes held without Juana's consent "*sabía a traición*". If, at the moment, Juana did not wish to govern, she might later change her mind.[81]

On 6 November, the southern lords who had earlier expressed support for the queen declared at Tocina (Seville) that to convoke a Cortes without the royal signature was not "in the service of God and the Queen." While urging Juana to govern, they declared that no one should do so for her without her consent, and would disregard orders lacking the queen's signature or the signatures of those who clearly worked for her.[82] Galician nobles, gathered at Samos, similarly declared their opposition to a Cortes that lacked the "true signature and true command of the queen our lady." They engaged in a series of defensive pacts with the cities of Santiago, Coruña, Betanzos, Lugo, Orense, Mondoñedo and others, based on service to Juana.[83]

Early in December, Juana left for the constable's hunting lodge of La Vega, outside Burgos. Although Martire describes this as an attempt to further isolate herself, she held audiences there, and it is more likely that she wished to profit from the imminent expiry of the ninety-day truce. She asked Lazárraga for advice about whom in the Council she could trust and chose a quorum of four to administer affairs: Dr. Pedro de Oropesa, an expert on canon and civil law, and one of the witnesses to Isabel's will; Dr. Galíndez de Carvajal; licentiate Luis González Polanco; and Dr. García Yáñez de Mújica, brother of Juana's former treasurer and steward. She asked these four to administer justice "as they had done in the time of the king and queen her lords" and told Lazárraga that Philip's and Manuel's appointees should be dismissed.[84]

Juana's councillors endorsed her first and most important initiative, a pragmatic law of 18 December that aimed to restore the royal patrimony by revoking all Philip's grants and privileges. This had the constable's and, in all probability, Villaescusa's strong support. The law was sweeping in scope, if traditional in language.[85] Addressing the Royal Chancery, nobles, *regidores* and municipal and fiscal officers, Juana invested the measure with all "the force and vigour of law, as if approved and promulgated by the Cortes." It "revoked, stopped, annulled and considered void and without force and validity" all privileges and grants awarded in *juros*, revenues and jurisdictions made by Philip since Isabel's death. Juana stated that Philip's measures had been taken "without my knowledge" and "to the great prejudice and impoverishment of my royal patrimony and the public good of these my kingdoms."[86]

The law targeted Philip's most important collaborators. More broadly, it signalled that Juana alone was empowered to dispense honours, grants and privileges. Its central expression of concern was to unburden her conscience by recovering the royal patrimony and, thereby, addressing a main concern of the Cortes of Valladolid: the plundering of Castile by a foreign elite. Her warning of the harm that would befall her kingdoms if she did not act has a prophetic ring, given subsequent comunero grievances.

Juana's law has variously been seen as electrifying, irresponsible and revolutionary. It tried to restore the "lost bon ton" in Castilian politics, writes Ruiz-Domènec. It was a "legal earthquake," triggered by a flash of conscience, in the view of García Oro. Prescott describes it as having an electrifying effect on her husband's adherents. For Cauchies, it was a rigorous measure that spurred many Flemings and Burgundians into leaving Castile. For Aram, it showed a first determined attempt to rule and exercise royal authority.[87]

Zurita remarks that Juana was insistent that the law be published and was also "very bent" on a complementary law, returning to their former allegiances the fortresses and military posts distributed to Philip's chief supporters. But, after much discussion, both laws were put on ice, to the anger of both the queen and constable.[88] Although he had helped formulate these laws, Lazárraga was a key figure in postponing them, perhaps because of the volatile situation in Burgos and lack of armed back-up. Despite the high opinion he expressed for Juana, he might also have wanted to smooth the path home for Fernando. Although Juana's law targeted Philip's measures, Fernando's right to bestow favours was implicitly denied by her assertion of the royal prerogative. There seems ultimately to have been a compromise between a readiness to draft these laws and their promulgation by Fernando the following year. But this allowed Fernando, not Juana, to reap the credit.

The procurators seem to have been concerned less with the opening of a Cortes than with getting Juana to clarify her position. They were left momentarily baffled and frustrated. Seville's representatives, Guillén de Casaus and Juan Serrano, and Madrid's Francisco de Vargas, were sent to enlist the help of Juana of Aragon in arranging an audience.[89] On another occasion, Cortes secretaries were persuaded to accompany procurators to Juana's door to notarise her remarks, an initiative that irritated the constable: "What sort of testimony do you expect to take from the Queen?" he snapped over dinner with the procurator from Guadalajara: "I'd like to see you take it somewhere with a dozen poplars where a dozen procurators can be strung up as a reminder!" On one occasion when asked about the Cortes, she said: "I shall let you know sooner than you think," and, on another occasion: "Go to the Council members and tell them what you want, and they will tell me, and then I'll tell you what to do."[90] While Juana seemed to talk in pythic riddles, the procurators' reluctance to initiate Cortes proceedings without her consent led to angry exchanges with Cisneros and some councillors, who threatened serious repercussions for their cities.

On 20 December, Juana finally made her position clear. She summoned the procurators to Miraflores, along with the bishops of Jaén, Málaga, Mondoñedo and Burgos, the papal nuncio, Ruffo dei Teodoli, and ambassadors Ferrer and Borgo. She ordered the procurators to disband because the case for a Cortes had not been made. She declared she was leaving Burgos to take Philip's body to Granada. The next day, Cisneros made a fresh appeal to the procurators. The queen "does not [govern] or say what she wants." If she refused to open a Cortes, "*then it is for you to do it to preserve the kingdom and prevent the spread of more evils than already exist*" [my emphasis].[91]

This was a speech with revolutionary implications. Fernando and Philip had based their claim to the throne on Juana's unfitness for office. But the archbishop went further, asserting that, with the future of Castile at stake, procurators were morally obliged to transfer government into their own hands. Cisneros' actions at the end of 1506 set a precedent that would be recalled in the febrile climate leading up to the events of 1520–1522. Significantly, he said nothing about Juana's new laws, which would have done much to clarify her position. In reality, to the partisans of Fernando, Cisneros and Maximilian, the queen's desire and ability to govern meant her willingness to support the interests of others.

## Notes

1. Martire (López de Toro, ed. 1955), 10, 312, 7 September 1506; Bernáldez (Gómez Moreno/Mata Carriazo, eds. 1962), appendix 1.
2. AGS, RGS-9, f. 317, September 1506.
3. See Chapter 8.
4. Zurita (Canellas López, ed. 1994), 4, 66.
5. 'Instrucción,' in González Olmedo (1944).
6. Relation du Deuxième Voyage de Philippe le Beau (Gachard, ed. 1876), I.
7. ADN. B 18846. 29656–29659, 31 August 1506.
8. ADN, B 18826. 24293 (July 1506).
9. "In year seven get out of Spain." Rodríguez Villa (1892), 163–169; Ladero Quesada (2016), 100–101. This letter is dated 1 July 1506 but reads as though written later.
10. Zurita, 4, 74; Danvila (ed. 1897–1900), Admiral to Junta of Tordesillas (1520), II, 336–344.
11. Relation du Deuxième Voyage, I, 447–448.
12. Martire, 10, 312, 7 September 1506; Santa Cruz (Beltrán y Rózpide, ed. 1920–1925), 2, 57–58; *Deuxième Voyage*, 447–448.
13. Galíndez de Carvajal (Floranes Robles y Enzina, ed. 1787), 316n., cites Alvar Gutierrez de Torres' *Sumario de las maravillosas y espantosas cosas* (1523).
14. Alcocer (Gamero, ed. 1872).
15. Knighton (2006), XXXIV, 3, 427–441; Picker (1993), 16, 5, 132–143.
16. AGS, PR 27, f. 85 (Jubileos y Gracias), 'Auténtica de las reliquias de los 10.000 martires que se trajeron de Roma para la princesa Doña Juana por facultad para poderlas colocar en las iglesias,' Rome, 27 October 1500; Galíndez de Carvajal, 316.
17. *Relation du Deuxième Voyage.*
18. CODOIN, 8, 11 October 1506, 397.
19. Santa Cruz (Mata Carriazo, ed. 1951), 2, 59.
20. Molinet (Doutrepont/Jodogne, eds. 1935–1937), II, 585–587; Vallejo (De la Torre y del Cierro, ed. 1913).
21. Giesey (1960), 7.
22. Gachard (ed. 1876), I, 493–496.

23. Cauchies (2003), 210.
24. Zalama (2010), 206.
25. Relation du Deuxième Voyage, 458–461; Burton (Jackson, ed. 2001), 3, 287.
26. "Where could you find/anyone more unfortunate?/I lost my mother,/ My brother was taken from me,/by my father, I'm forgotten ...". RB II/617, f. 136v., 'A la Reyna doña Juana'.
27. Cota (Kenniston, ed. 1964), 'Esclamación a España,' 91–93.
28. Gómez de Castro (Oroz Reta, ed. 1984); Martire, X, 316, 28 September 1506.
29. Silleras-Fernández (2015), 216; 232–233.
30. Zurita, 4, 96.
31. Alcocer, 20.
32. CODOIN, 8, 400–406, "Copia del Testimonio de Convenio celebrado entre los vecinos de la villa de Simancas y los señores de la chancillería de Valladolid ..."; Zurita, 4.
33. Vallejo, 103–107.
34. Zurita, 4, 79; García Oro (2005), 128–129.
35. Martire, 10, 318, 29 November 1506.
36. Albaladejo (1992), 31.
37. Carretero Zamora (Foronda/Genet/Nieto Soria, eds. 2005); Ladero Quesada (2016).
38. Martire, 10, 320, 19 December 1506; Maldonado (Fernández Vargas, ed. 1975), 44; Gómez de Castro, 196.
39. Valera (Monti, ed. 1982).
40. Peters (1970), 244.
41. Palencia (Tate/Lawrance, ed. 1998), Decas I.
42. Zurita, 4.
43. Earenfight (2005), xvi.
44. Cisneros told (Querini, ed. Höfler) that Fernando had compared Juana favourably to Isabel at the same age: '... *'im zoventu [Isabel] per ziloxia se trovo im assay pezor termene che al presente non si atrova questu sua fiola. tamen, suportata da luj ritorno en si: et fu la rezine che tuto el mundo ha cognoscuto* ...' Querini, 120, 7 July 1506.
45. Mary's response was to warn that if her husband "wished to encroach in the government of the kingdom she would be unable to permit it." (Castor 2010).
46. Yonan (Levy, ed. 2003), 113. As a woman, Maria Theresa could not be crowned Holy Roman Emperor but ruled by virtue of the Pragmatic Sanction of 1713.
47. BL, Egerton Ms. 309, 'Relación,' ff. 152–152v., 1 November 1506;
48. Zurita, 4, 89; CSP. Sp. 1, 501, to Henry, 15 March 1507; CSP (Queen Juana), 13, to Katherine, 15 March 1507; Alcocer (Martín Gamero, ed. 1872), 23–24.

49. Ochoa Brun (2003), IV.
50. Martínez Millán (ed. 2000), I, 105.
51. Ferrer to Murcia, 12 November 1506, Gomaríz Marín (ed. 2006), 256.
52. Martire, X, 320, 19 December 1506; Maldonado, 44; Zurita, 4, 145, 163; BL, Egerton Ms 309, 'Relación,' ff. 155v.–157, 'Carta.'
53. Zurita, 4, 96.
54. AGR, CSR 14, 1, f. 46, 'Orden de pago a Gonçalo de Salcedo,' 24 October 1506.
55. Zurita, 4; García Oro (2005).
56. Zurita, 4, 97.
57. Galíndez de Carvajal, 418.
58. Zurita, 4, 153.
59. BL, Egerton Ms. 309, 'Relación,' f. 156, 'Carta'; Martire, X, 323, 21 December 1506.
60. Z. ADP. 787. 77, Ferrer to Fernando, 10 August 1511.
61. Martire, 10, 320, 19 December 1506.
62. Prawdin (1938), 169.
63. Aram (1998), 331–358.
64. Zurita, 4; Azcona (2007).
65. Fagel (1996).
66. BL, Egerton Ms. 309, 'Relación,' ff. 155v.–156.
67. BL, Egerton, Ms. 309, 'Relación,' ff. 155v.–156v.
68. Zurita, 4, 157.
69. Urcelay Gaona (2009).
70. RAH, Salazar, A-12, ff. 127–129, Conchillos to Almazán, 7 March 1507. (If, however, the duchess of Roa died before 1506, as elsewhere reported, María's identity remains a mystery.)
71. Z. ADP. 787. 77, Ferrer to Fernando, 10 August 1511.
72. Meconi (2003).
73. AGS CSR, 14, f. 2. 88, Cédula, 23 June 1507.
74. Knighton (2001). The motet begins: "Remember not the sins of his youth or his transgressions, my Lord …".
75. Fernández de Oviedo (Pérez de Tudela, ed. 1983–2002), II; RAH, Salazar, A-12, ff. 86–87, Conchillos to Almazán.
76. Sanuto (Fulin, ed. 1969–1970), 6, 1 November 1506.
77. Zurita, 4, 115.
78. BL, Egerton Ms. 309, 'Relación,' f. 135v.
79. BN, Ms. 18761, 'Noticia de lo que al presidente y oidores del consejo real les pasó con la reina doña Juana,' 26 September 1506.
80. AGS PR 7, f. 72, Instructions of duke of Alba.
81. Zurita, 4, 125.

82. AHN, Osuna, 1523, f. 1, 6 November 1506, 'Escritura de compromiso'; Santa Cruz, *Crónica*, 2, 70–71; Zurita, 4, 106–107; Santa Cruz, II, 70–78.
83. García Oro (1994), 277–278; AGS, Cámara-Pueblos (La Coruña), 6, f. 340, 'Alianza de las ciudades de La Coruña y Betanzos con Don Fernando de Andrade'.
84. Zurita, 4, 156; Santa Cruz, II, 79–80.
85. It resembles a pragmatic law of 21 November 1504 on the abuse of sales taxes (*alcabalas*) and the diversion of revenues into private hands.
86. AGS, Cámara de Castilla, Diversos, 1.12.10, 18 December 1506, inserted in 'Sobrecarta de la Reina Doña Juana,' Palencia, 30 July 1507.
87. Ruiz-Domènec (2004), 148; García Oro (2005), 131; Prescott (1908), 636; Cauchies (2010), 130–131; Aram (2005), 88–89.
88. Zurita, 4, 155.
89. BL, Egerton MS. 309, 'Relación,' f. 135 and 135v., 'Carta de los procuradores de Sevilla al cabildo de ella,' 18 December 1506.
90. BL, Egerton, Ms. 309, 'Relación,' f. 137, 18 December 1506; ff. 142–146, 'Carta de los procuradores de Cortes Guillén de Casaus y Juan Serrano,' 21 December 1506.
91. BL, Egerton Ms. 309, 'Relación,' ff. 142–146, 21 December 1506.

## References


Albaladejo, Pablo Fernández. 1992. *Fragmentos de monarquía*. Madrid: Alianza.

Alcocer, Pedro. 1872. *Relaciones de algunas cosas que pasaron en estos reynos*, ed. A. Martin Gamero. Seville: Sociedad de Bibliófilos andaluces.

Aram, Bethany. 1998. Juana "The Mad's" Signature: The Problem of Invoking Royal Authority, 1505–1507. *Sixteenth-Century Journal* 29 (2): 331–358.

———. 2005. *Juana the Mad: Sovereignty and Dynasty in Renaissance Europe*. Baltimore and London: John Hopkins University Press.

Azcona, Tarsicio de. 2007. *Juana de Castilla, mal llamada la Beltraneja*. Madrid. La Esfera de los Libros.

Bernáldez, Andrés. 1962. *Memorias del Reinado de los Reyes Católicos*, ed. M. Gómez Moreno and J. de Mata Carriazo. Madrid: Real Academía de la Historia.

Burton, Robert. 2001. *The Anatomy of Melancholy*, ed. H. Jackson. New York: New York Review of Books.

Carretero Zamora. Juan Manuel. 2005. La crisis sucesoria y problemas en el ejercicio del poder en Castilla (1504–1518). In *Coups d'État à la fin du Moyen Âge? Aux fondements du pouvoir politique en Europe occidentale*, ed. François Foronda, Jean-Philippe Genet and Juan Manuel Nieto Soria. Madrid: Casa de Velázquez.

Castor, Helen. 2010. Exception to the Rule. *History Today*, October 10, vol. 60.

Cauchies, Jean-Marie. 2003. *Philippe le Beau: Le dernier duc de Bourgogne*. Turnhout: Brepols.

———. 2010. Les Lendemains de la Mort de Philippe le Beau à Burgos (25 septembre 1506): Retraite ou Débandade? In *Rencontres de Madrid-Tolède*. Basel: Centre Européen d'Études Bourgignonnes.

Danvila y Collado, Manuel (ed.). 1897–1900. *Historia crítica y documentada de las Comunidades de Castilla*. Madrid: Memoria Histórico Español.

Doutrepont, Georges, and Omer Jodogne (eds.). 1935–1937. *Chroniques de Jean Molinet*. Brussels: Académie Royale de Belgique.

Earenfight, Theresa (ed.). 2005. *Queenship and Political Power in Medieval and Early Modern Spain* (preface). Aldershot: Ashgate.

Fagel, Raymond. 1996. *De Hispano-Vlaamse Wereld: De contacten tussen Spanjaarden en Nederlanders, 1496–1555*, vol. 52. Brussels: Archives et Bibliothèques de Belgique/Achief en Bibliotheekwezen in België.

Fernandez de Oviedo, Gonzalo. 1983. *Batallas y Quingquagenas*, ed. Perez de Tudela. Madrid: Real Academia de la Historia.

Fulin, Rinaldo (ed.). 1969–1970. *I diarii de Marino Sanuto, 1466–1536*. Bologna: Forni Editore.

Gachard, Louis-Prosper (ed.). 1876. Relation du Deuxième Voyage de Philippe le Beau en 1506, par un Anonyme. In *Collection des Voyages des Souverains des Pays-Bas*, vol. I. Brussels: Commission Royale d'Histoire.

Galíndez de Carvajal, Lorenzo. 1787. *Anales breves de los Reyes Católicos don Fernando y doña Isabel*, ed. Rafael Floranes Robles y Enzinas. Madrid.

García Oro, José. 1994. *Don Fernando de Andrade, Conde de Villalba (1477–1540)*. Santiago: Xunta de Galicia.

———. 2005. *Cisneros: Un cardenal reformista en el trono de España (1436–1517)*. Madrid: La Esfera de los Libros.

Giesey, Ralph E. 1960. *The Royal Funeral Ceremony in Renaissance France*. Geneva: Droz.

Gomariz Marin, Antonio (ed.). 2006. Documentos de Juana I (1505–1510). In *Colección de Documentos para la Historia del Reino de Murcia*. Murcia: Real Academía Alfonso X el Sabio.

Gómez de Castro, Alvar. 1984. *De las hazañas de Francisco Jiménez de Cisneros*, ed. José Oroz Reta. Madrid: Fundación Universitaria Española.

González Olmedo, S.I., Félix. 1944. 'Instrucción' and 'Cuatro Diálogos'. In *Diego Ramírez Villaescusa (1449–1537), fundador del Colegio de Cuenca y autor de los Cuatro Diálogos sobre la Muerte del Príncipe Juan*. Madrid: Editora Nacional.

Höfler, Constantin R. (ed.). 1848. *Depeschen des Venetianischen Botschafters Dr. Vincenzo Querino, 1505–1506*. Vienna: Österreichische Akademie der

Wissenschaften, Archiv für Kunde österreischer Geschichts-Quellen, Band 66–67.

Kenniston, Hayward (ed.). 1964. *Memorias de Sancho Cota*. Cambridge, MA: Harvard University Press.

Knighton, Tess. 2001. *Música y músicos en la corte de Fernando el Católico, 1474–1516*. Zaragoza: Instituto Fernando el Católico.

———. 2006. Music, Why Do You Weep? A lament for Alexander Agricola (d. 1506). *Early Music* XXXIV (3): 427–441.

Ladero Quesada, Miguel-Ángel. 2016. *Los últimos años de Fernando el Católico, 1505–1517*. Madrid: Dykinson.

López de Toro, José (ed.). 1955–1957. *Petrus Martyr Anglerius: Epistolario*. CODOIN, 9–12. Madrid: Imprenta Góngora.

Maldonado, Juan. 1975. *La Revolución Comunera*, ed. Valentina Fernández Vargas. Madrid: Ediciones del Centro.

Martínez Millán, José. 2000. *La Corte de Carlos V*, vol. I. Madrid: Sociedad Estatal para la Conmemoración de los Centenarios de Felipe II y Carlos V.

Meconi, Honey. 2003. *Pierre de la Rue and Musical Life at the Habsburg-Burgundian Court*. Oxford: Oxford University Press.

Ochoa Brun, Miguel-Ángel. 2003. *Historia de la Diplomacia Española*, vol. IV. Madrid: Ministerio de Asuntos Exteriores.

Palencia, Alfonso de. 1998. *Gesta Hispaniensia*. Decas 1, ed. Brian Tate and Jeremy Lawrance. Madrid: Real Academía de la Historia.

Peters, Edward. 1970. *The Shadow King: Rex Inutilis in Medieval Law and Literature, 751–1327*. New Haven and London: Yale University Press.

Picker, Martin. 1993. Musical Laments for King Philip of Castile and His Musician Alexander Agricola. *Revista de musicología* 16 (5): 12–143.

Prawdin, Michael. 1938. *Johanna die Waansinnige: Habsburgs Weg zum Weltreich*. Vienna: Otto Lorenz Verlag.

Prescott, William H. 1908. *The History of the Reign of Ferdinand and Isabella*. London: Swann Sonnenschein.

Rodríguez Villa, Antonio. 1892. *La Reina Doña Juana La Loca. Estudio histórico*. Madrid: Librería de M. Murillo.

Ruiz-Domènec, José Enrique. 2004. *Isabel la Católica o el Yugo del Poder*. Barcelona: Ediciones Península.

Santa Cruz, Alonso. 1920–1925. *Cronica del emperador Carlos V*, ed. Ricardo Beltrán y Rospide and Antonio Blazquez y Delgado-Aguilera. Madrid: Imprenta del Patronato de Huerfanos de Intendencia e Intervencion Militares.

———. 1951. *Crónica de los Reyes Católicos*, ed. Juan de Mata Carriazo. Seville: Escuela de Estudios Hispano-Americanos de Sevilla.

Silleras-Fernández, Nuria. 2015. *Chariots of Ladies: Francesc Eiximenis and the Court Culture of Medieval and Early Modern Iberia*. Ithaca and London: Cornell University Press.

Urcelay Gaona, Hegoi. 2009. *Los Sarmiento, Condes de Salinas: Orígenes y Elevación de una Nueva Clase Señorial, Siglos XII–XVI*. Bilbao/Zarautz: Universidad del País Vasco/Euskal Herriko Unibertsitatea.

Valera, Diego de. 1982. *Doctrinal de principes*, ed. Silvia Monti. Verona: Università degli Studi di Verona.

Vallejo, Juan de. 1913. *Memorial de la Vida de Fray Francisco Jiménez de Cisneros*, ed. De la Torre y del Cerro. Madrid.

Yonan, Michael E. 2003. Conceptualizing the *Kaiserinwitwe*: Empress Maria Theresia and Her Portraits. In *Widowhood and Visual Culture in Early Modern Europe*, ed. Allison Levy. Aldershot and Burlington: Ashgate.

Zalama, Miguel-Ángel. 2010. *Juana I: Arte, Poder y Cultura en torno a una Reina que no gobernó*. Valladolid: Centro de Estudios Europa Hispánica.

Zurita, Jerónimo. 1994. *Historia del Rey Don Hernando el Católico. De las empresas y ligas de Italia*, vol. 4, ed. Ángel Canellas López, Magdalena Canellas and Antonio J. López. Zaragoza: Gobierno de Aragón.

CHAPTER 8

# The Personal Rule of Juana I (1506–1507)

## 8.1 Flight of a Funeral Cortege

A famous painting by nineteenth-century artist Pradilla Ortíz depicts the queen on a stormy meseta. Her veil streams in the wind as she stares down at a coffin draped in the Habsburg arms and a Carthusian monk intones the mass of the dead. Pradilla drew inspiration for *Doña Juana La Loca* from a letter in which Martire relates how, as Philip's cortege crossed a bridge over the Pisuerga, a storm forced it to shelter in a neighbouring religious establishment. But the queen:

> immediately ordered that the coffin be removed from there and, in the open fields, under the naked sky, by the weak light of the flaming torches, which were almost extinguished by the violence of the wind, she commanded that the corpse be removed. Some workmen came to open the wooden and lead caskets. After contemplating the body of her husband and summoning the nobles as witnesses she ordered that it be shut up again and carried to Hornillos.[1]

The story of this funeral journey has delighted the romantic imagination, with poets and novelists vastly extending its distance and accelerating its rate of progress. The poet, Edith Sitwell, has Juana rushing "like a comet across Spain," appearing "now like a pillar of fire, now like a blackened ruin." Historians too have been tempted into flights of fancy. Mattingly compares her to a "thief stealing a holy relic," and escaping



G. B. Fleming, *Juana I*, Queenship and Power,
https://doi.org/10.1007/978-3-319-74347-9_8

with it "through the mountains"; Williams has her travelling "only by candlelight … so that no one should know that her husband had died …".[2]

This is fun but bears no relation to the reality. In fact, the journey covered little ground. The first stage, to Torquemada, halfway between Burgos and Valladolid and south of Palencia, was followed by a side-step to Hornillos de Cerrato. The third, to Tórtoles de Esgueva, was marked by the reunion of Juana and Fernando. Thereafter, the cortege moved north to Arcos de la Llana (Burgos). Here Juana remained until she was taken to Tordesillas (Valladolid).

There was nothing secretive about the journey itself, although it had a fugitive element. Juana realised that it would be risky to bring about, which explains the semi-secrecy with which she planned it and haste of her departure. The first and most evident of her objectives was to fulfil her vow to Philip and ensure his burial at Granada.[3] The second—but, in the short term at least, the more important—was to secure a measure of political and personal freedom.

It has been seen as a symptom of her insanity that Juana left Burgos in the heart of winter (albeit a relatively warm one) and when heavily pregnant. But, from Juana's perspective, escape was essential. In troubled times, the capture of the royal person had become almost a "political ritual" of Trastámaran Castile.[4] While Enrique IV eluded capture several times, his Portuguese queen and their daughter fell into the possession of various nobles. Juana had, of course, been her husband's hostage and her younger son had narrowly escaped becoming Guevara's. As the ninety-day agreement drew to a close, fernandinos and former felipistas plotted to carry the queen off to their respective strongholds of Arévalo and Escalona, while Juana seems, most of all, to have feared that Cisneros might seize her and her baby. Juana's later comment to Ferrer, often overlooked, makes it clear that she left Burgos to escape the archbishop. The cortege can, thus, be seen as a vehicle of flight.[5]

Juana's last-minute declaration of her intentions was deliberately designed to catch people unawares. She angrily overrode objections to the removal of Philip's body and, Martire notes, no one dared defy her for fear that she might abort in fury and vexation.[6] After an awkward delay, caused by the need to find a more solid cart on which to carry the bier, the cortege left in a foggy dusk. Juana sat in a chair behind the *chariot d'armes*. A multitude surrounded her: "It was truly astonishing to see how many notables, including the most distinguished of illustrious men, accompanied the Queen, attending with care to her allusive comments, when she, content only with her husband's coffin, had abandoned all other responsibilities," Maldonado writes unsympathetically.[7] Among her retinue were Fray Romero, prior of Miraflores, the bishop of Jaén and Royal Council president (Fuente del Sauce), and the bishops of Málaga (Villaescusa), Mondoñedo (Muros) and Burgos (Ampudia).

Juana feared an ambush. Informed that Nájera and Velasco were waiting by the bridge out of Burgos, she ordered a detour, but Velasco subsequently joined her.[8] The cortege wound through the limy uplands of the Palentine Cerrato, overnighting at Cabia. It reached Torquemada on Christmas Eve. This, as indicated by an order of 19 December about travel expenditure, was where Juana had planned a temporary stop.[9]

"There is no-one, great or small," Conchillos told Almazán, "who does not say she is not ruined, and has not lost her mind…". Her "nonsensical" departure was "very damaging for everyone…". Conchillos' views about Juana were invariably coloured by the impact of her actions on Fernando. He describes the admiral's anger with Lazárraga for helping fund the journey: "You're doing more harm than you think." Cárdenas meanwhile exclaimed: "Look what a life I lead for the sake of our master!"[10] Clearly, her *mayordomo mayor* saw the queen's authority as essentially provisional. But the alarm of Fernando's supporters related less to Juana's state of mind than to her intended destination. No one had forgotten the declaration of support for Juana by southern nobles and, if she slipped beyond fernandino control, she would complicate Fernando's chances of regaining power in Castile.

Apart from the timing, most attention has focused on the duration and nocturnal aspect of the journey, together with Juana's periodic inspection of Philip's embalmed body. In Spain, embalming was rare and haste, therefore, essential. Isabel's funeral journey, which reached Granada in twenty-one days, moved fast, "soaking up the leagues and drinking the wind," in Azcona's memorable phrase.[11] Martire described the journey as the most "horrible" thing that had happened to him: "Do you think we travelled by land?" The cortege "almost swam" through the valleys and across the plains and tottered across the sierras, shedding baggage in the rocks. Even allowing for Martire's characteristic colour, the need for rapidity and weather conditions far more severe than those of 1506 converted it into a moving catastrophe: "Ay, how many wretched bodies, how many mules swept away in the torrents!"[12]

Philip's cortege was comparatively sedate and, as Juana intended, more characteristic of the funeral journeys of Burgundian dukes than of Spanish princes and monarchs. It was this alien aspect that made it so noteworthy to early sixteenth-century onlookers. "In my opinion," Martire wrote, "no epoch has witnessed a body being taken from its tomb to be carried off by a team of four horses, surrounded by funereal pomp and a swarm of clerics intoning the Office of the Dead. As in triumph, from the city of Burgos, in a carriage pulled by four horses, in nightly stages, we brought it and here watch over it."[13]

The procession's nocturnal quality is another supposed symptom of Juana's madness. The classical and medieval mind gendered day and night, sun and moon. In the *Roman d'Enéas*, for example, Camille, queen of the Vulcanes, is portrayed as "king by day, queen by night" ("*Lo jor ert rois, la nuit raïne*").[14] Martire, a Milanese humanist probably familiar with Hesiod's *Theogony*, whose Nyx is the powerful pre-Olympian goddess of the night, dwelling in shadow and only fitfully glimpsed, pursued the theme of queenship and the night. Throughout his *Epistolario*, he associates a transgressive Juana with night and sunlessness. Night was the medium in which *Beowulf*'s monstrous queen, Grendel, operated, while in Spenser's *Faerie Queene* "griesly Night" wears a "foule blacke pitchie mantle" and rides an iron chariot drawn by coal-black steeds of "hellish brood." Nashe, Spenser's contemporary, remarks that: "Well have the poets termed the night the nurse of cares, the mother of despair, the daughter of hell."[15]

Martire recorded Juana as declaring that: "Widows should not see the light of day," at least when they travelled.[16] Given the queen's propensity for laconic utterances and her occasional daytime appearances, this remark may have been slightly tongue-in-cheek. However, noble widows did follow certain norms. Margaret of Austria's chronicler relates how, recently widowed, but still in Castile, she was sometimes obliged to await nightfall in the shade of olive trees so that her appearance would not elicit inappropriate acclamations.[17] Juana was similarly anxious to avoid celebrations that sprang from a natural desire to greet her, but which could entail an improper regard for her widowhood and disrespect to the body and memory of a controversial foreign prince. She did not therefore think it proper to enter "embellished cities" and "magnificent plazas."[18] After leaving Burgos, the cortege went by rural and sometimes misty byways, as Juana steered a narrow path between her rejection of Philip's political legacy and her obligations to the ritual remembrance of a husband, lord and father.

Just as court celebrations were often nocturnal, so were rites of passage. In his study of royal death rituals in Spain, Varela notes that journeys from place of death to place of burial customarily began at sunset, when life had ebbed away, and ended with the first rays of the resurrecting sun. Such journeys placed a "metaphorical stress on the transitions in the otherworldly journey of the king: body and soul, night and day, death and resurrection." Only in 1818 did this practice change.[19] It is possible that Juana's night journeys were linked to this metaphorical aspect. As for her insistence that women should not approach the coffin, the presence of Carthusians offers, as Aram suggests, a rather more likely reason than necrophiliac jealousy for Juana's withdrawal of the bier from the convent of Bernardine nuns of Santa María de Escobar in April 1507.[20] Fray Romero would have accompanied the queen on condition that he and his companions would continue to inhabit the "desert of Chartreuse"—a spiritual, essentially woman-free space. Only Juana as monarch, not as woman, could enter this "desert."[21]

Finally, tradition also played its part in the ceremonies of identification. These would customarily take place when a royal body, moved from one point to another, reached a resting place or destination. Similarly, royal bones were often inspected during visits to ancestral pantheons. Thus, after mass at Miraflores in February 1502, Juana and Philip had together viewed the remains of Juana's maternal grandfather, Juan II of Castile, while care was taken to limit air entering the vault.[22]

In short, many rational explanations may be found for the funeral journey. Yet there is no question that, for witnesses like Martire and Maldonado, unfamiliar with northern European customs, and living on the temporal frontier of dynastic change, the cortege made a deep impression. Both clerics remarked on the four, spirited jet-black Friesian horses with their thick, flowing manes and feathery feet, possibly unaware they were a staple of the fourfold symbolism of aristocratic Burgundian funerary rites.[23] Striking in another way was the journey's ultimately circuitous path, largely owing to Fernando's desire to return to Burgos. But the true uniqueness of the cortège lay in the status and gender and (in its earliest stages) the heavily pregnant condition of the chief mourner. Juana's role is reminiscent of *Beowulf*'s queen Hildeburh, who commands her brother's and son's funeral pyre and who, while embodying desolation and family loss, is responsible for organising and presiding the cultural rituals of death, mourning and conservation of memory, even at the risk of a de facto exclusion from government.[24]

Martire was among those guarding Philip's bier at the church of Santa Eulalia in Torquemada, where Juana had organised a rota: "The constant smoke from the lighted torches has given us the colour of Ethiopians …".

Martire was, however, delighted with the riverbanks, ilex woods and thickets full of violets, which offered relief from the stifling tensions of Burgos.[25] Whether Torquemada's status as a *behetría*, governed by its inhabitants rather than by an overlord, was significant for Juana, who had visited the town with Philip in 1502, is unclear.

Catalina, named for Katherine, was born on 14 January 1507 after a difficult labour in which Juana's life was momentarily at risk.[26] Four days later, Martire told Ruffo that plague had struck Torquemada. Later, he informed Talavera that a maidservant of Juana's and eight servants of Villaescusa's had died.[27] This prompted Villaecusa to provide funds for the foundation of a chapel in his native pueblo of Villaescusa de Haro (Cuenca) where Juana and Philip are thought to feature among the guests in a beautiful polychrome representation of the wedding of Mary and Joseph.[28]

Cisneros reached Torquemada with a force of pikemen, halbadiers and musketeers. Still hoping for a Cortes, he officiated at Catalina's baptism at Santa Eulalia. Juana paid for a polychromed wood interior for the church font.[29] Her choice of Velasco and Villaescusa as Catalina's godfathers may well relate to their support for her in the months after Philip's death.

While plague inhibited Juana's progress south, Martire stressed her indifference to events. On 26 February, without mentioning that she was still in quarantine, he commented that she "does not care in the slightest whether her kingdoms prosper or perish …".[30] The queen offered twenty gold ducats at her churching on 4 March, which she attended with the constable and marquis of Villena. Afterwards, she appeared frequently in public. Martire continued, nonetheless, to emphasise her uselessness: she "does nothing but walk to and from the church, where people flock to see and speak to her. She deals amiably with some, sadly with others. The former withdraw satisfied and full of joy, the latter heads down, eyes fixed on the earth, and frowning. But the result is the same."[31]

Other evidence shows a queen engaging with affairs. Lazárraga told a cousin that he and Juana had much work between them, though admitting that Juana gave him the major part.[32] On 7 March, Ferrer found Juana busy with "the king's affairs, in which she daily improves," and Conchillos noted the arrival of "Nicolás, maestro de la Cámara"—possibly Dr. Nicolás Tello, royal accountant and councillor. After his departure, Juana ordered Lazárraga to obtain more funds: "for the first time [she] signed a *cédula*, then another four, I don't know what about," writes

Conchillos, who kept a close watch on the queen, observing that various books were being taken into her. But he thought it unlikely she would stick at the work.[33]

In fact, Juana had signed a series of *cédulas* before leaving Burgos. Although these were concerned almost entirely with household payments and journey costs—some also showing her scrupulous adherence to Isabel's testamentary request that Fernando receive half the revenues from the Indies—they demonstrate her desire to obtain the funds that were absolutely necessary in order to confer favours and patronage and, in general, to govern. Juana looked to the influx of gold from the New World, which, from about 1503, had begun to become profitable for the crown. She told the Casa de Contratación in Seville that she rejoiced at the good news sent her "about the abundance of gold that Our Lord has been pleased to provide in those islands [of the Indies]" and asked the Casa "not to pay out my half without receiving my signature, and as for the eight thousand pesos of gold and pearls which, in your letter, you told me have arrived, and the six thousand pesos newly brought in by the ship *la Garça*, I order you to give and pay the half of the one and of the other that belongs to me to Ochoa de Landa [royal treasurer]."[34] The approximately thirty *cédulas* in the archives of Simancas, dated between January and July 1507 and signed by Juana, are also concerned in the main with relatively mundane matters, but again show her desire for funds. She refers to the arrival of more gold and peals from the Indies as well as to her "very great pleasure" that the plague had receded from Seville.[35] In one order, she notes the return of two ships from La Española—possibly those mentioned by Cisneros' military captain, Vianello, as forming part of the expedition that had found the coastal mouth of a great river, with serpents, dragons and a king and his retinue in gold masks.[36]

On 30 April, plague finally forced Juana out of Torquemada. The cortege chanted its way to Hornillos de Cerrato, arriving at cock-row. This was a relatively short move across high moorland to a hamlet in an arroyo below a cliff where gypsum was mined and baked in the little ovens from which the pueblo took its name. Martire calls it a dump (*villorrio*) of no more than twenty-eight "hovels." These clustered around the honey-coloured church of San Miguel Arcángel, whose services Castilians customarily called upon when building a church over a mosque. Towering above stands the hermitage of Nuestra Señora de Belbis and, nearby, a ruined fortress, once held by the Enríquez clan and which, with its neighbouring fortresses of Baltanás and Palenzuela, played a part in an uprising against Juan II and in the war of succession. Juana settled into a place identified by local tradition as an outlying *finca* called El Bosque. It was in these unlikely surroundings, from which Cisneros kept his distance, that Juana again seized the political initiative.

## 8.2 The Queen's Council

Azcona compares Juana and her councillors to "disorientated walkers in an entangled landscape" of chaos and disorder. For Prescott, the period after the lapse of the provisional government left Castile "without even the shadow of protection afforded by its cortes, and with no other guide but its crazy sovereign." Thus, her kingdoms drifted "at random amidst the winds and waves of faction." More recently, Haliczer has described the "wave of confusion and near panic that gripped many Castilian towns after Juana's mental breakdown."[37] How true are these pictures of the first months of 1507?

As earlier noted, historians have resorted to a confusing periodisation for the tumultuous years between 1504 and 1522. References to the period between 1506 and 1507 as the "first Cisneros regency" ignore the existence of a reigning monarch who had neither abdicated nor formally delegated power.[38] Nor do such references take account of the shift away from Cisneros and towards queen and Council early in 1507. But if the period is remembered as a reign, two distinct phases come more clearly into focus: the first dominated by Cisneros' interim coalition, the second by a re-constituted Royal Council that began asserting its role under a more assertive queen.

By the beginning of 1507, Cisneros' relations with the Royal Council, never easy, were growing strained. García Oro mentions manifest splits between those who had earlier agreed to his "improvised regency."[39] Having accepted his arbitration in the panic surrounding Philip's death, the royal councillors feared that a Cisneros-led regency council could undermine their authority. They objected that, while other militias had been banned, Cisneros flaunted his own, and they resented his attempts to block royal provisions he disliked. In March, the Council finally backed Juana's decision to dissolve the Cortes and "went about their business without taking much account of him."[40] A measure of Cisneros' loss of influence was the fact that, in early January, after expiry of the ninety-day truce, Nájera led a militia into Torquemada to "free" the queen. Juana called on royal councillors for help and these royal councillors, with Ferrer, Villena and Ureña, negotiated Nájera's withdrawal.[41]

This time of uncertainty and instability was also one of experimentation, when members of the urban elite, who struggled to maintain a measure of political independence in the face of royal centralising tendencies, grabbed opportunities to reinforce foral tradition and try alternative methods of local government.[42] This sharpened the edge of municipal unrest in the fall-out from the power struggle between Fernando and Philip, further aggravated by Philip's ousting of *corregidores* before their terms of office had expired. But if Seville's procurators at Burgos, Guillén de Casaus and Juan Serrano, are to be believed, unrest in the cities was due less, as Haliczer maintains, to Juana's "breakdown" than to the Royal Council's failure to mesh with her desires.[43]

A major task of royal councillors was to intervene in the nomination of *corregidores*, and Casaus and Serrano questioned the Council's support for a Galician ally of Philip's, Fernando de Andrade, count of Villalba, whom Philip had appointed *asistente* to Seville. By the end of 1506, Andrade was still poised to assume the position, despite Seville's opposition and the fact that, according to the procurators, it was "well known" that Juana had not supported the appointment. The councillors replied that Philip's orders had been co-signed by Juana. The procurators objected that Juana's signature was false for "at that time she was not signing." They illustrated their argument with other examples. The Council had sent Enrique de Acuña, count of Valencia de Don Juan, to Asturias (Oviedo) "and he was not received, and others who had been sent to other cities had also been rejected."[44] Murcia's *regidores* had forcibly rejected Philip's *corregidor*, Garçi Tello, snatching the wands of office from his officials and handing them to Murcia's *adelantado*, Pedro Fajardo. Yet on 14 October, the Council, speaking as Juana, intervened to claim it was "my pleasure and will" that Philip's appointment be upheld and threatening reprisals if she were not obeyed. As in Cartagena and Lorca, reprisals were threatened if the local officials refused to comply.[45] In Cuenca, much of the urban patriciate refused to cooperate with Philip's *corregidor*, Martín de Acuña, a Leonese *regidor* who had clashed violently with the procurator for Toledo, Pedro López de Padilla, at the Cortes of Valladolid of 1506.[46] In the teeth of Cuenca's opposition, the Council again insisted that it was Juana's will that Philip's order be obeyed.[47] But it could not dislodge Diego Hurtado de Mendoza, who bore the military title of *guardamayor* and had stepped in on the grounds of restoring good governance in Juana's name.[48] The Council's action on Cuenca was, in Zurita's view, "very dangerous at a time when weapons could do more than laws" and when the Council lacked adequate military backing.

Segovia provides a particularly striking example of the way in which queen and Council were at odds. After yielding the fortress to Philip in 1506, Isabel's old friends, the Moyas, had returned to besiege it. The Council had contemplated declaring the Moyas rebels and confiscating their assets but the Moyas took the fortress in May. A procession of nobles, military captains, soldiers, municipal officers and local inhabitants wound through the streets and the royal pennant was raised to cries of "Castilla, Castilla, for Queen Doña Juana!" Zurita describes Juana's pleasure—"the most welcome event of her reign so far."[49]

The Council had been able to uphold the fiction that Juana agreed with Philip's decisions because her crucial laws rescinding them remained on ice. That December, she had tried, unsuccessfully, to oust Philip's councillors. Beyond thoughts of vengeance, this was a point of honour for the queen, whose authority and name were being tossed about between opposing factions. On 5 May, freed of Cisneros' presence and in a fresh attempt to bring an end to the diverging affinities in political and financial structures, she summoned the councillors. "She retained those she knew, chosen in former times by her parents," writes Martire; "she dismissed the ones chosen by her husband and ordered everyone to find lodgings. Neither pleas nor warnings could persuade her to modify her intention by permitting some of the new ones to remain. She entrusted those she chose with the task of governing until her father's arrival. So, here we stay with her, in the hovels and military-style tents put up for us. The rest returned to Palencia."[50]

Among those dismissed were Dr Francisco de Ávila, Alonso de Castilla and licenciates Miguel Guerrero, Fortún Ibañez de Aguirre and Francisco de Sosa. The president also withdrew after a meeting with the queen. She took similar action with respect to Philip's *contadores*, who governed the public finances and were empowered to preside over and judge litigation. The new royal treasury division created by Philip after the treaty of Salamanca, and which Manuel had led, was disbanded while her parents' appointees remained. The signatures of Guerrero, Ávila and Sosa disappear from royal provisions in June 1507, while the last two reappear among Fernando's nominations for 1508.

Juana discussed these dismissals with the men affected in the church of San Miguel Arcángel. They argued that Juana herself had endorsed their appointments. Juana denied it. They had not, she said, served her honourably. When Villena, who accompanied them, intervened on their behalf she retorted that he, with his *agudezas*, his slipperiness, had also dishonoured her, and insisted that everything "return to the state in which it had been before she disembarked in Spain …". An exchange between the queen and Alonso de Castilla became well known. When Juana asked him where he came from and learned that he had formerly lived in Salamanca, she advised him to return to his studies. "It seemed," Zurita comments, "such a pertinent and sensible remark … because of his poor reputation as a *letrado*."[51] A biographer of one of the more longstanding councillors, Palacios Rubios, describes her action as a demonstration of "great proof of sanity," occurring in an "interval of lucidity."[52] Similarly for Prescott, Castilla's dismissal reflected one of her "partial gleams of intelligence, directed in this peculiar way."[53] But on 26 September 1516, long after Juana's imprisonment at Tordesillas, Cisneros reappointed Castilla to the Royal Council on advice, or under pressure, from Brussels.[54]

Juana reinstated Dr. Martín Fernández de Angulo and licenciates Francisco de Vargas and Luis Zapata. The first, an archdeacon, doctor of canon and civil law, Cortes assistant, ecclesiastical expert and bibliophile, had witnessed Isabel's will and helped oversee Prince Juan's princely apprenticeship at Almazán. Galíndez de Carvajal describes Zapata as highly experienced, "honest," although not particularly scholarly. He thought Vargas self-regarding, self-interested and "extremely covetous."[55] A formidable financial operator, Conchillos describes him as having his "hands in the dough."[56] The signatures of Vargas, Angulo and Zapata on royal provisions start to appear in May 1507, as, for example, on one ordering Andrade to withdraw his men from the *behetrías* of Ontoria, Zazuán and Fresnillo, near Aranda.[57]

The queen's orders "scared everyone" and no-one dared countermand them. They were, Zurita observes, of "great importance" to the resurgence of the fernandino 'party'. This lost her the support of some former allies and, amid rumours of a plot to "kill the queen with herbs"—reportedly revealed to Cisneros by a monk during confession—the dismissed councillors met in Burgos with Manuel, Borgo and Nájera to discuss the establishment of a parallel administration operating in

Juana's name.[58] In April and June 1507, Borgo informed Margaret, regent of the Low Countries since April 1507, about his consultations with Nájera and Villena and the need for funds to sweeten them.[59] He advised Galician noble Pedro Bermudez to prepare for Charles's arrival in Spain that spring, when the prince would take Bermudez's sons and relatives into his household. The letter was accompanied by a covering message of 7 February in which the signature, *El Príncipe*, is followed by the formula "by order of the prince with the authority of the emperor, grandfather and father of his highness."[60]

Despite his industry, Borgo could not compete with the momentum building in Fernando's favour. On 11 May 1507, Benavente swore loyalty both to Juana and Fernando after receiving promises from the latter. Villena held out a little longer before also capitulating.[61] Zurita did not conceal the beneficial effect for Fernando of Juana's actions. Fernando was clever but also very fortunate that Castile did not break apart in his absence, "especially owing to some provisions that the queen began to take," whether on her personal initiative or through the Council.[62]

Martire praises Juana for her intelligence while criticising her for failing to act upon it: "She has much ability and a very good memory, this sovereign of ours. She penetrates acutely not only into women's affairs but into those of great men." However, she did not explain herself and was erratic.[63] Martire describes government as being in the hands of Cisneros and the constable, while Maldonado notes, with greater precision, that "the kingdom was governed by the Royal Council, to whom the Archbishop of Toledo … and Bernardino de Velasco … lent support and resources…".[64] An anonymous Spanish chronicler described the Council's heroic and solitary endeavours, asking whether the ten or eleven Spanish councillors who governed alone in 1507 should not be held in yet greater esteem than the 320 Roman councillors in the biblical book of Maccabees. Despite being "ill-treated by some grandees," they worked intensively, "continually dripping with sweat," to punish disobedience and villainy.[65]

In his study of the Royal Council, Dios maintains that Juana's "incapacity" meant councillors had to assume "extraordinary functions of government" and could only resume normal work after Fernando's return.[66] This, however, begs the question as to what 'normality' meant. Most government activity did not require the royal signature and councillors had worked intensively too during the crises of the dual monarchy.

The output of royal provisions is broadly comparable. For June 1502, for example, the Registro General de Sellos at the General Archive of Simancas contains over 300 provisions, compared with over 400 in June 1507. The exceptional number of almost 900 in October 1506 (compared with the already busy month of September 1506, when almost 700 were issued) may reflect the agitated political aftermath of Philip's death. In January 1507, the number drops to 266; while in February 1507, it rises to almost 600; and, in March, to almost 700, slightly diminishing between May and August 1507.

The wide range of issues covered in 1506–1507 shows the Council's frequent engagement with relatively mundane matters: repairs to the bridge at Tordesillas; outstanding monies owed Juana's sister, María, queen of Portugal; bread distribution in Granada; alleged acts of ill-treatment by the count of Salvatierra; financial support for students; perennial questions of *moneda forera*—the tribute paid to the monarch every seven years in recognition of royal dominion, and so on. Councillors worked with Lazárraga on Isabel's will and opened an inquiry into the conduct of the *corregidor* of Medina del Campo, Pero García Sarmiento, who declared that Fernando had done "nothing but rob" Castile and that Isabel had gone to hell.[67] The chanceries, too, appear to have functioned, and on 5 February, an order (*cédula*) from Juana in respect of justice administration in Vizcaya was incorporated in the Royal Chancery ordinances.[68]

This does not mean that government necessarily ran smoothly. While noting the beneficial effects of her actions, Zurita thought the Council "feared to deal with matters with authority and vigour because it did not know if Juana would take contrary actions."[69] This implies insufficient contact between queen and Council. There was, nonetheless, an important shift in relations in 1507 and, particularly after May, a recovery of dynamism and coherence. Juana met with the councillors at Torquemada between January and April. Between May and August, councillors signed documents in Palencia, Magaz and Antigüedad and their presence at Hornillos on 11 May, 16 May and 18–19 May can only be explained by the need to discuss matters with the queen.[70] Although Magaz and Palencia were their main places of residence between May and August, some may have travelled to Hornillos to see the queen more frequently. She ordered councillors to meet her in early July, as a brief message from Ferrer to the councillors shows:

"Her Highness would like you to send whomever you think best to come here today. I told her I did not know whether it would be possible to get here today because of the distance involved. She said if it could not be today it should be tomorrow. It being Sunday, I was unable to speak to her Highness until after mass. I told her what your worships wrote me, and with letter in hand in case she wished to see it." Juana wanted the councillors to join her at Hornillos because of plague in Palencia. Ferrer objected that they had gone to Palencia because of plague at Magaz, but Juana seems to have been aware that some councillors were still there: "She said she knew perfectly well what she was talking about, told me to be quiet and accept the order as she gave it." Juana, he adds, was thinking of leaving Hornillos, "and from what we can interpret this would be for the frontier with Aragon or kingdom of Toledo." Because she was speaking "boldly" about Toledo (and a resumption of her journey south), he felt the councillors should not delay.[71]

Ferrer's self-imposed role as intermediary between Council and queen clearly irritated Juana. Whether trying to distance councillors and queen from one another, or urging them to dissuade her from heading south, Ferrer's task was to prevent any initiative that might undermine Fernando's position.

## 8.3 The Perils of Widowhood

The king of Aragon ignored Juana's rights by distributing largesse among her subjects. This infuriated the constable, who declared that since the queen had revoked Philip's grants, Fernando's actions were similarly prejudicial to the crown.[72] Philip's former ally and ambassador, Antonio de Acuña, was among those whose allegiance Fernando wished to attract. He therefore encouraged Pope Julius II to nominate him to the see of Zamora. The Council, now acting more coherently in Juana's name, saw this as a flagrant abuse of her entitlement under the *Patronato Regio*, the royal prerogative allowing monarchs the right to nominate to ecclesiastical posts. Fernando was asked to urge the pope to "conserve the queen's pre-eminence and *patronazgo real*" in respect of Zamora, although, significantly, Fernando did not do so.[73] The Council also sent Judge Ronquillo y Briceño to remove Acuña from the bishopric. But Acuña encircled and set fire to Ronquillo's lodgings and imprisoned the judge and his *alguacil*. The Council sent reinforcements. These were ambushed, disarmed and stripped. This time the Council sent in cavalry and a fresh judge, and asked the city of Salamanca, duke of Alba and others to help free the royal officials and demolish the fortress that Acuña had begun building in Fuentesauco.[74] It also ordered the confiscation of the bishopric's assets.[75] On 2 May, in Juana's voice, it set out the royal case against Acuña, who had taken advantage of the fact that "after the death of the king my lord I was secluded and did not deal with government affairs." The dean, chapter, city council and other councils of the area were ordered to withdraw support for Acuña or be deemed traitors, with consequent loss of assets, posts and favours, and destruction of property.[76] This brought the release of the justice officials. But, counting on the support of some fellow nobles, Acuña held out in Fuentesaúco until 1508. Fernando then ceded him the bishopric.[77]

The Zamora case illustrates the difficulties faced by a monarch with insufficient military muscle to implement crucial laws. It also shows how the Royal Council fell back on the device of eliciting support and sympathy through the topos of vulnerable widowhood. Strife-ridden cities and countries were often compared to grieving widows. Lamenting the ills that had befallen Castile under Juan II, Valera exclaims: "How the lady of the people is alone! It is as if she had become a widow and there is no-one among all her friends to console her."[78] This was to echo Dante's lament for a stricken Rome: "How doth the city sit desolate, who was filled with people! The mistress of nations hath become a widow."[79] Now a flesh-and-blood widow embodied the concept of vulnerable kingdoms crying out for protection.

The Council made full use of the theme during the Galician crises of April and May. When the count of Lemos seized the fortress of Ponferrada in May 1507, he faced a coalition of nobles, episcopates and militias from across Castile, while the Council re-assumed Juana's persona, reprimanding Lemos for profiting from the "sad death of the king … leaving me a widow and my kingdoms in much danger."[80] Inevitably, though, the theme of widowhood was open to all to exploit. In 1506, Lemos and Andrade had based their alliance with surrounding cities and towns on the need to act in the face of the "anguish and sorrow" of the queen, who, for this reason, "does not wish to govern … nor has wished or wishes to delegate government to any person or persons …".[81]

Recourse to the theme of vulnerable widowhood was hardly a substitute for the laws that Juana had hoped to implement months earlier, and which, already drawn up by the queen, were implemented on Fernando's return. On 30 July, after he had disembarked at Valencia, *sobrecartas* (documents implementing laws already passed) were issued to the chanceries of Valladolid and Granada and Galician authorities, promulgating Juana's measures. These helped Fernando recover the fortresses of Burgos, Jaén, Plasencia and Mirabel. Juana was meanwhile limited to sending councillors (Oropesa, Mújica, Carvajal and Polanco) to negotiate Lemos's withdrawal on her behalf. Always mindful of Cisneros' interference in her affairs, she ordered them not to consult with him and, when hearing that Cisneros had sent his own deputation to Lemos, signed an order summoning her four councillors back for further talks as to the next steps to take. Since the order to which Zurita refers has not been unearthed, we do not know exactly in what context it was issued and dated. Nevertheless, the circumstances again illustrate Juana's concern about Cisneros' interference in her affairs.

In mid-June, Cisneros and Benavente met at Reinoso with Alba, Velasco, Ferrer and councillors. They then moved to Hornillos, where Juana agreed to appoint Benavente and Alba as captains general. The appointments were confirmed in a royal provision of 16 June, signed in Magaz, and an additional order of 22 June, signed in Benavente.[82] Ponferrada, writes Bernáldez, was besieged by order of queen and Council, until, on 30 July, he surrendered the fortress.

On 3 June, in a separate move, the queen ordered that the infante be brought to Hornillos. It seems she had been contemplating the reunion for a while, since she refers to a previous order not followed through because of uncertainty about the plague. She sent Cárdenas to escort the infante "by the places and paths that are most salubrious, so that, with the help of our lord there is no detrimental effect on his health."[83] This initiative, combined with her actions vis-à-vis royal councillors and accountants, was widely interpreted as reinforcing her authority. With Fernando on the point of returning, it was seen as a signal that she "wished and was able to make orders and govern."[84]

## 8.4 Juana's Triumvirate

This brief overview of Juana's effective period of government outlines the challenges that royal authority faced from *corregidores*, prelates and nobles and from the king of Aragon. On another issue, too, the Inquisition's activities in the south, the queen's Council and closest advisers diverged from Fernando's.

Fernando had ordered Martire to watch the queen.[85] Thus, at Torquemada and Hornillos she was accompanied by Martire and two bishops: Villaescusa, whom he describes as "researcher of the secrets of the skies," and Diego de Muros III, bishop of Mondoñedo, and "more acute than Mercury." The "triumvirate," as Martire calls them, had common literary, theological, political and educational interests. They shared Cisneros' criticisms of aristocratic abuse of power and an interest in Erasmian ideas and were influential in the birth and development of Spanish humanism. All three had been protégés, or close associates, of Isabel's former confessor, and Juana's erstwhile teacher, Talavera. Muros, like Villaescusa, was a former student of Salamanca and future founder of a college there. In 1494, he became dean of Santiago de Compostela and was the first administrator of the Hospital Real for pilgrims. In 1507, he was at court, at least in part to try to recover diocesan property from local nobles.[86] Villasescusa, as bishop of Málaga, a suffragan diocese of Seville, had clashed with Seville's archbishop, Diego de Deza, who had slipped back into his role as grand inquisitor after Philip's death. The archbishop had claims on Antequera, and Villaecusa was troubled by Deza's inquisitorial activities in the diocese.[87] In an unpublished treatise, *De christiana religione*, dating from around 1502, Villaescusa had set out the view that the Inquisition should draw a clearer distinction between simple error and ignorance on one hand and the wilful and conscious preference for Mosaic over Christian doctrine on the other.[88]

Juana's 'triumvirs' discussed a number of religious, ecclesiastical and political topics with her.[89] Martire, who stressed Villaescusa's ascendancy over her, boasted that they were "the only people whom the Queen allows to be seated in her presence …" and declared in June that he could not leave court because she "does not consent that anyone beyond us three … should take part with her in the ceremonies … She does not tolerate the presence of any cleric, apart from ourselves, except for the cantors."[90] Juana's favours conferred prestige upon Villaescusa and his friends at a time when the zealous inquisitor for Córdoba, Diego Rodríguez Lucero, had, with the backing of Fernando and Deza, charged Talavera with involvement in a network of "Judaising" *conversos* in Córdoba and Granada.[91]

Since Granada remained Juana's destination, her discussions with the triumvirs would, inevitably, have touched on the situation in the south. In an appeal to their "native-born mistress" the Cordoban municipal and church authorities claimed that they had substantiated allegations that

Lucero used torture, threats and extortion to extract false confessions and that he and Deza had brought "infamy" to Córdoba and offended Juana's royal person by arresting Córdoba's emissary to Juana, Alonso de Toro, on the royal road to Burgos. Juana was urged to order Deza to place judicial proceedings in the hands of bishops or judges of integrity and persuade Rome to replace Deza as inquisitor general. In a hint of revolutionary days to come, city and church authorities warned Juana that, pending a royal remedy, it would, if necessary, confederate with other cities to resist the inquisitors.[92] She received another appeal from the relatives of prisoners of the Inquisition at Jaén, who wanted her to suspend an auto de fé, pending an impartial inquiry.[93] Talavera himself appealed to Juana, among others, to "defend the honour of God." He claimed that Lucero and Lucero's allies wanted to expel *conversos* from Castile against the wishes of the church, "which did not seek a distinction between Jew and Greek."[94] Significantly, when a spokesman for the cathedral chapter of Granada was charged with drafting a defence plea to Rome on Talavera's behalf, he asked that Villaescusa be among those to whom the case might be transferred.[95]

Did Juana sympathise with the views of her triumvirate on this issue? After all, it had been to Philip's credit rather than to Juana's that the inquisitorial reign of terror in the south was temporarily halted, and Talavera's death on 15 May 1507, only a day after his appeal to Juana, obviated the need for a personal response from her. Juana's personal view is thus unclear. Nevertheless, it was in her court that moves were again made to stop Lucero. The papers of the inquiry into Talavera's alleged heresies have been lost or destroyed. However, Martire records his collaboration with Talavera's envoy to the court, canon Gonzalo Cabezas, and his defence of Talavera before the inquisitorial judges in March 1507.[96] Villaescusa, for his part, provided a home for members of Talavera's persecuted family, left destitute upon his death.[97]

Juana's councillors shared her advisers' sympathies. When a merchant brought news of Talavera's posthumous miracle working, Nicolás Tello exclaimed to a crowded Council chamber that he was unsurprised. Vargas compared him to St Jerome and the hermit Hilarion.[98] As the Córdoba crisis threatened to spill well beyond Andalucia, Juana and her councillors summoned Deza to Toro, where he failed to impress.[99] Protonotary apostolic Martín de Azpeitia reported to the Congregation of Burgos in 1508 that, in Palencia, "with great application [the royal councillors] completed examination of all the witnesses who had been brought from Córdoba, and also inquired into events in Toro."[100] Carvajal noted that the Council, intervening to calm the political turbulence generated by the inquisitors, "acted with all possible diligence" until June 1507. Declared innocent, the prisoners were released on the eve of the feast of St John (23–24 June).[101] Thus, we cannot "safely assume," with Lea, that under Juana "greed and cruelty claimed their victims"—not, at least, if her Council's record is taken into account.[102]

In conclusion, it is not without irony that the period almost universally described as marking Juana's collapse was actually the period in which she intervened in government as never before, rising to, and overcoming serious challenges to her right to act independently. She managed to block a Cortes that had been unlawfully convoked and which she believed was not only "unnecessary" but could harm her rights and interests and, perhaps, Fernando's. By reconstituting the Royal Council and treasury departments, she helped bring a halt to the paralysis caused by competing political agendas and, in conjunction with the Council, was credited with doing much to prevent Castile breaking apart. She prepared two key laws that sought to restore good practice and the royal patrimony, while dismantling the 'Flemish' party and easing the way for Fernando's return.

Yet her successes also brought the seeds of her destruction. Her relations with the powerful archbishop of Toledo could not have been worse and her instincts and interests as proprietary monarch sometimes clashed with Fernando's. Her effective reign was dominated by the prospect of his return, pending which she failed to draw from initiatives that would have done much to clarify her agenda. A re-energised Council began, from May onwards, to act on Juana's behalf to protect royal authority and impose justice. But despite her appeal to her councillors to serve her as loyally as they had served Isabel, she was hindered by huge fernandino pressure and did not, or could not, use the short time of relative freedom available to her to build a grouping loyal, above all, to herself.

## Notes

1. Martire (López de Toro, ed. 1955), 10, 339, 1 May 1507.
2. Sitwell (1946), 104–105; Mattingly (1942), 71–72; Williams (2013), 155.
3. That Juana had made such a vow is clear from a later papal brief allowing her to break it (AGS, PR 2.7, f. 52, 27 September 1507).

4. Foronda (Foronda, Genet and Nieto Soria, eds. 2005).
5. Z. ADP 787.77, f. 3, Ferrer to Fernando, 10 August 1511. Ferrer records Juana as saying that: "*se fue solo por aquello de Burgos por apartarse de [doña María] y del arzobispo.*" Since María de Ulloa accompanied the queen, the "doña María" in question may refer, as earlier suggested, to the constable's sister. Cisneros and "doña María," Juana later told Ferrer, meddled in her affairs and aimed to take control of her entire household.
6. Martire, 10, 324, 24 December 1506.
7. Maldonado (Fernández Vargas, ed. 1975), 44–45.
8. BN, Ms. 3238, 'Orígen'.
9. AGS, CSR 53, f. 447, Cédula, 19 December 1506.
10. RAH, Salazar, A-12, ff. 86–87.
11. Azcona (2002), 604.
12. Martire, 10, 280, 25 December 1504.
13. Martire, 10, 332, 26 February 1507.
14. Pratt (2002).
15. Koslofsky (2011).
16. Martire, 10, 359, 25 August 1507.
17. Lemaire de Belges (Masconnais, ed. 1549).
18. Martire, 10, 339, 1 May 1507.
19. Varela (1990), 88.
20. Aram (2005).
21. See Colinas (2003), 85.
22. *Reise* (Chmel ed. 1840), 615. The author names Enrique IV, who was, in fact, buried at Santa María de Guadalupe (Cáceres).
23. See, for example, Vale, *The English Historical Review*, 111 (September 1996), 920–938.
24. Ingham (Vaugh and Dickson-Bruckner, eds. 2003).
25. Martire, 10, 325, 8 January 1507; 326, 12 January 1507.
26. Santa Cruz (Mata Carriazo, ed. 1951), 2.
27. Martire, 10, 329, 18 January 1507; 335, 12 March 1507.
28. Millán Martínez (Martínez Soria and Millán Martínez, eds. 2009).
29. Bustos Rojo (2007).
30. Martire, 10, 332, 26 February 1507.
31. Martire, 10, 335, 12 March 1507.
32. AGS, CSR 12.7, f. 292, Lazárraga to Diego Martínez, 28 January 1507.
33. RAH, Salazar, A-12, f. 127, Conchillos to Almazán.
34. AGS, CSR, 14, f. 1.31, cédula, 15 December 1506.
35. AGS, CRS 14.1, ff. 29–30, 23 June 1507.
36. AGS, CRS 14.1, f. 31, 21 June 1507; Sanuto (Fulin, ed. 1969–1970), 23 December 1506.

37. Azcona (1960), 179; Prescott (1908), 636; Haliczer (1981), 107.
38. Arribas (2004), 36.
39. García Oro (2002), 164.
40. Zurita (Canellas López, ed. 1994), 4, 190; 222–223.
41. Martire, 10, 331, 21 January 1507; Santa Cruz, 2; Zurita, IV.
42. Diago Hernando (2004), 195–223.
43. Haliczer (1981), 107.
44. BL, Egerton Ms 309, 'Relación', ff. 139–140. Andrade's biographer, García Oro (1994), wonders whether his ultimate failure to take up the post was connected to Juana's law of 18 December 1506 but the meeting with the Council may also have had its effect (87–88).
45. Gomariz Marín (ed. 2006), 157, 240–241; 164, 250–251 and 167, 253–255.
46. Calderón (2001).
47. AGS, RGS 2-1507, f. 336 (Cuenca).
48. Mariana (1853), 3, 95.
49. Zurita, 4, 190; 230.
50. Martire, 10, 339, 1 May 1507.
51. Zurita, 4, 226.
52. Bullón y Fernández (1927), 99.
53. Prescott (1908), 636.
54. Dios (1982), 155n. See also AGS, Cámara de Castilla, 4, ff. 27–28, 9 June 1516/1517. Cisneros was advised to reappoint Castilla as a '*buena persona y… bien estimado en las cosas de Ytalia*.'
55. CODOIN, I, 'Informe', 122–127.
56. RAH, Salazar, A-12, 86v.
57. AGS, RGS 5-1507, f. 7.
58. Zurita, 4, 226; 235.
59. ADN, B. 244495; 24496; 24497; 24576, Borgo to Margaret.
60. Rodríguez Villa (1874), xxiv–xxvii.
61. AGS, PR 7, f. 102, 'Juramento de fidelidad'; AGS, CCA 11, f. 12, 'Escritura otorgada por D. Diego López Pacheco, Marqués de Villena'.
62. Zurita, 4, 233.
63. Martire, 10, 351, 5 July 1507.
64. Martire, 10, 350, 28 June 1507; Maldonado, 45.
65. BL, Additional Ms. 15568, 'Como el Rey', ff. 23–24v.
66. Dios, 156.
67. AGS, Estado 1-2, f. 192, 'Pesquisa contra algunos que hablaron mal de la Reyna Católica y su marido', 17 May 1507.
68. AGS *Ordenanzas*, lib.1, tit. 4, f. 51, 5 February 1507 (Palencia).
69. Zurita, 4, 233.
70. Rumeu de Armas (1974).

71. AGS, E 2-1, f. 32, 'Negocios de Galicia', 4 July 1507.
72. Zurita, 4.
73. Azcona (1960), 184; 356–357; Castro Lorenzo (Valladolid, 2007).
74. AGS, RGS 4-1507, f. 226, 20 April; f. 63, 23 April (Zamora); AGS, RGS 4-1507: f. 54; 55; 60; 62 (Zamora).
75. AGS, RGS 4-1507, f. 59 (Zamora).
76. AGS, RGS 5-1507, f. 240 (Zamora).
77. Castro Lorenzo, 61.
78. Valera (Penna, ed. 1959), II, 5–7.
79. Baskins (Levy, ed. 2003), 197–209.
80. AGS, Estado 1-2, f. 341, June 1507, 'Provisión del Infante de Granada'; AGS, RGS, 6-1507, f. 5, to Lemos; RGS, 6-1507, f. 359, to Medina del Campo; RGS, 6-1507, f. 360, to Lemos, among others; AGS, RGS 6-1507, f. 05, 15 June 1507 (Ponferrada).
81. García Oro (1994), 278.
82. AHN, Osuna, C. 420, D. 1. 2, 'Provisión de la Reina Juana'.
83. AGS, CSR 12, 10, f. 438. This copy records Juana's signature ("Yo la Reyna") alongside that of her secretary.
84. Zurita, 4, 252.
85. Martire, 10, 310, 7 July 1506.
86. García Oro (1976).
87. Saéz Olivares (Millán Martínez and Martínez Soria, eds. 2009), 155–166.
88. Olivari (1999), 39–56.
89. González Novalín (1981).
90. Martire, 10, 339, 1 May 1507; 349, 17 June 1507.
91. On 9 June 1506, Fernando had declared his belief that Talavera was indeed involved in creating secret synagogues. See Márquez Villanueva (1960).
92. AGS, PR 28, f. 40, 'Memorial de la ciudad de Córdoba a la Reina' [undated].
93. AGS, PR 28, f. 39 (Inquisición).
94. Azcona (Pérez Villanueva, ed. 1980), 103–104.
95. Azcona (1960).
96. Martire, 10, 333, 7 March 1507; 334, 7 March 1507.
97. Martire, 10, 457, 6 July 1511.
98. Martire, 10, 345, 31 May 1507.
99. Azcona (1960).
100. Document of 1 June 1508 in Azcona (Pérez Villanueva, ed. 1980), 134.
101. Azcona (1980), 146.
102. Lea (1906).

# References


Aram, Bethany. 2005. *Juana the Mad: Sovereignty and Dynasty in Renaissance Europe*. Baltimore and London: John Hopkins University Press.

Azcona, Tarsicio de. 1960. *La Elección y Reforma del Episcopado Español en tiempo de los Reyes Católicos*. Madrid: CSIC.

——. 1980. La Inquisición española procesada por la Congregación General de 1508. In *La Inquisición Española: Nueva Visión, Nuevos Horizontes*, ed. Joaquín Pérez Villanueva. Madrid: Siglo Veintiuno de España Editores.

——. 2002. *Isabel la Católica. Vida y Reinado*. Madrid. La Esfera de los Libros.

Baskins, Christelle L. 2003. Trecento Rome: The Poetics and Politics of Widowhood. In *Widowhood and Visual Culture in Early Modern Europe*, ed. Allison Levy. Aldershot and Burlington: Ashgate.

Bullón y Fernández, Eloy. 1927. *El doctor Palacios Rubios y sus obras. Un colaborador de los Reyes Católicos*. Madrid: Librería General de Victoriano Suárez.

Bustos Rojo, Ricardo de. 2007. *Doña Catalina de Austria. Centenario de su nacimiento* en Torquemada. Palencia: Ayuntamiento de Torquemada/ Diputación de Palencia.

Calderón, José Manuel. 2001. *Felipe el Hermoso*. Madrid: Espasa Calpe.

Castro Lorenzo, José de. 2007. *Don Antonio de Acuña y su época*. Valladolid: Diputación Provincial de Valladolid.

Chmel, Joseph (ed.). 1840. Reise des Erzherzogs Philipp nach Spanien. In *Die Handschriften der K. K. Hofbibliothek in Wien*, vol. 1. Vienna: Carl Gerold.

Colinas, Antonio. 2003. *Viaje a los Monasterios de España*. León: Edilesa.

Diago Hernando, Máximo. 2004. El papel de los corregidores en los conflictos políticos en las ciudades castellanas a comienzos del siglo XVI. In *En la España Medieval*, no. 27.

Dios, Salustiano de. 1982. *El Consejo Real de Castilla (1385–1522)*. Madrid: Centro de Estudios Constitucionales.

Foronda, François. 2005. S'emparer du roi: Un ritual d'intégration politique dans la Castille trastamare. In *Coups d'État à la fin du Moyen Âge?* ed. François Foronda, Jean-Philippe Genet, and José Manuel Nieto Soria. Madrid: Casa de Velázquez.

Fulin, Rinaldo (ed.). 1969–1970. *I diarii de Marino Sanuto, 1466–1536*. Bologna: Forni Editore.

García Oro, José. 1976. *Diego de Muros III y la Cultura Gallega del Siglo XV*. Vigo: Galaxia.

——. 1994. *Don Fernando de Andrade, Conde de Villalba (1477–1540)*. Xunta de Galicia.

——. 2002. *El Cardenal de España*. Barcelona: Ariel.

Gomaríz Marín, Antonio. 2006. Documentos de Juana I (1505–1510). In *Colección de Documentos para la Historia del Reino de Murcia*. Murcia: Real Academía Alfonso X el Sabio.

González Novalín, José Luis. 1981. Pedro Mártir de Anglería y sus "Triunviros" (1506–1522). *Hispania Sacra* 33 (67). Madrid: CSIC.

Haliczer, Stephen. 1981. *The Comuneros of Castile: The Forging of a Revolution (1475–1521)*. Madison and London: University of Wisconsin Press.

Ingham, Patricia Clare. 2003. From Kinship to Kingship: Mourning, Gender, and Anglo-Saxon Community. In *Grief and Gender, 700–1700*, ed. Jennifer C. Vaught. London and New York: Palgrave Macmillan.

Koslovsky, Craig. 2011. *Evening's Empire: A History of the Night in Early Modern Europe*. Cambridge: Cambridge University Press.

Lea, Henry Charles. 1906. *A History of the Inquisition in Spain*. London: Macmillan.

Lemaire de Belges, Jean. 1549. *La Couronne Margaritique*, ed. Antoine du Moulin Masconnais. Lyons: Jean de Tournes.

López de Toro, José (ed.). 1955–1957. *Petrus Martyr Anglerius. Epistolario*. CODOIN, 9–12. Madrid: Imprenta Góngora.

Lorenzo Arribas, Josemi. 2004. *Juana I de Castilla y Aragón (1479–1555)*. Madrid: Ediciones del Orto.

Maldonado, Juan. 1975. *La Revolución Comunera*, ed. Valentina Fernández Vargas. Madrid: Ediciones del Centro.

Mariana, Juan de. (ed.). 1853. *Historia General de España por el Padre Mariana*, vol. III. Madrid: Gaspar y Roig Editores.

Márquez Villanueva, Francisco. 1960. *Investigaciones sobre Juan Álvarez Gato*. Madrid: Anejos del Boletín de la Real Academía de la Historia.

Mattingly, Garrett. 1942. *Catherine of Aragon*. London: Jonathan Cape.

Millán Martínez, Juan Manuel. 2009. Villaescusa y los Ramírez en los siglos XV y XVI. In *Diego Ramírez de Villaescusa: obispo y mecenas*, ed. Juan Manuel Millán Martínez and Carlos Julián Martínez Soria. Cuenca: Universidad de Castilla-la Mancha.

Olivari, Michele. 1999. Hernando de Talavera i un tractat inèdit de Diego Ramírez de Villaescusa: Notes sobre un afer politicoreligiós entre el Quatrecents i el Cine-cents. *Manuscrits* 17, 39–56.

Penna, Mario (ed.). 1959. *Tratado de las Epístolas enviadas por Mosén Diego de Valera*. Madrid: Biblioteca de Autores Españoles.

Pratt, Karen. 2002. The Image of the Queen in Old French Literature. In *Queens and Queenship in Medieval Europe*, ed. Anne J. Duggan. Woodbridge: Boydell Press.

Prescott, William H. 1908. *History of the Reign of Ferdinand and Isabella the Catholic*, ed. John Foster Kirk. London: Swan Sonnenschein.

Rodríguez Villa, Antonio. 1874. *Bosquejo biográfico de la reina Doña Juana*. Madrid: Aribau.

Rumeu de Armas, Antonio. 1974. *Itinerario de los Reyes Católicos, 1474–1516*. Madrid: CSIC.

Saez Olivares, Alejandro. 2009. Patronazgo artístico de Diego Ramírez en el obispado de Málaga. In *Diego Ramírez de Villaescusa: obispo y mecenas*, ed. Juan Manuel Millán Martínez, and Carlos Julián Martínez Soria. Cuenca: Universidad de Castilla-La Mancha.

Santa Cruz, Alonso. 1951. *Crónica de los Reyes Católicos*, ed. Juan de Mata Carriazo. Seville: Escuela de Estudios Hispamo-Americanos de Sevilla.

Sitwell, Edith. 1946. *Fanfare for Elizabeth*. London: Macmillan.

Vale, Malcolm. 1996. A Burgundian Funeral Ceremony: Olivier de la Marche and the Obsequies of Adolf of Cleves, Lord of Ravenstein. *English Historical Review* 3: 920–938.

Varela, Javier. 1990. *La Muerte del Rey. El ceremonial funerario de la monarquía española (1500–1885)*. Madrid: Turner.

Williams, Patrick. 2013. *Katharine of Aragon: The Tragic Story of Henry VIII's First Unfortunate Wife*. Stroud: Amberley.

Zurita, Jerónimo. 1994. *Historia del Rey Don Hernando el Católico. De las empresas y ligas de Italia*, ed. Ángel Canellas López, Magdalena Canellas and Antonio J. López, vol. 4. Zaragoza: Gobierno de Aragón.

CHAPTER 9

# Entrapment (1507–1511)

## 9.1 Return of the King

We have seen the changes in Juana's political position through time. As princess she had begun to think about the kind of advisers she would like beside her as queen. But after Philip's highly controversial departure from Castile in 1502, governorship by Fernando seemed a more viable option than joint rule with Philip. After Philip's death, she saw Fernando either as future co-ruler, or as auxiliary. The fact that, by the end of 1506, she had seized the political initiative and begun to govern on her own account and that Maximilian, anxious to ensure Charles's succession, was talking of setting sail for Castile, prompted Fernando to leave Naples.

As earlier noted, monarchy in medieval and early modern Spain was invariably a partnership of some kind. This, in Earenfight's words, included "a repertoire of collective norms, institutional structures, and strategies for participation …".[1] But the problems posed to a reigning monarch by a father-king who had long ruled those same kingdoms are probably unique in European history. Juana saw Castile as hers. But her hesitations, and even the direction of her successes, reflect a perception in her own mind, and among much of the political elite, that she was, at best, the junior partner of the king of Aragon. In July and August 1507, she faced the unprecedented task of welcoming back to her shores a father who had discarded the royal title but not his regal ambitions, and whose future role was as yet undefined. According to Conchillos, she asked royal councillors Oropesa, Polanco and Mújica for advice on "how to proceed



G. B. Fleming, *Juana I*, Queenship and Power,
https://doi.org/10.1007/978-3-319-74347-9_9

in such cases." They replied that the decision was hers.[2] A document of 17 August states that Juana sent for various councillors and ordered them to inform nobles and prelates of Fernando's arrival and to set out to welcome him as "the king my lord and father of these kingdoms."[3]

In his *Glosa castellana al Regimiento de Príncipes*, a 'mirror of princes' with which Juana may have been familiar, García de Castrojeriz indicates that the title *padre del Reino* stresses a king's role as effective physician and guardian (*tutor*) of the land's "orphans." Valera's *Tratado de las Epístolas* offers a more muscular—and in this context, a more ominous—interpretation: a king, as *padre de la tierra*, is a good father who loves his children, but who also knows how to punish them, either with words or whips, and even, in a last resort, with death.[4] The role of kings as parents also emerges from Villaescusa's *Cuatro diálogos* (see Chapter 4), in which he urges Isabel to remember she is a mother, not a stepmother, and Juana may well have looked to her father's authority and experience to help her bring a remedy for her kingdoms. But her use of the title—if indeed the choice was hers and not the Council's—seems also to deliberately fudge the difference between Fernando as king of Aragon and king of Castile and between Fernando as guardian-king and co-king.

This was the moment at which a queen who subsequently showed her desire to engage with her kingdoms needed to signal publicly and clearly her intention to rule. It was evidently not easy. She was surrounded by fernandinos, who drew no distinction between the interests of daughter and father and, while her failure to bury Philip at Granada before Fernando's return had not prevented her taking a hand in government, it allowed her little margin for manoeuvre. Fernando had last seen Juana in 1504, when, as a rebellious daughter, her preoccupations as wife and mother had prevailed over her duties as princess. At this point, she seemed anxious to show, with an emphatic display of filial reverence, that she was again, above all, a king's daughter.[5] Laureola's comment in *Cárcel de Amor*—"It is better to die in obedience to [my father] than to live in his enmity"—comes inevitably to mind.

Yet it soon became apparent that Juana's obedience was not unconditional and that she hoped Fernando would respond to her great display of reverence by respecting her as more than a titular queen. Aram rightly notes that she struggled for a measure of royal authority within the prescribed role of filial submission.[6] But, rather than help negotiate the conditions of her own retirement, as Aram goes on to argue, the evidence demonstrates that Juana bitterly regretted the mistakes and hesitations that paved her way to Tordesillas.

On 20 July, Fernando and Germaine disembarked at Valencia. Fernando received Juana's emissaries, royal councillors Angulo, Zapata and Tello. On 11 August, he left Germaine in Valencia as lieutenant-general and advanced on Castile with an army of soldiers and officials. Alcocer associates his return with the end of the drought and greening of the land. Martire compares it to the sunrise, banishing Juana's reign of sorrow and lamentation. An anonymous Spanish chronicler actually inverts the situation of the two monarchs, comparing Juana to the visiting queen of Sheba and Fernando to the host king, Solomon, under whose male rule Castile would prosper.[7]

The same chronicler observes that, before leaving Hornillos, the queen ordered the singing of a *Te Deum*. It was doubtless sung with relief by the inhabitants of Hornillos, for whom Juana's sojourn had brought all the havoc traditionally associated with itinerant royal courts, and probably more, and at the end of July a royal investigator was asked to examine compensation claims for razed elm groves, slaughtered chickens, stripped orchards, wheat-fields, dovecotes, apiaries and vineyards.[8] The church, from which, or from parts of which, women had been banned, had also been badly burned in a fire caused by overheated wax.[9]

Juana set out for Tórtoles del Esgueva (Burgos) with her children and behind the bier. At Baltanás, she invited Juana of Aragon and the marchioness of Denia, who had been waiting there, to join her. She was reunited with Fernando on 29 August. By leaving her residence to greet him, she showed extreme respect. Fernando doffed his bonnet. Juana flung back her hood, revealing her white *tocas*, and threw herself at his feet. Fernando bowed so low that he had to kneel "and for a while they remained in one another's arms, and went hand in hand into the palace."[10] Juana "revealed her soul a little in those moments of joy. They conversed well into the night …".[11]

The only commentaries about the reunion derive from Fernando himself, from Almazán and from other sources sympathetic to Fernando. Zurita reports that Fernando emerged cheerful and pleased from a two-hour conversation, attended also by Cisneros, from which "it was understood that she wished to honour him in all things and was of greater judgment and intelligence than was published."[12] Fernando himself told Katherine that, after long discussion with Juana, he "had done whatever seemed requisite for the administration of justice, and for the peace and security of the kingdom, whereat the people were greatly rejoiced."[13] Martire observes that, despite having divested himself of the kingly title, he retained the rights of a monarch in their entirety.[14]

Such comments depict a serene, de facto transition of power. But no act of government confirmed them. There was no move to convoke a Cortes now, and no reference to unrest at Tórtoles. But, after Fernando's death, Juana's dueña, María de Ulloa, in a report to Cisneros, made a tantalisingly brief reference to such unrest. A witness had recalled to her "how, being in Tórtoles the day of the disturbances (*ruido*) some were crying 'Long live the queen!' and others 'Long live the cardinal [Cisneros]' and this with the king at the door …".[15]

The first crack in the façade of royal unity was Juana's insistence that the investiture of Cisneros as cardinal be held elsewhere than at the church of Santa María del Campo, then being prepared for the first anniversary of Philip's death. On 8 October, the court left for Arcos de la Llana, near Burgos, but Juana stubbornly refused to re-enter the city. Bitter memories apart, re-interment of Philip's body at Miraflores would have made a mockery of the cortege she had led into the Cerrato the previous December. As signs grew that Juana would not remain forever subservient, Fernando set about the gradual but systematic process of stripping away her regal attributes. Five stages can broadly be distinguished: the effective transfer of the Royal Council's allegiance to Fernando; the removal of key Castilian members of the queen's household and their dismissal, or absorption into, Fernando's entourage; the rejection of marriage suitors; the removal of the infante from his mother's guardianship; and, finally, her imprisonment at Tordesillas.

Aragonese officials filled key Castilian posts. Juana's Basque secretary, Lazárraga, retired, or was retired, and on 6 October was granted governance of the fortress of Alegría in Álava (Vizcaina).[16] Almazán and Conchillos, so scathing about Lazárraga's admiration for Juana, replaced him. Juana's signature no longer appeared on even mundane household orders and Fernando's angular signature replaced Juana's feathery one.[17]

Her *mayordomo mayor*, Cárdenas, asked Dr. Soto to back his departure on medical grounds but "did not dare" take leave of her in person.[18] Fernando had no intention of allowing another Castilian to replace him, as protocol demanded. Cárdenas therefore retained his title, while Fernando's Aragonese steward and ambassador, Ferrer, assumed effective control as *cerero mayor* (chief cirger). A special symbolic loss to Juana was her king-of-arms, Miguel Franco ('Granada'). Heralds were not only ceremonial tokens of the royal presence during celebrations, city entries and solemn occasions like the opening of a Cortes, but proclaimed the monarch's will and acted as diplomats and messengers. In November 1510, Fernando offered him to Maximilian and Margaret.[19]

A pay list for November 1507 shows Juana's household numbering about 120, although not all staff were necessarily present at one time or continued to serve her at all. An unusual predominance of armed units reflects security concerns.[20] But, in contrast to the number of ladies in Isabel's household in 1504, Juana had just two dueñas: María de Ulloa who, apart from her *asiento* as dueña, was paid separately as *camarera mayor*, and Beatriz de Mendoza, wife of Juana's master of horse, Diego de Castilla. Like the dismissal of Granada, the paucity of dueñas meant that Juana was not expected to appear in public. Staff lists for October 1508 and April 1509 refer to a handful of female servants of lower status.[21]

At the same time, suitors were discouraged. We cannot be sure if it was curiosity or apprehension (possibly both) that had motivated the queen to ask her half-sister whether Fernando was accompanied by Ferdinand, duke of Calabria.[22] But Philip's body was not yet buried; Maximilian opposed any move that might endanger Charles' claims on Castile and Fernando needed at all costs to avoid clashes with a newly empowered proprietary queen and son-in-law.

The most important suitor for Juana's hand was Henry VII, whose affection for Juana was real, according to his biographer, Chrimes.[23] Fernando used the notion of Juana's mental instability to resist Henry's overtures. In the vivid language characteristic both of the king of Aragon and his daughter, Fernando wrote that "to obtain anything from her requires great long detours, and even then scarcely anything can be obtained ... One can only approach her by degrees. I have done everything possible to persuade the queen ... to bury the body ... and have not succeeded; each time she tells me 'Not yet' ('*No aún*'). If it were done against her will, she would bring down the sky with her hands. It would utterly destroy her health."[24]

Henry thought Fernando an inveterate liar who held Juana prisoner against her will to "take everything from her." He recalled his favourable impression of her in 1506 and expressed bafflement at the un-Christian hint of necrophilia in Fernando's responses.[25] This owes much to the fact that at no point in the diplomatic exchanges between Henry and Fernando did the latter admit to the real bone of contention with Juana:

her determination to escort Philip's body to Granada. Juana wanted to fulfill her vow. But Fernando rejected the idea that Philip's body should lie beside Isabel's. Above all, he could not let Juana go south.

In the spring of 1508, Fernando made a gesture of 'friendship' by granting Henry's resident ambassador, John Stile, a rare audience with her. She was, however, non-committal. Henry brushed this aside as meaningless; Juana was a prisoner and had been rehearsed.[26] Regrettably, there are no details, but, at the time of Juana's imprisonment at Tordesillas, Stile attributes the failure to bury Philip's body to a cynical ploy. Philip's body went unburied "by cause that the peppyle maye derecte [detect] the les dyscreschyon [discretion] in the sayd qwyn, thys land now beynge perforce fully obedient unto the kynge of Aragon …".[27]

## 9.2 "Discretion" and "Natural Justice"

Fernando spent much on 'love.' But, as Rodríguez-Salgado observes, he would never again feel secure in the regency of Castile.[28] In the short term, he faced numerous problems. A new peace treaty between Maximilian and Henry VII committed the latter to help secure Charles' rights in Castile. Henry also granted the emperor a colossal injection of funds, which would help finance his proposed Roman coronation. But there was no guarantee that Maximilian might not invade Spain from Galicia if Fernando moved to subdue the rebellious south, and that Juana would not flee to Maximilian's side. Manrique had meanwhile thrown up defensive bulwarks at Nájera and refused to appear at court—tired, he said, of serving and unsure "under what law he had to live in these kingdoms and who was his *dueño*, if the queen his lady did not wish to be."[29] Eventually, faced with an army of infantrymen, cavalry and artillerymen and with the prospect of exile in Portugal, the old duke yielded all his fortresses but that of Nájera itself into Alba's hands. But the central tenet of his argument—that Fernando's interests were not necessarily the same as Juana's—persisted among the nobility.

As always, Juana was the mainspring of Fernando's problems. Her direct challenges became more frequent. She felt isolated and neglected at Arcos and her unhappiness may have trickled down to household servants. One of her *porteros*, Pedro de Tordesillas, was executed at Burgos in March 1508 for an alleged attempt on Fernando's life.[30] As the king of Aragon indulged in the court festivities that helped strengthen his grip on power, and which Henry VII did not fail acidly to note,[31] Juana became increasingly suspicious of her father's intentions. Fernando had stepped up security at Arcos and, in February, Venetian senator Sanuto copied into his diary an extract from a letter by an agent called Rossi: "The queen … has had certain words with the king; and this [arose] because she herself beat certain pages who were sleeping in her highness' antechamber, and she ordered that they be beaten for hardly any reason, and the king did not agree; and big words followed, in which she said: '*This kingdom is mine*,' etc."[32] The circumstances are unclear, but reminiscent of her reaction when, in Brussels, bowmen had guarded her door. Her "big words" suggest her fear and anger as she found herself again a captive, surrounded by guards.

News of these tensions reached other European courts. Some concerned Fernando's alliance with France. Stile wrote excitedly that, amid rumours that Fernando was committing troops to an invasion of the Low Countries, the grandees had risen in arms for Juana "because the queen had said she would not agree to troops leaving her kingdoms to fight her children's grandfather." Fernando had therefore secluded her.[33] After the queen of Aragon's arrival in Burgos that October, Juana received Germaine graciously.[34] But Germaine was pregnant and the French alliance, which Germaine embodied, added to Juana's concerns for her children.

Fernando was now the only conduit through which Juana could be approached. Early in 1508, Francesco Corner had come to Castile to negotiate a new alliance between Spain and Venice, but, like Querini, was embarrassed by his failure to meet the proprietary monarch, and felt unable to approach Germaine before he had paid his respects to Juana. When Corner mentioned his predicament to Fernando, he was told that Juana "had not been visited by any ambassador."[35]

Fernando proceeded with his plan to escort Juana to Tordesillas (Valladolid), urging her to meet him at Mahamud. But she had become extremely wary. Corner describes Juana setting out with her children, then turning back: "We'll go another day."[36] On 22 July, after waiting six days, Fernando returned angrily to Arcos, seized the infante and surrounded the house with troops. Later, he wrote Juana a mellifluous message: "God is witness to the regret that I feel in separating, Lady, from the place where you are, because there is nothing I like better than to be near you and to see you sometimes." But he had to travel south, for God would be most offended if he did not act to preserve "your justice." As for the infante, Arcos was unsuited to his health and she should not mind her aged father having the pleasure of "seeing [the infante] while I cannot see you. For you know there is no-one I love as I love you and those of my own blood."[37]

Fuensalida suspected Stile and his agents of stirring trouble: "It is not certain with whom [they deal], but they are continually quizzing the grandees, and asking who is who and what is their affinity, and [Stile] has written that you have taken the Infante away from the Queen, and that the Queen and grandees are unhappy…".[38] Fernando had a genuine love for the infante but, as Almazán noted, everyone "liked to see the descendants of the King and late Queen."[39] The infante's presence was particularly useful to Fernando on his forthcoming expedition to Andalucia, while Juana's enforced separation from her son, and her apparent desertion by Fernando, devastated her.[40] Ferrer describes the onset of what would become a nocturnal pattern of conduct, with an agitated queen repeatedly waking him with complaints, questions and demands to know the infante's whereabouts, to which Ferrer replied vaguely that he was well.[41] However, Juana had reason to worry. Letters from fray Ruíz and Dr. Parra, dating from long afterwards, reflect concern about the boy's persistent fevers.[42] Worst of all, his abduction confirmed that Fernando would not respect the queen's rights, either as guardian or sovereign.

With Arcos well guarded and the infante under his control, Fernando could focus on Andalucia, where Pedro Fernández de Córdoba y Pacheco, marquis of Priego, personified the hostility to the king of Aragon of many southern lords, knights and senior city officials.[43] The house of Aguilar, to which Priego belonged, had jurisdiction over a swathe of towns and territories and had long protected Córdoba's large, wealthy *converso* population. From this, in turn, the Aguilars drew support, submitting only reluctantly to the rule of the dual monarchy.[44] But they had contributed substantial funds to the conquest of Granada. The death in 1501 of Alonso Fernández de Córdoba, or Aguilar, elder brother of the Great Captain, Gonzalo, when fighting Moorish rebels in the Sierra Bermeja, featured in a new crop of ballads to rival those of the Granadan campaigns. One opened with the evocative lines:

*Rio Verde, Rio Verde*
*Tinto vas en sangre viva,*
*Entre tí y Sierra Bermeja*
*Murió gran caballería …*

Alonso's son, Pedro, who had fought gallantly beside him and had been severely wounded, was subsequently granted the office of *alcalde mayor* of Córdoba and marquisate of Priego, and was among the lords gathered at Tocina in November 1506. That October, he and the count of Cabra had seized the wands from the officials of Philip's absent *corregidor*, marched into the alcázar, where the tribunal of the Inquisition was based, and freed its prisoners, forcing Lucero to flee. In 1508, he was involved in a dispute between the *corregidor*'s men and servants of Juan Daza, bishop of Córdoba. Priego, close to Daza and prominent with him in the campaign against Lucero's abuses, challenged the authority of the court magistrate Fernando had sent to investigate on the grounds that Juana had not signed the warrant. The dispute ended with the arrest and momentary detention of the judge at Priego's castle of Montilla. Priego then drove him out of Córdoba.[45] He had, noted Corner, the backing of nobles across Andalucia.[46]

Fernando arrived in Andalucia in September 1508 with an army of thousands. Resistance was minimal and, at Niebla (Huelva), quickly crushed. Many of Priego's supporters and allies were flogged or executed. Priego himself was imprisoned at Trasierra, tried by royal councillors for high treason and sentenced to death. Fernando mixed *ira regia* with clemency, commuting the sentence to perpetual banishment, a heavy fine and deprivation of all royal offices. Priego's fortresses were demolished; even Montilla, ancestral home of the Aguilar clan, was razed. Priego had escaped death but his treatment rankled among the nobility, for whom the sacrifice of southern lords in the Sierra Bermeja was a recent and often personal memory. Resentments about the legitimacy of Fernando's position, particularly in the absence of a Cortes that sanctioned his authority, were re-ignited by the Royal Council's action in finding Priego guilty of lèse-majesté, or treason. Treason, they asked, against whom?

Fernando's response to such a question was to merge himself with Juana into a single, indivisible monarchical entity. But the duke of Nájera was not alone in repudiating the idea. The constable was a close friend of the Great Captain and also, by extension, of Priego. He was also a prospective son-in-law of the Great Captain, since, after the recent death of Juana of Aragon, he planned to marry his daughter, Elvira. To what extent these marriage plans—furiously opposed by the king of Aragon for reasons that need not concern us here—played a part in the deteriorating relations between Fernando and Velasco over Priego's punishment and the queen's ill treatment, is unclear. But, as we have seen, the constable had long opposed Fernando's disregard for Juana's rights. When Fernando reprimanded him for subordinating service to the crown to his own interests, Velasco's heated response was that to serve Fernando was a relatively small matter of discretion (*gracia*). To serve Juana, on the other hand, was a matter of natural justice (*razón natural*) and necessity (*premia*). To imply that he had fallen short of such service touched his honour so deeply that he felt minded to quit the kingdom "honestly," like a good soldier.[47]

The distinction that Velasco drew between service to the guardian-king and to the legitimate monarch shook Fernando at a time when a (territorial) dispute with yet another troublesome son-in-law, Manoel of Portugal, led the latter to question the "legitimacy of [Fernando's] right to the government of Castile."[48] As for Priego, Zurita is among various historians, then and since, to attribute his attitude to resentment that Fernando had not granted the southern lords anticipated favours.[49] Priego may also have underestimated the ruthless will to govern of a king whose actions were generally tempered by prudence. But his appeal against his punishment, couched in the discourse of lineage, honour and reputation and fired by a burning sense of what he thought right, again cannot be reduced to a mere defence of personal privilege or expression of petty ill-will. All his challenges—against Philip's lone rule; municipal abuse and inquisitorial persecution; Cisneros' illegalities and Fernando's usurpation—were carried out in the name of Juana I, whose pennant had been raised from the Tower of Lions of Córdoba's *alcazar* in 1504. In Priego's appeal of 1509, he argued that, as a representative of the crown, Fernando's conduct had confused him. When Juana and Philip had disembarked in 1506 he, as Córdoba's senior justice official, had lowered his wand of office in token of lawful obedience to the new monarchs. Yet, after Philip's death and Fernando's return to Castile, ostensibly ("*segun decián*") to console the queen, Fernando had started governing alone and appointing his own officials, "and, with all respect to his highness, I did not know, nor do I know yet, by what title and for what motive and reason he does so …".

In November 1506, Priego had opposed the Royal Council' s convocation of a Cortes as unlawful. Now he made another crucial legal point: Fernando had failed to demonstrate his right to govern. Juana was fully entitled to do so in her own right should she wish, and as she had done, "and if she has abandoned [the reins of government] because of indisposition, that is new to me; on the contrary, I have been informed that her highness is disposed to govern." Even if that were not the case, the fact that the matter concerned the governance of great realms and lordships meant that it was "only just and should and would be a reasonable thing" for himself and for the knights, grandees, cities and towns to join together as vassals and loyal servants of the queen to decide what should be done. But until the will and disposition of the queen were known, he was not obliged to obey the king of Aragon.[50]

## 9.3 To Tordesillas

In October 1508, Villaescusa, who had remained with Juana at Arcos, told Fernando that she had not washed or changed since the infante's departure. She slept and ate on the floor and her irregular meals meant that she often missed mass.[51] This was, as Aram indicates, a protest.[52] It may also have been a breakdown. Fernando's presence in the south without her, the loss of the infante and the gradual stripping away of her regal household had put an end to any illusion that she and Fernando might co-govern. Once again, she had lost control of her life and household—even of her musical consolation. In August 1508, Ferrer dismissed her treasured northern chapel. Apart from its high cost of maintenance, Fernando may have suspected that it supplied Juana with a channel of information to the Low Countries and Maximilian.[53] Anchieta lingered on, as did Alonso de Alva, whom Duggan describes as a "skilled contrapuntalist" and "one of Spain's best composers."[54] Still, the loss of her northern chapel was another blow.

Martire compares Fernando's attempts to dislodge her from Arcos by a mixture of reward and punishment to grappling with a "tall elm tree with roots stretching to the very centre of the earth." Fernando's own simile was more martial. It cost him more trouble, he told Corner, to move Juana than to "convey the whole of the artillery of the King of France, the Signoria of Venice and my own combined …".[55] It seems unlikely that he did not recall, at some point during the journey to Tordesillas, the laborious trans-Pyrenean journey that his father had made in 1462 when abandoning his own daughter, Blanca—"tremendous proprietary victim"—to the prisons of the Foix. Vicens Vives has described the event as "the blackest of all the acts that one can impute to Juan II."[56]

Whether Fernando had yet decided on Tordesillas as the definitive place of confinement for Juana is uncertain. As late as 7 February 1511, a warrant underwritten by secretary Juan Ruíz de Calcena ordered Villaescusa to prepare for a change of Juana's place of residence every six months, based on the recommendation of one of Fernando's officials, Francisco de Soria.[57] Nothing came of it, but the order's existence suggests that Fernando was still considering where or how best to maintain his daughter in security. At the time, Corner thought that Fernando might deposit Juana at the convent in Madrigal de las Altas Torres, where two illegitimate half-sisters (both called María) were enclosed as nuns. But "most people say they will go to Tordesillas *until his Highness feels the time is right for them to go on to Granada*" [my emphasis]. Since "without the body the Queen would not go," they would ride to Tordesillas by night behind the bier.[58] This implies that Fernando lured Juana there on the understanding that it was a temporary stop on the road to Granada.

The cortege set out on 14–15 February 1509. Crowds flocked from Burgos and elsewhere to see if the queen was still alive.[59] The constable and duke of Alba came to kiss hands before the procession wound its way through Villahoz, Villafruela and the Esgueva valley to Renedo. Here, between 24 February and 10 March, it halted while Fernando went to Valladolid to sign a new treaty with Maximilian. The emperor's recent reversals in Italy had brought about a radical shift in alliances and he now sought Fernando's help against Venice. The treaty of Cambray, of which Juana was probably kept unaware, reinforced Fernando's hold on Castile, formally accepting that Juana's "defects" granted him the right to rule through power of tutelage. It also confirmed Charles' right to the succession. When Fernando re-joined the cortege, it made a detour of Valladolid, travelling via Simancas, Geria and Matilla de los Caños. The exact day of arrival at Tordesillas is unspecified, but it was before 24 March.[60] Juana later recalled her stay at Renedo as the moment at which she should have made a last stand.[61]

Her imprisonment was doubtless facilitated by the customary seclusion of noble widows. The royal monastery of Santa Clara followed an austere regime of enclosure known as the Congregation of Santa Clara, and Ferrer later claimed that "during the seven or eight years in which I have been the governor of this royal household and court, it has, God be thanked, been governed like a monastery and order of most honest friars …".[62] While Philip's body was taken to the monastery Juana occupied rooms overlooking the Duero in the palace's eastern wing: "possessed as she is by Saturn," Martire writes, "resistant as she is to movement, she refused to leave … those exposed to the blizzards for those protected from the storms. She was moved neither by paternal blandishments nor by the threats he sometimes mixed with them. She refused to obey her father, whom, on other occasions, she respects, venerates and reverences…".[63]

Even imprisoned, Juana cast a shadow. Some even suspected, in the spring of 1509, that her imprisonment was linked to Germaine's pregnancy and a possible prelude to assassination: "The deliverance of the quwn of Arragon of child … ys ourely lo[kyd] for to be," writes Stile, "and of a swerty the qwyn of Castyl ys sore seke and yn grete jober[dy of] hyr lyf."[64] During a long conversation with Corner, in a "remote part" of the church of San Francisco, Valladolid, the Great Captain told him that Juana was "very ill and not expected to live many months more …". He added bitterly that the king, whom he came close to calling a usurper, had forced him to look on as his ancestral home was razed and as Fernando "acted against his very blood." The Great Captain, who felt utterly betrayed, had prepared ships and intended to offer his services to Venice.[65] But his plans were thwarted only days later by the defeat of Venice at Agnadello.

Fernando continued to reinforce his position. In December, the treaty of Blois followed that of Cambray, confirming him as governor in Juana's lifetime, or, should she die, until Charles reached the age of twenty-five. Fernando agreed to send the infante to Maximilian (a promise indefinitely delayed). He also agreed to allocate the huge sums owed to Juana from her marriage settlement, which Philip's will had requested that she receive, to the maintenance of her children's households in the Low Countries.[66] Juana's consent was not sought. In October 1510, a Cortes finally opened at Madrid with the aim of endorsing the treaty and confirming the succession. It was held in the presence of Habsburg representatives, such as Mercurino Gattinara and Claude de Silly. Cisneros and Ruffo were there. So were some of Fernando's most reliable allies, such as the duke of Alba and marquis of Denia, and at least two lords with whom Fernando had a troubled history: Priego and the Great Captain.[67] These attended, almost certainly, to witness the promulgation of Priego's pardon on 30 November 1510 and also, perhaps, because Priego had argued for a Cortes so forcefully.

It is not known whether Priego and his uncle were among the deputation of nobles, prelates and ambassadors that visited Tordesillas on 12 November, six days after her thirty-first birthday. Before agreeing to ratify the treaty of Blois some nobles may have urged Fernando to provide concrete evidence of Juana's incapability. This seems the only rational explanation for the visit. Fernando was careful to assure himself, with an initial lone visit, that her appearance bore witness to her indisposition. She was, writes Zurita, "disfigured" by melancholy and by her refusal, or inability, to eat or sleep. As the illustrious company burst into the room all were "*muy maravillados.*"[68]

Zurita argues that Fernando intended the "shame" of it to shock the queen into improving her habits of dress and conduct. "Greatly affronted," she tried to recoup prestige by demanding a female entourage which, freely chosen by herself, would have signalled her intention to act as monarch. Unhappy with the names Fernando suggested, she recommended others of greater "authority," such as Violante de Albión, who had accompanied Juana on her first voyage and managed her wardrobe, and Inés Manrique de Lara, countess Paredes. Inés was the widow of Juan Chacón, *adelantado* of Murcia, former *camarera mayor* of Isabel and later *aya* of Prince Philip. She was also the stepmother of the "mad" friend of Juana's youth, María Manrique Chacón. But Fernando did not accede to Juana's demands, as would have been logical if shock therapy were his real intent. Ulloa and Mendoza remained her only dueñas, while key staff continued to drain away.

Stile suspected that Juana would be imprisoned there "for the terme of hyr life." A tight knot of Aragonese servants surrounded her, while Villaescusa and Muros, were held at bay: "the bysschop of Malaga and the bysschop of Mondonedo … be there for a countenance, but they speke not wythe the qwyn, nor to any man except Monsen [Mosen] Ferrer."[69] Stile's claim was only partially true, for Villaescusa did manage to visit her now and again.[70] Nevertheless, Fernando's wish to distance him from Juana was, Villaescusa believed, linked directly to his attempts to "serve [her] with the same fidelity as before, and to see that she was well served and restored to health (*curada*)."[71] As in the case of Lazárraga, the granting of rewards and new positions was followed by alienation from the queen. In 1510, Villaescusa was elevated to the ranks of the lower nobility for the "great perils" he had endured while serving Juana at Philip's court.[72] On 12 August 1512, he was named inspector (*visitador*) of the university of Salamanca. And in 1514, his nomination to the presidency of the Chancery of Valladolid took him away from Juana's side for good.

## 9.4 "Mad Things"

The royal palace of Tordesillas, built by Enrique III, sat on the bluff rising over the Duero and was surrounded by precipitous walls of stone and earth. Enrique's son, Juan II, had been imprisoned there. Below the walls, the river flows widely through the town. Laurent Vital praised its delicious taste and trout and barbels. From the left bank, the plain stretches southward toward Medina del Campo. To the north lies Valladolid, and—to the west—Salamanca, Toro, Zamora and Portugal. A sketch by Anton van den Wyngaerde, dating between 1565 and 1570, shows Tordesillas from the south or left bank. The stone bridge has a central watchtower, where the river toll was paid, and there is a weir with water mills. Three of several extramural hermitages are marked: Santa Marina, San Cristóbal and the Christ of Battles. The townscape is dotted with towers and belfries. Toward the eastern end of the north bank, the great bulwark of the royal monastery of Santa Clara, to this day a Clarisan convent, looms over the river. West of Santa Clara is the palace, long since demolished—a two-storey building with a mirador overlooking the river. There was a plazuela on the riverfront—"a wide and beautiful space either to walk or gallop the horses in when they had been watered." Interior galleries surrounded two patios, one bigger than the other. At the eastern end was an orchard and kitchen garden, teeming with rabbits. Vital was surprised by the sheer height of the building.[73]

Various reports describe Juana's presence at Tordesillas as voluntary. Juana, writes Martire, in somewhat contradictory phrasing, was "secluded of her own accord and always will be while she lives."[74] Zurita thought Tordesillas well suited to someone who "abhorred the name of the kingdom as if it were death ...". But he adds that, by enclosing her in Tordesillas, "an infinite number of evils and scandals were miraculously avoided."[75] Maldonado made a similar comment, adding that Juana busied herself in domestic duties, educating Catalina and repeating funeral ceremonies for Philip.[76] Aram has more recently suggested that Juana (albeit with some reluctance) agreed to move to Tordesillas as long as she could take Philip's remains with her and dedicate herself to a spiritual life.[77]

The reality seems far more terrible. All the evidence points to a bitter war of attrition between Juana and her captors. Enraged by her imprisonment, she hungered for engagement with her kingdoms. But Almazán had already hinted that lone rule was preferable to joint rule (see Chapter 4) and, as Zalama indicates, Fernando could never have relied on Juana not taking a decision, either *motu proprio* or influenced by others, that could have toppled him from power.[78]

Her attitude emerges in many subsequent letters, and not least from an eight-page missive that Ferrer wrote to Fernando just months after that shocking November visit. This document, hitherto overlooked in most studies of Juana, grants a vivid insight into her life, thoughts and conduct in 1511, and provides invaluable clues to her attitude to her gaolers—Fernando included—and to the related problem of her spiritual practices.[79]

Ferrer described Juana's depressed state after a visit by Fernando had left questions important to her unresolved. For about ten days she stayed in bed. Her hair was uncombed and had lice. Later, she reversed her routine, staying up and dressed, "for everything she does is by extremes and laziness …". On the evening of Friday, 8 August, her Flemish servant, Cornelia, helped her wash before visiting Santa Clara. Going downstairs with Ferrer, she saw her dueña, Mendoza, in the patio, but Ulloa was absent and Juana wanted to know why. When Ferrer 'played the innocent' Juana turned to her master of horse, Diego de Castilla, who did likewise. She ordered a *montero* to go to Ulloa's posada. The *montero* replied, as evidently pre-agreed, that Ulloa was absent on business. This angered Juana. Ferrer intervened: persons with houses, children and lands must sometimes attend to their affairs.[80] Juana retorted that doña María went off daily without leave; doña María had more affairs than don Fernando and more still in the offing, while she (Juana), with only two dueñas, was now reduced to one.

When Juana returned, at around two a.m., she was still vexed that Fernando, though nearby, had not returned. She asked after his health and itinerary. She then:

> began so long a story … that I thought I would not get out of there alive; and this was that when the king her husband died in Burgos the grandees there were all minded to serve and obey her and daily urged her to deal with government matters … and that she, out of respect for your highness, and as an obedient daughter, had always intended to await your highness so that he would assist her and her children and kingdoms, and this, she said, I knew very well because I was always present … and still the archbishop [Cisneros] by which she means the cardinal, but never calls him cardinal, and the constable and the late lady doña María wanted to meddle in her affairs … and that when your highness came from Naples she [*aquella*]

expected, with your highness' favour, to govern all Castile, and that doña María de Ulloa, much under her influence, also intended to claim her part.[81]

Was the mysterious "doña María" that *aquella* who, not content with trying to govern Juana's household, dreamt of governing her kingdoms? Or was Juana, as Fernández Álvarez believes, referring to herself?[82] Language structure and context create ambiguity here. The probability that Juana was criticising someone else's ambitions, not expressing her own, does not, however, invalidate the fact that the queen felt thwarted in her expectations. As Gómez de Castro admits: "Sometimes [Juana] complained about being deprived of the reins of government and being shut in that prison."[83]

Juana exclaimed that she wished that she and her children "were all dead." Whether she had seen the infante again is unclear but she complained that both he and Catalina were being neglected. Returning to the events of 1506–1507, Juana regretted her hesitations about governing. She could have turned for help to Maximilian, about whom she said "a thousand good things," praising his "dignity," "lineage" and "valour." She wished she had acted more forcefully with the grandees. If they had accompanied her to Tordesillas, they could return now to free her. About this she said a "hundred thousand mad things."

Ferrer describes a woman imprisoned against her will, brooding over past events and her mistakes. As a queen who had lived with, defended, and perhaps at times abused her slaves, Juana spoke angrily in terms of slavery and emancipation, clearly resenting her subjection to overbearing parental power. She cursed her father and vented her spleen on those she saw enjoying the freedom and privileges denied to her. It seems that she had often retraced in her mind the road from Brussels to Burgos and from Burgos via Renedo to Tordesillas, pondering alternative scenarios.

Because of her imprisonment, she said, she had been unable to take control of her affairs, discharge her responsibilities and surround herself with "honourable women." Fernando had ceased to pursue the matter of the marriage settlement. He:

> treated her like a dog, and not like a daughter, nor like a slave, because even slaves were taken more account of, and she should have adopted the view that, the day they married her, her obligation to obey had ceased and … that she was freed (*que liberta era*), not least as regards her conscience and soul, because for years now she had not been able to confess or receive communion …[84]

This was, she said, Fernando's fault. It was he who had placed her in the company of the women who "obstructed" her and God would punish him for the evil he did her.

Juana clearly saw her freedom in terms of the ability to preside over an independent royal household and court. As she had told Villena toward the end of 1506, she had expected Fernando to help complete the process of re-forming her household. This, as the nucleus of a royal court, was a primary demand of future Cortes gatherings and politically crucial because, by this means, the queen would become accessible to her subjects, gain financial independence and honourable accompaniment. She could then intervene in Castile's affairs and in her children's and be free to perform her spiritual duties unmolested. This last problem would assume increasing significance over time.

"All her enmity," wrote Ferrer, "is focused on those serving her." These, in her Juana's view, were no more than guards, as Ferrer and Ulloa point out in their letters to Cisneros in 1516.[85] Juana had favoured Ulloa, but she resented her ability to lead a separate life. She was the queen's dueña but also the hard-working guardian of her own son. This gave Ulloa a measure of independence from Juana, while Juana remained dependent on Ulloa. Her absence without Juana's leave signalled that she was answerable not to Juana but to Fernando, Cisneros and the Velascos—those to whom she looked to defend her family's assets, estates and lineage.[86]

The queen did not know, that August night, where Ulloa had gone. But we do, and this may help us understand Juana's bitterness. On 22 July, Cisneros told secretary Diego López de Ayala: "I am determined, God willing, to be in Burgos for the eve of Our Lady of August, and as you wrote me that the old Countess [Villandrando] will be in the house of the Count of Salinas, and María de Ulloa will be there too, and the whole house will be full, I have agreed not to move my lodgings." In a letter of 13 August, on the same theme, he added: "and everyone will be fine there [in Burgos], and it has particularly pleased me that the lord Infante will be very well accommodated in the house of the Count of Salinas."[87] In other words, Ulloa could play hostess to Ferdinand while Juana remained locked up.

Her remarks about her female entourage made "your hair stand on end," writes Ferrer. She "said things about [Ulloa] that made you want to die from laughter." She mocked Ulloa's relatively low rank.

Ulloa carried her head as though "stuck on a spike," always tossing it. She never stopped talking. She was unbearably meddlesome. As for Mendoza, she was of high rank—granddaughter of the famous marquis of Santillán and daughter of the duke of Infantado—but stupid. It made Ferrer want to die from laughter to hear the queen casting around for enough adjectives to describe her stupidity. Catalina's *ama* was a shameless whore. The women who brought medicine for Catalina's cough were "*eslizeras.*" The word is obscure but not dissimilar from Ovid's "*strigas*"—supernatural beings who robbed cradles or drank children's blood while their nurses neglected them.

Juana's remarks reveal a cruel, colourful mixture of acidity, sarcasm, satire, disdain and imaginative verve. Characteristic of the queen, and of her facility with language, they reveal her all-consuming resentment with her isolation and lack of control over her life. She needed women, she said, more "suited to her estate." But these could only come when the others had gone, so that there would be no contamination. Ferrer warned Fernando that he had agreed to ask him to dismiss the women and "*restore her to freedom*" [my emphasis].

When Juana was in this agitated state, "complaining about your highness and talking big and threatening that [Fernando] has to do a thousand things," Ferrer found it best wait until the storm had blown over. That night, Juana ordered that her bed be made, and she ate. The next Saturday, she went again to Santa Clara and remained silent. Ferrer was trying, meanwhile, to ensure that the women did not spread news about Juana's unhappiness and "do not say or do anything more than I tell them." But, being women, and thus imprudent, this was difficult.

"These words of hers are very malicious," Ferrer concludes, but "have no foundation; everything is madness and raving." Today she was looking "very well and very humble." But the great heat of the last few days had made her irritable. She quarrelled with one of her servants, Anastasia, who was pregnant, and smacked her. He writes: "since she is not sane, she is nothing, and whatever she says or can do amounts to nothing." In a postscript, he adds: "it is close to midnight [and] they have come to tell me that the queen is already at the bottom of the stairs with her mantle and *capirote*, to leave for the church. And if she gives us these bad nights too often we shall lack the health to go on serving her."

Important as Ferrer's letter is for understanding Juana's state of mind in 1511, it also reveals much about Fernando and Ferrer himself, and the web of deceit they wove around the queen. Ferrer linked the degree of Juana's health and sanity to the degree of her humility and obedience, while casting himself in the role of assistant in a wider enterprise: "I played the innocent"; "she had me dead from being two hours on my knees"; "she is nothing," and so on. Fernando's tolerance of, and complicity with, servants who felt able to express themselves in this way—whatever his daughter's condition—is possibly the most surprising element of the letter. It is, quite simply, stunning.

Martire, who accompanied Fernando and Germaine when they visited Juana in January 1513, describes Fernando attempting to coax her from the rooms overlooking the river into the palace interior. Again, she refused. She would not wear furs; delayed food and drink for "extraordinary" lengths of time. Such behaviour, he adds, was unrelated to the antique idea of contempt for earthly empires and things, for she cared for bagatelles. Though unwell, "she lives more happily and with greater serenity" than those "tormented by the ambition to reign."[88] Yet Ferrer's letter shows a queen indeed tormented by that ambition.

Juana was not the only child of the Catholic Kings to display irregular eating habits.[89] But in Juana's case, the "extraordinary delays" in eating and drinking that Stile, Martire and Ferrer mention were hunger and thirst strikes with specific objectives. The queen, who sometimes spoke of killing herself, sought to enforce her will by the only means available to her—the infliction of harm on her own body. Her bouts of refusal to eat and drink were linked to an overwhelming sense of frustration at her own powerlessness.

Juana's situation as a sovereign queen confined within a prison-palace was virtually unique.[90] The degree to which her 'melancholic' symptoms resemble those of modern maximum-security prisoners deprived of sympathetic social contact, or held in long-term, small-group isolation, is discussed later. But Juana's objectives were clear and she could collect herself before the outside world. When expecting visitors or wishing to attend mass at Santa Clara, she washed, dressed and recovered her regal manner. In 1516, Ulloa told Cisneros that whenever Juana thought people were coming to see her she washed, dressed and put on shoes.[91] Ironically, this was the last thing Fernando wanted, and why, in November 1510, he took such care to ensure that Juana was not forewarned of the nobles, prelates and ambassadors who had demanded to visit her.

## Notes

1. Earenfight (2005), xvi.
2. RAH, Salazar, A-12, f. 167, to Almazán, 20 August 1507.
3. RAH, Salazar, A-12, f. 166, 'Órdenes de la Reina Juana,' 17 August 1507.
4. Nieto Soria (1988).
5. Martire (López de Toro, ed. 1955), 10, 365, 4 October 1507.
6. Aram (2005).
7. Alcocer (Gamero, ed. 1872); Martire, X, 363, 5 September 1507; BL, Additional Ms. 15568, 'Como el Rey Don Enrique fue alçado Rey de Castilla,' ff. 25, 26.
8. AGS, Cámara de Castilla-Pueblos 9, ff. 179–181.
9. Zalama (2003). During the obsequies for Duke Philip the Good, the windows of the nave and choir of the church of St Donat had to be broken to allow the heat from the wax to escape.
10. Zurita (Canellas López, ed. 1994), 4, 258–259.
11. Martire, 10, 363, 5 September 1507, 213.
12. Zurita, 4, 259.
13. CSP, Sp. 1, ed. Bergenroth, 554, November 1507.
14. Martire, 10, 363, 5 September 1507.
15. AGS, Estado 3, f. 113, 'Relación de María de Ulloa' [undated; February 1516].
16. Galíndez de Carvajal (Rafael Floranes Robles y Enzinas, ed. 1787).
17. Compare, for instance, Juana's order to her treasurer, Ochoa de Landa, of 20 December 1506 and Fernando's similar order to Ochoa de Landa of September 1507: AGR, CSR 14, f. 1 ('*Yo la Reyna*') and AGS, CSR 14, f. 2 ('*Yo el Rey*,' and, underneath, '*por mandato de su alteza*').
18. RAH, Salazar, A-12, f. 208, Ferrer to Fernando [undated].
19. Domínguez Casas (1993).
20. AGS, CRS 55, ff. 14–18, 'Oficiales de la casa de la Reyna,' 5 November 1507.
21. AGS, CRS, 14-4, ff. 182–187, 20 October 1508; AGS, CRS 14, f. 431–434, April 1509.
22. RAH, Salazar, A-12, f. 255, Conchillos to Almazán, 17 August 1507.
23. Chrimes (1999), 320.
24. Fuensalida (Berwick y Alba, ed. 1907), 18 April 1508, 437.
25. Fuensalida, 27 April 1508, 442–444.
26. Fuensalida, 18 April 1508.
27. Pollard (ed. 1914), III, 34, Stile to Henry VII, 26 April 1509. (Henry had died five days before).
28. Rodríguez-Salgado (Belenguer, ed. 2000), III.

29. Zurita, 4, 263–269.
30. Ladero Quesada (2016), 352n. The motives of this *portero*, who had shown heroism in rescuing Prince Juan from the flames at Santa Fé in 1491, are unclear.
31. Fuensalida, 26 July 1508, 469–472.
32. Sanuto (Fulin, ed. 1969–1970), 7, February 1508, 371.
33. Fuensalida, 21 March 1508, 480; 27 April 1508, 443.
34. Martire, 10, 368, 5 November 1507, 218; AGS, PR CC 4, f. 75, Juana's address to procurators, 1520.
35. Corner, 'Dispacci, Spagna,' BNM (Venice), IT. VII. 1108 (7448), f. 322, to Senate, 18 March 1508; f. 324v., 29 March 1508.
36. Corner, 'Dispacci,' f. 346v., 16 July 1508.
37. Rudolf (Sabadell González, ed. 2003), 51.
38. Fuensalida, 5 July 1508, 463.
39. Canestrini (ed. 1859–1868), II, 15 January 1514; 9 August 1508.
40. Zalama (2003); Zurita, 4. Álvaro de Osorio, the infante's chaplain, confirms Juana's protests (Rudolf).
41. RAH, Salazar, A-8, ff. 120–122, Ferrer to Fernando [undated; probably July 1508].
42. RAH, Salazar, A-13, f. 115, 13 May 1510, Ruíz to Almazán; Rudolf, 'Yo el Infante,' 51–52.
43. See Edwards (1982) for a detailed description of the situation in Córdoba.
44. Muñoz Vásquez (Ortíz Juárez/Salcedo Hierro, eds. 1983), 64–76.
45. Edwards (1976, 165–172; 1982).
46. Corner, 'Dispacci,' ff. 340–341, 28 June 1508; 343v., 6 July 1508.
47. Zurita, 4, 321–322.
48. Doussinague (1944), 158.
49. Zurita, 4.
50. '*Porque si la reina nuestra señora quiere administrar puede y ha podido hacerlo por si si quisiera, é si lo deja por indisposición de su persona, esto yo no lo sé, antes he sido informado que s. a. está en disposición de governar* ...' See Martínez Marina (1813), II, 161–163.
51. RAH, Salazar, A12, f. 262, to Fernando, 9 October 1508.
52. Aram (2005).
53. AGS, CSR 14, 3, f. 172, 'Lista de la capilla flamenca despedida,' August 1508.
54. Duggan (1976), 73–95.
55. Martire, 10, 410, 7 March 1509; Corner, 'Dispacci,' f. 363, 25 February 1508 [1509].
56. Vicens Vives (1953), 267.
57. RB, II/2205, f. 13, Cédula, 7 February 1511.
58. Corner, 'Dispacci,' f. 358v, 17 February 1508 [1509].

59. Zurita, 4.
60. Zalama (2010).
61. Z. ADP 787. 77, Ferrer to Fernando, 10 August 1511.
62. AGS, Estado 1-2, f. 298, 6 March 1516.
63. Martire, 10, 431, 24 October 1509.
64. Stile (Pollard, ed. 1914), 34, 26 April 1509, 150.
65. Corner, 'Dispacci,' f. 373, to Council of Ten, 1 May 1509. On 3 May Juan of Aragon was born, but died the same day.
66. Le Glay (ed. 1845), I, LXXXIII, 15 December 1509.
67. Carretero Zamora (1988).
68. Zurita, 5, 121–122.
69. Stile, 34, 26 April 1509.
70. In April 1510, Fernando thanked Villaescusa for letting him know about a conversation the bishop had with Juana about a visit by the prior of Miraflores. Fernando's request that he be kept informed of anything "of note" shows that Villaescusa was in at least occasional contact with Juana (RB II/2205, 12, Fernando to Villaescusa, 7 April 1510).
71. González Olmedo (ed. 1944), 'Instrucción,' 144.
72. González Olmedo, 'Carta de privilegio de hidalguía,' Tordesillas, 30 January 1510; Madrid, 27 February 1510.
73. Vital (Gachard, ed. 1881), III, 1-303; Martín González (1994).
74. Martire, XI, 516, 17 January 1513.
75. Zurita, 4, 356.
76. Maldonado (Fernández Vargas, ed. 1975).
77. Aram (2005, 2008).
78. Zalama (2003).
79. Z. ADP 787. 77, Ferrer to Fernando, 10 August 1511. This was transcribed in *Fuentes de Zurita* (1969), 60, 155–159. Fernández Álvarez cites some salient points in *La Cautiva de Tordesillas* (2006), although leaving much else unexamined.
80. In the summer of 1510, María de Ulloa and Marina de Villandrando were in arbitration over family "lawsuits and differences" (Urcelay Gaona 2009, 216 and 216n).
81. Z. ADP 787. 77, ff. 2v.–3.
82. Fernández Álvarez (2006).
83. Gómez de Castro (Oroz Reta, ed. 1984), 429.
84. Z. ADP 787. 77, ff. 4–4v.
85. AGS, Estado 1-2, f. 298, Ferrer to Cisneros, 6 March 1516; Estado 3, f. 113, Ulloa, 'Relación.'
86. See AGS, Estado 1-2, f. 287, 1516, re Ulloa's protests to Cisneros that various payments for her services to Juana had been suspended; Estado 4, f. 77, 1517, Charles's reinstatement of these payments.

87. Gayangos/de la Fuente (eds. 1867), Carta XXXI, 69; Carta XXXIV, 72.
88. Martire, 11, 516, 17 January 1513.
89. See Tremlett's biography of Katherine (2010). The eldest daughter, Isabel, seems also to have suffered from irregular eating habits.
90. Although the illnesses of the imprisoned queen of Scots would also be exacerbated by inactivity, stress and depression and she had an amethyst ring "*contra la melancholie*," her prison conditions are not strictly comparable. (See Guy 2004).
91. AGS, Estado 3, f. 113, February 1516, 'Relación.'

## References


Alcocer, Pedro. 1872. *Relaciones de algunas cosas que pasaron en estos reynos*, ed. A. Martín Gamero. Seville: Sociedad de Bibliófilos andaluces.

Aram, Bethany. 2005. *Juana the Mad: Sovereignty and Dynasty in Renaissance Europe*. Baltimore and London: John Hopkins University Press.

———. 2008. Queen Juana: Legend and History. In *Juana of Castile: History and Myth of the Mad Queen*, ed. María A. Gómez, Santiago Juan-Navarro and Phyllis Zatlin. Lewisburg: Bucknell University Press.

Bergenroth, G.A. (ed.). 1868. *Calendar of State Papers, Supplements to Vol. I and Vol. II of Letters, Despatches and State Papers Relating to Negotiations Between England and Spain, Preserved in the Archives of Simancas and Elsewhere*. London: Longmans, Green, Reader and Dyer.

Berwick y Alba (ed.). 1907. *Correspondencia de Gutierre Gómez de Fuensalida, embajador en Alemania, Flandes y Inglaterra (1496–1509)*. Madrid: Alemana.

Canestrini, Giuseppe (ed.). 1859–1868. *Négociations diplomatiques de la France avec la Toscane*. Paris: Imprimerie Royale.

Carretero Zamora, Juan Manuel. 1988. *Cortes, monarquía, ciudades: Las Cortes de Castilla a comienzos de la época moderna (1476–1515)*. Madrid. Siglo veintiuno de España Editores.

Chrimes, S.B. 1999. *Henry VII*. New Haven and London: Yale University Press.

Domínguez Casas, Rafael. 1993. *Arte y Etiqueta de los Reyes Católicos: Artistas, residencias, jardines y bosques*. Madrid: Alpuerto.

Doussinague, J.M. 1944. *La Política International de Fernando el Católico*. Madrid: Espasa Calpe.

Duggan, M.K. 1976. Queen Joanna and Her Musicians. *Musical Quarterly* 30: 73–95.

Earenfight, Theresa (ed.). 2005. *Queenship and Political Power in Medieval and Early Modern Spain*. Aldershot and Burlington: Ashgate.

Edwards, John. 1976. La révolte du Marquis de Priego à Cordoue en 1508. *Mélanges de la Casa de Velásquez*, vol. XII.

———. 1982. *Christian Córdoba: The City and Its Region in the Late Middle Ages*. Cambridge: Cambridge University Press.

Fernández Álvarez, Manuel. 2006. La Cautiva de Tordesillas. In *Doña Juana, Reina de Castilla*. Madrid and Barcelona: Fundación Rafael del Pino/Real Academía de la Historia/ Marcial Pons.

Fulin, Rinaldo (ed.). 1969–1970. *I diarii de Marino Sanuto, 1466–1536*. Bologna: Forni Editore.

Galíndez de Carvajal, Lorenzo. 1787. *Anales breves de los Reyes Católicos don Fernando y doña Isabel*, ed. Rafael Floranes Robles y Enzinas. Madrid.

Gayangos Pascual and Vicente de la Fuente (eds.). 1867. *Cartas del Cardenal Don Fray Francisco Jiménez de Cisneros dirigidas a Don Diego López de Ayala*. Madrid: Real Academía de la Historia.

Gómez de Castro, Alvar. 1984. *De las hazañas de Francisco Jiménez de Cisneros*, ed. José Oroz Reta. Madrid: Fundación Universitaria Española.

González Olmedo, S.I., Félix. 1944. *Diego Ramírez Villaescusa (1459–1537), fundador del Colegio de Cuenca y autor de los Cuatro Diálogos sobre la Muerte del Príncipe Don Juan*. Madrid: Editora Nacional.

Guy, John. 2004. *My Heart is My Own: The Life of Mary Queen of Scots*. London: Fourth Estate.

Ladero Quesada, Miguel-Ángel. 2016. *Los últimos años de Fernando el Católico, 1505–1517*. Madrid: Dykinson.

Le Glay, André Joseph Ghislain, ed. 1845. *Négociations diplomatiques entre la France et l'Autriche durant les trente premières années du XVIe siècle*, vols. I–II. Paris: Imprimerie Royale.

López de Toro, José (ed.). 1955–1957. *Petrus Mártyr Angelrius. Epistolario*. CODOIN, 9–12. Madrid: Imprenta Góngora.

Maldonado, Juan. 1975. *La Revolución Comunera*, ed. Valentina Fernández Vargas. Madrid: Ediciones del Centro.

Martín González, J.J. 1994. Tordesillas, un conglomerado social. In *Tordesillas 1994*. Madrid: Sociedad V Centenario del Tratado de Tordesillas, 1994/ Sociedad Editorial Electa España, 1994.

Martínez Marina, Francisco. 1813. *Teoría de las Cortes ó Grandes Juntas Nacionales de los Reinos de León y Castilla*. Madrid: Fermin Villalpando.

Muñoz Vásquez, Miguel. 1983. Córdoba durante el Reinado de los Reyes Católicos. In *Córdoba. Colonia romana, Corte de los Califas, Luz de Occidente*, ed. José-María Ortiz Juárez and Miguel Salcedo Hierro. León: Everest.

Nieto Soria, Juan Manuel. 1988. *Fundamentos ideológicos del Poder Real (siglos XIII–XVI)*. Madrid: Eudema.

Pollard, A.F. (ed.). 1914. *The Reign of Henry VII from Contemporary Sources, III*. London and New York: Longmans, Green.

Rodríguez-Salgado, María José. 2000. La Granada, el León, el Águila y la Rosa. In *De la unión de coronas al Imperio de Carlos V*, vol. III, ed. Ernest

Belenguer Cebriá. Barcelona: Sociedad Estatal para la conmemoración de los centenaries de Felipe II y Carlos V.

Rudolf, Karl Friedrich. 2003. Yo, El Infante – Fernando, "Prinz in Hispanien". In *Fernando I. Un infante español emperador*, ed. Nuria Sabadell González. Valladolid: Universidad de Valladolid.

Tremlett, Giles. 2010. *Catherine of Aragon: Henry's Spanish Queen*. London: Faber and Faber.

Urcelay Gaona, Hegoi. 2009. *Los Sarmiento, Condes de Salinas: Orígenes y Elevación de una Nueva Clase Señorial, Siglos XII–XVI*. Bilbao/Zarautz: Universidad del País Vasco/Euskal Herido Unibertsitatea.

Vicens Vives, Jaime. 1953. *Juan II de Aragón (1398–1479). Monarquía y Revolución en la España del Siglo XV*. Barcelona: Editorial Teide.

Vital, Laurent. 1881. Premier Voyage de Charles-Quint en Espagne de 1517 à 1518. In *Collection des voyages des souverains des Pays-Bas*, vol. III, ed. Louis-Prosper Gachard. Brussels: Commission Royale d'Histoire.

Zalama, Miguel-Ángel. 2003. *Vida cotidiana y Arte en el Palacio de la Reina Juana I en Tordesillas*. Valladolid: Universidad de Valladolid.

Zalama, Miguel Ángel. 2010. *Juana I. Arte, Poder y Cultura en torno a una reina que no gobernó*. Madrid: CEEH.

Zurita, Jerónimo. 1994–1996. *Historia del Rey Don Hernando el Católico. De las empresas y ligas de Italia, 4 and 5*, ed. Ángel Canellas López, Magdalena Canellas, and Antonio J. López. Zaragoza: Gobierno de Aragón.

CHAPTER 10

# Coup (1516–1519)

## 10.1 The Death of Fernando of Aragon

Although Fernando couched his authority in fatherly terms of protection and guardianship, the absence at his side of the lawful monarch, in whose name many acts of government were still issued, confused channels of communication, tainted the legitimacy of his government and sharpened dissent. Cisneros' later letters to Brussels highlight Fernando's controversial appointments of *corregidores* to important cities like Toledo and Valladolid as one of the most destructive aspects of his rule.[1]

On the other hand, the years between 1509 and 1512 marked the peak of his international and military success. The treaty of Blois reinforced his position. Spanish victories followed in north Africa. Aragonese power was consolidated in Naples. Navarre, annexed in 1512, was incorporated into the crown of Castile in 1515. Fernando boasted to Maximilian that the "crown of Spain" had not been as great or powerful in 700 years, and "all, after God, through my own agency and labour."[2] A long-cherished belief in his divine mission, further fuelled by the prophecies of María de Santo Domingo, the young *beata* de Piedrahita whom Cisneros had brought to Burgos in 1508, helped drive his political ambitions. In 1516, he reminded his Dominican confessor, Juana's former confessor, Tomás de Matienzo, that he could not die before he had conquered Jerusalem.[3]

Fernando fought off declining health with hunting and falconry, but lost his merry look.[4] The long-desired son eluded him. In his wills of



G. B. Fleming, *Juana I*, Queenship and Power,
https://doi.org/10.1007/978-3-319-74347-9_10

1512 and 1515 he conferred Castile's governance on the infante. He was haunted by the thought of Charles, who had become sovereign of the Low Countries in 1515. Although Charles stood also to inherit Maximilian's possessions in Austria, Tyrol and parts of Germany, and would be a candidate for the imperial crown, the Trastámara legacy proved as irresistible to him as to Philip.

In January 1516, on the road to Guadalupe, Fernando was forced to stop at Madrigalejo (Cáceres). Charles's envoy, Adrian Florizoon Boeyens of Utrecht, bishop of Tortosa, who had arrived as his ambassador, and who has been described as pursuing Fernando through Extremadura like the spectre of death, was sent away, but later recalled.[5] The dying king dictated his last will. Royal councillors persuaded him to drop his plan to make the twelve-year-old infante governor. And doña Juana, whom Fernando had not seen since 1513 was, they reminded him, still alive. Once again they conjured the spectacle of civil war—one that would pit Charles and Ferdinand against one other, and either or both against the queen. Fernando yielded, on the verge of tears. Could the infante not have the revenues from the military orders? But this too was controversial. "He will be very poor then," he said. When Cisneros was proposed as interim governor, "it did not seem that the King had taken the nomination well and he said quickly, 'You know his condition,' and for a moment there was silence, but no one replied."[6]

Fernando's death on 23 January turned Juana into the first (and last) sovereign queen of Aragon. But her nomination was purely formal: "according to everything we have, in our life, been able to know of her," reads the will, "she is very separated from the governing and administering of kingdoms, nor is disposed to do so." He left temporary governorship of Aragon to her half-brother, Alonso of Aragon, archbishop of Zaragoza.[7] Fernando's body, in a Dominican habit, was escorted to Granada, where it joined Isabel's in the church of San Francisco in the Alhambra. Throughout the journey, obsequies were held and in Córdoba the marquis of Priego and count of Cabra took part.

Fernando felt cheated, to quote Elliott, "by a malignant fate which had placed his masterwork in the hands of alien descendants."[8] It was, however, a fate Fernando himself had helped shape. During her brief effective reign Juana had helped stabilise royal administration and smoothed the path for his return and Villaescusa was not the only member, or former member, of the queen's household to regard her restoration to health as a matter of political will. In 1516, the Royal Council itself expressed doubt over the extent and permanence of Juana's incapability.

Cisneros knew that Juana mattered to Castile and acted to stifle dissent within the infante's and queen's households and elsewhere. The infante was moved to Madrid and thereafter to Aranda de Duero. He was placed under strict surveillance and changes made to his household. In order to impose them Charles resorted to the argument, formerly used both by Philip and Fernando, that Juana's and his sovereign interests were indistinguishable and that conspiracy against himself and the queen would not be tolerated.[9] He replaced key officials with Lachaulx and Guevara. These, ironically, were the very same men who had tried to seize control of the infante on the day of Philip's death.

As for Juana, both Cisneros and Adrian, with whom the cardinal had now to work, feared that Juana might be stirred into action by Fernando's death. An information blackout was imposed on Tordesillas and grandees and soldiers had to obtain a special licence to enter town.[10] On 30 April, the bishop of Catania wrote from Brussels that Charles' priority was "the custody of the Queen which, on account of the diversity of opinions, is very necessary …". She was to be treated well but guarded and watched with great vigilance.[11] At first, Charles did not seem aware of the news blackout and, on 16 February, sent his mother commiserations on Fernando's death. Cisneros and Adrian blocked the letter.[12] Meanwhile, the *corregidor* and council of Tordesillas, in alliance with Diego de Castilla, Juana's master of horse, planned to seize the queen. But when halbardiers rushed the stairs, *monteros* blocked the way.

Sensitive to the commotion, Juana winkled the truth about Fernando's death out of her Franciscan confessor, Fray Juan de Ávila. She demanded to see Cisneros. She asked the whereabouts of the grandees and who among them had attended Fernando. Ulloa embarked on a damage-limitation exercise. She told the cardinal that Fernando's miraculous recovery had been conveyed to the queen, and that staff had been ordered not to approach her. She also alluded to fears that the cardinal, "who loved [the queen] so little," would want to "tether her" and move her to a fortress.[13] Some believed she was possessed. In late February, a deputation from Tordesillas begged Cisneros and other prelates and nobles to permit them to embark upon a three-month cure. Stile names Dr. Soto as being among those who undertook to cure the queen for the "honour, comfort and weal" of all her lands:

> these sayd persons have browzghte testymonyalys and wryteyngys that there be serten persons, prystes, fesecyons, and other, amongys the which one ys the Doctwr Sotto, the sayd Qwyns fesecyon, the whyche he and the other prystys, with clergy and fesyke, apon payne of theyr lyvys, havey-ing licence, wyl undertake for to remedy the Qwyn of hyr dyseas wythyn the space of thre monthys, seyeing that sche ys cumberyd with spretys by wycchecrafte.[14]

The response is unknown, but Juana's master of horse, Diego de Castilla, and his allies, took matters into their own hands. They summoned a "sorcerer," who, surrounded by *monteros*, and stationed out of earshot and sight of Juana, chanted "spells."[15]

Villaescusa, unlikely to have approved of these methods, hoped that Juana would fare better with her son than her father. In his *Instrucción*—a briefing addressed to his nephew, about to seek patronage at Charles' court, but written mainly for Charles' benefit—the bishop and Chancery president described Juana as weak and ill, unable to govern or give counsel. But he tried to exploit the old argument of indivisibility of interests in her favour:

> as I consider that the queen's affairs … and his are one and the same, he should know that the queen … has been badly served and not well treated, that his highness must order that her health requires that she be well served and treated …[16]

Ulloa meanwhile advised Cisneros to dismiss Ferrer: "by the life of my children, if he stays, our lordship will see a thousand revolts and vexations."[17] In his letter to Cisneros of 6 March 1516, in which Ferrer seeks to defend his conduct, the derisive tone he had adopted in letters to Fernando is absent. Ferrer begged the cardinal to honour and reward him; he had only obeyed orders. Cisneros knew that Juana was incurable and if they had given her "the rope"—a reference to forcible feeding—it was to save her life.[18]

Cisneros' dislike of Juana must account for the fact that, while governing in her name, he did not visit her once between January 1516 and his death in October 1517. He did, however, send Rodríguez Sánchez de Mercado, bishop of Mallorca, to inspect conditions at Tordesillas, and replaced Ferrer with Hernán Duque de Estrada, Prince Juan's former steward and a former ambassador. As Charles pondered whether to replace him with a governor of his own, Cisneros' emissary in Brussels,

López de Ayala, argued that Duque's appointment had been good for Juana's health; she had been seen in public, in suitably royal garments, and was communicating with people.[19] But this, he later realised, was precisely the wrong argument: "Thinking to render a service to Hernán Duque, I am now ruining him. For according to what I see they speak here *proeter formam* of her health, and that not because they wish for it. They are very dangerous people, and one must hold one's tongue here."[20]

## 10.2 Prince or King?

Isabel's will, successive gatherings of the Cortes and the treaties of Cambray and Blois had granted Charles the crown only *after* Juana's death. But Charles knew that his chance of inheriting the imperial mantle would be greatly enhanced as king. Juana might live for years and, as mere prince, his position seemed vulnerable. Maximilian appealed to the imperial estates to support Charles' claim to the kingship and, after much debate, they agreed that Charles and Juana should share the royal title.

In a letter of 4 March the Royal Council argued that the decision was unlawful, gratuitous and rash. It was not Fernando's death, but Juana's, that determined Charles' rights. By seizing the crown Charles risked undermining the "honour and reverence that divine and human law owes to the queen our lady, your mother …". In fact he risked splitting the monarchy apart. He had to remember that Juana was "not born wholly incapacitated" ("*no nació impedida del todo*"). In other words, her ill-health was not necessarily irreversible. "For the love of God," they urged Charles, "and the honour a son owes a mother it would be well to leave her the title in its entirety …".[21]

The Council's warning is crucial for understanding the depth of the shadow that Juana cast over her kingdoms. But it was ignored in Brussels. On the night of 14 March 1516, the holy hill of St Gudula blazed with light as Charles threw off his black mourning mantle and hood and grasped the sword of justice from the bishop of Badajóz. The church resounded with the cry, "Long live the Catholic Kings!"[22]

Faced with a fait accompli, Cisneros laboured to enforce Spanish compliance. He and Carvajal scrambled to re-assemble arguments that, shortly before, they had picked to pieces. Ironically, they resorted to precedents once used by Isabel's advisers to back the female right to govern. Some sons, they argued, had ruled by consent in their mother's lifetime, as in the case of Berenguela, who had been acclaimed sovereign ruler by the Cortes of Valladolid of 1217, but immediately conferred the royal title on her son, Fernando III.[23] Others had taken the crown owing to their mother's "unfitness" ("*defecto*"), as in the case of Alfonso VII, son of Urraca I. Charles had, moreover, been obliged to bow to imperial and papal persuasion. Even if Juana were in full possession of her faculties, "the extension of our empire, its size and multitude of regions … are such that you would find yourselves obliged to deliberate, and to doubt, whether the resolution of such great problems could be confided to any woman, however capable."[24]

The Council's reference to the "unfitness" of Urraca I, (r. 1109–1126), provides a clue as to how 'defects' in female rulers were understood. Both Juana and Urraca had stormy marital relations, widely described in purely personal terms but characterised in reality by profound political conflict. Urraca struggled to retain control of her patrimony against an Aragonese husband who, in the belief that his marriage entitled him to claim them, laid waste to swathes of her kingdoms and at one point imprisoned her. Supporters of her son, Alfonso, argued that Urraca's sex, female instability and caprice prevented her from being able to protect her kingdoms from the Moors and designs and depredations of her husband. She was criticised for her sexual conduct (extramarital affairs rather than the *rage d'amours* attributed to Juana). Clerics and chroniclers saw Urraca as a Jezebel, ruling with the reins of female tyranny (*tirannice et mulierbriter*), fomenting civil war. Her reign was seen as accidental, anomalous, sulphurously marked by determination to rule without regard for her son's rights. In recent years Urraca's reign has been sympathetically re-examined.[25] In 1516, however, few disputed the use of Urraca as a warning to opponents of Charles' seizure of the kingly titles. This, Pérez has argued, was an "authentic coup d'état."[26]

Aside from the specific reasons for the attempt to justify the "coup," it may more generally be seen as a symptom of that complex process of substituting new dynasties for old to which Peters has referred, and in which "the traditional sense of dynastic legitimacy could only be overcome by the … attribution to the old dynasty of a quality of powerlessness or incompetence which rendered its individual members unfit to rule."[27] It was no easy matter, however, to overcome that "traditional sense of dynastic legitimacy" and many resented the proclamation of Charles as king. Juana might have lost her most powerful ally among the nobility in

1512, with the sudden death, in disputed circumstances, of Bernardino Fernández de Velasco, constable of Castile, but both the admiral and duke of Alba disliked the view that the kingdom's fundamental laws should be changed and its rights violated because of the dramatic growth in Spain's empire. It would, they argued, set a bad precedent for a new ruler to annul laws long recognised as sacrosanct.[28] Elsewhere, Enríquez expressed his opposition more vividly: to concede the title to Charles was to declare "the living queen dead."[29] His words closely resemble those later used by Bartholomé Leonardo de Argensola—poet, chronicler and chaplain to Juana's granddaughter, María. Argensola—who shows some sympathy for Juana, and who continued Zurita's history where it ended in 1516. He reports Charles' advisers as saying that "owing to the duration of her impediment the Queen … should be counted for dead and that it was a good thing that, by resorting to the use of the title of King, so pious and obedient a son should be freed from having to await his Mother's death …".[30]

Cisneros called a meeting at the house of Madrid's *corregidor* to explain Charles' position. When this got heated, he ordered Pedro Laso de Castilla to raise the standards for Charles at once.[31] A similar order to all Castilian cities laid stress on the scale of international support for Charles and his deep filial reverence and care for Juana.[32] Thus, where Juana's filial reverence had led to her downfall, that same supposed reverence in Charles was used to back him as ruler and king. In a later letter to the comunero junta of Tordesillas, Enríquez described his surprise:

> When the letters came in which the king called himself king and the grandees were called to Madrid to discuss [the matter], the platforms had been erected, the trumpets were at the door … and I thought, what a strange novelty! Such a thing should not be done without thought and without the whole kingdom being informed. I resisted until there was no grandee or city left that did not call him king, and, in that realisation, I took the same path, but not post-haste … and they wrote from Flanders to complain …[33]

An authoritarian but ailing Cisneros struggled in wobbly tandem with Adrian, his position undermined on two fronts. Cisneros' relations with the Royal Council were never good and his authority was further weakened by a Brussels-based administration, which included a number of Aragonese officials hostile to the cardinal. His defence of crown authority against both Castilian nobles and the intrigues of Charles' court has often been praised. But this begs the question as to the source of that crown authority. Indeed, his attempt, in 1506, to override the rights and desires of the legitimate monarch and convoke a Cortes against her will set a precedent for independent action by the cities, and this they would recall when, a decade later, he tried to stifle constitutional debate. Meanwhile, in Stile's words, nobles, prelates and lawyers could "in no wyse" agree that:

> the Prynce shuld be proclamyd Kyng, the Quwn hys moder beyng alyve, onles that the Prynce were her[e] personally. And the astatys here have and do take grete dysplesure and dysdayne that the Flemyngs have proclaymeyd thayr prynce Kyng of Castyl with oute the asent of the astatys of Castyl ...[34]

If Aragon, famously intractable, would not bend the knee, Castile showed great reluctance to do so. Like Enríquez, Priego noted the lack of consultation: "In my view ... the grandees should have been informed [beforehand] ...".[35] Sandoval observes that: "While everyone complied, their hearts did not."[36] Several cities were slow to hold the ceremonies of proclamation. The *ayuntamiento* of Jerez de la Frontera complained that, while its officers had obeyed the orders from the governors, Royal Council and Chancery of Granada, they had received none from Juana.[37] Standards were only raised in Zamora on 18 May after much pressure from Cisneros and its *corregidor*.[38]

Cisneros' attempt to raise a standing army, the *Gente de Ordenanza*, to suppress political and economic unrest, met with failure and, as Pérez observes, led to the accumulation of weapons in the local *ayuntamientos* and would facilitate recourse to weaponry by former *Ordenanza* captains, soldiers and city officials during the comunero uprising.[39] Meanwhile, the cardinal faced a serious rising in Málaga against the fiscal policies of the admiral, whose jurisdiction had been extended there by Fernando and Isabel. Enríquez' gallows were dismantled and the city briefly declared autonomous.

Charles' proclamation as king, without the agreement of the estates and in the teeth of resistance, could not long be sustained in his continuing absence. That July, expecting his arrival imminent, the *corregidor* of Valladolid ordered that facades and windows be plastered and whitewashed and stone pillars replace the wooden posts around the plaza.[40] At the same time, memories of Philip's rapacious entourage and *Landsknechten* were still fresh, and a secretary of Cisneros reported that even children were threatening to send the "Flemings" to the devil.[41]

As Royal Chancery president, Villaescusa repeatedly warned Cisneros, Chièvres and Charles about "scandalous" sermons by Franciscan friars and demands that Juana be brought there from Tordesillas.[42] The unlawful imprisonment of the legitimate monarch was the common cause around which agitation revolved. As a historian of the comunero uprising has pointed out: "Many cities, although convinced by Cisneros that they must accept the new monarch, continued to consider Juana the legitimate sovereign."[43]

Cisneros warned Charles that the cities were tinder-dry. Their "juntas" could not be stopped and there was unrest everywhere.[44] Disturbances, often building on long-standing resentments, broke out in Toledo, Guadalupe and Burgos. In Seville, there was "division and tumult."[45] In Baza (Granada), a group of *conversos* warned Cisneros that the whole kingdom could ignite "as some of us, from experience, have seen in past times."[46] Former royal cities like Huéscar (granted by Fernando to the duke of Alba) and Arévalo (granted by Charles to that "turbulent woman," Germaine[47]), took the chance to throw off lordly control. A *morisco* from Baza described an action led by Juana's first *mayordomo mayor*, who had sailed with her to the Low Countries: "Last Friday … don Rodrigo Manrique, *comendador* of Yeste, entered Huesca [Huéscar] at midnight with twenty-five cavalrymen and twenty five infantrymen … crying 'The Queen! Liberty!' They went to the fortress, or rather, fort, and took it and with ropes threw the fortress governor out of the window … and another day ordered the arming of all the *moriscos* …".[48] On 18 February, the chief justice officer of Baeza (Jaén), licentiate Francisco Cano, warned Cisneros about constant "*diversydad y quistyones*" and urged him to investigate whether the queen should not be "better served," and temporary reinforcements sent to Baeza.[49] Cisneros' secretary, Diego López de Ayala, describes a dispute over the priorate of the military order of San Juan (Toledo), in which Brussels supported the candidacy of Antonio de Zúñiga, brother of the duke of Bejar, and Rhodes—seat of the Order of St John—supported Diego de Toledo, son of the duke of Alba. Ayala told Cisneros: "everyone is up in arms about it, and all these places clamour for the Queen."[50] In June 1516, in a throw-back to the times of Juan II and Enrique IV, a group of nobles, including the admiral and new constable of Castile, the count of Benavente and the dukes of Infantado and Albuquerque, met at Pedraza (Segovia), reportedly to conspire to overthrow Cisneros, seize control of the queen and set up a new government with Juana beside them.[51] Exactly a year later, representatives from Burgos, Valladolid, León and Zamora met to consider the potentially revolutionary move of themselves convoking a Cortes to debate the position the kingdom should take in the continuing absence of a king who had so far shown no urgency in fulfilling his contractual obligations.

Although the realms of Aragon are not the focus of this book, the tumult in Sicily, sometimes called 'the second Vespers,' should be given a brief mention. On 6 March 1516, an uprising in Palermo forced the viceroy, Hugo de Moncada, supporter of Fernando's controversial fiscal and religious policies, to flee to Messina—like Burgos, a mercantile city with Flemish links. There, Moncada was further isolated by the refusal of Naples' viceroy, Ramón Folc de Cardona, to accept Charles's "coronation." Standards in Palermo and much of Sicily were raised only for Juana, and a new, Palermo-based 'princes' parliament,' led by the marquis of Geraci and marquis of Licodia, claimed to represent all Sicily in Juana's name.[52] Having ousted the viceroy, they declared loyalty to her "under whom all aspire to live and die."[53] Dissent, caution and confusion with respect to the true locus of royal authority emerge from the correspondence coming out of Naples and Sicily. Whether or to what extent high officials and juanista nobles were aware of Juana's true situation remains unclear. But they chose to address her as the *live* legitimate sovereign who heard complaints, pored over despatches and intervened directly in Sicilian affairs.

It was against this simmering background that Charles finally, and importantly, obtained pope Leo X's endorsement as 'Catholic King.' Leo's bull of 1 April 1517 (*Pacificus et aeternus rex*) snubbed Juana by awarding Charles (*Carolus Hispaniarum rex*), and his posterity, the right to inherit the title of 'Catholic' from his maternal grandparents, while skipping any reference to the lawful queen.[54] That same year, Adrian was appointed a cardinal—partly, perhaps, to strengthen his authority as Charles' adviser.

Charles followed this political coup with a monetary one. Coins minted to raise funds for his journey to Spain were designed to promote and reinforce his kingship and bore the legend: "JOANNA ET KAROLUS D[EO] G[RATIA] RE." Simultaneously, however, the single crown over two initials, which had symbolised the extension of Isabel's authority to her husband, was replaced with two crowns over two initials, reinforcing Charles' personal claim.[55]

## 10.3 Mother and Son

Juana had long suspected Fernando's death. But it was forcefully denied. She was kept unaware of Charles' proclamation as king, although both Argensola and Sandoval report occasional slips of the tongue in her presence and Juana's emphatic rebuke that she alone was the monarch. "She felt it deeply," Argensola remarks, "but not as someone who is irrational but with clear awareness."[56]

Juana had not seen her 'Flemish' children for over a decade and then only fitfully and in trying circumstances. Margaret of Austria's guardianship of Eleanor, Charles, Isabeau and Mary at her cultivated humanist court of Mechelen is celebrated in a beautiful woodcut from Maximilian's *Weiß Kunig* in which she and they stand before the emperor and his jester. Their mother tongue was French and the court in which they grew up was wholly Burgundian.[57] Juana had, in former times, been keen to ensure that Charles had Spanish servants and tutors, but, although he received early lessons in Spanish and Dutch, his grasp of both languages remained poor. When he was nine, Guillaume de Croÿ-Chièvres, a former governor of the Low Countries, was appointed his tutor and Charles became as reliant upon him as Philip had formerly relied upon Busleyden and Manuel. In 1512, Adrian of Utrecht took responsibility for his education and became his spiritual adviser.

As Rodríguez-Salgado has commented, it is difficult to form a clear impression of Charles at this early stage, when the tool of his advisers and "cocooned by rituals and by his household." Nonetheless, he was "as keen as any young ruler of his age to seize power from the old guard, and made no attempt to protect Margaret when his advisers demanded that she relinquish authority over the Netherlands." Though quiet, indolent and awkward as a youth, there were gritty moments of determination to impose his will. Anxious, above all, to control family members, he demonstrated little affection for them while closely supervising them and, where thought necessary, punishing them. Years later he came close to incarcerating his daughters.[58] Blockmans agrees that Charles was "authoritarian, cool and manipulative with the female members of the dynasty." After marriage, he subjected his daughters to "a life of seclusion that was incomprehensible even to his contemporaries."[59] Margaret eventually recovered her eminence as councillor of state, a position from which Charles had demoted her when he came of age in 1515; but his treatment of his aunt is significant for the clue it provides to the steel in his character and subsequent treatment of his mother and brother.

"As the King's coming was repeatedly postponed," writes Charles' biographer, Karl Brandi, "two flames of discontent flared up into a single blaze. There is always a smoulder of unrest when a foreign ruler ascends a throne; but in Spain another fire was piled on this and with it a draught to fan the flames, for doubts were soon raised as to who was really ruling – the native regent or foreigners."[60] Here, as so often, the struggle is seen as one between two forces, obscuring the significance of the *third* force—a shadow force, perhaps, but a powerful one, under which he would live for most of his life.

Charles and his sister, Eleanor, set sail on 12 September 1517. Despite storm, fire and the tragic loss of humans and horses, most of the fleet reached Santander in safety. But, blown off course, Charles and Eleanor disembarked at Tazones, near Villaviciosa (Asturias), on 19 September. They moved slowly south through fog and rain to Tordesillas, arriving on 4 November. During this time, Cisneros lay gravely ill at Roa de Duero. It has sometimes been seen as a snub to the cardinal that Charles did not visit him immediately, but it was natural that his first destination should be the monarch in whose person the kingdoms of Castile and Aragon were embodied. Charles and Chièvres had to make their own assessment of the situation before embarking on a series of politically sensitive encounters. Above all, they needed to secure, or appear to secure, Juana's consent to Charles' assumption of royal power.

Both Martire and the Flemish chronicler, Laurent Vital, who wrote a fascinating account of Charles's first journey to Spain, note Juana's delight in the visit.[61] The quality of the tapestries that Juana had hung in their chambers astounded Vital, who describes how some seemed to come alive by torchlight. In Charles's *retrete* were the "golden tapestries" of the life of the Virgin, commissioned at the time of Juana's *juramento* as princess in 1502, and it is tempting to see in them a reminder to her son of her pre-eminence.

Vital shows the careful engineering that went into that first encounter. Charles and Chièvres were briefed about Juana's "solitary life" and how to approach her. It was arranged that Juana's confessor, Fray Juan de Ávila, would inform her of the arrival of Chièvres. Chièvres would then prepare (and, if necessary, try to enthuse) Juana for the encounter with Charles and Eleanor, and signal, by opening the door to her antechamber, the moment at which her children should enter the room.

A beaming grand chancellor bowed low to the queen and, after the customary pleasantries, the signal was given. Snatching a torch from a bracket, an inquisitive Vital tried to light the way, but Charles brushed him aside. Thus, regrettably, Vital did not directly witness the meeting, which took place in the presence of a handful of courtiers. Among them were people familiar to Juana from years before, including Ana de Beaumont, who had accompanied her to the Low Countries in 1496. The queen stood at the far end of what appears to have been a long and simply-furnished room. Charles advanced with measured step. Eleanor followed a pace behind and to his left. Both made progressively deeper reverences. At the halfway point, Charles bowed low, then, sinking to the floor, reached to kiss her hand. But, in a gesture of respect, she refused the *besamanos*, embracing them both. Charles made a small, formal speech, ending with an expression of obedience. The queen listened with a smile and nodded. Then she took their hands in hers, exclaiming: "*Mais êtes-vous mes enfans? Et que vous êtes en peu de temps devenuz grants*!" This, Vital, adds, was a rhetorical question, for she knew perfectly well who they were.[62]

During this first audience, Juana, speaking throughout in French, showed warmth, dignity and courtesy. Afterwards, Chièvres lingered, conversing with Juana and with Ávila and Duque for over half an hour. This was the most crucial part of an encounter in which genuine emotion on Juana's part mixed with elaborate charade on that of Chièvres. The latter had to take into account not only Juana's extreme sensitivity to her status but the fact that Fernando's death had never been confirmed to her. He stressed that Charles was no longer the child of fond memory but ready to learn to *share the burden* of government with Fernando and herself, as though this would be a three-way endeavour. As at Tórtoles, Juana's part in the conversation went unrecorded. Perhaps she agreed to this innocuously worded proposition on the grounds, or in the hope, that the apprentice prince would fully restore her royal household, regularly consulting with her, allowing her freedom of action and mediating for her with her father.

## 10.4 "Everything Must Be Kept Secret"

On 8 November, news came of Cisneros' death. Chièvres successfully petitioned Charles for the vacant archbishopric of Toledo for his seventeen-year-old nephew and namesake, Guillaume de Croÿ, already a cardinal. On 10 November, a memorial service for Philip was held at Santa

Clara. The next day the royal caravan moved on to Mojados (Valladolid) for Charles's first meeting with his brother.

Vital describes Ferdinand's sense of fun, lively mind and intellectual curiosity ("*il est à tout faire, et veult tout oyr et sçavir* …").[63] His treatment after Fernando's death had devastated and enraged him but he made dutiful reverence to Charles at Mojados on 18 November. Charles subsequently made a spectacular appearance in Valladolid for the opening of the Cortes. He wore yellow, white and red cloth of gold and silver, slashed with love knots, and a white Austrian plume in a jewelled black velour bonnet. His horse had a "gay and fierce countenance" and "most of his legs were always in the air." Jousts and junketing followed. The count of Benavente brought an Indian elephant. Villaescusa laid on a lavish banquet, the centrepiece of which was a fountain spouting red and white wine. But outside the Chancery, where Villaescusa asked him to preside over one of his cases, the atmosphere was heavily charged. Vital found local priests rude, rebellious and inhospitable. He saw *libelles diffamatoires* on church portals: "Accursed are you, Castile, for allowing and suffering your children, friends and citizens to be killed and murdered every day with impunity by foreigners!"[64]

The city buzzed with polemic. Between the opening of the Cortes and the oath taking of 3 February 1518 there had been weeks of political wrangling as to whether and under what conditions Charles should be sworn-in, and the appointment of a Fleming, Jean Le Sauvage, to co-preside the Cortes did not augur well for native law and tradition. Juana's absence was felt. Castilians "professed much love and respect for Queen Doña Juana," writes nineteenth-century historian, Manuel Colmeiro, of the opening of the Cortes, "whether because they sympathised with her misfortune or because they saw in her the legitimate heir of the Catholic monarchs, to whom, in good or bad health, the crown belonged."[65] Juana's unique proprietary status was upheld, and before Charles was sworn-in as king—but only in effect as a tutelary one—he had to promise that if Juana's health improved he would return her to power. He was asked to observe a "tacit contract" ("*contrato callado*") with his subjects. These would serve him with their wealth and persons in exchange for good and fair royal administration and protection of the patrimony.[66] The pact, though not new, would assume fresh significance in the light of future events.

The procurators' primary *petición* was for the queen to receive the "household and establishment that is owed her Royal Majesty as Queen and mistress of these Kingdoms." As earlier noted, this meant more than might appear. Charles was urged to marry and to ensure that the infante stayed in Castile until Charles had children of his own. Foreigners were to be banned from Castilian benefices and offices, and gold, silver and minted coin stopped from flowing abroad. Charles' responses were vague and, in any event, unfulfilled. Many were disappointed. The Venetian ambassador, Marco Minio, reported that "*non è de alcun valor*" and that Chièvres managed everything.[67] The French ambassador told François I of the Castilian nobles' great frustration with a king to whom they had just sworn fealty, adding that he (the ambassador) was obliged to keep a full table to provide for the malcontents who filled his lodgings.[68]

Catalina appeared briefly in Valladolid. Keen to include his youngest sister in his marital diplomacy, Charles had her secretly extracted from Tordesillas on the night of 13 March, through a hole cut in the soft masonry behind the tapestry in her room. Hesitant, she had wept "because of her love for the queen" but was ordered to obey the king. Her appearance at court, her sheepskin cast momentarily aside for violet and gold satin, has all the ingredients of a fairy tale. But it was a fleeting one. Juana discovered the hole and went on hunger and thirst strike, sitting up all night. On 15 March, Charles felt obliged to return Catalina to their mother, but he was irritated and exploited the occasion to enforce changes to Juana's household that could not have been further removed from those desired by the Cortes.[69]

Charles replaced Duque with Fernando's cousin, Bernardo de Sandoval y Rojas, second marquis of Denia, who became governor and administrator of both palace and town.[70] Beatriz de Mendoza and her husband, Castilla, who had tried to 'cure' the queen after Fernando's death, were dismissed, while Ulloa, unwell, may already have left.[71] An element in Charles' choice of Denia as de facto mayordomo was the unwavering loyalty that the marquis had shown to Fernando. In 1469, the marquisate of Denia (Valencia), together with the town of Lerma in the Esgueva valley, had been awarded to his father for services in the war of succession. The son's prospects were reinforced by his marriage, in 1492, to Francisca Enríquez, daughter of Fernando's chief steward, Enrique Enríquez, and one of the noblewomen whom Conchillos had described in 1507 as not being to Juana's taste. In 1502, Bernardo succeeded his father and in 1516 was among those accompanying Fernando's body to Granada.

Vital glimpsed Denia at the jousts in Valladolid, dressed in cloth of silver with golden florets. There he was the gentle knight. But, at Tordesillas, he was Charles' intransigent servant. His position, although it would prove lucrative, was, in some respects, unenviable. Like Ferrer, he became a hate figure within the town and palace, and there were moments when, despite his total loyalty to Charles, he seemed shaken by Juana's plight and by the theatre of cruelty, deceit and absurdity that he found himself building around her. His many letters to Charles reveal none of the derision, bordering on obscenity, that Fernando allowed Ferrer to express. Yet, while Catalina's situation improved, Juana's worsened. Denia's true mission, performed, as Zalama notes, with extraordinary cruelty, was to muffle the voices coming out of Tordesillas and ensure that Juana was forgotten.[72] His occasional doubts about his role may have contributed to the waspish, schoolmasterly tone he adopted when Juana put him on the defensive. He had difficulty explaining the ban Charles had placed on her visits to Santa Clara—visits that, under Ferrer and Duque de Estrada, had allowed her a modicum of contact with the outside world and a measure of sensory stimulus and control. But Charles was adamant that she must not be seen.

Most visitors were thus forbidden, including the queen's half-brother, Alonso, archbishop of Zaragoza, whom Fernando had appointed governor of Aragon. Alonso was refused an audience with Juana in 1518, presumably because Charles did not want to risk him forming a favourable impression of Juana and defending her rights at the forthcoming Corts of Aragon.[73] The infante was another *persona non grata*. Despite Cortes demands, he had to leave for Flanders on 26 May. Most of his servants, bitterly disillusioned, would join the war of the Comunidades on the comunero side. Although it was customary for family members and nobles to leave the country only with the licence of the proprietary monarch—as Juana herself would have had reason to remember—personal contact between mother and younger son was the last thing Charles wanted. Denia told Charles that the infante had been informed that Juana was "better treated than she used to be" and that he had been told this because "it seemed to me to be in your Highness' service that in these realms, and everywhere, it is known that this improvement in her royal person is owing to you … *but even if [Ferdinand] were to have stayed here a hundred years I should never have written or told him what is happening here*" [my emphasis].[74]

By July 1518, Denia was struggling to plug awkward rumours within the Royal Council. These originated, he believed, with one of Juana's attendants, Leonor Gómez, a "known gossip" and wife of Royal Council rapporteur Alarcón. Denia sourly remarked that there was no baptism, wedding or funeral in town that Juana's servants did not attend and the buzz of excitement they brought back with them unsettled the queen. Some were rebellious and showed insolence to the marchioness; "they have combined and mutinied like soldiers, saying that what is done to one is done to all." Reminding Charles of the imperative of secrecy ("everything relating to this place must be kept secret"), Denia urged Charles to threaten Gómez and others with dismissal.[75] In October 1518, Fray Ávila intervened on behalf of several servants, distressed at the prospect of dismissal, and urged Charles to show compassion.[76]

If Denia faced uneasy royal councillors and rebellious servants he had also to deal with the force and tenacity of the queen's struggle against captivity. Finding her in clean outdoor clothes, ready to go out, he admitted to the startling effect her appearance and words had on him. Her ingenuity and eloquence ("*tantas buenas palabras*") often got the better of both Denia and his wife.[77] Charles insisted that the exchanges between queen and marquis take place out of earshot. Letters had to be confided only to trusted messengers "because the case is so delicate and concerns me so much."[78]

Denia told Juana she could not leave the palace because of the spread of plague. But Denia's main problem was security. Tumult could ensue if Juana were seen on the road. He argued against Charles' suggestion that she should be moved to San Pablo de Moraleja (Valladolid) when plague did reach Tordesillas. So many visited the Carmelite monastery to venerate the virgin there, and receive indulgences, that they might be alerted to her presence.[79] Charles then suggested that Denia alert Juana to the perils of the plague by organising religious processions that could pass to and fro before the palace windows. Her women, he added, should work to fill her with "fear."[80] Such proposals were not far removed from the "consort of madmen" paraded before Juana's Italian cousin, Giovanna d'Aragona, in John Webster's drama *The Duchess of Malfi*.

Denia's reports, and the lies he told, and was ordered to tell, show that Charles was worried less about his mother's indisposition than about her latent power. They also show that, contrary to the view that she lacked curiosity about the world, she was avid for news. Cut and thrust between marquis and queen could last five or six hours. Faced with Juana's constant demands for the restoration of her rights, Denia became entangled in deceit. From this he tried occasionally to cut himself with a curt reminder that Fernando or Charles were in charge, not herself:

> The Queen our lady called for me and told me to write to the King her lord [Fernando] and that His Highness order that she be better treated and give her the things she wanted with less difficulty, because she did not want to show him disrespect, as many grandees of the kingdom would like. I said: 'His Highness treats you as is reasonable and Your Highness should show him the respect you owe him and not mind what the grandees want, for their own interests ... Your Majesty may believe that she speaks words to lift stones. No-one knows it and no-one must ...[81]

Juana sought information from others, such as her steward, Arzeo; her doctor, Soto; her treasurer, Landa. If her demands to see them were refused, as they usually were, she responded with hunger strikes over days. Juana struggled to maintain her regal functions. Denia anticipated, for example, that, she would ask if Dr. Soto were still receiving the supplementary payments (*ayuda de costa*) that Isabel had granted him, but that Charles had not authorised. Denia told Soto that he must assure the queen that everything was in order. Juana duly asked him if he was getting these payments: "Your Highness may believe," Denia told Charles, "that if [Juana] knew the contrary she would be extremely upset ...".[82] When Denia refused to allow a visit from her treasurer, she stopped eating. Denia also refused to send for a physician when Juana, who had a strong fever and chill for ten days, requested one.[83]

She never ceased to fret about the infante, as she invariably called him. Informed that he had left Spain to help the emperor, she constantly urged his return. Denia's inventive responses were peopled with the living dead. Fernando was busy in Málaga. Maximilian, who had died in January 1519 was, where Tordesillas was concerned, still alive, but he had abdicated in Charles' favour. Juana quickly replied that, in that case, the infante could come home, for she "very much wanted to see him." Denia countered that Maximilian was old and tired, and needed Ferdinand's company. "That's good," the queen replied but "remained a long time thinking without saying a word."[84]

She often asked to see the grandees. She wanted to know who accompanied Fernando and who was with Charles. "I distributed them around as well as I could," Denia admitted after a four-hour audience, adding that the eloquence of her arguments meant that no-one must see her: "the truth is that she speaks words which would deceive them all."[85]

Juana struggled to make sense of life. Why did Fernando never visit? And what of relations between Fernando and Charles? She repeatedly addressed demands to her father for the restoration of her liberty, unconvinced about the authority of the 'prince.' Towards the end of 1519, she ordered Denia to tell Fernando that:

> she cannot bear the life she leads, that she has been so long a prisoner, that … even if, as his daughter, she had to respect him, he should treat her better, that she should be where she could engage with her affairs (saber de sus cosas), should she wish it, as many grandees had advised …

Again she expressed anxiety about the infante. Although he was, she said bitterly, "in a better land than this, she wanted to have her son where she could see him." Again she demanded to visit Valladolid and see the grandees. When Denia objected that Tordesillas was the best place for her she retorted that she would go where she liked. She would go where *convenient*, Denia snapped back, at which "she remained silent." She constantly asked for Catalina, threatening that, if she, like the infante, were to be taken away, she would "throw herself out of the window or stab herself to death."[86]

## Notes

1. De la Fuente/Gayangos (eds. 1867), Carta LXXVII, 155.
2. Doussinague (1950), Instructions to Pedro de Quintana.
3. Ladero Quesada (2016).
4. BL, Additional, 15568, f. 38.
5. Villacañas Berlanga (2008), 538.
6. BN, Ms. 1778, fs. 1–22 (2v.), 'Memorial y suma de algunas cosas que sucedieron después de la muerte del Rey Católico que fue en Madrigalejo a 23 de enero de 1516,' ff. 1–22 (2v.); Galíndez de Carvajal (Floranes Robles y Encinas, ed. 1787), 341–347.
7. González Sánchez (ed. 2001), 268–269.
8. Elliott (1990), 142.
9. Fernández Álvarez (ed. 1973), Charles to Fernando, XII, 7 September 1517, 71–74.
10. Pérez (1999), Adrian to Cisneros, 77n.

11. CSP (Queen Juana), ed. Bergenroth, 26, 30 April 1516.
12. Zalama (2010).
13. AGS, Estado 3, f. 133 [1516], 'Relación.'
14. Brewer (ed. 1920), 1 March 1516, 450.
15. AGS, Estado 3, f. 133.
16. González Olmedo (ed. 1944), 'Instrucción,' 114.
17. AGS, Estado 3, f. 133.
18. AGS, Estado 1-2, f. 298, Ferrer to Cisneros.
19. López de Ayala (ed. 1921–1928), I, 163.
20. CSP (Queen Juana), 27, to Cisneros, 12 July 1516.
21. BN Ms. 1778, ff. 7–8, 'Memorial.'
22. Argensola (Lanaia, ed. 1630); Brandi (1970); Blockmans (2002).
23. For Berenguela, see Bianchini (2012).
24. BN, Ms. 1778, f. 8, 'Memorial'; Galíndez de Carvajal, 370–377; Gómez de Castro (Oroz Reta, ed. 1984), 389–390.
25. Pallares/Portela (2006).
26. Pérez (2000), 21.
27. Peters (23).
28. BN, Ms. 1778, f. 8; Galíndez de Carvajal, 370–377.
29. Aram (2005), Francisco Pacheco to Priego, 113.
30. Argensola, 155.
31. Galíndez de Carvajal, 374.
32. López de Ayala (ed. 1928), II, LXVIII, 3 April 1516, 136–137.
33. Danvila (1897–1900), II, Admiral to Junta, October 1520, 338.
34. Brewer (ed. 1920), I, 1732, 3 April 1516, 486.
35. Paz y Mélia (ed. 1915–1922), I, Undated paper [1516], 113.
36. Sandoval (ed. 1955–1956), 80, 83.
37. AGS, Estado 3, f. 24, 'Actas de la Ayuntamiento de Jerez de la Frontera.'
38. Pérez (1999), 79n.
39. Pérez (2000).
40. AGS, Estado 8, f. 14 [1516], Regidores of Valladolid to Charles; AGS, Estado 1-2, f. 277, Jorge de Mesa to Bartolomé Ruiz de Castañeda, 20 July 1516.
41. De la Fuente/Gayangos (eds. 1867), I, Jorge Varacaldo to López de Ayala, 23 August 1516, I, 18–19.
42. AGS, Estado 1–2, f. 296, Villaescusa to Cisneros, 23 December 1516; AGS, Estado 4, f. 65, to Cisneros, 20 January 1517; AGS Estado 5, f. 30, to Chièvres, 20 April 1518; AGS, Estado 5, f. 80, to Charles, 15 May 1518.
43. Berzal de la Rosa (2008), 39.
44. De la Fuente/Gayangos (eds. 1867), 'Minuta de un Memorial dirigido al Rey en 18 de marzo de 1517' (appendix VII), 268.

45. AGS, Estado 3, f. 29, chief justice officer Juan de Ribera to Cisneros, 26 June 1516.
46. López de Ayala, II, López de Ayala to Cisneros, 4 February 1516, 8–9.
47. Gómez de Castro, 427.
48. Paz y Mélia, I, António de la Cueva to Priego [undated; 1516], 108.
49. López de Ayala/Alvarez de Toledo, II, 48–51.
50. De la Fuente/Gayangos (eds.), Francisco de Ruiz to López de Ayala, 3 September 1516, 252–255.
51. Suárez Varela (Szaszdi León-Borja/Galende Ruiz, eds. 2015), 277n.
52. Rivero Rodríguez (2005), 73–74; and in Martínez Millán (2000), 1, 150–158; Cancila (2007), 47–62.
53. CODOIN, 24, 'Carta de los marqueses de Irache y de Licodia á la Reina Doña Juana,' Palermo, 15 May 1516, 176. The presidents of the 'parliament of princes' were subsequently lured to Naples, where Cardona kept them pending the appointment of a new viceroy in Sicily.
54. Carretero Zamora (Nieto Soria/Foronda, eds. 2005), 575–593. Still, Juana was frequently referred to as 'Reyna Católica,' not least by Charles himself.
55. Francisco Olmos (2003), 139n.
56. Argensola, 186.
57. For Margaret's court, see, for instance, Dagmar Eichberger, 'A Cultural Centre in the Southern Netherlands: the Court of Archduchess Margaret of Austria (1480–1530) in Mechelen.' 2003. Martin Gosman/Alasdair Macdonald/Arjo Vanderjagt, eds., *Princes and Princely Culture, 1450–1650*, I. Leiden/Boston: Brill.
58. Rodríguez-Salgado (Soly, ed. 1999), 55.
59. Blockmans (2002), 122.
60. Brandi (1970), 73.
61. Martire (López de Toro, ed. 1955–1957), CODOIN, 11, 602, 10 November 1517; Vital (Gachard, ed. 1881), III, 1–303.
62. Vital, 134–136.
63. Vital, 147.
64. Vital, 234.
65. Colmeiro (ed. 1883–1884), XXIV.
66. Colmeiro; Sandoval (ed. 1955–1956); Francisco Olmos (2003); Pérez (2000). See also 'Ordenamiento de las Cortes de Valladolid de 1518' (www.cervantesvirtual.com).
67. CSP, Ven., II (1509–1519), ed. Brown, 969, Marco Minio to the Signoria, 16 September 1517.
68. TNA, PRO 31/3, French Transcripts, ff. 87–203 [undated letter: 1518].
69. Vital, 237–246.
70. AGS, Estado 33, f. 112, Charles to Denia, 15 March 1518. Cárdenas retained the title of *mayordomo mayor*.

71. AGS, Estado 1-2, f. 287, 1517; Estado 4, f. 77, 29 April 1517.
72. Zalama (2003).
73. Ibidem.
74. AGS, Estado 5, f. 290, 27 April 1518.
75. AGS, Estado 5, f. 339, 'Lo que Pedro de Arayz, mi secretario, ha de decir …,' 30 July 1518; CPS (Queen Juana), 34.
76. AGS, Estado 5, f. 313, Ávila to Charles, 30 October 1518; CPS (Queen Juana), 40.
77. AGS, Estado 5, f. 311 [1518].
78. AGS, Estado 5, f. 294, 19 April 1518; CPS (Queen Juana), 30.
79. CSP (Queen Juana), 39, Denia to Charles, 13 September 1518.
80. Aram (2005). The appendices to the original Spanish-language edition (2001) incorporate the letter from Charles of 30 October 1518 in full.
81. AGS, Estado 5, ff. 340–341 [undated; October 1519].
82. AGS, Estado 6, f. 18, 6 June 1519.
83. AGS, Estado 5, f. 337, 26 September 1519; AGS, Estado 5, f. 323 [undated; October 1519]; AGS, Estado, ff. 340–341 [undated; October 1519].
84. AGS, Estado 5, ff. 340–341.
85. Ibidem.
86. AGS, Estado 5, f. 343 [undated; end 1519].

## References

Aram, Bethany. 2005. *Juana the Mad: Sovereignty and Dynasty in Renaissance Europe*. Baltimore and London: John Hopkins University Press.

Argensola, Bartolomé Leonardo de. 1630. *Primera Parte de los Anales de Aragón que prosigue los del Secretario Gerónimo Çurita*, ed. I. de Lanaia. Zaragoza: I. de Lanaia.

Bergenroth, G.A. (ed.). 1868. *Calendar of State Papers, Supplement to Vol. I and Vol. II of Letters, Despatches and State Papers Relating to Negotiations Between England and Spain, Preserved in the Archives of Simancas and Elsewhere*. London: Longmans, Green, Reader and Dyer.

Berzal de la Rosa, Enrique. 2008. *Los comuneros. De la realidad al mito*. Madrid: Sílex.

Blockmans, Wim. 2002. *Emperor Charles V, 1500–1558*. London: Arnold.

Bianchini, Janna. 2012. *The Queen's Hand: Power and Authority in the Reign of Berenguela of Castile*. Philadelphia: University of Pennsylvania Press.

Brandi, Karl. 1970. *The Emperor Charles V: The Growth and Destiny of a Man and of a World-Empire*. Hasssocks: Harvester.

Brewer, John Sherren (ed.). 1920. *Letters and Papers, Foreign and Domestic, of the Reign of Henry VIII*. London: HMSO.

Brown, Rawdon (ed.). 1867. *Calendar of State Papers Relating to English Affairs in the Archives of Venice (1509–1519)*, vol. 2. London: HMSO.

Cancila, Rossella. April 2007. Congiure e Rivolte nella Sicilia del Cinquecento. *Mediterranea: Ricerche Storiche* IV, 47–62.

Carretero Zamora, Juan Manuel. 2005. Crisis sucesoria y problemas en en ejercicio del poder en Castilla (1504–1518). In *Coups d'État à la fin du Moyen Age? Aux Fondements du pouvoir politique en Europe occidentale*, ed. Jean-Philippe Genet, François Foronda and José Manuel Nieto Soria. Madrid: Casa de Velázquez.

Colmeiro, Manuel (ed.). 1883–1884. *Cortes de los antiguos Reinos de León y de Castilla*. Madrid: Rivadeneyra.

Danvila y Collado, Manuel (ed.). 1897–1900. *Historia crítica y documentada de las Comunidades de Castilla*. Madrid: Memoria Histórico Español.

De la Fuente, Vincente, and Pascual de Gayangos (eds.). 1867. *Cartas del Cardenal Don Fray Francisco Jiménez de Cisneros*. Madrid: Real Academía de la Historia.

Doussinague, J.M. 1950. *El Testamento Político de Fernando el Católico*. Madrid: CSIC.

Elliott, John. 1990. *Imperial Spain, 1469–1716*. Middlesex: Penguin.

Fernández Álvarez, Manuel (ed.). 1973. *Corpus Documental de Carlos V, I (1516–1539)*. Salamanca: Universidad de Salamanca.

Francisco Olmos, José Maria. 2003. Estudio documental de la moneda castellana de Carlos I fabricada en los Países Bajos (1517). *Revista General de Información y Documentación* XIII (2), 133–153.

Galíndez de Carvajal, Lorenzo. 1787. *Anales breves de los Reyes Católicos don Fernando y doña Isabel*, ed. Rafael Floranes Robles y Enzinas. Madrid.

Gómez de Castro, Alvar. 1984. *De las hazañas de Francisco Jiménez de Cisneros*, ed. José Oroz Reta. Madrid: Fundación Universitaria Española.

González Olmedo, S.I., Félix. 1944. *Diego Ramírez Villaescusa (1459–1537), fundador del Colegio de Cuenca y autor de los Cuatro Diálogos sobre la Muerte del Príncipe Juan*. Madrid: Editora Nacional.

González Sánchez, Vidal (ed.). 2001. Testamento del Rey Don Fernando el Católico. In *El Testamento de Isabel la Católica y otras consideraciones en torno a su muerte*. Madrid: Instituto de Historia Ecclesiástica 'Isabel la Católica'.

Ladero Quesada, Miguel-Ángel. 2016. *Los últimos años de Fernando el Católico, 1505–1516*. Madrid: Dykinson.

López de Ayala, Jerónimo (ed.). 1921–1928. *El Cardenal Cisneros, Gobernador del Reino*. Madrid: Real Academía de la Historia.

López de Toro, José (ed.). 1955–1957. *Petrus Martyr Anglerius. Epistolario*. CODOIN, 9–12. Madrid: Imprenta Góngora.

Pallares, María del Carmen, and Portela Ermelindo. 2006. *La Reina Urraca*. San Sebastián/Donostia: Nerea.

Paz y Mélia, Antonio (ed.). 1915–1922. *Series de los más importantes documentos del archivo y biblioteca del exmo. señor duque de Medinacieli*, vol. I. Madrid: A. Paz y Mélia.

Pérez, Joseph. 1999. *La revolución de las Comunidades de Castilla (1520–1521)*. Madrid: Siglo Veintiuno de España Editores.

———. 2000. *Carlos V*. Madrid: Temas de Hoy.

Rivero Rodríguez, Manuel. 2005. *Gattinara: Carlos V y el sueño del Imperio*. Madrid: Sílex.

———. 2000. Crisis sucesoria en la Corona de Aragón (1516–1517). In *La Corte de Carlos V*, ed. José Martínez Millán, vol. I. Madrid: Sociedad Estatal para la Conmemoración de los Centenarios de Felipe II y Carlos V, 150–166.

Rodríguez-Salgado, María José. 1999. Charles V and the Dynasty. In *Charles V: 1500–1558*, ed. H. Soly. Antwerp: Fonds Mercator.

Sandoval, Prudencio de. 1955–1956. *Historia de la Vida y Hechos del Emperador Carlos V*, ed. Madrid: Biblioteca de Autores Españoles.

Súarez Varela, Antonio. 2015. La Comunidad de Valladolid y la cuestión conversa: el caso del procurador Alonso de Saravia. In *Carlos V. Conversos y Comuneros*, eds. István Szaszdi León-Borja and María Jesús Galende Ruíz. Valladolid: Centro Estudios Camino Santiago Sahagún/Marcial Pons.

Villacañas Berlanga, José Luis. 2008. *La Monarquía Hispánica (1284–1516)*. Madrid: Espasa Calpe.

Vital, Laurent. 1881. Premier voyage de Charles-Quint en Espagne de 1517 à 1518. In *Collection des voyages des souverains des Pays-Bas*, III, ed. Louis-Prosper Gachard. Brussels: Commission Royale d'Histoire.

Zalama, Miguel-Ángel. 2010. *Juana I: Arte, Poder y Cultura en torno a una Reina que no gobernó*. Valladolid: Centro de Estudios Europa Hispánica.

———. 2003. *Vida cotidiana y Arte en el Palacio de la Reina Juana I en Tordesillas*. Valladolid: Universidad de Valladolid.

CHAPTER 11

# The Giants' War (1519–1520)

## 11.1 Tyrants and Traitors

After much argument and some violence, Charles was sworn-in as king, co-regnant with Juana, at the Corts of Zaragoza on 29 July 1518. He did not reach Barcelona until the new year. There he was told of Maximilian's death, at Wels, in Austria, on 12 January. Maximilian had spent huge sums persuading the seven imperial electors to accept Charles as his imperial heir, but had died with the issue still open.

Although essentially Burgundian, Charles had German blood and his *Hausmacht*, together with Margaret's tireless work, gave him a head start over his main rival, François I. The deciding factor, however, was his Spanish 'coronation' and the money and metals it brought him, of which no reminder was more spectacular than the gold and silver fruits of the 'Indias' displayed (to Dürer's admiration) during the electoral period. Charles spent colossally and his main creditor, merchant and financier, Jacob Fugger, was paid with Castilan funds, including tax income from Spain's extensive territories, and control of its silver and mercury mines. In 1525, the Fuggers were granted the income from the Spanish military orders for three years.

Charles was elected at Frankfurt am Main on 28 June 1519. He cut short his stay in Aragon, suspended the Corts of Valencia and returned, via a smouldering Castile, to prepare his coronation journey to Aachen, city of Charlemagne. Inevitably, his election changed his relationship with Spain. Henceforth, he was to be addressed as 'Sacred Catholic



G. B. Fleming, *Juana I*, Queenship and Power,
https://doi.org/10.1007/978-3-319-74347-9_11

Caesarean Majesty,' not, according to Spanish tradition, as 'your Highness.' From September 1519, his imperial title preceded Juana's on government documents. The reference to Juana was sandwiched uncomfortably between repeated references to himself:

> "*Don Carlos por la graçia de Dios Rey de Romanos, Emperador semper augusto, doña Juana su madre y el mismo don Carlos por la divina clemençia reyes de Castilla, de Aragón, de las dos Seçilias, de Iherusalén* …", and so on.

The imposition on Castile of an alien and plundering government of Flemings, Burgundians and Germans had been Juana's main political concern in 1506. Now blatant examples of malpractice again fuelled resentment. The settlement of Castilian income on German bankers and Charles' acquiescence in granting Cisneros' mighty see to a young kinsman of Chièvres cut to the quick of Castilian sensitivities. An ironic rhyme about the increasing rarity of the high-value gold *ducados de a dos*, minted during the dual monarchy, captured popular concern about the draining away of wealth. The Spaniard who finds the precious coin in his hand lifts his bonnet in greeting, with the words:

> *Salveos Dios ducado de a dos,*
> *Que monsieur de Xevres no topó con vos.*[1]

Eager to combine further funds with a swift departure, Charles snubbed tradition by summoning a Cortes to Galicia. Conflict broke out in Toledo, whose procurators, instructed to oppose demands for a new emergency tax (*servicio*), hesitated to depart. Charles summoned three of the city's most militant *regidores*, including militia captain Juan de Padilla, to Galicia. But crowds blocked their path. Men disguised and with lanterns went by night around the houses of political leaders, "persuading them to liberty."[2] A furious crowd besieged the *alcázar*, symbol of royal authority and the *corregidor* fled two days later.

Salamanca's procurators were expelled from the Cortes for refusing to swear allegiance to Charles unless he met their demands. Meanwhile, rebellion spread to Segovia. On 29 May, Hernán López Melón, a police functionary who antagonised critics of the absent *corregidor*, was lynched and strung up on an improvised gallows. A colleague called Portal met the same fate. So, later, did one of Segovia's procurators, Rodrigo de Tordesillas, who braved an enraged crowd on his return from Galicia.

The record of his deliberations at the Cortes was torn from his hand and a noose thrown around his neck. Despite desperate interventions on his behalf, he was strangled and hung upside down beside the others.

Throughout Castile, events followed a similar pattern. On 10 June, the procurators of Burgos fled; their houses were razed and the fortress, symbol of royal authority, was occupied. Garci Jofré de Cotannes, a royal purveyor of French origin to whom Charles had controversially granted tenancy of the fortress of Lara, was beheaded, hung upside down and his house set alight. Guadalajara's fortress was attacked and, although the procurators escaped, their properties were gutted and decontaminated with salt. The effigies of Zamora's absent procurators were dragged through the streets and burned in the plaza. These ferocious acts were also rituals, imitating the customary practices of the ruling elite. To seize a fortress was to proclaim its occupants traitors. Upside-down hangings and the burning and salting of houses were recognised punishments for treason. On 1 June, the poet and royal physician, Francisco López de Villalobos, wrote from Valladolid that the "republic of Spain" had been turned topsy-turvy, with defendants sentencing judges and lords serving their vassals. Even the most ruinous villages gave themselves airs.[3]

This was the background against which Charles set sail, leaving Adrian to the thankless task of damage-limitation. Persisting unease about Charles' seizure of the crown combined with his *bobito* image and insatiable retinue to light a long fuse that, as we have seen, had been laid years before, winding from Toro through Tórtoles to Tordesillas. Clearly, many different social and economic factors contributed to the explosive situation in 1520. Unease with foreign rule and fear of heavy fiscal measures were but the catalysts for an uprising that Fernández-Armesto is among other historians to describe, *inter alia*, as the consequence of years of accumulating resentments, including "the unfulfilled rebelliousness of two generations of declining civic autonomy."[4]

The imprisoned Juana—whether as individual, symbol or embodiment of a dream—was at the heart of this agitation, which began to assume revolutionary proportions. In Galicia, the procurators again demanded that her household be placed "in the order that her royal person and the honour of these kingdoms require."[5] Humanist cleric Juan Maldonado noted that, in Toledo, Padilla was declaring that Charles reigned unjustly as long as Juana lived, and again, that everyone aimed "*a que reinase la democracia mientras la reina Juana viviese.*" The inhabitants of Zamora "ran in arms, appealing to queen and people."[6] Fearing that a successful appeal to Juana would encourage the cities to defend their demands in blood, Adrian sought to divide and rule by offering protection to those willing to declare their loyalty to Charles.[7]

Preachers linked Juana directly with the events that became known as the war of the Comunidades. In May, a priest proclaimed Charles a tyrant and usurper, born not of Juana, but a slave; Juana's rightful heir was Ferdinand.[8] In July, a friar from Valladolid was gaoled for preaching that Charles had bought an empire his heirs must not inherit.[9] In September, the influential Dominican, Alonso de Medina, declared in Valladolid that Juana was issuing orders in the interests of the realm.[10] Enthusiastic in Juana's support, he was later blacklisted as "one of the principle traitors and subversives of the whole kingdom," along with bishops Acuña and Villaescusa and a host of clergy and "bad monks throughout the kingdom."[11]

Mounting agitation was often expressed in terms of wounded honour—that keyword of the emotional and political vocabulary of the time. Demands from successive Cortes had linked it with the restoration of the queen's household, and the *libelles diffamatoires* mentioned by Vital also referred to it. But 'community,' 'commune,' *comunidad*—the 'open councils' of 'good men' and taxpayers (*pecheros*)—was the word on everyone's lips. These councils had flourished, if unevenly, in areas under crown control before being gradually replaced by a more restrictive, authoritarian system of urban *regimiento* under the dual monarchy. But by 1519–1520, the crushed seeds of *comunidad* began to blossom again as city, town and village councils, cathedral chapters and communities of friars formed around specific political demands and goals. In the spring of 1520, the word appeared in a manifesto from Franciscan, Augustinian and Dominican friars at Salamanca. This, widely disseminated, contained two main demands, fiscal and political, and a warning: there must be no fresh *servicio*. If Castilian resources were squandered for Charles' personal, dynastic and imperial purposes, the *comunidades* would take matters into their own hands.[12]

The comunero movement was diverse and, as the character known as the 'Toledan' points out in Maldonado's contemporary book about the uprising, involved all classes. It attracted "Old Christians" alongside *conversos* and *moriscos*; lords as well as peasants and artisans; bishops and mendicant monks. The involvement of women from all social ranks was remarkable. Its nature remains controversial. Nineteenth-century supporters of a liberal constitution saw it as the embryonic expression of patriotic nationalism and liberty, stifled by Habsburg despotism. For others it was an essentially rear-guard response by traditionalists with vested feudal interests. Pérez places it within a panoramic context of conflicting social and economic forces. Elliott, while remarking on its positive elements, sees it as a largely confused and often negative revolt. Maravall emphasises its strikingly progressive political objectives: a detailed written constitution and the formation of a group of institutions designed to protect the public interest against imperialism.[13]

Certainly, the existence in comunero ranks of numerous traditionalists does not infer lack of radicalism. Revolutionary movements look back, as well as forward, to reclaim lost or disappearing rights and privileges, real or imagined, both as a means of expressing what might otherwise be almost impossible to express, and of driving forward fresh agendas for political, economic and social change. Comunero leaders, drawn from the patrician elites of Castile's heartland—as well as similar leaders of the Germanías of Aragon—looked to forms of medieval communitarian self-government as antitheses of absolutism and to the golden myth of Italy's communes.[14] In general, the uprising stemmed from a movement in which a strong sense of the historic memory, however recreated, was used to propose a strengthening and reshaping of a broken contractual relationship—that *contrato callado*, drawn to Charles' attention in 1518, between rulers and *res publica*. Although the movement was suppressed before it could flower into full-blooded revolution, it was unquestionably powered by a revolutionary energy that drove demands for specific reform into subversive, wide-ranging projects, affecting the whole nature of government and monarchy. In this sense, it can be seen as a precursor of the English, American and French revolutions of the seventeenth and eighteenth centuries.

Despite the growth in comunero demands to limit the monarchy's power, the movement cannot be called anti-monarchist as such; nor was it anti-imperialist in principle. That is to say, it opposed Castile's submergence in the Holy Roman Empire rather than the process of Hispanic expansionism already underway during the dual monarchy. It became increasingly anti-aristocratic, despite the active involvement of some members of the nobility and the initial neutrality of various magnates, unhappy with Charles. During this period a number of *behetrías*, targeted by predatory lords and caught in their crossfire, sought royal status and protection. Such was the case of Becerril de Campos, caught between the Manriques and Velascos. In 1507, Juana had confirmed her parents' decision to bring Becerril under crown protection. Now the town again found itself up against the Velascos.[15] There were armed uprisings in Madrigal, Arévalo, Olmedo and elsewhere. The early modern chronicler of Segovia, Diego de Colmenares, refers to the particular hatred inspired by the Moyas, "sons of the Bobadilla," and seen as tyrants who had extended their territory by force and intimidation.[16]

Against the advice of some fellow councillors, Antonio de Rojas, archbishop of Granada and hardline Council president, urged Adrian to exact severe reprisals against the perpetrators of the lynchings in Segovia; otherwise the "carders of Segovia and bonnet-makers of Toledo" would think they could act with impunity.[17] As judge Ronquillo (who, in 1507, had been sent against Acuña) bore down on Segovia, its militia, under Juan Bravo, formerly a captain of Cisneros' failed *Gente de Ordenanza*, joined with the militias of Toledo and Madrid, led by Padilla and Juan Zapata, to block his path.

On 8 June, Toledo outlined five objectives: annulment of the *servicio* voted at La Coruña; re-introduction of the *encabezamiento*, under which taxes were paid per head of population; restriction of public posts and ecclesiastical benefices to Castilians; prohibition on the export of currency; and designation of a Castilian to head the government in Charles' absence. Subsequently, Toledo appealed to sister cities to gather in Ávila, couching its call to arms in loftier terms. This was an attempt to renew the initiative taken in June 1517 by Burgos, Valladolid, León and Zamora, and build on the precedent set by Cisneros in 1506. But Toledo's appeal was more radical yet, seeking to distance the monarchy and common good from a tyrannical, even demonic, Royal Council and repudiating outright the Council's participation in the Junta. Toledo's leaders declared they were not the slaves of Chièvres but the subjects of the king. They were not mutineers but "*otros Brutos de Roma*" and saviours of the *patria*. They were not traitors but would live on as immortals. They might lose everything. But in danger was safety, in theft wealth, in exile glory, in defeat victory and in persecution a crown.[18]

On 29 July, in Ávila's cathedral sacristy, representatives from Toledo, Segovia, Salamanca, Toro and Zamora gathered around a table, on which they placed the gospels and a cross, and swore to defend and reform Castile in God's name. "From henceforth," writes Sandoval, "the members of the Comunidad called those of the Council tyrants, and the members of the Council called those of the Comunidad traitors."[19] Pedro Laso de la Vega, Toledo's honey-tongued *regidor*, and Alonso de

Pliego, dean of Ávila, presided over the assembly, soon to be termed the Junta General or Holy Junta.

Adrian and Rojas hoped that, with only a handful of cities responding to Toledo's call, a hard response to Segovia might stamp the uprising out. But the treasury had been drained by Charles' insatiable demand for funds and military forces had to guard the ever-sensitive borders of Navarre from French depredations. The artillery was stored at La Mota of Medina del Campo and would be hard to extract. Adrian finally ordered Charles' captain general, Antonio de Fonseca, to move on Medina. Fonseca's troops, reinforced by Ronquillo's, reached the city on 21 August. The *corregidor* welcomed them, but the city in general did not. A parley achieved nothing. Fonseca's adjutants decided that to reach the artillery they would need to cause a distraction. It was a fateful decision. A fire deliberately lighted in the street of San Francisco, where the merchants stored their wares between the international May and October fairs, consumed the whole town. Few have described it more passionately than Pedro de Ayala, comunero count of Salvatierra, who, in language characteristic of the contemporary rhetoric, told the Junta that: "neither Mohammed nor his hosts of Moorish dogs, nor pagan Nero nor accursed Herod committed such cruelties against their enemies … as these … against their fellow Christians …".[20] Maldonado describes women abandoning their children to the flames amid lugubrious howls and ululations as they urged their menfolk to protect the artillery. The fire raced toward the convent of San Francisco, which it devoured, together with houses, workplaces and merchants' stores. The sacred host was snatched from the blaze and placed in a tree hollow in the convent orchard, where it became a focus for prayer and imprecation. Fonseca fled to Portugal and from there to the Low Countries, where Ronquillo joined him.

The conflagration, from which Medina del Campo would never fully recover, set Castile alight. In Valladolid, there were sackings and burnings and a community was established under Juan, infante of Granada, descendant of its last Nasrid kings, who sent three procurators to Ávila. One after another, and as far as Extremadura, Murcia and Andalucia, new communities sprang up. The balance of power swerved toward the Junta. Militia captains Padilla, Bravo and Zapata arrived at Medina on 24 August and, from the smoking ruins, looked northward across the plain to the rocky outcrop of Tordesillas. With the new community established there, and with the Junta, they discussed Juana's liberation. If they could convince her of the rightness of their cause, then victory, surely, would be theirs.

## 11.2 The Appeal to Juana I

Calderón de la Barca's philosophical play, *La vida es sueño*, written over a century later, describes a conflict between the forces of predestination and free will. Fearing the prophecy that his son and heir, Segismundo, will become a tyrant, the king of Poland imprisons him in a tower. When Segismundo is momentarily released, the gaoler kneels before him, pleading that he has acted purely in his interests. Later, Segismundo is returned to captivity as unfit to govern and his reflections give rise to the play's most famous lines, in which he concludes that dreams are life and life a dream. But the people refuse to accept the alternative: foreign rule. As tumult spreads, a group of militiamen visit Segismundo to beg him to claim his inheritance. Instead, the prince imprisons his liberators as traitors, and offers allegiance to the father against whom he had earlier sought vengeance. The king confirms Segismundo's succession and dynastic values are upheld. Whether Calderón had Juana and the comuneros in mind when he wrote his masterpiece, striking parallels between Segismundo's situation and the queen's in 1520 cannot have escaped him.

Opinions with respect to Juana's role in the uprising diverge widely. Prawdin believes the struggle between comunero leaders and Castile's governors to win over the queen was of greater transcendence than any battle waged outside Tordesillas. Pérez states that Juana's confused obstinacy saved Charles, while "the comuneros who desired most ardently to confer power upon her had to renounce their wish. Is that not the best proof of the queen's incapacity?" Haliczer sees a "convalescent" queen, "eager to play a part in the kingdom's affairs once again," and whose refusal to sign comunero documents showed a recovery of sanity. For Zalama, she was "a person incapacitated to govern the fate of a kingdom, even though her own." Aram stresses Juana's "apparent support for the imperialist cause." Espinosa sees Juana as sympathetic to comunero grievances, without questioning her madness.[21] Given such diversity of views, it is important to look attentively through the window opened into the palace of Tordesillas in 1520.

This was an increasingly surreal world, in which a caged queen struggled to make sense of exchanges with her captor. She knew that Denia withheld information vital to her interests but her repeated attempts to draw him out or break him down proved fruitless. When she demanded to go to Valladolid, he told her she could not do so without Fernando's permission. When she asked for funds so that she could carry out her regal duty to grant favours, Denia told Charles: "I am of the opinion that no money should be given to her ... Everyone here must know that he has to serve her Highness but the rewards are to be received from your Majesty ...".[22]

Denia's responses filled the queen with anguish. Why continue denying that Fernando was dead when the matter affected her so crucially? Why, if Charles was going to the Low Countries, could the infante not return? What of Eleanor? And how could the grandees go abroad without seeking her permission? Though she added: "It's such a long time since they were here it's no wonder they go without my leave." She wanted to summon them. Denia insisted she had first to obtain permission from Fernando or Charles.[23]

Adrian and Rojas meanwhile knew that a royal order signed by Juana and sanctioning reprisals against Segovia would deal a heavy blow to the comuneros. Though surely aware that this amounted to accepting Juana's ability to govern, they probably thought it a risk worth taking in the belief that, with a return to normality, the royal initiative would be forgotten. Once Rojas met Juana, in August 1520, Fernando's death could no longer be concealed. Juana welcomed the deputation. But the sudden, formal revelation of what she had long suspected shook her to the core. Like Segismundo she felt she was dreaming:

> she complained, saying that for fifteen years she had been lied to and her person not treated as it should have been. And turning to the Marquis of Denia, who was present, she said: 'Foremost of the liars is the marquis.'
>
> The marquis knelt and, with tears in his eyes, said: 'It is true, señora, that I lied to you; but I did it to prevent you succumbing to your passions, but I must confirm that the king your father is dead and I buried him.'
>
> She answered: 'Bishop, believe me, all I see and am told is like a dream.'
>
> The president replied: 'Señora, in your hands, after God's, lies the remedy for these kingdoms, and Your Highness would perform a greater miracle in signing [these papers] than St Francis.'[24]

The captive queen showed how closely she clung to Isabel's world. When Rojas asked if he and his delegation could sit, she ordered: "Not chairs, benches, as in the time of the Queen my lady, and give the Bishop a chair." Rojas begged her to sign the measures. She prevaricated. The next day, she presided a six-hour meeting but remained wary, insisting that, on so serious a matter, the whole Council should come to a decision before she approved it.[25] Juana may have wished to prolong and savour this opening to the outside world. But on 23 August, before Rojas could return, the inhabitants of Tordesillas rose, clamouring to "see their Queen." Denia could not prevent a meeting between Juana and local officials, who offered her an utterly different version of events. Unsure what to believe, Juana asked her treasurer to send for Villaescusa and royal councillors Polanco, Aguirre and Zapata.[26] Both Martire and the author of the "*Relación de las Comunidades*" mention that these talks took place. Martire states that nothing much came of them, but peace-making initiatives were almost certainly discussed with Juana and may well have influenced Villaescusa's subsequent attempts to bring opposing sides together.[27]

News came of an uprising in Jaén, supported in the first instance by Rodrigo de Mexía, the procurator who had met the admiral on the road to Mucientes in the summer of 1506, and had helped defend Juana at the Cortes of Valladolid; "and what is worse," reported Adrian, "they are appealing in everything to the Queen's authority …". Yet, he added, they could hardly be called rebels while claiming to obey her.[28] The militias of Toledo, Segovia and Madrid marched to Tordesillas, entering the town on 29 August. Padilla told Toledo that:

> Her highness went to one of the corridors that overlook the plaza between the palaces and the river and ordered the whole army to pass before her, and her Highness stayed watching for two hours, looking at all the infantry and cavalry … and as I passed with these general captains of Segovia and Madrid before her Highness, and made the reverence due to her Majesty, her Highness ordered us to come up [to her apartments]. And not content with that, she summoned us with a gesture of the hand, although we could not hear her words over the great hubbub of people …[29]

Elliott describes Padilla as "disgruntled and embittered," slighted in the distribution of favours, goaded on by an ambitious wife.[30] This was also the (predictable) view of Charles' supporters. Yet Padilla's charisma is evident and his father-in-law, count of Tendilla and governor of the Alhambra, describes his conversation as "so sweet that we all adore him."[31]

Padilla, who would have remembered Juana from the tumultuous summer of 1506, surely introduced himself in words not dissimilar from those imagined by a poet of the comuneros:

*Señora, Juan de Padilla,*
*que os presenta sus respetos,*
*es hijo de Pedro López*
*quien os salvo del encierro*
*hace ya catorce años,*
*exponiéndose a ser muerto …*[32]

Padilla realised how little the queen knew of "all the deceptions that had been practiced on her until now …". She had, he writes, received them "with *increíble alegría*" and he begged her to "visit and console the cities" and govern. His lengthy conversation with her filled him with emotion: "as regards all that her Highness said I have never heard anything better or more considered." Juana also spoke to Bravo and Zapata, then to "all our captains and their people." Padilla was struck by her regal memory for people and places: to each she "said something in particular, and spoke so well that there was no one without tears in his eyes." Juana's ladies looked "the most glad and delighted in the world, all saying aloud … that they need no longer be deceived or imprisoned."[33] She met the captains again for two hours on 1 September, together with the *corregidor* and others.

When she refused to sign the order approving the Junta's transfer to Tordesillas, notaries recorded her words: "Let them come here, I want that," and again, "Yes, let them come." This was interpreted as an order to the Holy Junta to gather at the palace as the Cortes and General Junta of Tordesillas.[34] At an inquiry into the Denias' treatment of Juana, members of her household testified that she had been forcefully held "as if not in her right mind, but she is of sound mind and as prudent as at the outset of her marriage," and as willing and ready to govern as Isabel.[35] The inquiry ended with the Denias' expulsion from the town on 20 September.

On 24 September, procurators from fourteen Cortes cities gathered at Tordesillas in an atmosphere of public euphoria.[36] "The people," writes Sandoval, "thought it a miracle that the Queen, after so many years of imprisonment, so far removed from government affairs that she was seen by almost no one, should sally forth at this moment of such need, with such lucidity and clarity of judgment, to govern these realms …".[37] Beside Juana were Catalina, Fray Ávila and some ladies. She faced over fifty officials, procurators and *regidores*, ranging from deans and noble knights to chandlers and drapers. In extraordinary circumstances, attempts were made to follow traditional procedure. Pedro Laso spoke at length, declaring that Toledo, first and principal city of Castile, had risen in her service and the kingdom's, and entreating her to take confidence and govern.

Dr. Alonso de Zúñiga, a cleric and law professor from Salamanca, seems to have particularly impressed the queen. Holy zeal and divine inspiration had, he said, inspired the procurators to visit their lawful sovereign. The foreigners who had entered Castile after Fernando's death—"foreigners whom your highness knows better than anyone"—had left her subjects almost penniless and their native queen a captive. Now her subjects "humbly beseech your highness to take courage, to rule and govern and command your kingdoms, for there is no one in the world to forbid or impede you. As the most mighty queen and lady in the world, you can command in everything, and should not forsake all your kingdoms and subjects, who are ready to die for you and in your service. On this point I appeal to the royal conscience of your highness."

Juana, who was standing, with Zúniga at her feet, was visibly moved. "Stand up," she interjected at one point, "so I can hear you better." She turned to her attendants: "Bring me a cushion because I want to sit and listen to him properly." Zúniga resumed his speech—again falling to his knees—and the queen looked "very pleased" with it. His appeal to her to inaugurate her personal rule elicited a response that the Junta's secretaries, Juan de Mirueña and Antonio Rodríguez, describe as "long and very detailed" and which they summarised and signed.[38] This is the only known record of a speech by Juana, unless one includes Querini's bullet-point summary of her dealings with the procurators at Mucientes in 1506.

Despite Juana's bitter criticisms of Fernando, made privately to Ferrer, Juana upheld the royal and dynastic practice of defending family members in public, and praised Fernando, as Isabel was wont to do, at her own expense.[39]

> After God took to himself the Queen my lady I always obeyed and respected the King my lord and father, for he was my father and husband of the Queen my lady and for as long as he lived I had no concerns regarding him because no-one would have dared act wrongly and when I was told that God had taken him I was very sorry and should have preferred not to know and that he was alive and I there [in his place], for his life was more necessary than mine, but since I needed to know of [his death] I would have wished to know it sooner in order to remedy everything that it was in my power to do …

Yet she had never really understood Fernando's treatment of her, and wondered if Germaine ("*la mujer*") had played a part:

> I love all the people very much and am deeply sorry for any injuries and wrongs they have suffered, but I have always had bad company. I have been fed falsehoods and lies and been deceived with double-dealing. I always wanted to be in a position where I could occupy myself with the affairs that concerned me, but since the King my lord put me here – whether because of the woman who took the place of the Queen my lady, or for other considerations that [only] his highness would know I could do nothing more.

She rebuked the procurators, whether or not wittingly deflecting onto them the phrase about desire and ability that had so often been used to disqualify her from government:

> By the time that I heard of the influx of foreigners they were already here, and it much aggrieved me and I was under the impression that they had come here to protect my children's interests. But that was not the case, and I am greatly surprised that you have not avenged such ill-doing for had you wished to do so you should have been able to do so (*quyen quyera lo pudieran hazer*)...

Juana then returned to her own faults, raising the possibility that fear of possible repercussions on her children had played a part in her hesitations about seizing the initiative:

> If I have not take the initiative in this it is because I was afraid that, here or there [in the Low Countries], they might harm my children and even now, although I am assured they have gone, I can hardly believe it; and [you should] try to see whether any are still here, although I cannot believe that harm will come to them, for I am the second or third proprietary queen and mistress and the fact that I am the daughter of a King and Queen should alone have sufficed to ensure that I was not ill-treated. And I am very pleased with you for taking it upon yourselves to remedy such wrongs and if you fail to do so it will be on your consciences ...

She promised to involve herself in "these matters" as much as she could, whether in Tordesillas or elsewhere. She warned that she would also "need time to comfort my heart and console myself for the death of the king," by whom she presumably meant Fernando, whose death had just been confirmed to her, and asked them to choose "four of the wisest among you" to confer with her whenever necessary. When Fray Ávila attempted a clarification—"Your highness will hear them once a week"—she repeated: "I shall speak with them as often as necessary."[40]

From this and Padilla's euphoric letter—an extremely rare example of juanista (if also comunero) propaganda—the emerging picture is of a cautious but sympathetic monarch, who welcomes the comuneros as assistants in a reform process she will encourage as best she can. According to the author of the *Relación de las Comunidades*, the comuneros used Padilla's letter as a template on which to found their "diabolic and disloyal attempt to tyrannise the kingdom."[41] Some have queried whether Juana's speech was truly hers. However, its general tone and register; the personal detail; the simplicity; the occasional tone of bewilderment, naiveté and confusion; the fact that, here and there, words seem only half-heard, give it the ring of authenticity. Had the speech been fabricated, it would probably have conformed more exactly to a coherent political text.

## 11.3 Juana I and the Junta of Tordesillas

Juana's speech contained an implicit hint that her swings of mood might not allow her to be consistently or regularly involved in the process of political reform but that she would do what she could and what she thought right. Yet, from the outset, she found herself facing dissension in comunero ranks—dissension stemming as much from internal differences of view about the queen's status as from her failure to sign Junta documents.

The eight letters drafted by the community of Jaén after joining the Junta reflect the confusion about whom to address. One was addressed to Juana; others to her chaplain; the archdeacon of Jaén; the Junta; the procurators of Toledo and Valladolid; and Villaescusa. A seventh, to Charles, lamented that he could not hear in person the grievances of Andalucia, while the eighth asked Adrian (as well as Juana) to approve the procurators' nominations.[42] Many early comunero letters and documents, like Toledo's patriotic appeal to sister cities, and the *Capítulos de los que ordenaban de pedir los de la Junta*—probably drawn up at the time of the Junta of Ávila and before the appeal to Juana was made—refer to, or address, only Charles. In any case, the *Capítulos* were not exactly written with Juana's approval in mind, given that they begin by demanding an end of the right of women to succeed to the throne.[43] On 23 September, before Juana's meeting with the procurators, Adrian reported that the Junta was deliberating whether orders should be issued only in Juana's name.[44] On 24 September, Zúñiga addressed Juana as "the most powerful Queen and mistress of the world" and referred to Charles as "prince." But only a day later, he was involved in the drafting of a document that referred to Charles as "king," and, although Juana never publicly rejected Charles' claim on the title, it is unlikely that this was her doing. In whose name, then, were acts of government to be issued? Leaders in Toledo, Salamanca, Madrid and Segovia led a majority urging the exclusive use of Juana's name. But Valladolid asked a commission of jurists to clarify, *inter alia*, whether Juana's authority sufficed. On 8 October, the Burgos city élite, traditionally pro-Flemish, argued that Charles, though absent, had the right to appoint whomever he wished.

Although the Junta sought to legitimate itself through the queen, it was not she who sanctioned the changes to her household (see Chapter Sect. 12.3) or the decision of 11 October to replace Padilla as captain general with Pedro Girón, son of the count of Ureña. Nor did she give Padilla, whom she liked, licence to withdraw from her side.[45] It is likely that she became rapidly aware that decisions were being taken behind her back, and that her strongest advocates were Charles' most vehement adversaries. But, despite the private rebukes she had formerly made to those who referred, in her presence, to Charles as king, he remained her heir and she defended him publicly from the charge of usurpation. One anti-comunero source has her declare that: "no one turns me against my son, and everything I have is his."[46] According to another, she justified Charles' action from precedent: "in the states of Flanders there is a land called Friesia and the lord of Flanders is called king of Friesia." When her interlocutors testily objected that Charles was calling himself king of Castile, not Friesia, she replied that: "when the proprietary queens of the kingdom became widows their eldest sons always called themselves kings of Castile." She cited Urraca's son, Alfonso, and Berenguela's son, Fernando.[47]

This reads as though she had studied the arguments made by the Royal Council in 1516 after Charles had overridden its initial objections. This is, of course, highly improbable. While Juana may have had some knowledge of Castilian history, and the apparent uncertainty arising from her speech as to whether she was "second or third proprietary queen" may have related to understandable confusion over the circumstances in which, in 1217, Berenguela had conferred the kingship on her son as soon as she herself was declared sovereign, we cannot be sure that Juana used these precedents to justify Charles' conduct. What *is* clear is that she had no wish to abandon her royal prerogatives and continued to see the Royal Council as the backbone of government. Since she wanted the Junta to work in partnership with the royal councillors, she attached importance to her right to summon them and, if she thought necessary, dismiss some and appoint others, as she had done or tried to do in 1507. In other words, she attached important to her right to govern. But the Junta accused the Council, under the intemperate presidency of Rojas, of driving the repression of just demands, and even of outright malevolence.[48] Many nobles broadly agreed. Rojas wanted only to "slash and burn," Velasco wrote. Enríquez claimed the Council had "destroyed the kingdom."[49]

Juana's engagement with the Junta was complicated by the fact that, while she seemed amenable to discussion of reform, a radical shift in events took place only a day after the opening of the Cortes, with the order to dissolve the Royal Council. The queen insisted that only *she* had that power. The Junta thought otherwise. On 30 September, it sent a delegation to Valladolid to arrest those councillors who had not already fled. On 20 October, the Junta, now known as Cortes and Junta General, drew up a plan envisaging a Cortes with authority drawn directly from the cities (although only those same eighteen cities that traditionally had votes in the Cortes). After urging that Charles return to Spain and marry and, again, that the queen's royal household be restored, the *Proyecto de Ley Perpetua*, or *Capítulos de Tordesillas*, proposed that the cities assemble every three years, or as often as desired, without the need for royal sanction or the royal presence. The cities (or those, at least with votes in the Cortes) would determine taxation and act as a check and balance on government activity. The law envisaged, *inter alia*, the introduction of justice reforms, with an automatic appeal mechanism in cases of sentences of death or mutilation. Cities, towns and communities would themselves decide whether to accept *corregidores* and all awards grants or mercedes made by Charles, Philip and Fernando since the reign of Isabel would be revoked.[50] The revocation of Philip's *mercedes* was, it will be remembered, the cornerstone on which Juana had tried to form her government in 1506–1507. In short, the *Proyecto* envisaged a real structural shift in Castile's political fabric, with legitimacy passing from the monarchy to the Cortes as ultimate body of authority and voice of the kingdom.

The revolutionary tenor of such proposals alarmed peripheral communities like Burgos, which withdrew from the Junta. A contemporary work by Trinitarian friar Alonso de Castrillo reflects a movement divided against itself. His *Tractado de República*, published at Burgos early in 1521, shares general grievances and expresses a belief in the undesirability of perpetual or dynastic governance, whether royal or not. But it compares the uprising to the doomed Gigantomachy of Greek myth. In Ovid's *Metamorphoses*, the rebel giants "gathered themselves together in concert and maintaining that there was no reason for the supremacy exercised by the heavens over the earth sought to storm the former, intending to precipitate Zeus from his throne and the minor gods from their houses." Piling mountains together, raising them to the stars, they were eventually crushed beneath the weight of their own hubris.[51]

Sensing the serious implications for royal authority of comunero actions, Juana clung to a defence of the *status quo (ante)*—the Castile of the Catholic Kings as she had known it. A secret report attributed to Fray Francisco de León, and enclosed with a covering letter of 13 November from Adrian to Charles, shows Juana reading, or having read to her, the acts she was being asked to sign and arguing over them at length:

> her Highness, seated on her *estrado*, was talking with them a long time, as they read out their provisions before bringing them to her to sign, and after they had read everything, she told them that before she could sign them the provisions must be signed on the back by the members of the Council, and [only] afterwards could her Highness sign them, and that was why she had to communicate with the [royal] councillors, and her Highness said she had sent for them and they would soon arrive, and she said this because her Highness had secretly ordered a servant of hers to go in search of them, but he never went.[52]

Juana tried to defend the reputations of the royal councillors and of Adrian and Iñigo Fernández de Velasco, who had succeeded his brother as constable. She pointed out that the councillors:

> dated from the time of the Catholic king. They could not be bad, or at least there must be some who were good, and that was why she wanted to

speak and communicate with them, because they were experienced people and knew the form of good government from the time of the Catholic kings, and if there were some who were bad, her highness [not the Junta] would order their punishment.

The procurators objected that there was no need for the Council; she had legal experts at Tordesillas who knew how to govern. That, Juana insisted, was for *her* to judge. Repeatedly the procurators returned to the fray. At the same time, she faced pressure from some household members to withhold her signature. Adrian told Charles that, had she not been warned of the difficulties that might follow, she would have signed the Junta's documents long ago, adding in cipher, "*[and] all the kingdoms would have mutinied.*"[53]

León's account shows that, seasoned by an interminable series of conflicts and arguments throughout her reign, Juana fielded pleas and demands with caution, skill and subterfuge, and repeated attempts at dialogue as well as with an insistence on the pre-eminence of her royal authority. But, while the Junta agreed to talk to councillors as individuals, it objected to Juana's attempt to summon the entire Royal Council, as she had asked Rojas to do before the Junta's arrival, so that she herself could discuss matters with councillors and decide, as in 1506–1507, who to keep or discard and what to do next.

Thus, if a first distinction should be drawn between Juana's defence of Charles and her belief in her own right to govern, a second should be drawn between the comuneros' wish to exploit her authority and grant her real power. There is no indication that Juana was being offered the genuine freedom of manoeuvre that Pérez imagines or that Prawdin envisages when referring to the comuneros' offer of "*Freiheit, Reich und Krone.*"[54] Had they capitulated to Juana's desire to recall familiar advisers, royal councillors and grandees they would have run the risk of surrendering everything so far gained. Had Juana, on the other hand, awarded the Junta procurators the charismatic weapon of her signature, she would have risked becoming the cipher of forces beyond her control.

The Junta's claim to represent royal legitimacy masked an impossible struggle between queen and comuneros that continued through the late summer and autumn.[55] Some believed that the queen's failure to support them by signing their acts of government could only be explained in terms of demonic possession. If Castile was to be saved, heavenly forces had to be called upon to help the Junta rescue the queen from herself.

## 11.4 Juana I and the Body Politic

Juana's mental health had been a key component of successive power struggles within the wider crisis of legitimacy and the opening lines of the Junta's *Provisión*, addressed to Valladolid on 26 September, place the question at centre stage: "*It is well known to everyone that the root and first cause of all the evils and injuries suffered by these kingdoms has been the lack of health of the queen our lady* ..." [my emphasis]. The *Provisión* declares a threefold remedy by "humane" means. Following the Denias' expulsion from Tordesillas, all the "most distinguished and excellent" doctors in the realm would be invited to advise the Junta and priests would be asked to hold "solemn and devout processions" throughout Castile to pray for Juana's health.[56]

For years, the queen's mental health had been plotted upon a gendered graph of female obedience. Every sign of improvement or deterioration was judged in terms of the degree of cooperation, obedience and respect she showed to father, husband and son. Thus, in December 1506, Conchillos had referred to Juana's decision to depart for Granada as an act of insanity that would bring ruin on her kingdom. In August 1507, by contrast, her alleged capitulation to Fernando at Tórtoles was interpreted as a sign of health and intelligence. In 1520, many comuneros saw the transgressions of the body politic reflected in Juana's years of ill treatment and consequent indisposition.

In her biography of Juana, Aram adapts the idea of the king's two bodies to the notion of a divergence between Juana's "personal and institutional selves" that sanctioned the rule of others in her name. But, as shown above, Juana herself fought to retain the right to exercise royal power, while the concept of the 'mystical body'—the notion that Juana formed a single inextricable link with her kingdom and, indeed, *embodied* it—seems particularly appropriate to the situation in 1520.

The idea of the 'mystical body' was rooted in classical Greek literature and early Church exegesis, notably in the writings of Paul. Adaptations of the corporal metaphor abound in medieval writings, including the *Siete Partidas*, where kings, as God's deputies, are compared to the head that animates the limbs of the body politic. When the '*farsa*' of Ávila of 1465 tore royal attributes from an effigy of Enrique IV, González de Mendoza declared that: "every kingdom is held to be a natural body, and we regard the king as its head, and the rest of the kingdom as its members. And if the head, because of some inability (*ynabilidad*) is sick, it would seem better counsel to apply those medicines which reason suggests than to remove the head, which nature forbids."[57] The king's 'illness' or 'inability' not only contributed to, but reflected, the illness and division of the kingdom, just as the wound or mysterious lethargy of the Fisher King of the Grail legends, reflected the wasting of the land. Early in her reign, Isabel had lived the corporal metaphor in her own person, galloping alone to the admiral's fortress of Simancas to secure the punishment of his son (the current admiral). Believing that an act of serious disobedience had affected the health of the body politic, Isabel then went to bed, declaring: "My body suffers from the blows that Don Fadrique delivered yesterday against my guarantee." His punishment (imprisonment, followed by a period of exile in Sicily) brought Isabel's recovery.[58]

The *Provisión* follows immediately after the declaration, on 25 September, of a "perpetual union and brotherhood" of confederated cities and towns, according to which, if one town or city were attacked, the rest must come to its defence with arms.[59] The notion that the towns and cities of Castile formed an organic whole—an idea notably discussed in Sánchez de Arévalo's fifteenth-century work, *Suma de la Política*—is vividly encapsulated by a letter of 24 August 1520 from the community of Segovia to Medina del Campo, immediately after Medina's devastation: "Let our Lord God be witness that, as the houses of that town [Medina] were set alight, so our own entrails burned … But, señores, be assured that, as Medina perished for Segovia, so the memory of Segovia will either perish or Segovia will avenge Medina …".[60] In a later letter to Burgos, on the verge of breakaway, the Junta recalled the views of Athenian statesman and legal reformer Heredotus Solon, hero of ancient Greek democracy: "Solon said that the city or the kingdom was a body, and thus that when one member of the body hurts, so do all."[61]

The declaration of an alliance of cities, together with the contents of the *Proyecto de Ley Perpetua*, appear to see the Junta as the commonwealth's embodiment, effectively replacing Juana or Charles in that role. On the other hand, the *Provisión*, in identifying the evils and injuries suffered by Castile with Juana's ill-health, draws a sympathetic equation between the burning entrails of Castile's communities as they wept for the destruction of Medina del Campo and the queen's melancholic distress. It remained, nonetheless, at a loss to know how best to cure and treat her. On 30 August, Martire characteristically declared that affairs of state meant as much to Juana as the "birth of new stars."[62] On 6 November, English prelate and diplomat Cuthbert Turnstall wrote to cardinal Wolsey about rumours of comunero disillusionment: "the queen of Spain … hath not such use of reason as they had [been told], so that by her they might have colored an[d] supported their said rebellion as they intend[ed], now begin to repent of their folly."[63]

A more complex picture emerges from Tordesillas itself. It had long been known that Juana responded well to external stimulation and she had been "much seen and visited, especially by one of those *letrados* they [the Junta] had here, to the extent that every day and every hour they wanted to talk to her Highness …".[64] On 19 September, Portuguese ambassador João Rodrigues reported that it was the "greatest novelty" to "see what the Queen does." She was listening to many and her responses were "not altogether beside the point." Her rooms were clean and well appointed; she had ordered new clothes and headgear.[65] She had become accessible, wrote a Venetian agent, "and they say she is in good form."[66] On 8 October, Adrian reported (from Valladolid) that Juana had never been in so poor a state, surrounded by plates of cold and rotting food. Yet on 13 November, he observed that "on many matters her Highness speaks very sensibly …". On 16 November, he reported that she was wearing fine clothes and dressing Catalina well, so that the infanta could accompany her to Santa Clara.[67] Two days earlier, the Junta wrote to the Merindades, encouraging visits to Tordesillas, where Juana's health had much improved. Venetian secretary Geronimo Dedo reported rumours from Naples that Juana had written to the viceroy and city that she wanted to govern ("*lei vuol essere Raina*") and was allowing the cities control over municipal government and revenues. She had been asked to visit Valencia.[68]

The variation and chronology of these reports demonstrate the essentially intermittent nature of Juana's 'illness' or 'illnesses.' She functioned at times effectively, at others not. It is also possible that Juana used 'illness' strategically, as various female descendants would do. Adrian, who did not know her in person, took her incurability for granted; yet his letters, and Fray León's report, suggest that, when unable to control matters or exert authority, Juana used 'tiredness' and 'illness,' as well as the weapon of her signature, in a tactical sense, adapting the wits evident in her tussles with Denia to a drawn-out strategy of evasion, alternately raising and dashing hopes.

A commission of three—Toledan deputy Pedro de Ayala; a canon of León, Juan de Benavente, and Fernán Diáñez de Morales, dean of Soria—was set up in October to investigate the queen's health.

It decided to call on a renowned Aragonese exorcist. He and his team duly arrived, but concluded that Juana was not possessed, and that "for what she was suffering there was no remedy."[69] This perplexed Junta members, who persisted to the end in their belief that a cured queen would endorse their actions and that her restoration to health was essential to the welfare of the body politic. As the admiral later put it, when the cities lost her they felt it "to the depths of their soul."[70]

## Notes

1. 'God bless, *ducado de a dos*/for escaping the clutches of M. de Chièvres.'
2. BL, Ms. Egerton 309, 'Relación,' f. 35v.
3. Villalobos (SBE, ed. 1886), XIII, 7 June 1520.
4. Fernández-Armesto (Carr, ed. 2000), 131.
5. Sandoval, (ed. 1955–1956), 216.
6. Maldonado (Fernández Vargas, ed. 1975), 71, 109, 148.
7. AGS, Estado 8, f. 113 [deciphered fragment]. Also in Danvila (ed. 1897–1900), I, 444–445, as part of a letter of 28 July 1520 from Adrian to Charles.
8. Danvila, IV, Adrian to Charles, 23 May 1521.
9. Danvila, I, Adrian to Charles, 24 July 1520.
10. Danvila, II, Adrian to Charles, 1 November 1520.
11. AGS, Estado 8, f. 171, "Memorial de los malos asi eclesiásticos y Religiosos como cavalleros y letrados y otras personas" [undated]. The list is headed by Acuña ('*el peor de todo el Reino*'), followed by Villaescusa ('*no tan malo, pecó por liviandad*').
12. Pérez (2001), 'Carta de los frailes de Salamanca.'
13. Pérez (1999), Elliott (1990) and Maravall (1963).
14. Danvila, 1, 30 June 1520.
15. Gutiérrez Nieto (1973).
16. Colmenares (Baeza González, ed. 1970), 196; see also Gutiérrez Nieto.
17. Santa Cruz (Laiglesia y Auser, ed. 1920), 1, 239.
18. Ferrer del Rio (2007), 'Carta de Toledo a las demás Ciudades, invitandandolas a reunir en Junta' (1520), 326–327.
19. Colmenares; Sandoval, LXXX, 271.
20. Danvila, II, Salvatierra to the Junta and others, 22 September 1520.
21. Prawdin (1938), Pérez (1999), Haliczer (1981), Zalama (2010), Aram (2005) and Espinosa (2009).
22. AGS, Estado 5, f. 287, [May?], 1520; CSP (Queen Juana), Bergenroth, ed. 49.
23. AGS, Estado 5, f. 288, [May?], 1520; CSP (Queen Juana), 50.

24. Sandoval, 271–272.
25. Ibidem.
26. AGS, PR 3, f. 20, "Cartas de Alonso Martyn de Balboa para el Obispo de Cuenca y los licenciados Zapata, Polanco y Aguirre," 23 August 1520; Danvila, I, "Testimonio de la entrevista que el teniente corregidor, Alonso Saravia ... tuvo con la Reina Doña Juana el 23 de agosto de 1520," 467–469.
27. Martire (López de Toro, ed. 1953–1957) 12, 684. For Villabrágima, see Chapter 12.
28. Danvila, II, 4 September 1520.
29. BL, Egerton 390, 'Relación,' ff. 59v.–60.
30. Elliott (1990), 150.
31. Fink de Backer (Nader, ed. 2004), 71–92.
32. López Alvárez (1977), 34.
33. BL, Ms. Egerton 309, 'Relacíon,' ff. 59v.–61, Padilla to Toledo, 1 September 1520.
34. *'y vengan aquí que yo huelgo dello'; 'sí, vengan'*. AGS, PR, CC 4, f. 73, 1 September 1520.
35. Danvila, II [undated; September 1520]; AGS, PR 2-1, f. 18, Adrian to Charles, 4 September 1520; AGS, PR 2-1, f. 20, to Charles, 14 September 1520.
36. There was no representation from the south. As Maldonado observes, this did not imply a lack of comunero agitation, but it had been stifled '*ya con promesas, ya con el terror ...*' (112).
37. Sandoval, 279.
38. AGS, PR 4, f. 75, 'De lo que pasó con la Reina nuestra señora,' 24 September 1520; CSP (Queen Juana), 61. See also Sandoval, 276–279. For Dr. Zúñiga, see Möller (Szaszdi León-Borja/Galende Ruiz, eds. 2015), 499–524.
39. After the attempted assassination of Fernando in 1492, Isabel told Talavera, "And this is one of the sorrows I felt: to see the King suffer what I deserved, not meriting it, but paying for me ...". Ochoa (ed. *Epistolario Español*, 1850), 14–15, Liss (2004), 349 and Sesma Muñoz (2006), 191–193.
40. AGS, PR 4, f. 75.
41. BL, Ms. Egerton 309, 'Relación' ff. 61v.–62.
42. Arboledo (1993).
43. "*Sucesión*. La primera [condición] que después dél [Charles] no pueda suceder muger ninguna en el reino: pero que no habiendo hijos, que puedan suceder hijos de hijas é de nietas siendo nacidos é bautizados en Castilla; pero que no puedan suceder sino fueren nacidos en Castilla" (*Capítulos*).

44. CSP Sp. 2, 60, Adrian to Charles, 23 September 1520.
45. BL, Egerton, Ms. 309, 'Relación,' f. 61v.
46. AGS, PR 2, f. 36, Lope Hurtado to Charles.
47. BL, Egerton Ms. 309, 'Relación,' f. 55.
48. Pérez (2001), *Provisión de la Santa Junta a la Comunidad de Valladolid*, 26 September 1520, 90–93.
49. Danvila, I, to Charles, 24 June 1520.
50. Carretero Zamora (Martínez Gil, ed. 2002), 245–256; Martínez-Sicluna y Sepúlveda (Szaszdi León-Borja/Galende Ruiz, eds. 2015), 451–484.
51. Fernández-Santamaria (1977).
52. AGS, PR 2-1, f. 166, Fray Francisco de León to Adrian (November 1520).
53. AGS, PR 2-1, f. 169.
54. Prawdin, 296.
55. In his book about Juana of Castile ("la Beltraneja"), Azcona considers the possibility that some comuneros, either during a mission to Portugal, or in exile, "fluttered like butterflies around the flame of the Excelente Señora." (Azcona 2007), 250.
56. Pérez (2001), 'Provisión de la Santa Junta,' 90–93.
57. Pulgar (Mata Carriazo, ed. 1943), I; McKay (1985).
58. Pulgar, I, 441–444.
59. Danvila, II, 'Alianza y hermandad jurada que las ciudades y villas del Reino realizaron en Tordesillas el 25 de septiembre de 1520,' 76–81.
60. Sandoval, 249.
61. Danvila, II, 30 October 1520.
62. Martire, 12, 51, 30 August 1520.
63. Brewer (ed. 1920), 3, 1043, 384.
64. AGS, Estado 8, f. 32, Licenciate Polanco to Charles, 17 January 1521.
65. Partially cited in Pérez (1999), 194n; in full in Aram (Szászdi León-Borja/Galende Ruíz, eds. 2013), 51–57.
66. Sanuto (Fulin, ed. 1969–1970), 24, 7 September 1520, 290.
67. Danvila, II, to Charles.
68. Sanuto, 24, 3 November 1520, 406.
69. Portuguese ambassador's letter, 28 October 1520, in Alba (1975), 122–123 and Aram (2013), 57–60.
70. Danvila, II, admiral to Luis de la Cuvea (undated).

## References

Alba, Ramón. 1975. *Acerca de algunas particularidades de las Comunidades de Castilla, tal vez relacionadas con el supuesto acaecer terreno del Milenario Igualitario*. Madrid: Editora Nacional.

Aram, Bethany. 2005. *Juana the Mad: Sovereignty and Dynasty in Renaissance Europe*. Baltimore and London: John Hopkins University Press.

———. 2013. La Reina Juana, Fray Juan de Ávila y la Infanta Catalina ante los Comuneros. In *Imperio y Tiranía. La Dimensión Europea de las Comunidades de Castilla*, ed. István Szászdi León-Borja and María Jesús Galende Ruiz. Valladolid: Universidad de Valladolid.

Arboledos, Pedro Andrés Porras. 1993. *Ciudad de Jaén y la revolución de las comunidades de Castilla: 1500–1523*. Jaén: Diputación de Jaén.

Azcona, Tarsicio de. 2007. *Juana de Castilla, mal llamada La Beltraneja*. Madrid: La Esfera de los Libros.

Bergenroth, G.A. (ed.). 1868. *Calendar of State Papers, Supplement to Vol. I and Vol. II of Letters, Despatches and State Papers relating to Negotiations Between England and Spain, Preserved in the Archives of Simancas and Elsewhere*. London: Longmans, Green, Reader and Dyer.

Brewer, John Sherren (ed.). 1920. *Letters and Papers, Foreign and Domestic, of the Reign of Henry VIII*. London: HMSO.

Carretero Zamora, Juan Manuel. 2002. Las Cortes en el Programa Comunero: Reforma Institucional o Propuesta Revolucionaria? In *En Torno a las Comunidades de Castilla*, ed. Fernando Martínez Gil. Cuenca: Universidad de Castilla- La Mancha.

Colmenares, Diego de. 1970. *Historia de la Insigne Ciudad de Segovia y Conpedio de las Historias de Castilla*, ed. T. Baeza González. Segovia: Academía de Historia y Arte de San Quirce.

Danvila y Collado, Manuel (ed.). 1897–1900. *Historia crítica y documentada de las Comunidades de Castilla*. Madrid: Memoria Histórica Español.

Elliott, John. 1990. *Imperial Spain, 1469–1716*. London, Middlesex: Penguin.

Espinosa, Aurelio. 2009. *The Empire of the Cities: Emperor Charles V, the Comunero Revolt, and the Transformation of the Spanish System*. Leiden and Boston: Koninklijke Brill.

Fernández-Armesto, Felipe. 2000. The Improbable Empire. In *Spain: A History*, ed. Raymond Carr. Oxford. Oxford University Press.

Fernández-Santamaría, J.A. 1977. *The State, War and Peace: Spanish Political Thought in the Renaissance, 1516–1559*. Cambridge: Cambridge University Press.

Ferrer del Rio, Antonio. 2007. *Historia del levantamiento de las Comunidades de Castilla, 1520–1521*, ed. Jesús Gascón Pérez. Pamplona: Urgoiti.

Fink de Backer, Stephanie. 2004. Rebel with a Cause: The Marriage of María Pacheco and the Formation of Mendoza Identity. In *Power and Gender in Renaissance Spain: Eight Women of the Mendoza Family, 1450–1650*, ed. Helen Nader. Chicago: University of Illinois Press.

Fulin, Rinaldo (ed.). 1969–1970. *I diarii de Marino Sanuto, 1466–1536*. Bologna: Forni Editore.

Gutiérrez Nieto, Juan Ignacio. 1973. *Las Comunidades como Movimiento antiseñorial*. Barcelona: Planeta.

Haliczer, Stephen. 1981. *The Comuneros of Castile: The Forging of a Revolution, 1475–1521*. Madison and London: University of Wisconsin Press.
Liss, Peggy K. 2004. *Isabel the Queen: Life and Times*. Philadelphia: University of Pennsylvania Press.
López Álvarez, Luis. 1977. *Los comuneros*. Barcelona: Editorial Laia.
López de Toro, José (ed.). 1953–1957. *Petrus Martyr Anglerius. Epistolario*. CODOIN, 9–12. Madrid: Imprenta Góngora.
Maldonado, Juan. 1975. *La Revolución Comunera*, ed. Valentina Fernández Vargas. Madrid: Ediciones del Centro.
Maravall, José Antonio. 1963. *Las Comunidades de Castilla. Una primera revolución moderna*. Madrid: Revista de Occidente.
Martínez-Sicluna y Sepúlveda, Consuelo. 2015. La Ley Perpetua: Ley fundamental del Reino en la revuelta comunera. In *Carlos V: Conversos y Comuneros*, ed. István Szászdi León-Borja and Maria Jesús Galende. Valladolid: Centro Estudios Camino Santiago Sahagún/Marcial Pons.
McKay, Angus. 1985. Ritual and Propaganda in Fifteenth-Century Castile. *Past and Present* 107 (1), 3–43.
Möller Recondo, Claudia. 2015. El doctor Alonso de Zúñiga; catedrático de Derecho y comunero. In *Carlos V: Conversos y Comuneros*, ed. István Szászdi León-Borja and Maria Jesús Galende. Valladolid: Centro Estudios Camino Santiago Sahagún/Marcial Pons.
Ochoa, Eugenio (ed.). 1850. *Epistolario Español*. Madrid: Rivadeneyra.
Pérez, Joseph 1999. *La revolución de Comunidades de Castilla (1520–1521)*. Madrid: Siglo XXI de España.
———. 2001. *Los Comuneros*. Madrid: La Esfera de los Libros.
Prawdin, Michael. 1938. *Johanna die Wahnsinnige: Habsburgs Weg zum Weltreich*. Vienna: Otto Lorenz Verlag.
Pulgar, Fernando de. 1943. *Crónica de los Reyes Católicos*, vol. I–II, ed. Juan de Mata Carriazo. Madrid: Espasa Calpe.
Sandoval, Prudencio de (ed.). 1955–1956. *Historia de la Vida y Hechos del Emperador Carlos V*. Madrid: Biblioteca de Autores Españoles.
Santa Cruz, Alonso. 1920. *Crónica del Emperador*, ed. Francisco de Laiglesia y Auser, vol. I. Madrid: Imprenta del Patronato de Húerfanos de Intendencia e Intervención Militares.
Sesma Muñoz, J. Ángel. 2006. *Los idus de diciembre de Fernando II*. Zaragoza: Nogara Libros.
Villalobos, Francisco López. 1886. *Algunas obras del doctor Francisco López Villalobos*, ed. Sociedad de Bibliófilos Españoles. Madrid: Imprenta de Miguel Ginesta.
Zalama, Miguel-Ángel. 2010. *Juana I: Arte, Poder y Cultura en torno a una Reina que no gobernó*. Valladolid: Centro de Estudios Europa Hispánica.

CHAPTER 12

# Vengeance (1520–1522)

## 12.1 The Battle for Tordesillas

Charles wrote in October 1520 that the Denias' expulsion from Tordesillas had upset him more than any other thing.[1] Reports about Juana's unfitness to govern remained contradictory. She had not endorsed the Junta but she had engaged with procurators and lawyers and, whether under pressure, or of her own volition, could have caused his downfall at any time. She had defended Adrian as, by all accounts, a "good man" of moderate habits.[2] But no Castilian institution had sanctioned his governorship and Charles' partial response was to appoint native-born Castilians, the constable and admiral, as co-governors. These were obliged, under the terms of their appointment, to proscribe the comuneros as traitors—"*rebelles, alebes y traydores, ynfieles a nos y a nuestra Corona* …".[3]

The spread of comunero discontent through rural Castile and eruption of the movement of the brotherhoods, or Germanías, in Valencia and beyond, had driven recalcitrant nobles into the imperial fold. By the end of November, the governors had assembled an army of some 8000 infantry and over 2000 cavalry. But Enríquez refused to formally assume the governorship until 3 January 1521. This was partly because he feared that, as the emperor's direct representative, he would draw fire upon his heartland of Medina de Rioseco, Castromonte and Torrelobatón, all within relatively easy distance of Valladolid, and partly because he wanted to strike a reasonable stance in his ongoing negotiations with the comuneros.



G. B. Fleming, *Juana I*, Queenship and Power,
https://doi.org/10.1007/978-3-319-74347-9_12

At the end of November, another would-be negotiator, accompanied by judges and magistrates, visited comunero and Caroline camps. Pérez concludes that Villaescusa's initiative was purely personal.[4] He had, however, been Juana's most important adviser and envoy and in his recent talks with her she had probably granted him authority to negotiate. At Villabrágima, to the south-east of Rioseco, he announced that he had come "on behalf of the Queen and King, our lords" (in that order) to command the comuneros to withdraw from their positions pending readiness to negotiate.[5] He was, however, unfortunate in his interlocutor, Antonio de Acuña, one of the last and most extraordinary of the Spanish warrior bishops. Acuña had defied the queen's Council over the see of Zamora in 1507 and, whatever the motive for his adoption of the comunero cause, there is no doubting the adoration of his congregations and the dread he inspired among his adversaries. His extreme restlessness created around him an almost supernatural sense of extreme mobility.

Villaescusa's attempt to coax Acuña into accepting a ceasefire failed and he had no better luck among the lords gathered at Medina de Rioseco. He knew the admiral personally, having sailed with him in the armada of 1496, and he shared an understanding of comunero grievances. But Enríquez disliked the actions that Villaescusa had taken against lordly self-interest as Chancery president and suspected him of being too close to the Junta. Charles' envoy, Lope Hurtado de Mendoza, agreed: "The President of Valladolid is here," he told Charles, "and has been speaking to me … and thinks it would be better if your Highness settled with the Junta, because the Grandees always placed your Highness in difficulties."[6] Villaescusa told the admiral he thought a peace deal could be reached if some royal councillors were dismissed and Pedro Laso appointed as (fourth) governor.[7] In a meeting rife with insults, Enríquez snarled: "And so? Are you saying that you sympathise with the Junta's proposals? You'll be thrown out of the magistrature!"[8]

Stalemate followed. But disagreements, misgivings and hesitations among the Junta's military leaders proved fatal to the comunero cause. In early December, Girón decided to move his men westward to the constable's territory of Villalpando, where they would be better sheltered from winter snows and well placed to sabotage convoys heading for Rioseco. But, unaccountably, he left the road to Tordesillas exposed, and on the night of 4 December, Charles' men marched down it, led by the constable's son, Pedro Fernández de Velasco, count of Haro. The first detachments arrived at about ten o'clock in the morning of the next day. Though vastly superior in numbers, the assailants lacked heavy artillery. The walls seemed impregnable, and most casualties on the Caroline side occurred early on, with cavalry over-exposed below. Eventually, however, a weak spot, smeared over with earth and lime, gave way to the firepower of four falconets. Those who eventually forced their way through faced ferocious attack and some were overwhelmed by fire and smoke from neighbouring houses, set deliberately alight. Others succeeded in raising a standard to the cry of "Victory! Victory!" The standard was shot to shreds but the point made.[9]

Word reached Haro that Pedro de Ayala, procurator for Toledo, had taken Juana and Catalina from the palace, intending either to display the queen on the battlements to stop the assault, or escort her across the bridge to Medina del Campo. Haro decided against storming the bridge. Darkness was falling. The river was fast, deep and dangerous and the banks steep. If Juana was, gone they would find her later. At two o'clock next morning, the gate was broken open and the artillery dragged into the town. Hand-to-hand fighting and shooting ensued amid raging fires and the clang of church bells. Among the fiercest fighters were up to 300 of Acuña's priests. Fray Antonio de Guevara later claimed he had witnessed one shoot eleven dead from behind a battlement while blessing them with the sign of the cross.[10] Some *junteros* fled to Valladolid and Medina del Campo. Others were captured. After Tordesillas fell, the killings ceased but the plunder of houses, churches and monasteries continued and was generally acknowledged to have been "so general that not a single servant of her Highness escaped." Even Catalina's mule was taken.[11]

According to Maldonado, Juana was discovered in the main palace patio, holding Catalina by the hand. Gómez de Santillán, who, as procurator of Granada, had defended Juana at the Cortes of Valladolid in 1506, and fought in Charles's cavalry at Tordesillas, relates that, with Catalina and a chest of jewels, and amid general confusion, Juana had gone to Santa Clara and ordered that Philip's coffin be prepared for a quick escape.[12] There are problems with this story but, if true, the queen may have worried that the fire would spread there, engulfing Philip's remains.

## 12.2 The "Dance of Discord"

Juana, who had long demanded the right to see "her" grandees, enjoyed the bustle around her.[13] Several lords, including Haro and Fernando de Vega, knight commander of Castile, remarked on the graciousness of her reception. But while, for both sides, possession of the queen was crucial, opinions were divided as to whether to exploit it. This author has preferred to describe the victors of Tordesillas as 'Caroline' or 'imperial' rather than 'royal,' given the complex implications of the latter word, and the fact that many comuneros too could be described as upholders of royal authority. But even the victors were not a coherent force. Divisions existed between the followers of the (hardline) constable and the admiral.[14] Some had close comunero links, and although various nobles and knights, including the sixty-year-old Enríquez, sweating in armour he had never thought to have to wear again, fought bravely, they were, as the queen drily, if amicably, pointed out, rather late.[15]

Comments about the queen's affability mingled with others about her confusion.[16] But, although the length and conditions of her captivity had put her at the mercy of bewildering claims and counter-claims and made it difficult for her to emerge from the world of the past, she had shown flashes of energy and resourcefulness. Her earlier remark to the Junta that she "loved all people" smacks less of empty rhetoric than of a genuine desire to mediate. Villaescusa's initiatives, and her attempts to bring royal councillors to Tordesillas for talks with herself and the Junta, had failed. But this did not invalidate her efforts. Above all, her protection of Charles, like her former protection of Fernando, had ensured his political survival in Spain. From Rioseco and Tordesillas, respectively, Adrian and Lope Hurtado praised Juana's conduct. Charles owed a "great debt" to his mother, Adrian told him, for her defence of his "person and succession" and for "other things." Lope Hurtado told Charles she had said "many good things" in his defence.[17] Juana may have believed she had done enough to secure her freedom. But the marquis of Denia would later maintain that she had been spoilt by all the attention and become haughty "in consequence of the offers made her" so that "there is no man who does not have great difficulty with her."[18]

For Denia and the constable, Juana's "liberation" meant her definitive political erasure. Others hoped to exploit the queen's legitimacy and latent power. The loss and sacking of Tordesillas had fuelled comunero wrath against the nobility, who lived in heightened fear of reprisals, and when Juana told Enríquez, worried about his estates, that she had ordered the comuneros to avoid bloodshed and disband their troops, he persuaded her to repeat her words before a "great many knights," ordering that they be recorded.[19]

Enríquez was not alone in believing that an appeal from Juana could be converted into royal measures. Santillán told Adrian that he had witnessed Juana dictating orders to Pedro de Girón and to comunero cities to disband and refrain from violence and thought these measures, transcribed by two notaries in the presence of the grandees, could work.[20] Vega managed, however, to block the initiative, arguing that to take such action would be tantamount to acknowledging the existence of two monarchs—the "worst thing that can happen in a realm."[21] Fray Antonio de Guevara agreed. For the "good and loyal knights of Spain," he told Acuña, victory meant only one thing: a return to the natural order under a *single* monarch—only traitors served a plurality of monarchs. Whereas, in 1516, the Royal Council had used this same argument against Charles, Guevara used it now against the proprietary queen: "As for us and for our friends, we want no other God but Christ, nor any other law but the Gospel, nor any other King but Don Carlos."[22] The consternation of Charles' most loyal servants when faced by the question of co-rule is a measure of the importance of the issue at stake. Despite the fact that, until Juana's death, acts of government bore the names both of Charles and Juana, to exploit Juana's authority in this situation was to uphold her sanity and thus to undermine Charles as king.

The debate—or, to use the admiral's phrase, the "*dança de la discordia*"—continued. On 22 January 1521, Adrian reassured Charles that, although the subject had been discussed at length, both as regards "what has happened and what will happen," no use had been made of Juana's orders.[23] But a month later, an exasperated Denia remarked that: "Four days ago the Admiral went into the Queen our Lady and asked her Highness to sign or the kingdom would be lost … I told him before the Cardinal [Adrian] that he must not beg her Highness to sign because he knows what a disservice it would be to God and his Majesty. He answered, 'I'm not asking the Queen of Fez to sign, but *my* Queen!'[24] I said that if her Highness were disposed to it we would all do it and work for it and the King our Lord would beg us to do so, but being as she is, it's not even worth thinking about. What he then said I cite the Cardinal [Adrian] as my witness. Believe me, your Majesty, your servants have more trouble enduring the Admiral and repairing what he does to the detriment of our undertaking than fighting the traitors twenty times over …".[25]

Denia was fortunate that, although willing to give verbal orders and have them notarised, Juana still withheld her signature. The admiral and count of Benavente spent hours talking with Juana.[26] She assured Benavente that she would sign documents once she left Tordesillas.[27] Perhaps this was, again, a delaying tactic. On the other hand, to "leave Tordesillas" meant to regain her freedom. As far as we know, Juana never used her signature while in captivity or under constraint, and after the battle, she had become rapidly aware that she was being held "in the power of the Constable." Closely aligned to Denia, Iñigo Fernández de Velasco supported Charles' reinstatement of Denia as the person best suited for Juana's "punishment or satisfaction."[28]

But the admiral insisted that Juana was fit to govern.[29] Enríquez had never been consistent in this respect, and was swayed by emotion and by political contingency. In 1506, he had pressed Juana to consider co-rule, either with Philip or Fernando. But by 1520, he was, like Villaescusa, and like the comuneros, aware that neglect and cruelty had aggravated her mental state. To the comuneros of Valladolid, he argued that they must look to Juana's sons to govern.[30] Yet, in 1521, with Tordesillas again under Caroline control, he insisted once more on Juana's sanity. Despite their defeat at Tordesillas, the comuneros remained a formidable force, but one that might, as Adrian and Rojas had hoped months earlier, prove peculiarly vulnerable to a signed order from Juana. A governing queen might also, as Fernández Conti indicates, present a "golden" opportunity for the admiral's ambitions.[31] Yet the sheer persistence with which Enríquez pursued both the grail of the royal signature and the expulsion of the Denias—even after Charles' return and his hopes for political promotion had been dashed—suggests that he was genuinely uneasy about the queen's ill treatment.

During December and the first weeks of 1521, the struggle for control of the queen amounted to a new battle of Tordesillas. Enríquez told Charles that Denia was being very harsh to "the queen's people" and should consider the negative consequences of giving him free rein.[32] The emperor's envoy, Lope de Hurtado, also warned that Denia had returned "with more passion than was necessary for the times we're in" and that Charles "should command him to be far more temperate and try to be amiable with the servants of the Queen our lady … It is said that he is determined to turn everything upside down and given the passion he has and the ill-will with which he is received, I think what he is doing will not be good."[33] But Vega, concerned at the growth of a party within the palace that opposed Denia's reinstatement, warned Charles, without a trace of irony, to order the admiral, count of Benavente, marquis of

Astorga and count of Haro to stop promoting initiatives by Juana and restrict them to "seeing that she is at liberty, as she is at present …".[34]

Charles' wariness of the admiral was predictable. Despite his prominence in the uprising's suppression and the importance of Medina de Ríoseco as a refuge and military base and perhaps for the very reason that he was a subtle political player—an "old fox," as he was often called; a "free man of Spain" as he called himself—and the comuneros' most acute and feared opponent, he was seen by Charles (as he would later be seen by Charles' wife, Empress Isabel) as something of a nuisance. Enríquez believed that a monarch's role should be limited to "keeping the peace, administering justice, and, why not, granting rewards," and that absolutism broke the bond between monarch and realm.[35] He was too flamboyant, too subtle, too intelligent and, perhaps, too unpredictable to win Charles's trust. While he appealed to the emperor's good sense and humanity, it was Denia's appeal to his fear and insecurity that won the day. Charles urged the marquis to obstruct any move to exploit Juana's authority.[36] Denia scoffed at the admiral's frequent talks with Juana and plans to "raise Lazarus from the dead again."[37]

Ultimately, it was not the defeat of the comuneros at Tordesillas that sealed Juana's fate but the gradual desertion of grandees and royal councillors. The comuneros had opened a window that Enríquez and his allies fought to keep ajar. Their departure from Tordesillas meant Juana's final disappearance from public view, if not from public memory. Juana's clear desire to influence affairs; her rumoured comunero sympathies; the support for her of a magnate of the calibre of Enríquez; her continuing importance for the comuneros and the fear that a new struggle to possess her might follow; the fact that her public appearances had thrown into question the extent of her 'incapacitation' or 'incurability'—all these factors ensured that the queen would remain closely confined and under continual surveillance and that, to borrow Denia's biblical allusion, there would be no resurrection.[38]

## 12.3 Purge

As noted earlier, Juana had begun forming the embryo of her own household and administration in the autumn of 1506 and had hoped for Fernando's cooperation in completing the process. Instead, the king of Aragon had absorbed many of her Castilian servants and officials into his own household, while continuing to pay them out of the funds allocated to the queen. This practice had continued, so that nominations to Juana's household would never correspond with the actual number of staff working at Tordesillas. When, in 1518, Charles asked the newly appointed marquis of Denia to pare down Juana's household, Denia responded cautiously. Her staff already received only 'alms,' often paid well in arrears, and a third of the funds allocated for her household went instead to individuals drawn into the emperor's entourage.[39] Nonetheless, some servants, seen as security risks, faced dismissal.

During its occupation of Tordesillas the Junta had been unable, for evident reasons, to address the reconstruction of the queen's household as she herself desired—that is, along the lines of Isabel's. But the Junta had tried to restore some Isabelline associations. Denia had been replaced with Alonso de Quintanilla, a former servant of Juana's brother, and his wife, Catalina de Figueroa, and over seventy new *continos* had been nominated. Among these, several had former associations with Isabel and Prince Juan. Francisco Álvarez de Toledo and Pero Zapata were the sons of Isabel's former royal secretary. Fernando de Anaya was the son of Isabel's doctor, De la Reyna, and Juan Gaitán was a former servant of the prince. Some appointees were procurators, such as Alonso de Saravia of Valladolid and Pedro de Ayala of Toledo, who was described in an earlier-mentioned blacklist of comunero ecclesiastics, friars, knights and *letrados*, as a "*muy mala persona.*"[40] Others were army captains like Juan Bravo, Juan Zapata (another "*mala persona*") and Juan de Mendoza, son of Isabel's "inseparable" cardinal, Pedro González de Mendoza.

Most or all of those who feature on another list, compiled in April 1521 by the royal *contadores mayores*, had by then been captured or had disappeared.[41] Some, like Francisco de Álvarez de Toledo, died in prison. Others, like Alonso de Saravia, were executed after attempting to escape the country. Others, like Juan de Mendoza and Pedro de Ayala, had death sentences commuted. Denia returned, meanwhile, like an avenging angel, determined to purge the palace of the slightest trace of comunero infection. He began with the staff who had been instrumental in ousting him, such as Juana's longstanding *despensero mayor*, Fernando de Arzeo, Juan de Carquijano and Carquijano's son, recommending that, out of a total of 169 household members in July 1521, a core of twenty-two should be dismissed.[42] These dismissals, to which Charles agreed, further embittered relations with the admiral, who had released from prison the ringleaders of the palace revolt against Denia and reinstated Carquijano's son in his position as *repostero de plata*. Treasurer Ochoa de Landa and chamberlain Diego de Ribera were placed under close scrutiny. So too was the queen's confessor, Fray Ávila, embarrassed by "defamatory" reports that he had encouraged Juana to govern.[43]

Denia also maintained that some (troublesome) female attendants served no purpose now that the marchioness had rejoined him. The marchioness herself complained to Charles that servants like Juana Cortes and the infanta's *ama*, Leonor de Alarcón, and "another two or three who entertain the same opinions," hampered her in her duties, for the queen allowed only these to enter her rooms and Catalina's.[44] The marchioness did not clarify what these "opinions" were but long-standing hostility between the Denias and Juana's servants was tainted with the comunero brush.

The Denias implied that even fifteen-year-old Catalina had been contaminated by close proximity with *junteros*. In July 1521, Enríquez declared that the Denias were treating her so badly that she might, in desperation, take the veil.[45] In August, Catalina appealed secretly to Charles. She told him that her previous letters were written under strict surveillance, but she felt he must know the truth about the Denias' actions against the queen and herself. Catalina defended herself from Charles' allegations that she had sympathised with the comuneros. She protested that she could not have avoided talking to Junta members nor prevented them from contacting the queen. She had signed a letter urging Padilla's return to Tordesillas (after he had left for Toledo) because she had understood it was "in the service of the Queen …". She meant no harm. As for the Denias, they were "angry with everyone." They resented the infanta speaking to her mother's servants and disliked her rapport with Ana de Cabrera, countess of Módica, wife of the admiral, who had shown "great compassion" to her that January, and with whom she enjoyed corresponding. For this, the marchioness wanted to "tear out her eyes." She subjected her to body searches and inquired into the messengers who brought letters to and from the countess and her sisters. Servants were ordered to stop her speaking and writing and she was treated as if her status were no greater than that of Denias' own daughters. These same servants had rifled through her wardrobe. They "take everything, use it and spoil it, so that I have nothing of my own and nothing lasts me."

More grimly, Catalina revealed that Juana was not only being stolen from but subjected to severe restraint, even within the already restricted parameters imposed by Charles in 1518. The marchioness and her daughters used stealth to gain access to Catalina's room. Once concealed there, they ordered Juana's servants to lock the queen in her bedchamber "where no light enters other than candlelight …". Catalina begged Charles "for the love of God to provide that, if the Queen my lady wishes to walk for her recreation in the corridor over the river or the one where the sedge mats are, or if she wishes to take recreation by going into her reception room she should not be prevented." She was unlikely to try to escape, Catalina added, but if she did, the women could stop her.

Catalina also showed concern for Ávila, whom she called "the guardian." This was the elective title conferred, within the Franciscan order, on the superior of a community of at least a dozen priests, and Ávila was, or had been, superior of the monastery of San Francisco de Ávila. Catalina argued that Juana was distressed by the death of a beloved *camarera*, María de Cartama. If Ávila were dismissed, as she had heard might happen, she would have "no other person to comfort her …".[46]

A rush of letters from Ávila to Charles, in which Ávila often signs himself "your poor priest and chaplain" and sometimes "your poor priest and servant" or "slave" (*siervo*)—a formula attaching as much to the professed humility of his order as to the conditions of his service—glimmer with pathos as he describes his tribulations at the hands of the avenging Denias. He did everything for Juana, he wrote in June. But the marquis wanted him to stop seeing her: "As he does not dare to tell me this in words, he endeavours to let me understand it by the manner in which he impedes and molests me, as the most reverend cardinal has seen." Referring to himself and the priests he supervised, he adds: "we are dead from hunger, as the last year nothing has been paid for our maintenance."[47] By August, nothing had changed. He was continually harassed and had been deprived of food, fuel and clothing.[48]

Such was the prevailing paranoia after the Denias' return that even Adrian—who had come to Tordesillas on 26 December 1520, to work more closely with his co-governor, Enríquez—was treated warily. Adrian had expressed exasperation with his former pupil in a letter that favourably compared Juana's conservation of the royal patrimony with Charles' squandering of it, and which, according to Martire, had been intercepted and publicly read out in Valladolid: "I assure you … that [Juana] is wiser in not underwriting [acts of government] and conceding nothing than your Majesty in conceding everything, because the former [approach] means that nothing leaves the Kingdom, but the latter means that the whole patrimony is being lost …".[49]

Suspicion of Adrian may explain his inability to see the queen. He complained to Charles: "As regards the queen's health, God knows it weighs on my mind that I have not seen her Highness, for every time [I try to do so] I am prevented on the grounds that she is indisposed, and I do not wish to insist with her Highness about this and annoy her."[50] However, the decision is unlikely to have been hers. On 17 January, Polanco assured Charles, in words more terrible than they might seem, that the grandees and other knights no longer saw Juana, "since that is most suitable from various points of view." He himself had not kissed hands "because it seemed unnecessary." Polanco agreed with Denia that the many visits she had received had made her "very importunate" and noted that, over the last four days, she had stopped eating—a probable reaction to the abandonment.[51] Even the admiral hesitated to see her, for "To see her is to pity her, with little means of doing anything about it, and from pure compassion we do not see her."[52] Yet his struggle with Denia over use of Juana's signature continued through February. Denia declared that she would not sign anything "as long as I can help it."[53]

In December 1521, he lamented slow progress in punishing her servants and advised an investigation into their conduct. Ávila reported that the servants were much distressed by news that they were to be dismissed and entreated Charles to show compassion.[54] The emperor's response was to sack Ávila too. Denia confirmed that the friar had not visited Juana since receiving notice to quit and Charles had done her a big favour by divesting her of a "person who spoke to her as he liked" ("*a su voluntad*").[55]

## 12.4 The Legacy of Villalar

In the war of the Comunidades possession of the true source of royal authority meant everything. As the author of the *Relación de las Comunidades* writes: "The most important thing of all is to have her."[56] To lose her was to lose the claim to legitimacy. Contemporaries note the mixed shock and defiance with which the comuneros responded. "So great was everyone's astonishment and so great their sorrow," Maldonado comments, "that at one and the same time they lost both hope and judgment …".[57] Yet Tordesillas itself remained "pure community."[58] Councillor Vargas noticed an increase in popular anger and agitation.[59] Restored to favour after Girón's catastrophic leadership, and greeted like a star wherever he went, Padilla saw the queen's "liberation" as his priority.[60] Pero Laso de la Vega threatened war on the governors as "delinquents" if they did not grant Juana access to her subjects … . Francisco Maldonado, Salamanca's militia captain, whose tattered red banner with its blue fleur de lys still hangs in the old cathedral, demanded: "Above all things, the liberation of the Queen, so that everyone may visit and consult with her, given that, after all, she is the only legitimate sovereign."[61]

After defeat at Tordesillas the Junta moved to Valladolid. This became steadily more radical as its *cuadrillas*, or popular assemblies, assumed greater prominence in the city's decision making. The oaths of fidelity publicly sworn to the Junta that November were adaptations of the traditional oath of allegiance to the monarch, and clear expressions of belief in the popular legitimacy of *pueblo* and *Comunidad*.[62] Nonetheless, the queen was not forgotten. The liberation of the queen and (definitive) suppression of the Royal Council were the two conditions set by a *cuadrilla* in April for entering peace negotiations.[63]

The Junta drew Acuña from a monumental sulk over Tordesillas to stir up the north and inject new vigour into comunero administration. As the bishop and his priests streamed across the Tierra del Campo with their guns and their breviaries, Pedro de Ayala, count of Salvatierra, raised an army to raid northern Castile. These combined forces failed, however, to reap the advantage from pro-comunero agitation in Burgos and divisions and hesitations once more emerged over military strategy. At the end of February, in a daring move, Padilla's army moved out of Valladolid into the Montes de Torrijos and, after a four-day siege, seized the admiral's stronghold of Torrelobatón, which lies on a direct line between Tordesillas to the south and Medina de Rioseco to the north. But he needed to act quickly. Instead, logistical hesitations, combined with low morale—a certain weariness and even a moral repugnance with what he had seen of the evils of war, expressed in a letter to Valladolid—gave his adversaries time to regroup.[64] With Salvatierra's forces occupied to the north of Burgos, Velasco struck out for Tordesillas on 8 April and joined with Enríquez' troops near Torrelobatón. Although Padilla had infantry and artillery, he lacked cavalry and had decided to seek reinforcements at Toro. But, on 23 April, he was intercepted at Villalar. In fading light, torrential rain and a sea of mud, his infantry and cannons proved no match for Caroline horse. Padilla galloped this way and that, trying to animate his men, urging them not to abandon their banners. In a desperate last charge, lance in hand, upon Pedro Bazán, viscount of Valduerna, he was knocked down and captured, along with Juan Bravo, Francisco Maldonado and various other captains. The next day, the three

**Fig. 12.1** This oil on canvas painting by Antonio Gisbert Pérez (1860), and entitled *Los Comuneros Padilla, Bravo y Maldonado en el patíbulo*, shows the execution of the three comunero leaders at Villalar on 24 April 1521. It hangs in the Congreso de los Diputados, Madrid (*Source* ART Collection/Alamy Stock Photo)

leaders were summarily beheaded for treason in the plaza of Villalar, and their heads stuck on pikes (Fig. 12.1).

Villalar became a metonym for comunero defeat. But fighting continued. Attempting to profit from the situation, François I sent troops across the Pyrenees and, with imperial resources focused on the north and east, a second revolutionary cycle broke out south of the Guadarrama, in and around Toledo, Madrid and Guadalajara. Acuña's mercurial appearance in the southern meseta re-ignited its towns and villages. "This accursed sect of liberty," Enríquez warned Charles in May, "is very much imprinted on the people's hearts and it will take a long time and many good works to bring forgetfulness."[65]

Juana's native city, first to adopt the comunero cause, was the last to abandon it. On 29 March, Good Friday, weeks before the battle of Villalar, Acuña had made a triumphal entry into Toledo and was placed, by popular acclaim, on the archbishop's throne. Thereafter, he engaged in hostilities with Antonio de Zúñiga, prior of the military order of St John of Jerusalem. An inconclusive battle took place at Romeral in April. In April Zúñiga's troops advanced on Mora and set fire to the church in which numerous non-combatants had taken refuge. The flames and explosion of a gunpowder magazine led to the collapse of the choir. Maldonado, who describes women jumping from on high to escape the flames, estimates the number of deaths at around 3000.[66] An infuriated Acuña pursued Zúñiga's men across La Mancha. But, in the tidal wave of emotion that followed news of the executions at Villalar, the focus of attention shifted towards Padilla's remarkable twenty-four-year-old widow, María Pacheco de Mendoza, daughter of the count of Tendilla and niece of the marquis of Villena. In a mixture of grief and determination, Pacheco subsequently seized the alcázar, nominated new city officials, oversaw security, imposed new taxes and had bells melted down for cannon.

Her actions drew the ire of contemporary chroniclers, who depict her as a tyrannical virago.[67] Having earlier commented that she dominated her marriage as the "husband of her husband," Martire links her protagonism to madness, and even to demonic possession; Santa Cruz relates it to witchcraft.[68] Like Juana's *moriscas* in earlier days, Pacheco's were looked upon askance. Fray Guevara describes Pacheco working with a "mad" slave or "great witch," who stoked her ambitions.[69] He associates her *locura* with political disobedience and inordinate ambition—transgressive conduct that betrayed her noble blood.

With Acuña in retreat from Toledo the forces of the prior of St John set siege to the city. Pacheco was eventually drawn into negotiations and on 25 October an agreement relatively favourable to the comunero 'rebels' was reached at the monastery of La Sisla and celebratory lamps and candles were lit across the city. But on 9 December, after French forces withdrew from Spanish territory, leaving only the fortress of Fuenterrabía provisionally in French hands, Castile's emboldened governors ordered the prior to renegotiate and "thin out" the agreement's provisions to "preserve the authority of H[is] M[ajesty]."[70] On 2 February 1522, night of Candlemas, the cathedral chapter called for the celebration of Adrian's election as pope. But this ended in prolonged rioting and violence. As the new terms of the pardon were publicly announced, Pacheco called out a warning from her balcony: "Look, brothers! This pardon is not real ...". In the tumult that followed, demands for Pacheco's head were plainly heard. The next morning, in peasant's disguise, she took the road to Portugal. Her property was demolished and decontaminated with salt. A column was later placed there, testifying to the "tyranny" of its former inhabitants.

The collapse of Toledo marked the beginning of the end of the comunero uprising, although the resistance of the Germanías of Aragon continued into 1523, with points of conflagration in Catalonia, Valencia and Mallorca. In July 1522, the emperor, who had spent much of this period in Germany and the Low Countries, disembarked in Castile with thousands of German mercenaries and a long artillery train and on 28 October signed a general amnesty, proclaimed at Valladolid on 1 November. It seemed generous. Given the thousands who had militated in comunero ranks, only 293 persons—mainly captains, procurators and some nobles—were *exceptuados*, or excluded.[71] Of these, twenty-three were executed for rebellion, treason and lèse-majesty. Others died in prison or, like Pacheco and Ayora, in exile. Some paid their way into rehabilitation or were cleared of charges. Others, expelled from their homes, fled to the Germanías or made their way to Navarre, where they hoped to restore their fortunes by joining with imperial troops.

The systematic destruction of comunero documents means that the full extent of the repression may never be known. The general pardon did not apply to those already convicted and still awaiting punishment. Both before and after the pardon, and in its margins, summary hangings, garrottings, mutilations and beatings affected, in particular, the lower ranks of Castilian society. There was fierce persecution of comuneros in Toledo, Cuenca, Madrid and elsewhere. The Consejo de Órdenes, which governed the military orders, punished a number of knights of the habit, who went into exile or languished in captivity, like the infante's former *ayo*, Núñez de Guzmán. The Inquisition was also used for punitive ends, placing various *conversos* under investigation. Assemblies were banned. Individuals and communities were subjected to severe and extraordinary taxes. Fiscal repression in the Castilian heartland was particularly harsh. Enormous quantities of money changed hands in one-sided compensation deals. The faltering economy of central Castile, a main cause of the uprising, suffered a severe and lasting blow. Traditional communitarian and representative institutions went into decline. Former comuneros were disqualified from holding public office and the voices calling for a more limited monarchy and for elective government were silenced.

Comunero defeat at Villalar and Toledo marked the failure of an important political gamble, amounting from a later liberal perspective, to no less than an "expulsion from Paradise."[72] The last of the great comunero leaders and rebels against empire, Antonio de Acuña, bishop of Zamora, was arrested on the road to Logroño in 1522 and garroted at Simancas on Good Friday, 23 March 1526, in the presence of the judge Rodrigo Ronquillo, whom Acuña had himself imprisoned a decade before. Acuña's long and increasingly bitter struggle to obtain a pardon as a prince of the church came to an end when he killed his gaoler, Mendo Noguerol, in an escape attempt that went wrong.

Administrative reforms were carried out after the emperor's return to Castile. New meetings of the Cortes were held. But they would never put an effective check on imperial ambition and the ever-rising costs of war. In his end-of-mission report to the Venetian Senate of 16 November 1525, Contarini remarked that the attitude of the Spanish towards "his Casaerean majesty" could not be worse ("*non è buono, anzi direi meglio quando dicessi ch'è pessimo*"). As for Caesar's mother, she was still alive but "shut up on that rock" and, like her son, melancholic. She was also invisible: "*no se vede mai.*"[73] The memory of Juana was linked inextricably to the memory of revolutionary conflict. The wounds inflicted never truly healed. Many were left with a profound sense of lost opportunity, while down the decades, and indeed the centuries, those in power were haunted by the spectre of "democratic" revolt. Charles's belief in the primacy of dynastic interests meant that he rarely succumbed to sentiment. But what emerges, in particular, from the bullying of his little sister in 1521, and from the letters of Juana's gaolers in general, is that he could never throw off the terrible image of the Junta at Tordesillas and, in particular, of Padilla and his mother the queen engaged in congenial conversation. Padilla was dead. But, as Enríquez had reminded the emperor, Padilla's ghost lived on.

## Notes

1. Danvila (ed. 1897–1900), II, Charles to Adrian, 7 October 1520.
2. AGS, PR, CC, 2-1, f. 166, Fray León to Adrian, November 1520.
3. Suárez Varela (Szászdi León-Borja/Galende Ruíz, eds. 2013).
4. Pérez (1965).
5. Martire (López de Toro, ed. 1957), 12, 705, 11 December 1520; González Olmedo (1944); see also Fleming (Szaszdi León-Borja/Galende Ruíz, eds. 2015), 103–122.
6. Gutiérrez Nieto (1973), 311.
7. Danvila, II, Enríquez to Seville, 28 November.

8. Martire, 12, 705, 11 December 1520.
9. For accounts of the battle see Maldonado (Fernández Vargas, ed. 1975); BL, Ms. Egerton 309, 'Relacion,' ff. 69v.–79 (see also Díaz Medina, ed. 2003); Sandoval (ed. 1955–1956), LXXX; Danvila, II; CSP (Queen Juana), Bergenroth, ed.
10. Guevara (Ochoa, ed. 1850), XIII, Carta XLIII, 20 December 1520.
11. AGS, PR 2, f. 36, Lope Hurtado to Charles, 10 December 1520; CSP (Queen Juana), 76.
12. AGS, PR 3, f. 40, Gómez de Santillán to Adrian, 9 December 1520; CSP (Queen Juana), 75.
13. AGS, Estado 8, f. 32, Licentiate Polanco to Charles.
14. Danvila, III, to Charles, 4 January 1521.
15. AGS, PR 3, f. 36, Fernando de Vega to Charles, 10 December 1520; Danvila, II, 634.
16. "*bien creo que no se le acordara a su alteza de mandarnos llamar oy antes de comer*," Danvila, II, Fernando de Vega to Charles, 6 December 1520, 634–636.
17. AGS, PR 2, f. 101, 10 December 1520.
18. CSP (Queen Juana), 96, to Charles, 25 January 1522.
19. CSP (Queen Juana), 72, Haro to constable, December 1520.
20. AGS, PR 3, f. 40, to Adrian, 9 December 1520.
21. CSP (Queen Juana), 73, Vega to constable, 8 December 1520. A letter from Vega to Charles of the same date refers only to Juana's unfitness, probably on the grounds that a reference to the dangers of a dual monarchy was thought impolitic (Danvila, II, 8 December, 636).
22. Guevara, 20 December 1521, XLIII.
23. CSP (Queen Juana), 81, 22 January 1521.
24. AGS, PR 3, f. 39, Denia to Charles, 22 February 1521. According to Martire (XI, 668, 28 April 1520), the queen of Fez fled her husband with the help of a freed slave and was baptised on 27 April 1520. Charles and Germaine de Foix were her godparents.
25. AGS, PR 3, f. 39.
26. CSP (Queen Juana), 78, Lope Hurtado to Charles, 16 December 1520.
27. CSP (Queen Juana), 78, Lope Hurtado de Mendoza to Charles, December 1520.
28. Sanuto (Fulin, ed. 1969–1970), 24, letter from Alvise Marin (Milan), 2 January 1521; Danvila, III, constable to Charles, 25 January 1521.
29. AGS, PR 3, f. 96 [undated, unsigned]; CSP (Queen Juana), 79, attributed to Lope Hurtado, December 1520.
30. Santa Cruz (Laiglesia y Auser, ed. 1920), 1, 31 October 1520, 341–342.
31. Fernández Conti (Martínez Millán, ed. 2001), II, 29–51.

32. Danvila, III, "Creencia que el Almirante dió á Angelo de Bursa (pariente) de lo que debia decir a S.M.," 28 January 1521.
33. CSP (Queen Juana), 70, Lope Hurtado to Charles, December 1520.
34. CSP (Queen Juana), 74, Vega to Charles, 9 December 1520.
35. Gutiérrez Nieto (1973), 294–297.
36. CSP (Queen Juana), 84 [March 1521?].
37. Danvila, III, to Charles, 21 February 1521.
38. Fleming (2015).
39. For the complex interrelation between the households of Charles and Juana, see Carlos Morales in Martínez Millán (ed. 2000), Zalama (2003) and Aram (2005, 2006).
40. AGS, Estado 8, f. 171, "Memorial de los malos asi eccelesiasticos y religiosos como cavalleros y letrados y otras personas" [undated].
41. Danvila, III, "Relación formada por los contadores mayors de la Reyna Doña Juana, consignando los Continos que fueron despedidos por comuneros," Tordesillas, 18 April 1521.
42. Danvila, III, 2 April 1521; CSP Sp. 96, 25 January 1522; AGS, CSR 24-6, ff. 85–90, 4 July 1521; Carlos Morales (Martínez Millán, ed. 2000) 1, 190–197; Aram (2006), 99–175.
43. CSP (Queen Juana), 57, Adrian to Charles, 14 September 1520.
44. Danvila, IV, Francisca Enríquez to Charles, 30 July 1521.
45. Danvila, IV, "Instrucción del Almirante a Sancho Martínez de Leyva," 5 July 1521.
46. AGS, Estado 8, ff. 122–127, 'Memoria de la s. yinfanta para su magt.'; CSP (Queen Juana), 94, Catalina to Charles, 19 August 1521.
47. AGS, Estado 8, f. 124, Ávila to Charles, 15 June [undated; 1521]; CSP (Queen Juana), 90.
48. AGS, Estado 8, f. 192, Ávila to Charles, 19 August [undated; 1521].
49. Martire, 12, 713, to Gattinara, 2 [?] March 1521.
50. Danvila, III, Adrian to Charles, 4 January 1521.
51. AGS, Estado 8, f. 32, Polanco to Charles, 17 January 1521.
52. Danvila, III, 'Creencia que el Almirante dió a Diego Hurtado,' January 1521.
53. CSP (Queen Juana), 83, Denia to Charles, 21 February 1521.
54. AGS, Estado 5, f. 313, Ávila to Charles, 30 October [undated; 1521/1522?].
55. AGS, Estado 10, f. 59, 2 October [undated; 1523?].
56. BL, Egerton Ms. 309, 'Relación,' f. 83v.
57. Maldonado, 177.
58. AGS, PR 5, f. 407, Adrian to Charles.
59. Danvila, II, Vargas to Charles, 13 December 1520.
60. Santa Cruz, 1, 421

61. Ferrer del Rio (2007), "Carta de Don Pedro Laso de la Vega a los gobernadores antes de volver Padilla a encargarse del mando," January 1521, 336–337; "Carta de credencia a Francisco Maldonado," 25 January 1521.
62. Súarez Varela (Szászdi León-Borja/Galende Ruíz, eds. 2015), 259–349.
63. AGS, PR 3, f. 138, 'Voto particular de una de las cuadrillas de Valladolid sobre los capítulos de paz que los Gobernadores trataban con los de la Junta.' 9 April 1521.
64. For Padilla's scruples, see his message to the council of Valladolid of 28 February 1521, in Martínez Gil (2005), 159.
65. Danvila, IV, "Creencia que el Almirante confió a Angelo de Bursa," 11 May 1521.
66. "*Los de Zúñiga ... recurrieron a medios inhumanos, a saber: arrojaron fuego al templo, pero con tal astucia, que prendiendo primero la llama en materias fáciles de incendiar, se comunicase luego al azufre que allí se guardaba*" (Maldonado, 200).
67. Martínez Gil (2005).
68. Martire, 12, 680, 23 July 1520; 727, 27 July 1521; Santa Cruz, 1, 463.
69. Guevara, XLV, to Juan de Padilla; XLVII, to María Pacheco.
70. Martínez Gil, 194.
71. AGS, Estado 10, ff. 25–28, 'Perdón general'; For more background, see, *inter alia*, Pérez (1999, 2001).
72. Álvarez-Junco (2011).
73. CSP. Ven. III (1520–1526), Rawdon Brown (ed. 1869), Gasparo Contarini to Council of Ten, 4 December 1524; Albéri (ed. 1839–1840), Serie 1, vol. II, 'Relazione di Gasparo Contarini,' 44–45, 64.

## References


Albéri, Eugenio, ed. 1839–1840. *Relazioni degli Ambasciatori Veneti al Senato*, Series 1. Florence: Società editrice fiorentina.

Álvarez-Junco, José. 2011. *Spanish Identity in the Age of Nations*. Manchester and New York: Manchester University Press.

Aram, Bethany. 2005. *Juana the Mad: Sovereignty and Dynasty in Renaissance Europe*. Baltimore and London: John Hopkins University Press.

———. 2006. La Casa de la Reina Juana, 1496–1556. In *Doña Juana, Reina de Castilla*. Madrid and Barcelona: Fundación Rafael del Pino/Real Academía de la Historia/Marcial Pons.

Bergenroth, G.A. (ed.). 1868. *Calendar of State Papers, Supplement to Vol. I and Vol. II of Letters, Despatches and State Papers Relating to Negotiations Between England and Spain, Preserved in the Archives of Simancas and Elsewhere*. London: Longmans, Green, Reader and Dyer.

Brown, Rawdon (ed.) 1869. *Calendar of State Papers relating to English Affairs in the Archives of Venice*, vol. 3, 1520–1526. London: HMSO.

Carlos Morales, Carlos Javier de. 2000. La cuestión de la financiación de la corte y la defensa del modelo de Casa castellana durante los Comunidades (109–197) and Los últimos años de las Casas de Castilla y Borgoña del Emperador (259–266) In *La Corte de Carlos V*, ed. José Martínez Millán, vol. I and II respectively. Madrid: Sociedad Estatal para la Conmemoración de los Centenarios de Felipe II y Carlos V.

Danvila y Collado, Manuel (ed.). 1897–1900. *Historia crítica y documentada de las Comunidades de Castilla*. Madrid: Memoria Histórica Español.

Díaz Medina, Ana (ed.). 2003. *Relación del discurso de las Comunidades*. Valladolid: Junta de Castilla y León.

Fernández Conti, Santiago. 2001. Carlos V y la alta nobleza: el almirante don Fadrique Enríquez. In *Carlos V y la quiebra del humanismo político en Europa (1530–1558)*, II, ed. José Martínez Millán. Madrid: Sociedad Estatal para la Acción Cultural Exterior, 29–51.

Ferrer del Rio, Antonio. 2007. *Historia del levantamiento de las Comunidades de Castilla, 1520–1521*, ed. Jesús Gascón Pérez. Pamplona: Urgoiti.

Fleming, Gillian Beatrice. 2015. Una ventana sobre Tordesillas: Juana I como mediadora. In *Carlos V: Conversos y Comuneros*, ed. István Szászdi León-Borja and María Jesús Galende Ruiz. Valladolid: Centro Estudios Camino Santiago Sahagún, 103–121.

Fulin, Rinaldo (ed.). 1969–1970. *I diarii de Marino Sanuto, 1466–1536*. Bologna: Forni Editore.

González Olmedo, S.I., Félix. 1944. *Diego Ramírez Villaescusa (1459-1537), fundador del Colegio de Cuenca y autor de los Cuatro Diálogos sobre la Muerte del Príncipe Don Juan*. Madrid: Editora Nacional.

Guevara, Antonio. (Eugenio de Ochoa, ed. 1850). *Epistolas familiares*. Madrid: M. Rivadeneyra.

Gutiérrez Nieto, Juan Ignacio. 1973. *Las Comunidades como Movimiento antiseñorial*. Barcelona: Planeta.

López de Toro, José (ed.). 1953–1957. *Petrus Martyr Anglerius. Epistolario*. CODOIN, 9–12, vol. 12. Madrid: Imprenta Góngora.

Maldonado, Juan. 1975. *La Revolución Comunera*, ed. Valentina Fernández Vargas. Madrid: Ediciones del Centro.

Martínez Gil, Fernando. 2005. *La Mujer Valerosa. Historia de doña María Pacheco, comunera de Castilla (1497–1531)*. Toledo: Centro de Estudios de Castilla-La Mancha/Almud.

Martínez Millán, José. 2000. *La Corte de Carlos V*, vol. I. Madrid: Sociedad Estatal para la Conmemoración de los Centenarios de Felipe II y Carlos V.

Pérez, Joseph. 1965. Le razonamiento de Villabrágima. In *Bulletin Hispanique*, LXVIII, 217–224.

———. 1999. *La revolución de Comunidades de Castilla (1520–1521)*. Madrid: Siglo Veintiuno de España.
———. 2001. *Los Comuneros*. Madrid: La Esfera de los Libros.
Sandoval, Prudencio de. 1955–1956. *Historia de la Vida y Hechos del Emperador Carlos V*. Madrid: Biblioteca de Autores Españoles.
Santa Cruz, Alonso. 1920. *Crónica del Emperador*, ed. Francisco de Laiglesia y Auser, vol. I. Madrid: Imprenta del Patronato de Húerfanos de Intendencia e Intervención Militares.
Suárez Varela, Antonio. 2013. La Mala Sedición. Una aproximación al discurso anticomunero. In *Imperio y Tiranía. La Dimensión Europea de las Comunidades de Castilla*, ed. Istvan Szászdi León-Borja and María Jesús Galende Ruíz. Valladolid: Universidad de Valladolid.
———. 2015. La Comunidad de Valladolid y la cuestión conversa: el caso del procurador Alonso de Saravia. In *Carlos V. Conversos y Comuneros*, ed. Istvan Szászdi León-Borja and María Jesús Galende Ruíz. Valladolid: Centro Estudios Camino Santiago Sahagún/Marcial Pons.
Zalama, Miguel Ángel. 2003. *Vida cotidiana y Arte en el Palacio de la Reina Juana I en Tordesillas*. Valladolid: Universidad de Valladolid.

CHAPTER 13

# The Politics of Penitence (1521–1539)

## 13.1 Hiding the Queen

As king-by-coup, Charles was strong enough to hide the queen away but not strong enough to allow her to be seen. In his anxiety to prevent all contact between his mother and the outside world, he became, from a distance, the director of a theatre of illusion designed entirely to conceal her from view. Within this parallel world, conflict continued but became an internal, dynastic and household affair. The more important members of Juana's household were, in theory, her subjects, but in reality her son's agents. Since they did not answer to her, she saw them as carrying out acts of lèse-majesté on a daily basis.

Denia kept Charles informed of Juana's "indisposition." By this he meant her refusal to accept her captivity and desire to engage with political affairs. In January 1522, he wrote in cipher that: "Her Highness speaks often with me and tells me often to call the grandees into her presence, because she wants to speak with them and to be informed of the affairs of the Kingdom and despatch them." Denia replied that the grandees were too busy in her service, adding that, since she "refuses to do anything required for her life and soul and does exactly the contrary," force would be required. Whether Charles consented is unclear but Denia justified it from family precedent: "*y la Reyna su ahuela asy le sirvió y trató la Reyna Nuestra Señora su hija.*"[1]

The Spanish wording lends itself to ambiguity. Bergenroth understood Denia to mean that Charles' grandmother, Isabel, had consented


G. B. Fleming, *Juana I*, Queenship and Power,
https://doi.org/10.1007/978-3-319-74347-9_13

to the use of forcible restraint on Juana. But Denia's earlier letter to Charles of July 1521 makes it as likely that he was referring to Isabel's use of restraint on Juana's grandmother, Isabel de Avís: "*asy se hizo con su aguela estando en su indispusicion* ..." ("and this was done to [Juana's] grandmother, when she was indisposed ..."). Denia's comment raises further questions about the grandmother's little-known widowed seclusion at Arévalo.[2]

In 1516, Ferrer had used the phrase "*dar cuerda*" when referring to the rope or strap used to force-feed or otherwise restrain Juana. Denia often referred to "*premia*" when referring to forcible restraint and punishment. Bergenroth rightly translates this as torture. While there is no suggestion that Juana was subjected to the rack (*escalera*) or some sixteenth-century equivalent of water-boarding, torture was certainly practiced at Tordesillas if this is understood as modern international law defines it: that is, the infliction by an official of severe pain or suffering, physical or mental, to punish, intimidate and coerce.[3]

We do not know if the emperor consented to Denia's request. But he was unmoved by pleas to soften Juana's prison conditions. A month after Denia's letter, Adrian VI advised Charles to treat his family with less "abstraction," showing greater "humanity" to Juana in her "continuing retirement."[4] The papal plea fell on deaf ears. Evidently, the maternal relationship was not easy, not least because it rested on that densely tangled web of lies and subterfuge. Charles tended to flee his mother whenever he suspected a difficult moment. On his return to Castile in 1522, he offered two reasons for visiting her, neither connected with filial sentiment: "We intend to hold the *cortes*," he told his ambassadors in England, "and then to go to Tordesillas to see our mother, in order to keep God's commandment and to satisfy the common people."[5] But the queen did not give him an easy time. Charles arrived at Tordesillas on 2 September, intending to stay for the anniversary of Philip's death, but on 7 September was back in Valladolid because the queen "*no estaba más tratable.*"[6]

In the concluding remarks to his work on Juana's life at Tordesillas, Zalama, although convinced of her "irreversible schizophrenia," nonetheless describes her treatment as incomprehensible, and asks why she could not have been allowed to live at liberty, with her "*manías.*"[7] The question is surely answered by the emperor's above remark to his ambassadors: Juana mattered to the "common people." In public, she could impress. Her arguments were often virtually impossible to refute. Even after 1522, there was no guarantee that the Junta would not re-form in some city or another and that recourse to the queen would not again be sought. Castrillo had compared the comunero uprising to the revolt of the giants. His Toledan humanist contemporary, Alejo Venegas, would liken it to the nine-headed hydra that haunted the swamps of Lerna.[8] Which of these heads would swing next into view? The Aragonese movement of the Germanías, which had comunero links, was not suppressed until 1523. In Sicily, a new uprising broke out.[9] Toledo was still being described in 1524 as a hotbed of "tonsured ruffians."[10]

Moreover, the rulers of Castile saw a new and important threat to the kingdoms' stability—Lutheranism—which they linked to comunero and *agermanat* agitation. In 1521, the nobles gathered at Tordesillas saw the political roots of the comunero movement as inseparably entwined with heretical religious ones. That April, a flurry of letters to Charles had emerged from Tordesillas and from elsewhere in Castile, even as the emperor, then presiding the Diet of Worms, prepared to hear Martin Luther recant or defend his beliefs. The constable had no doubt that *converso* opposition to the Inquisition and Dominican order "lay at the roots of the revolt of these Kingdoms." He and his fellow nobles and prelates warned Charles about the "malignant and diabolical cunning" with which Luther tried to "pervert and contaminate" the realm and weaken the Inquisition's power. "From a little spark, most Christian lord, may spring and burst forth a great fire." This could be less easily extinguished in the cities and towns with the strongest comunero traditions.[11] Charles himself would later say that he had always associated Lutheran rebels and heretics with comuneros.[12]

It was in view of continuing agitation and security fears, not least from the inhabitants of Tordesillas, with their possible contacts within the palace, that Denia and other nobles recommended that Juana be transferred to the relatively remote and strongly fortified town of Arévalo. But the operation would require the utmost secrecy. In an age when the personal and physical presence of the monarch remained so important and when the corporal metaphor was continually applied, Denia was terrified that the sight of a troubled queen would further aggravate her troubled kingdoms and that people who caught sight of her, and even managed to hear or speak to her, would "find the means to commit [yet] greater errors" than before. Denia also knew that Juana would resist a move to Arévalo, which conjured memories of the place where her grandmother had been confined, and in 1518, when a similar move was under discussion, he had envisaged packing her by force into a fast-moving litter that did not stop anywhere en route.[13]

This plan came to nought, but the need to keep the source of royal legitimacy out of sight, and thus, hopefully, out of mind, caused recurring headaches for the marquis. When plague erupted in October 1527, and Charles ordered Denia to escort Juana to Toro (Zamora), Denia justified the delay in departure by Juana's ongoing indisposition. She had eaten nothing but bread and cheese for the last five or six days, her habit "when her will on anything is not done." He would therefore ensure that, if necessary, she would set out at midnight for Pedrosa and stay hidden there until the following night, when, at the same hour, she would depart for Toro. She would arrive before dawn, after all precautions had been taken to confirm that no one had seen her, because "in truth, I am ashamed of myself for what I see her say and do." Scouts were sent to find suitable accommodation. The first houses were thought insufficiently secluded: "everyone would see Her Highness there, which would not be appropriate."[14]

In the end, Juana's only known departure from Tordesillas took place in the summer or autumn of 1533 when she was led along a south-easterly route via Geria to Tudela de Duero, full of memories of the feverish, plague-ridden summer of 1506. When Juan de Zúñiga, *ayo* of Prince Philip and *comendador mayor* of León, went there with a message from Charles, Denia asked him to see Juana on the emperor's behalf, "because she has always talked about Y[our] M[ajesty] not remembering H[er] Highness." In a rare outburst he added: "I could well be mistaken but it seems to me that we must all serve and see H[er] H[ighness] as ill and Y[our] M[ajesty] must treat and visit her as his mother and in good health."[15] The plague caught up with them at the end of May. Denia sought permission to transfer Juana to Mojados, where Charles visited briefly before she was returned to Tordesillas in the summer of 1534. Just how Denia managed to keep this strange, desultory ambulation around the backwaters of Valladolid a secret from the local population remains a mystery. The queen rode camouflaged against the night, but several dozen carts and people went too, and rumours were always rife.

## 13.2 'Madness' and 'Melancholy'

If even a glimpse of the living queen was thought sufficient to inflame the people, the queen's death was feared for the same reason. Thus, when at the end of 1524, Catalina prepared to leave Tordesillas to marry

João III of Portugal, the familiar pattern of deceit re-emerged. Charles' confessor, García de Loaisa, inquisitor and president of the Consejo de Indias, advised the emperor to be absent when Catalina left, so that he could not be directly blamed if "anything happens to endanger the life of the Queen."[16] On 18 December, Ferdinand's ambassador, Salinas, noting that Juana had still not been told, wrote: "Please God some vexation will not come from this, although I think that it cannot be prevented, because not an hour passes without her wanting to see [Catalina] and asking after her."[17]

Charles signed the marriage contract at Burgos on 5 July 1524 and stayed at Tordesillas between 3 October and 5 November, when he formed Catalina's dowry. His despoliation of Juana's possessions has been well documented elsewhere and is mentioned here only briefly to draw attention to the trickery and deceit by which the queen was again surrounded.[18] Many of Juana's possessions had already disappeared—some on the *Julienne* and bumpy roads of England, others given away but not registered, others stolen. But Tordesillas in 1524 was still a treasure house. Spanish art historian Fernando Checa describes Juana's tapestry collection, comprising about sixty pieces, as "remarkable in view of the brevity of her 'political' career."[19] Major individual gems bore names such as "the Jesus," "the Star," "the Heart," "the Ostrich," and "the Emperor." Many jewels had religious significance, such as an exceptional, solitary gold axorca of light, movable units enclosing the mysteries of the Passion.[20] In later years, Juana prized her jewels less as ornaments than as objects of memory and spiritual pieces, to hold, reflect upon and pray with.

The fact that Juana combined in her person that strangely toxic mix of vulnerability as captive and latent power as proprietary monarch meant that subterfuge, stealth and skullduggery were constantly applied, transforming what might otherwise have been normal family transactions into a series of thefts. When, thirty-five years later, the third marquis of Denia ordered an inventory of her few remaining goods, he inquired into the disappearance of a chest about which she had been especially protective. Alonso de Ribera testified that Charles, with Catalina and the Denias, had awaited nightfall before supervising the removal of chests or trunks through a door specially re-opened for the purpose, and down a staircase. The trunks were returned with worthless objects of similar weight. According to another witness Charles distracted Juana in conversation while the chests were removed. When, soon afterwards, she ordered her *camarero mayor* to open one in her presence, he and the queen found bricks and old pieces of cloth. The *camarero* feigned astonishment; he was, he cried, lost. "Jesus, Ribera!" Juana exclaimed, "what little spirit you have!" After discovering the culprit to be Charles himself, she closed the matter, thus preserving his honour and acting, in Zalama's words, "not only with prudence but intelligence."[21]

The celebration of the proxy marriage had similarly farcical elements. Catalina dressed in cloth of silver before reverting hastily to black before Juana could see her. Charles left for Madrid, although not without asking Enríquez to help mitigate the effects on the queen of Catalina's departure, and subsequently thanking him with the gift of a peregrine falcon, "the most beautiful bird I have ever seen."[22] On the night of 1 January 1525, Catalina finally asked her mother to bless her marriage. The next morning, she heard mass, breakfasted and made a secretive, but highly emotional departure.[23]

The admiral tried meanwhile to distract the queen, who ordered him to sit, "and we spoke about a whole range of very substantial things." Juana wanted to know what role Charles had played in the matter, and was unconvinced when Enríquez told her lamely that Charles knew nothing; "it could not be, they had deceived" him, she said. To argue otherwise was, after all, to convert Catalina's nuptial journey into an abduction and the head of the Franciscan order, who was present, into one of the kidnappers. Enríquez hoped nothing would happen, "I don't know, in her eating or something."[24] The meeting broke up after Juana discovered that Catalina had gone. Contarini reported that she stood for a whole day and a night in the corridor, gazing out of the window, then "entered her chamber and took to her bed, remaining thus for two days; and no wonder, for this daughter was her solace."[25]

On 15 January, the admiral made a last vain attempt to persuade Charles to expel the Denias from Tordesillas: "I spoke several times with the Queen, our lady, and, in truth, lord, with all her great troubles, her dissatisfaction with the marquis and marchioness is so great that she suffers more acutely from hearing them [talk] than from the departure of the queen [Catalina]; and as that seems to me a thing most worthy of compassion I am writing to you to tell your Majesty. On this matter she seems to be as sensible as anyone could be, although, when embarking on other matters she is as confused (*disconcertada*) as your Majesty has seen ...". She claimed, for example, that her attendants were out to kill her.[26]

Juana was overwhelmed by the horror of her situation: "The Queen our lady is as usual," Denia reported in May. "About a month ago she went into the corridor and began to scream. To prevent her Highness being heard I ordered the women to beg her to return to her room, and if she refused, conduct her there by force." In the last fortnight she had "undressed three times, gone to bed and dressed again." He reiterated the need for forcible restraint. "I have always thought that her Highness, being disposed as she is, in punishment for our sins, nothing could do her more good than some torture ...".[27] The following April, while Charles and Isabel of Portugal were married in Seville, Denia observed that Juana needed round-the-clock supervision: a complement of twelve women "to guard her person by day and night as well as for other things appropriate for her service." Since, however, many were ill or had died, replacements were needed.[28]

The stream of letters from Denia between 1518 and 1536, like a tide chart recording the ebb and flow in the queen's health, brings us to the point at which Juana's 'madness' or 'melancholy' requires further exploration. We have seen that 'madness' (*locura*) was used in many different contexts. It could be used to depict disobedience to and transgression of traditional norms, as in the case of María de Pacheco, who had leapt to political prominence after Padilla's execution. But 'melancholy' was the word more generally used to describe Juana's condition. Both Martire and Guicciardini refer to her saturnine disposition, while Guicciardini is careful to explain that she was unable to undertake the huge administrative task of governing Castile "*no tanto per la imbecilità del sesso, quanto perchè per umori malincolici* ...".[29] In 1550, when Ferdinand's ambassador, Juan Alonso Gámiz, referred to her "*grandísima imaginación y pensamiento*" he too meant her 'melancholy'.

In Juana's case, I have argued that an acute sense of loss in early life was further exacerbated by systemic stress and interminable, enforced idleness, imprisonment and abuse. With this came a sense of powerlessness that enraged the queen, sensitive as she was to her exalted status. At the same time, her forebears, including Enrique III, Juan II, Enrique IV, Isabel de Avís and Isabel I, were known for varying degrees of melancholy. Juana's daughter, Mary of Hungary, suffered incapacitating bouts of melancholy. So, famously, did Charles. Her granddaughter, María, was reputed, as widow and dowager empress, to have an "excess of melancholic humours which regularly interfered with her activities." She "had difficulty eating and sleeping; she was sorrowful, fearful, suspicious, and jealous …".[30] Before his death in 1564, Juana's son, Ferdinand, would drift into "melancholic fantasies." He would cry and throw things on the floor; pound his fists on the table; draw imaginary circles; sit in strange positions, and when returning to his senses could not think consecutively.[31] Juana's great grandson, Rudolf II, is well known for a 'melancholic' nature in which moods of energy and rage alternated with states of deep depression.

Much of what nowadays (perhaps inadequately) is termed 'depression' and might once have been called 'brainsickness'—a term used by Lady Macbeth in Shakespeare's play about illusion and distorted vision—would have been subsumed under the vast melancholic umbrella of early modern Europe. Thus, in the unhappy climate of Tordesillas between 1529 and 1531, Isabel de Albornoz, wife of Juana's treasurer, Ochoa de Landa, was thought, like Juana, to have succumbed to *imaginación de la cabeza* and "diabolical temptation." Physical and spiritual remedies were sought to help her banish Beelzebub, "prince of demons."[32] But a "woman of Simancas," probably a midwife who also cured women's illnesses, concluded that Albornoz suffered from "*mal de la madre*," a form of 'hysteria' known in sixteenth-century England as "suffocation of the mother."[33]

Burton's *Anatomy of Melancholy* (1621) presages a series of modern studies about the effect of isolation on prisoners when he relates melancholy to imprisonment. Burton observes that horses confined to stables and hawks penned in mews were especially vulnerable to disease. So too "this body of ours, when it is idle and knows not how to bestow itself, macerates and vexeth itself with cares, griefs, false fears, discontents, and suspicions; it tortures and preys upon his own bowels, and is never at rest."[34] Burton extends the analogy to confined women: "How are those women in Turkey affected, that most of the year come not abroad; those Italian and Spanish dames, that are mewed up like hawks, and locked up by their jealous husbands!"[35]

Melancholy, for Burton, is an "anguish of the mind" or "depravation" of mental functions, rather than—as in madness—their "abolition." Fear and sorrow are its inseparable companions. Sorrow "refrigerates the heart, takes away stomach, colour, and sleep; thickens the blood … contaminates the spirits …". Fear "makes our imagination conceive what it list, invites the devil to come to us … and tyrannizeth over our phantasy …". Referring to Dürer's famous engraving, *Melencolia I*, in which a winged female figure stares into space, oblivious to the rainbow and rays of cometic light streaming in through the open window of her mysterium, Burton remarks that melancholy could seem a sad woman, held by some to be "proud, soft, sottish, or half-mad … and yet of a deep reach, excellent apprehension, judicious, wise and witty." Thus, melancholics—and Burton mentions Juana several times—could be "of profound judgment in some things, although in others *non recte judicant inquieti* [people in a passion do not judge correctly] …".[36]

Juana's younger contemporary, Teresa of Ávila, would ask Juan de la Cruz to exorcise the melancholic "illnesses" of nuns who rebelled against enclosure and imprisonment. She too distinguished between madness and melancholy—"so subtle it plays dead." It created restlessness; darkened judgment; focused on trifles and caprices (what Martire had called in Juana "bagatelles") and manifested itself in constant mood swings. It was infectious and pined for freedom: "It is not definitely madness … but … sometimes is."[37]

In Juana's case, the symptoms of melancholy are extremely close to those identified in a range of modern studies of maximum-security prisoners subjected to long-term social isolation. One such study, carried out in the USA, lists among the effects of such isolation apathy; obsession; anxiety; aggression; surges of panic and rage; dreams of revenge; impulses to suicide, dirtiness and dishevelment; the sense of being in a fog; poor concentration; and disturbed sleeping patterns, such as an inability to rest at night or to stay awake during the day.[38] These findings post-date a pioneering study of the effects of isolation on small groups of German prisoners, in which this writer was involved, and which noted that very low blood pressure and circulatory problems led to dizzy spells and headaches and that intellectual and emotional disturbances included severe restlessness and inability to concentrate; irritability; hallucinatory phenomena; and depression and suicidal tendencies.[39]

In a "memoir of madness," American novelist William Styron describes experiences strikingly similar to those suffered by Juana and by modern maximum-security prisoners: stifling anxiety; disruption of sleep patterns; lack of appetite; loss of self-esteem; a world drained of colour; a sense of despair, resembling "the diabolical discomfort of being imprisoned in a fiercely overheated room"; a "smothering confinement" with no breeze and no escape; the development of "fierce attachments" to objects trivial in themselves; the sense of a "poisonous fogbank" rolling in on the mind and forcing one into bed.[40]

From the outset, Charles had accepted his mother's inability to govern as an article of faith and, after years of imprisonment and social isolation, combined with intense surveillance, that belief had doubtless become self-fulfilling. But moments of torpor alternated with alertness, and as late as 1538 the queen's nagging curiosity about "her affairs" ("*sus cosas*") was undiminished. Perhaps it was this very struggle to maintain her royal identity that kept her alive. The third marquis of Denia, who succeeded as Juana's gaoler when his father died in 1536, pursued the practice of fabrication and deceit. When telling Charles in 1538 that Juana was "always asking what your Majesty is doing and why the grandees have gathered for a Cortes" [the Cortes of Toledo] and a host of similar questions, he admitted to lacking the skill to bat such questions away, but replied "what he thought apposite to calm her down."[41]

## 13.3 Confession and Possession

On 3 March 1526, the bride of Charles V rode through Seville's Macarena gate, her white plumed headdress covered with pearls and precious stones that sparkled like stars, her white hackney stepping high. Isabel of Portugal was of a similar age to Charles and her fabulous dowry would help fund his plans for a Roman coronation. But, at least as importantly, a Portuguese marriage had been a comunero demand. Iberian-born and the daughter of Juana's sister, María, Isabel was familiar with the Spanish language, culture and customs and the uprisings of the early 1520s had impressed upon Charles the need to delegate power within the family during frequent and prolonged absences abroad. Altogether, Charles would spend in Spain only sixteen of his forty-two years as king, with the queen-empress governing Castile between 1529–1533 and 1535–1538.

Since he was not proprietary ruler of the Spanish realms, it was technically incorrect to call his deputies 'regents,' although in practice the term was used.[42] Charles addressed his wife in correspondence as "*Emperatriz y Reyna*," while Isabel signed herself "*La Reyna*" but paid respect to Juana as "*La Reyna mi señora*." As Rodríguez-Salgado has noted, Isabel had "firm views about life and duty" and "her rapid identification with the interests of the Castilian elites led to regular clashes with Charles and increased the distance between them."[43] At the same time, her letters to Charles provide glimpses of her moral severity and of the struggle that united them against religious change. She refers witheringly to the

Lutherans whom Charles faced at the Diet of Augsburg (1530–1531); expresses impatience with the children of condemned heretics whose documents of rehabilitation from Rome allowed them to resume their former position in Spanish society; and encourages provincials to impose the rules of Observance on wayward friars.[44] When Henry VIII initiated divorce proceedings against Katherine, Isabel, convinced that the matter "closely concerns the Christian religion itself," sent agents to scour Spain and Sardinia for evidence to undermine Henry's case.

In the Spanish realms a religious reform movement had long existed. The ground for new ideas was thus receptive. Isabel's periods of governance coincided with the gradual hardening of attitudes within a church hierarchy anxious to suppress potential subversion in the wake of Luther's publication of his theses on indulgences and three great treatises of 1520. As Rawlings points out, the Spanish Inquisition "deliberately set about associating innovative trends in religious and intellectual life with the 'heresy' perpetrated by Martin Luther, however far removed they were from such a definition in actual fact."[45] Among such trends was illuminism, which derived in part from the movement of spiritual contemplation known as the '*devotio moderna*,' a current of interior contemplation originating in the Low Countries and expressed in such works as Thomas à Kempis' *Imitation of Christ* and Ludolf of Saxony's *Vita Christi*. This was to deeply influence the founder of the Jesuits, Ignatius Loyola, who, after leading prayer groups in Castile, was arrested in 1526 and fled Spain in 1527. Inquisitors became particularly concerned about the spread of illuminism through areas formerly fertilised by comunero militancy, fearing that they threatened not only the church and papacy but the monarchy that sustained them.

The admiral had been among the lordly signatories of the letter sent to Charles in 1521. Yet his intellectual curiosity often prevailed over religious orthodoxy and some of his many verses touch upon the porous boundary between different forms of illuminism. He explains *recogimiento*, or meditative seclusion, as seeking purification through "the heart" and *alumbradismo* as advocating a form of abandonment ("*a Dios del todo dexarnos*"). This involved a cleansing of the soul from all thought and external influence so as to merge with, and become inseparable from, the divine will. *Alumbrado* groupings, in which women were prominent, spurned exterior forms of expression: fasting; acts of penitence and charity; visible states of ecstasy and supernatural visions; and aids to worship such as imagery and adoration of the cross. Enríquez was among several grandees to support or court forms of illuminism. They included the duke of Alba; the duke of Infantado and his wife, María Pimentel, daughter of the count of Benavente; the marquis of Villena and his wife, Juana Enríquez, the admiral's sister; and Enríquez himself and Ana, his wife, countess of Módica.

Argentinian historian and literary critic Avalle-Arce describes the spiritual crisis suffered by such nobles as a "generational phenomenon."[46] They had lived through the war of succession and Granadan wars, the dual monarchy and the turbulent years that followed. Some had supported Charles *in extrémis* but were disillusioned by a new dynasty that left little room for the "free men of Spain" they perceived themselves to be. Vital's description of the marquis of Villena on the road to Valladolid in 1518 provides the quintessential image of a member of that transitional generation. He rode in black satin amidst a glittering gold and silver entourage of at least 200 horse, a "Turkish" or "Jewish" turban wound several times around his head in traditional Castilian style, like one of the three biblical magi.[47] The presence at Villena's court at Escalona of some of the brightest stars of illuminism has been attributed to his search for salvation at the end of "an entire life of frustration and disillusionment."[48]

Enríquez shared that disillusionment. In 1522, he told Charles that his acceptance of the governorship had interrupted a spiritual retreat, connected to debts incurred during his voyage to the Low Countries with Juana in 1496—debts he does not specify but which had increased during the comunero uprising.[49] His anger about promises he had made as governor but which Charles had not honoured, was well known at the time. As he stood on the threshold of a radically changing Castile, he had a sense of a coming to the end of all things. To this he gave expression in the *Epístola Moral* of 1524, depicting a once prosperous land gone to waste through a series of calamitous royal deaths and the collapse of an honourable order of values, accompanied by apocalyptic events ("many massive famines and almost continuous plagues" and "horrible earthquakes").[50]

In 1525, the year of his lengthy last meeting with Juana, he recruited the illuminist priest, Juan López de Celain (subsequently burned as a Lutheran) to help evangelise his estates. Celain's disciples became known as the 'admiral's apostles.'[51] Later, the admiral adopted a magus called Eugenio Torralba, whose familiar, Zequiel, had prophesied, *inter alia*, the outbreak of the comunero uprising. Zequiel accompanied

Torralba on exploits later recalled by Quixote and reminiscent of the adventures of Dr Faustus in Marlowe's great, anti-Catholic play of that name. Torralba claimed that they had flown to Rome in an hour and had witnessed the Sack of Rome. In another version, they left the outskirts of Medina de Rioseco at dusk, astride two black ponies, and—on a journey bearing a partial resemblance to Maldonado's fantastic tale, *Somnium*, fruit of the comunero uprising—plumbed the Mediterranean and fringed the moon before reaching Rome.[52]

The admiral's quest for spiritual redemption intensified further after the death in 1526 of his beloved wife, whose gilded effigy may still be seen at prayer, beside her sister, Isabel, countess of Melgar, in the monastery church of San Francisco in Medina de Rioseco According to one of many references to his diminutive stature, Enríquez' mourning, worn for the remainder of his life, made him look like "a mouse with trappings."[53] The insatiable curiosity of this charismatic "mouse" took the form of multitudinous questions in verse: Do beasts have souls? Does devilish temptation originate in God? Where does the soul reside? What happens to guardian angels after the death of the humans they protect? Where was God before heaven? Would a poor or unlettered confessor, who "heard him but did not understand him," jeopardise his chances of salvation?[54]

The waves of spiritual unrest that washed over Castile in the 1520s, whether or not they permeated parts of the palace at Tordesillas, may help us understand why the queen's lack of demonstrable piety, and expressions of despair, became such a concern for the empress. Indeed, one historian describes Juana's family as looking with terror upon the prospect of her eternal damnation.[55] According to the Fourth Lateran Council of 1215, later confirmed at Trent, Christians had to confess at least once a year. But Juana had not done so for well over a decade and Denia was among those who believed she was swayed by demonic forces.[56] Not only did Juana refuse the rite of confession but often threatened to kill herself, and her continual hunger strikes, sometimes combined with thirst strikes, raised the spectre of despair and the sin of Judas—a sin so terrible that it ruled out any form of religious commemoration and burial in sacred ground. Certain mitigating circumstances existed in cases of suicide, as shown in sequences of the exquisitely illustrated thirteenth-century song cycles, the *Cantigas de Santa María*. These included killing oneself in a state of natural madness, and thus of 'innocence.'[57] But the lack of consensus about Juana's 'innocence' accentuated fears that she could die a 'bad' death. This mattered to dynastic reputation. It was also particularly important—as Denia, without any apparent hint of irony, acknowledged—for someone of her (pre-eminent) status.[58]

The paradox posed by a sovereign still invested with sacred legitimacy, yet who shunned the sacrament of penitence, became a long-term family dilemma. The persistence with which the family tried to persuade her to repent her sins shows that doubts persisted about the nature and extent of her mental incapacity, in turn raising questions about the degree of the family's responsibility for the situation. The empress drove forward the struggle to save Juana's soul, reinvigorating efforts to find a suitable confessor. But she came up against an important aspect of Juana's multi-faceted fight for sovereign authority: the right she felt was hers, and which her mother had enjoyed, to choose her own confessor.

As early as 1498, Juana's exchanges with the Dominican, Tomás de Matienzo, had sparkled with frost—partly, as Matienzo realised, because she suspected that her parents had imposed him upon her as inquisitor. Her subsequent confessor, Fray Ávila, was not a powerful political figure like Isabel's confessors, Talavera and Cisneros, but Juana trusted and cared for him and never gave licence for him to leave her. Following his departure, her repeated refusal to accept alternative confessors may be seen as a means of applying pressure to Denia and family members either to reinstate Fray Ávila or allow her to choose his successor. An undated letter from around 1530 casts light on Juana's attempt to retain a measure of independence in the matter: "Today," Denia told Isabel, "I have again spoken with the Queen our lady about her confessing. Her Highness said she wanted to do it but did not know anyone in the order of St Dominic. I told her Highness that both the former and present provincial are honourable men and she would be satisfied with either. Her Highness told me to send for them. I shall do so. Although I am such a bad man that I cannot believe that so good a thing will happen because I ask for it …".[59]

When dismissing Fray Ávila, Denia had put political expediency before religious interests. Yet he looked sourly on ad hoc confessions. Monks were best confined to their monasteries, he told Charles; if any "sensible and virtuous" monk could be found he would have to return at once to his cell after the act had taken place. Again, secrecy and deceit were essential; Juana must be assured that the monk was a person of status, provincial head of his order.[60] But Juana was well attuned to Denia's lies and extremely suspicious. She had ceased to favour Franciscans after suspecting the involvement in Catalina's departure of the order's minister general, Fray Francisco de los Angeles Quiñones, and nothing came of the proposal to send her a Dominican. Juana said she would like to confess but "had a lot of occupations that prevented her."[61]

After visiting Juana in February 1532, Isabel repeated that she *must* confess. But Juana's attitude to confession was not the only obstacle. The matter was entangled with the whole foundation on which her captivity rested. If her condition made her innocent of sin, any attempt to extract a confession would be pointless, even sacrilegious. This had presumably been the view of John Stile when commenting, in 1509, that: "the Qwyn of Castyl ys of no sadnys nor wisdom more then a yonge childe, and ys verry febyl, for sche etetythe nor drynkthe not some tyme yn twoo or thre days, and hyrethe no mas some tyme yn ayzghte days, nor myndeythe hyt not, but as a child having non order."[62] If, however, Juana performed the sacrament of penitence, it could be argued that her judgment was unimpaired.

When, in 1532, this thorny matter was discussed within the Council of State—an advisory council formed after 1521—some councillors suggested that if Juana were seen to confess, the inference could logically be drawn that "she is in another disposition than that which she has." Aware of the explosive nature of the question, Denia insisted that any act of penitence demonstrating her sanity had, for that reason, to be kept secret. Even if she had "as good a disposition as her mother no priest should ask her to do anything but what appertained to a woman."[63] This meant keeping her apart at all times, and at all costs, from political action or discussion.

After a fleeting visit to Tordesillas by Charles and Isabel in September 1538, Charles directed Pedro Romero, now *vicario* of the royal Carthusian monastery of Our Lady at Aniago, Valladolid, to confess the queen. Charles may have felt that Juana's formerly good relations with Romero would encourage her to accept him. But Denia again resorted to subterfuge: a *montero* would tell her that Romero happened to be passing and wished to kiss hands. Ever wary, the queen asked where he came from, where he was going and who was with him. She was very pleased he was nearby and would let him know if she needed him.[64]

This is the last known attempt by Isabel and Charles, acting together, to try to resolve the problem of Juana's troubled spiritual state, for Isabel died in childbirth at Toledo, on 1 May 1539, at the age of just thirty-five.

## 13.4 The Spiritual Life of a Political Prisoner

Defining Catholic orthodoxy in Spain in the late 1520s and the 1530s is no easy task. Even Cisneros, with his enthusiasm for Erasmus, and Isabel I, with her interest in the *devotio moderna*, might have been found wanting by the church and inquisitional standards of the time. Isabel I seems sometimes, indeed, to have been taken aback by striking manifestations of religious intransigence in her children, although this does not appear to have been the case with Juana—destined, in any case, for a land with no inquisition. Nor had Juana shown the spiritual restlessness of some of 'her' grandees, or the religious uncertainties of various relatives, like Ferdinand I, Mary of Hungary, Maximilian II or Rudolf II. It cannot, however, be excluded that Juana had heard something about Lutheranism, illuminism and the Jesuitism that would attract her daughter, Catalina, and granddaughter, Juana.

In all probability, the queen herself was conventional in her Catholic faith. She had followed family tradition in favouring the Franciscan order and, at the age of five, was admitted into the brotherhood of Friars Minor and Poor Clares.[65] She shared the family's commitment to the Observant movement and would certainly have approved of the labours undertaken by Villaescusa when reforming religious practice in his see of Cuenca during the 1530s.[66] She had bestowed relics and performed numerous acts of religious patronage. In 1510, she extended her protection to a small community of nuns at Tordesillas, belonging to the Augustinian order of St John of Jerusalem.[67] Both Aram and Zalama have documented her various acts of patronage, some small, others of greater import, with respect to the monastery of Santa Clara. When, in 1513, the nuns made alterations to the choir, Juana objected on the grounds that they "shortened the church," and she provided a solution to the problem, for which she paid in two installments. This large-scale operation lasted over a decade, but by the time it was completed her visits to Santa Clara had again been prohibited.[68] She continued to hear mass, if erratically, within the palace, made rosaries and prayed with them.[69]

A clue to her spiritual life, if an inevitably precarious one, may be found in her books of hours, which she kept with her at Tordesillas and which, like rosaries and jewels, served as vehicles for memory and meditation. One of the most well-known of these *horae*, now in the British Library, has some personalised features. The arms and mottoes of Philip and Juana ("*Qui vouldra?*" and "*Je le veus*") appear in the borders of the first of two images of Juana. Her book, on its protective chemise, lies open before her on a prie-dieu at the Office of a Guardian Angel—an office described as "exceedingly rare,"[70] but which may reflect the influence from her Spanish childhood of Eiximenis' *Natura angelica*. Juana's guardian angel stands behind her with John the Baptist, one of her patron saints, as she implores the archangel Michael to guard her from "the torment of my enemies." The rubric of the office of the angel is particularly thumbed, although whether from use by its first owner, or by subsequent ones, we cannot know.

This is a gorgeous manuscript, lavish in the use of liquid gold. Michael first appears in an ogee archway, thrusting Adam and Eve out of Eden and across the threshold of time, hustling them down the stairs toward the temporal world with its multitudinous wheel and clock-like mechanisms. The profusion of windows, turrets, stairs, columns and statues in the book's architectural borders, the motifs of flowers and butterflies, strawberries, birds, grasshoppers, and so forth, and the many drolleries, convey both a strange dream-like quality and sense of fun. A monkey drags a solemn-looking demon in a tub on wheels. Another, in a green hood, plays tennis. A stag's head emerges from a snail shell. A cherub in a feathered blue hat carries a flower in his downturned mouth. A bare-bosomed mermaid floats past with mirror and comb. A crowned cat walks hand in hand with a popish monkey. But, above all, Juana's book offers an inner space for interior prayer and contemplation. The book's concluding suffrages are dedicated to favourite saints, including Mary Magdalene; Barbara (shown with the tower in which her father imprisoned her) and Catherine of Alexandria, an image of whom Juana had purchased shortly before her first departure for the Low Countries, and whom she here invokes as "*Ave mater martyr regina*." (Fig. 13.1)

As earlier mentioned, Aram has influentially argued that Juana "retired" to Tordesillas to practice an ascetic form of spirituality beside the nuns of Santa Clara—a practice she may have developed under the influence of figures she knew personally, such as Margaret of York, or by reputation, such as the saintly Isabel of Portugal (1271–1336). Aram suggests that Juana's "retirement" or "semiretirement" helped her reconcile conflicting family commitments, and even that she helped project a legend of female debility as part of a strategy to protect her children.[71] She refers to her "sacrifice of the right to rule," her "contemplative piety," facilitating her exclusion from political power; her "inability or unwillingness to rule" and an "inaccessibility" both "voluntary and enforced."[72]

**Fig. 13.1** The second portrait of Juana in a book of hours now in the British Library (BL, Add. Ms. 18852, f. 288) shows her in gold brocade and ermine, and with a rosary at her belt, praying to the Virgin in the company of her patron saint, John the Evangelist. Juana is thought to have especially requested the prayer. The rubric reads: "*Oratio devoto de b[ea]ta virgine Maria vers*," followed by the incipit: "*Dignare me laudare te virgo sacrata* ..." ("Accord me grace to praise you, holy virgin ...") (*Source* Paul Fearn/Alamy Stock Photo)

However, the view that Juana accepted her alienation from her kingdoms both clouds and sweetens the bitter reality of Tordesillas, to which Juana time and again bore witness. The queen was, without any doubt, a political prisoner and continually challenged the denial of her proprietary rights. Had she not clung so fiercely to her royal attributes and desire to take part in political life, the need to uphold an alternative reality around the queen would have been less of an imperative. In a brief but perceptive overview of Juana's life, Lorenzo Arribas argues that there is, as yet, no demonstrable evidence that Juana sought, through "*recogimiento*," to reinforce a deliberate "strategy of State," while it is likely that she used the religious card to obtain certain modest objectives.[73]

This seems certain. Deprived of her visits to Santa Clara, Juana fought a rear-guard action over territory within the palace, refusing to hear mass in an inner room and struggling for access to the river corridor, where Denia eventually conceded to the erection of a makeshift chapel.[74] Once that struggle was won, she continued the fight elsewhere, as her resistance to all confessors after Ávila demonstrates. But such examples do not fully explain the gap between her expressed desire to confess and apparent inability to do so. The clearest clue to the conundrum remains Ferrer's letter of 1511 (see Sect. 9.4), in which Juana, though fresh from mass at Santa Clara, describes the worst aspect of her imprisonment as its *obstruction* of her spiritual life. This engendered in the queen a sense of outrage so great that it could find no relief in the sacrament of penitence.

Different as their cases are in so many respects, there is a sense in which the problems faced by Juana as a royal prisoner resemble those of Héloïse as a reluctant abbess centuries before. Writing to her former lover, Abelard, Héloïse asks how she can show genuine repentance for "sins" she has no genuine desire to disown: "How can it be called repentance for sins, however great the mortification of the flesh, if the mind still retains the will to sin and is on fire with its old desires? It is easy enough for anyone to confess his sins, to accuse himself, or even to mortify his body in outward show of penance, but it is very difficult to tear the heart away from hankering after its dearest pleasures."[75]

Juana and Héloïse were both the subject of nineteenth-century paintings that show them languishing over dead husbands and lovers. But the more important similarity between them lies in the question of penitential *honesty*—a question raised at Juana's deathbed by Domingo de Soto.[76] The queen's gaolers justified her imprisonment, and the alternative reality built around it, as a means of protecting her against herself. But Juana saw it as a material and spiritual offence that robbed her of her kingdoms and very soul. How was she honestly to "tear the heart away from hankering after" its dearest desire—the desire, that is, for her freedom and the effective recognition of her status? How to forgive a bunch of traitors whose crimes against her had no finite duration? How to draw the necessary distinction between offenders and offence when those same offenders were, at the same moment in which she was being asked to demonstrate her piety, "obstructing" her with their gossip, laughter, surveillance and mockery?

Juana excelled in saying no, and not yet. She did not fast; she went on hunger strike. Alternatively, she confined herself to days of bread and cheese. Juana once said that she was treated worse than a slave, "for even of slaves more account is taken." Yet the sense that she had of herself as the sovereign monarch still sang in her blood and marrow. She was, in Marlowe's words, a king whose regiment had gone. She was a perfect shadow in a sunshine day. But one thing that Isabel's daughter would, or could, not do was surrender to, or forgive, her captors, among whom her female guards formed the front line. This was what Juana meant when she told Ferrer that her captivity militated against her spiritual salvation.

## Notes

1. AGS, PR 3, f. 39, Denia to Charles, 25 January 1522; CSP (Queen Juana), 96.
2. Danvila (ed. 1897–1900), IV, Denia to Charles, 28 July 1521.
3. Article 1, UN Convention against Torture and Other Cruel, Inhuman or Degrading Treatment or Punishment, adopted by General Assembly resolution 39/46 of 10 December 1984.
4. Danvila, V, "Instrucción que el Cardenal de Tortosa, electo ya Papa, dió al Emperador acerca de que debia hacer á su regreso á España," February 1522.
5. Mattingly (ed. 1940), Charles to ambassadors, 11 August 1522.
6. Sandoval (ed. 1955–1956), 81, 10.
7. Zalama (2003), 415.
8. Venegas (Zuili, ed. 2001).
9. Giurato (2003).
10. Castañeda Tordera (Gómez Vozmediano, ed. 2008), 255–316.
11. Danvila, III, constable to Charles, 24 May 1521; CPS (Queen Juana), 86, Cardinal, admiral and grandees in Tordesillas to Charles, 12 April 1521; 87, Instructions of grandees to duke of Alba, 12 April 1521; 88, president of Royal Council and councillors to Charles, 13 April 1521; 89, bishop of Oviedo to Charles, 14 April 1521.
12. Pérez (1999). '*Siempre los comparé con los comuneros de Castilla*' (68).
13. AGS, Estado 5, f. 300, 12 May 1518.
14. AGS, Estado 15, f. 71, Denia to Charles, 16 October 1527; translated in CSP (Queen Juana) as "what I see and what is said and done."
15. AGS, Estado 36, f. 243, Denia to Charles, 20 February 1534.
16. CSP (Queen Juana), ed. Bergenroth, 97, Loaisa to Charles, 15 July 1524.
17. Rodríguez Villa (ed. 1903–1905), I, Salinas to Ferdinand, 18 December 1524, 90.

18. See Zalama (2003).
19. Checa (2008), 76. Charles took the famous "golden tapestries" in 1526.
20. Muller (2012).
21. AGS CMC 1ª Época 1544 [undated], 'Provança de Alonso de Ribera,' 20 August 1555; Zalama (2003); Aram (2005).
22. AGS, Estado 13, f. 323, admiral to Charles, 7 July 1525.
23. AGS, Estado 13, f. 270, admiral to Charles, 2 January 1525. "*La señora reina de portugal sintió tanto ell apartarse de su madre que le costó un buen desmayo.*"
24. Ibidem.
25. CSP. Ven., III, ed. Brown, 910, Contarini to Signoria, 9 January 1525.
26. AGS, Estado 13, ff. 14–15, 'Carta del Almirante a Carlos sobre estado de la Reina,' 15 January 1525.
27. CSP (Queen Juana), 100, Denia to Charles, 23 May 1525.
28. AGS, Estado 14–28, f. 2, Denia to Charles, 4 April 1526.
29. Guicciardini (ed. 1776), II, 134.
30. Sánchez (1998), 157–158.
31. Fichtner (2001), 59.
32. AGS, CSR 12, f. 19/566–567, 'Carta del Doctor Valladolid para el mal de la mujer de Ochoa de Landa,' 1529–1531.
33. AGS, CSR 24, f. 38/510, 'Recebta de la mujer de Simancas para el mal de mujer de Ochoa de Landa' [1531?]; J.T.R.D. (ed. 1994), 221; Porter (2002).
34. Burton (Jackson, ed. 2001), I, 243–244.
35. Burton, 345.
36. Burton, 260–262; 392.
37. Fernández Álvarez (2002), 292–293; Lisón Tolosana (1990), 126–129.
38. Grassian (1983); Schaler (2008). Both studies describe the effects of social (or small-group) isolation as well as solitary confinement.
39. *Amnesty International's Work on Prison Conditions of Persons suspected of politically motivated crimes in the Federal Republic of Germany: Isolation and Solitary Confinement* (AI Index: EUR 23/01/80). See also the later, more detailed study, *Cruel Isolation: Amnesty International's Concerns about Conditions in Arizona Maximum Security Prisons* (AMR 51/023/2012).
40. Styron (2001).
41. BN Madrid, Ms. 1778, 45–50v., Denia to Charles, 25 November 1538.
42. Rodríguez-Salgado (1988).
43. Ibidem.
44. Guisado (ed. 1987).
45. Rawlings (2002), 27.
46. Avalle-Arce (1994), 147.
47. Vital (Gachard, ed. 1881), 148.

48. Silva (2006), 112.
49. Danvila, V, admiral to Charles [1522], 337.
50. BN, Ms. 7075, "Epístola moral que el Sr Almirante de Castilla embió a un hombre docto, con su respuesta escrita en el año 1524."
51. Avalle-Arce (1994), 135.
52. Caro Baroja, I (1992).
53. The remark is attributed to Charles' jester, Francesillo de Zúñiga, in Baroja (1992), I, 264.
54. Avalle-Arce (1994).
55. Villacorta Baños-Garcia (2005).
56. AGS, Estado 24, f. 292, to Charles, 24 April 1532.
57. Guiance (1998). The verb '*suicidarse*' did not exist; instead '*matarse a se mismo*' or '*asesinarse*' were used.
58. CSP (Queen Juana), 104, Denia to Charles, 23 February [1531?].
59. CSP (Queen Juana), 103, Denia to Isabel, 23 February [1530?].
60. AGS, Estado 24, f. 290, 20 March 1532.
61. Ibidem.
62. Brewer (ed. 1920), I, 162, 9 September 1509, 86–87.
63. AGS, Estado 24, f. 290, 20 March 1532.
64. BN Madrid, Ms. 1778, ff. 45v.–50v., Denia to Charles, 25 November 1538.
65. AGS, PR 27, f. 70, "Carta de hermandad de la Orden de San Francisco a favor de la infanta Doña Juana de Aragón y Castilla," 19 August 1485.
66. González Olmedo (1944); Nalle (1992).
67. Zalama (2003).
68. See, for example, Zalama (2010); Aram (2005) mentions that, among other things, Juana herself sketched a device that she wished to have engraved on a lamp, for which she provided the Carthusians of Miraflores with gilded silver plate and funds (105).
69. AGS, Estado 22, f. 122, Denia to Charles, 10 May 1532.
70. BL, Add. Ms. 18852, Hours of Juana of Castile, f. 36; Morrison (E.M.) in Kren and McKendrick (eds. 2003), 14, 385.
71. Aram (Gómez, Juan-Navarro and Zatlin, eds. 2008), 41: "My own work suggests that a sixteenth-century emphasis on the passions and belief in female debility colored a legend that Juana projected in order to protect her children's inheritance."
72. Aram (2005), 103, 146, 165, 169.
73. Lorenzo Arribas (2004).
74. AGS, Estado 5, f. 315, to Charles, 13 September 1518; CSP (Queen Juana), 39.
75. Radice and Clanchy (eds. 2003), Letter 4, 68.
76. See Chapter 14.

## References

Aram, Bethany. 2005. *Juana the Mad: Sovereignty and Dynasty in Renaissance Europe*. Baltimore and London: John Hopkins University Press.

———. 2008. Queen Juana: Legend and History. In *Juana of Castile: History and Myth of the Mad Queen*, ed. María A. Gómez, Santiago Juan-Navarro, and Phyllis Zatlin. Lewisburg: Bucknell University Press.

Avalle-Arce, Juan Bautista de. 1994. *Cancionero del Almirante Don Fadrique Enríquez*. Barcelona: Quaderns Crema.

Bergenroth, G.A. (ed.). 1868. *Calendar of State Papers, Supplement to Vol. I and Vol. II of Letters, Despatches and State Papers Relating to Negotiations Between England and Spain, Preserved in the Archives of Simancas and Elsewhere*. London: Longmans, Green, Reader and Dyer.

Brewer, John Sherren. 1920. *Letters and Papers, Foreign and Domestic, of the Reign of Henry* , vol. VIII. London: HMSO.

Brown, Rawdon (ed.). 1869. *Calendar of State Papers Relating to English Affairs in the Archives of Venice (1520–1526)*, vol. 3. London: HMSO.

Burton, Robert. 2001. *The Anatomy of Melancholy*, ed. H. Jackson. New York: New York Review of Books.

Caro Baroja, Julio. 1992. *Vidas mágicas y Inquisición*, vol. I. Madrid: Akal.

Castañeda Tordera, Isidoro. 2008. La Proyección de las Comunidades. Memoria, Represión y Olvido. In *Castilla en llamas. La Mancha comunera*, ed. Miguel F. Gómez Vozmediano. Ciudad Real: Almud.

Checa, Fernando. 2008. *Tapisseries flamandes pour les ducs de Bourgogne, l'empereur Charles-Quint et le roi Philippe II*. Brussels: Fonds Mercator.

Danvila y Collado, Manuel (ed.). 1897–1900. *Historia crítica y documentada de las Comunidades de Castilla*. Madrid: Memoria Histórico Español.

Fernández Álvarez, Manuel. 2002. *Casadas, Monjas, Rameras y Brujas: La olvidada historia de la mujer española en el Renacimiento*. Madrid: Espasa Calpe.

Fichtner, Paula Sutter. 2001. *Emperor Maximilian II*. New Haven and London: Yale University Press.

Gachard, Louis-Prosper (ed.). 1881. Premier Voyage de Charles-Quint en Espagne de 1517 à 1518. In *Collection des Voyages des Souverains des Pays-Bas*, vol. III. Brussels: Commission Royale d'Histoire.

Giurato, Simona. 2003. *La Sicilia di Ferdinando el Católico: Tradizioni politiche e conflicto tra Quattrocento y Cinquecento (1468–1523)*. Messina: Rubbettino.

González Olmedo, S.I., Félix. 1944. *Diego Ramírez Villaescusa (1459–1537), fundador del Colegio de Cuenca y autor de los Cuatro Diálogos sobre la Muerte del Príncipe Don Juan*. Madrid: Editora Nacional.

Grassian, Stuart. 1983. Psychiatric Effects of Solitary Confinement. *Washington University Journal of Law and Policy* 22: 325.

Guiance, Ariel. 1998. *Los Discursos sobre la Muerte en la Castilla medieval (Siglos VII–XV)*. Valladolid: Junta de Castilla y León.

Guicciardini, Francesco (ed.). 1775–1776. *Della Storia d'Italia*. Florence: Friburgo.

Guisado, Maite (ed.). 1987. *Cartes Íntimes d'una Dama Catalana del S. XVI*. Barcelona: La Sal.

J.T.R.D. 1994. Memorial del tesorero de la Reina Juana, Ochoa de Landa, "a mi señor el Licenciado", remitiéndole la receta propuesta por una comadre de Simancas para curar la enfermedad de su esposa. (1531?) In *Tordesillas 1494*. Valladolid: Sociedad V Centenario del Tratado de Tordesillas, 221.

Kren, Thomas, and Scot McKenrick (eds.). 2003. *Illuminating the Renaissance: The Triumph of Flemish Manuscript Painting in Europe*. Los Angeles and London: J. Paul Getty Trust.

Lisón Tolosana, Carmelo. 1990. *La España Mental: Demonios y Exorcismos en los Siglos de Oro*. Madrid: Ediciones Akal.

Lorenzo Arribas, Josemi. 2004. *Juana I de Castilla y Aragón (1479–1555)*. Madrid: Ediciones del Orto.

Mattingly, Garrett (ed.). 1940. *Further Supplement to Letters, Despatches and State Papers Relating to Communications Between England and Spain, Preserved in the Archives of Vienna and Elsewhere (1513–1542)*. London: HMSO.

Muller, Priscilla E. 2012. *Jewels in Spain, 1500–1800*. El Viso: Hispanic Society of America.

Nalle, Sara T. 1992. *God in La Mancha: Religious Reform and the People of Cuenca, 1500–1650*. Baltimore and London: John Hopkins University Press.

Pérez, Joseph. 1999. *Carlos V*. Madrid: Temas de Hoy.

Porter, Roy. 2002. *Madness: A Brief History*. Oxford: Oxford University Press.

Radice, Betty, and M.T. Clancy (eds.). 2003. *The Letters of Abelard and Heloise*. London: Penguin.

Rawlings, Helen. 2002. *Church, Religion and Society in Early Modern Spain*. Basingstoke and New York: Palgrave Macmillan.

Rodríguez-Salgado, María-José. 1988. *The Changing Face of Empire: Charles V, Philip II and Habsburg Authority, 1551–1559*. Cambridge: Cambridge University Press.

Rodríguez Villa, Antonio (ed.). 1903. *El Emperador Carlos V y su Corte según las cartas de Don Martín de Salinas, embajador del Infante Don Fernando (1522–1539)*. Madrid: Real Academía de la Historia.

Sánchez, Magdalena S. 1998. *The Empress, the Queen, and the Nun: Women and Power at the Court of Philip III of Spain*. Baltimore and London: John Hopkins University Press.

Sandoval, Prudencio de. 1955–1956. *Historia de la Vida y Hechos del Emperador Carlos V*, ed. Madrid: Biblioteca de Autores Españoles.

Schaler, Sharon. 2008. *Sourcebook on Solitary Confinement: The health effects of solitary confinement.* London: Mannheim Centre for the Study of Criminology and Criminal Justice, 10–24.
Silva, Alfonso Franco. 2006. *Entre la Derrota y la Esperanza.* Cádiz: Universidad de Cádiz.
Styron, William. 2001. *Darkness Visible: A Memoir of Madness.* London: Vintage Classics.
Venegas, Alejo. 2001. *Agonía del Tránsito de la Muerte*, ed. Marc Zuili. Paris: Harmattan.
Villacorta Baños-García, Antonio. 2005. *La Jesuita.* Barcelona: Ariel.
Zalama, Miguel-Ángel. 2003. *Vida cotidiana y Arte en el Palacio de la Reina Juana I en Tordesillas.* Valladolid: Universidad de Valladolid.
———. 2010. *Juana I. Arte, Poder y cultura en torno a una reina que no gobernó.* Valladolid: Centro de Estudios Europa Hispánica.

CHAPTER 14

# The Demons of Tordesillas (1550–1555)

## 14.1 Family Quarrels and Family Visits

Government documents bore the *intitulatio* of the proprietary monarch and her son, the emperor, from 1516 until Juana's death. But Juana's imprisonment and Charles' involvement in seemingly endless wars abroad meant that most of the time there was no monarchical presence in Castile. Instead, it was ruled by a series of governors and 'regents' (as they were unofficially called). Isabel's two periods of government in the 1530s have been mentioned. When Charles left Spain at the end of 1539, the government was handed to a cardinal, duke and royal secretary. When, in 1543, Charles left Spain again, Philip became governor. When Philip went to Augsburg for a family summit, he was succeeded by the monarchs of Bohemia—his cousin, Maximilian, son of Ferdinand, and Maximilian's wife, María, daughter of Charles. After returning to the 'regency' Philip was succeeded by his younger sister, Juana of Austria.

This state of affairs increased tensions within government administration, whose leaders, bound by legal and financial restrictions, walked a tightrope between the need to be seen to represent and reflect the wishes of the sovereigns and the need to protect the subjects under their jurisdiction—in practice to protect them from the exactions of the emperor.[1] The period was also marked by strong dynastic tensions. Juana's embodiment of the Trastámaran inheritance meant that any move by Charles to dispose of her kingdoms and estates and titles within the crowns of Castile and Aragon remained dubious in law and Ferdinand and Maximilian were



G. B. Fleming, *Juana I*, Queenship and Power,
https://doi.org/10.1007/978-3-319-74347-9_14

highly sensitive to that fact. Thrown out of Castile in 1518, Ferdinand had become king of the Romans in 1531, ruling the Habsburg lands in central Europe and determined to advance the dynastic prospects of his numerous family. As Rodríguez-Salgado notes in her classic exploration of the division and near-collapse of Habsburg authority in the 1550s and the conflicts and difficulties that Juana's 'regents' faced, her survival mattered in terms of Charles V's policies with regard to the dynastic succession and consequent nature of the empire. If Charles died before Juana, would Philip or Ferdinand govern the Spanish realms? Since common law and practice favoured the rights of the eldest surviving son of the person incapacitated, Ferdinand had a much stronger claim than Philip to govern Juana's Spanish, Italian and American territories until her death.[2]

At the end of the 1540s, the emperor's health was in decline and he decided that he had to take action to protect Philip's rights. The dispute over the succession came to a head at the summit at Augsburg in 1550–1551. When Charles insisted that Ferdinand yield his longstanding claim to the imperial succession in Philip's favour, Maximilian rushed to Augsburg to stiffen his father's resolve. He was followed pell-mell by Mary, anxious to broker an agreement. The rows were acrid and prolonged. At one point, Ferdinand and Charles refused to speak to one another. Under heavy and sustained pressure, Ferdinand eventually capitulated to an agreement which, had it been implemented, would have seriously undermined the position of his successors, and which, in effect, meant the crown of Charlemagne being tossed about between family members. But on one issue, as Rodríguez-Salgado observes, Ferdinand ominously refused all compromise: the future of the Trastámara inheritance.

One potential trigger for dynastic conflict was the kingdom of Naples, bequeathed by Charles to Philip on the eve of his marriage to Mary I. Since Naples lay within the jurisdiction of the council of Aragon and Juana was still Aragon's rightful sovereign, only she had the right to dispose of it. Charles thus transferred to Philip only his own self-appointed regency powers. Philip drew up legal documents to ward off any possible rival claim to Naples by Ferdinand.[3] In October 1554, the pope agreed to invest Philip with the kingdom, but years of wrangling followed. Philip told the pope that Naples was in Juana's gift and that the transfer had been agreed by "the emperor and Queen my lords, father and grandmother, together and … both royal majesties have withdrawn from the administration of the said kingdom …".[4] Despite this fiction of royal togetherness, Juana, by her very hold on life, threatened to turn family differences into war.

Each time a new 'regent' took power, he, or she, visited Juana to secure her blessing on their work in her 'service.' This was, of course, all of a part with Tordesillas' theatre of illusion, but since the queen remained in law the mistress of her kingdoms, every regent was obliged to participate in the ritual process of drawing upon the source of royal legitimacy so that the hole at the heart of the monarchy was less apparent. Relatives made social visits too. These were, nonetheless, infrequent and, during Juana's forty-six years at Tordesillas, personal contact between the queen and her children, niece and grandchildren averaged out at barely more than one visit every two years.[5] The presence of Charles and Isabel at Tordesillas during the Christmas blizzard of 1536 illustrates one of those rare moments when the queen's prison became a court.[6] On such occasions, Juana's formal pre-eminence was honoured, but her sensitivity to her status may also have lent them a certain tension and piquancy. The lonely queen was torn between an eagerness to receive and a need to complain.

By the 1550s, her household numbered just over 150, very few of whom would have served her personally, and was managed entirely as a Denia family enterprise. When the second marquis of Denia died in 1536, his son, Luis Sandoval y Rojas, succeeded him as third marquis, governor and gaoler. He lived at Tordesillas with mother, wife, sisters, daughters, nephew and son. The latter, Francisco Gómez, was the future gaoler of Prince Carlos and father of the later duke of Lerma. The dueñas formed the front line of security around the queen (the second being the *monteros de Espinosa*). They included his wife, Catalina de Zúñiga y Cárdenas; the Rojas sisters, Ana Enríquez de Rojas, a *beata*, and Magdalena de Rojas, countess of Castro; the daughter, Francisca de Rojas, countess of Paredes; the cousin, Margarita de Rojas; and the daughter-in-law, Isabel de Borja, countess of Lerma and daughter of the duke of Gandía and later saint, Francisco de Borja.[7]

Juana had real affection for some of her servants but a visceral hatred for the Denias who guarded her. Prevented from exercising power and authority as she had wished, and, surrounded by captors whom, as such, she loathed, Juana lived increasingly in an inner world of the imagination. She could be cool with Charles but clearly cherished family contacts. She hungered and worried for news. After relatives' visits she was invariably curious about the route they had taken and how they comported themselves on horseback. Her many questions showed not only her alertness and responsiveness but the nostalgia of someone who had once herself been an 'Amazon'; who still remembered the sights, sounds and smells of the roads of her youth and who, in the words of the poet Machado, "*va soñando caminos.*" It was with her grandchildren that Juana seemed most able to relax, and, if the number of their visits as governors (1548–1551) is any indication, those who showed most affection for Juana were Maximilian and María. Their first visit to Tordesillas, in 1548, when Philip accompanied them, was the occasion of an unprecedented naval tournament on the Duero. They spent the first days of 1549 with Juana and were there again in July 1550. María visited alone in January 1551. She returned in July with her younger sister, Juana, and the queen's great-grandson, Carlos.

A report by Ferdinand's ambassador, Juan Alonso Gámiz, about a meeting between the queen and Maximilian in July 1550, at the time when the dispute over the Habsburg succession was reaching its climax, draws attention to several of the queen's characteristics: her extreme sensitivity to her proprietary status and concern to uphold it; her intense curiosity about her family; her love for her younger son (she asked "an infinite number of things") and the "*grandísima imaginación y fantasia*" with which she spoke about her ill-treatment. It also describes her attempts to use Maximilian as a conduit through which to press for certain (unspecified) provisions.[8]

The trigger for that display of "very great imagination" was a gift from Ferdinand—a gold crucifix, studded with diamonds, rubies and pearls that he hoped she would use in prayers for him and his family. Juana was intrigued by the design, examining it closely and commenting that she had seen many similar pieces in Flanders that had belonged to Charles the Bold. But this, Maximilian interjected, came from the house of Austria and, as she could see from the inscription on the case, it was dated 1451 and had originally belonged to Emperor Frederick. "In truth," Juana exclaimed, reading the inscription on the box, "my son gives me great pleasure by remembering me and sending me such a distinguished and devotional piece, which I am not worthy to have with me …!" She started to worry that she did not know where to keep it. Could she not hang it, Maximilian asked, from a strip of cloth in her chamber? No, she said, she would need to put it in a special chest, because so many of her belongings had been stolen.

This was a danger point for Maximilian, impulsive by nature, deeply unhappy with Charles and Philip and his lack of independence as governor and resentfully aware of the close watch being kept on him at all times (here through Gámiz). But to encourage the queen to speak further on the theft of her possessions would have been to risk raising embarrassing allegations. Maximilian switched tack. But the subject he broached was potentially as thorny, involving a fresh reminder of Juana's humiliating situation: "Señora, the King my lord [Ferdinand], has ordered, both in writing and verbally, to fulfil to the letter everything that you would wish or ask for… and because I understand that your Highness would like to have some money beyond what is settled on your household to give alms and do other things as you wish, without having to inform or ask it from your servants, I have ordered the licenciate [Gámiz] to bring 400 gold ducats for your Highness to keep and dispose of as you will." These, wrapped in a handkerchief, he placed in her lap.

Juana, though pleased, stood on her regal dignity; if the money did not come from her own estate she could not accept it. When Maximilian reassured her, she asked if it came in "doubloons or simple ducats." She questioned him again and in detail about Ferdinand and his family. The conversation, notes Gámiz, gave Maximilian much pleasure—even more so in that the queen "three times" called Ferdinand "my son"—"something she never calls the Emperor." When he was about to leave, and halfway down the room, Juana called Maximilian back, again expressing her joy that Ferdinand remembered her. She asked them not to forget her and repeated a request for favours for her servants, "naming some in particular."

In their message of the same date, María and Maximilian told Charles that the queen had entrusted them with a memorandum, requesting "certain things." They had felt obliged to forward it, urging him to fulfill her requests because "of the nature that they are" and "small things from which her Highness would receive satisfaction and for which we would ourselves be very grateful to your Majesty."[9] The fact that her grandchildren felt obliged to forward these modest requests speaks volumes about the tragedy of her situation, of which they seem to have been not entirely unaware.

Ferdinand had been told that Juana would leave a will in Charles' favour.[10] But while most of her treasure had long been accounted for, the very existence of a will would have testified to Juana's soundness of mind. What this meant is demonstrated by the later case of Philip II's artist, Juan Fernández de Navarrete, whom a childhood illness had left deaf and dumb. Navarrete's struggle for the right to leave a will, and thus to free himself from the world of the *muertes civiles*, the legally dead, by proving that, among other things, he had "acute understanding," could communicate and had an excellent memory, reflected the twofold significance of wills at the time.[11] In his widely read guide to a good Christian death, *Agonía del Tránsito de la Muerte* (1537), Alejo Venegas emphasises the spiritual importance of wills. More than a distribution of earthly goods, they were spiritual maps, professions of faith, expressions of desire, pleas for atonement, requests to the living for spiritual help on the journey beyond and pleas to God and his saints for forgiveness and intercession and passports, in short, out of purgatory and into heaven.[12] Isabel I's will is a classic example, entreating that Christ's "death and passion" be placed between her judgment and soul and asking Michael to receive, protect and defend her soul from "that cruel beast and ancient serpent who will then wish to swallow me…". Don Quixote, when at the point of death, testifies to the recovery of his sanity by calling for a priest to confess to and a scribe to take down his will, "for in such extremities as this a man must not jest with his soul."

What the "small things" in the little paper Juana handed to Maximilian were and whether they were attended to is unclear. Evidently, Juana had nothing much to give. Fernando had negotiated away the large sums owing from her marriage settlement in order to bolster his own position in Castile, and when on the eve of the comunero uprising, Juana complained to Denia about the little she could leave the infante, Denia had snapped that everything belonged to Charles.[13] This was, in effect, to proclaim her a *muerte civil*, null and void as a legal entity.

## 14.2 "House of Agonyes"

On the night of her grandchildren's departure, Juana could not sleep. She feared that Ferdinand's crucifix, or parts of it, would disappear. At two o'clock in the morning she called for Gámiz, who found her drained of colour, clutching the crucifix in its case. Would he keep it for her, she asked, until she had a special chest made to keep it safe? When he hesitated, she gave him her "royal word" that it would be ready in less than thirty days and would then call him back. Gámiz asked why she could not give the crucifix to her chamberlain, Ribera, or to Denia. Her reply was emphatic. She had already lost too many jewels of great value and her chests were empty. Eventually Gámiz agreed, but 'secretly' entrusted it to her treasurer.

In attributing Juana's claims to her "*grandísima imaginación*" Gámiz resorted to the traditional practice of deflecting blame from the Denias onto Juana's condition. As we have seen, the claim that demons possessed Juana had been made both by those hoping to restore her to health and those determined to hide her away. Francisco de Borja, the Jesuit who met her several times before her death, describes the continuing conflict between Juana and her guards, who accused her of throwing out blessed candles with "*mucha furia*," because they smelt, and shutting her eyes at the moment of the host's elevation. Borja tested these claims, but inconclusively. On one occasion, he had a chaplain approach her at the moment of elevation to see whether her eyes were open or closed. But Juana signalled to the priest to move out of her line of vision and later asked in irritation what he thought he was doing. "I thought," he said in confusion, "that your Highness had called for me."[14]

The Inquisition did not persecute sorcery and witchcraft to the same degree as heresy. But there had been a notable witch scare in Cuenca in the first decade of the sixteenth century and in 1519 several 'witches' were tried at Cuenca.[15] In Cervantes' later tale, *El coloquio de los perros*, drawn from the case of Córdoban witches investigated for entering into a pact with the devil, the witch Cañizares draws a distinction between witchcraft and sorcery—the art of invoking and consorting with demons. Although she has abandoned sorcery, she tells the mastiff, Berganza, it has proved impossible to abandon the vice and sensual delights of witchcraft, including night flight. She has made herself a reputation for piety and good works, and desires, as she approaches death, to return to God. But witchcraft has fettered her will and frozen her soul so that it cannot reach out for God's hand.

Juana's exact contemporary, the cleric and mathematician Pedro Ciruelo, tackled the subject of sorcery with a mixture of scepticism and belief in demonic power. He saw it as treason against God, the ultimate act of lèse-majesté. He thought demons could be conjured in circles, flasks of water, varnished mirrors, precious stones in rings, even the glimmer of fingernails. One remedy against diabolically manipulated clouds was to ring large church bells, fire artillery, light blessed candles and recite devotional prayers.[16] When a great storm broke over Tordesillas on 23 June 1550, killing ten people and sending a bolt of lightning through the roof of Juana's chamber, Denia brought blessed candles to her rooms, and, invariably cool in a crisis, Juana tried to comfort the marquis by assuring him that her Agnus Dei relic was proof against storms, plague and demonic forces. From her high vantage point over the plain, she improvised on the formula, "*Christus vincit, Christus regnat, Christus impera*," replacing it with: "*Christus vincit, Christas regnat, Christus* me defenda."[17] By doing so, she showed that ability to adapt and improvise on Latin that Vives had mentioned.

Juana's natural intelligence and memory were still sharp and she had retained her facility with language. During her "warm and honourable" reception of Prince Philip in November 1543 she even joked with his jester and there was "good conversation." In 1550, Maximilian took genuine pleasure in talking with her. But new lies and deceptions had settled onto the strata formed by older ones until her habitat had become a fantastically structured reef of falsehood over which she was condemned to drift, like Phantastes in Spenser's *Faerie Queene*, through a world thronged by "infinite shapes of things" that "were never yit." As she approached the end of her life, the boundary between real and imaginary, living and dead, began to waver, sometimes disappearing altogether. The "house of agonyes" in which Phantastes dwelt was Juana's too, the demons around her assuming corporeal form to threaten the queen and her closest relatives, living and dead.

In November 1551, Charles instructed Philip to engage with "*lo que tocaua a la confisión*" on his return from Augsburg.[18] Philip and his younger sister, deeply attracted to the Society of Jesus, looked to Borja for help. In May 1552, the queen made a "general confession" and Borja granted a "general absolution"—an exceptional means of forgiving sin in emergency circumstances. But he doubted that she had shown proper contrition.[19] This became more urgent as, by March 1553, Juana's long physical inactivity, contributing to her circulatory problems and swollen legs, meant that she became paralysed from the waist down. Denia told Charles that, if God needed a confession, "which I hope He does not," they could only pray for it.[20]

When Philip left Spain in 1554 to marry Juana's niece and England's first queen regnant, Mary I, the regency was handed to his younger sister, who had been named after the queen and is generally known as Juana of Austria and princess of Portugal. She and Philip visited Tordesillas to receive the queen's blessing on their respective missions. At the same time, Borja, now commissary general of the Society of Jesuits, made the first of three consecutive visits there. Philip's forthcoming marriage provided the Jesuit with a springboard into the troubled waters of Juana's spiritual state. The queen listened attentively as he outlined Mary's problems in gaining approval for the dominant features of English policy in 1554: reconciliation with Rome and her Spanish marriage. Philip, said Borja, was concerned that Juana's "way of life" could be exploited by her niece's enemies. Would they not argue that if "her Highness lived like them, without masses and without images and without sacraments," they could do likewise?

Juana responded to his plea to "unburden her royal conscience" by projecting back onto her female guards the accusations they brought against her. Formerly, she said, she had made confession, communed, heard mass, used images, prayed in the approved manner, but her "company" snatched away her prayer book, scolded and scrapped with her, mocked her devotions, spat on saints' images, and contaminated the water. At mass, they interposed themselves between her and the priest, turning her missal upside down, ordering him to say only what they wanted to hear. They had tried to steal her reliquaries and crucifix.

When Borja, whose own daughter was among the dueñas, expressed his doubts that they could be responsible for all that she accused them of, Juana replied evenly: "That could be, because they say they're dead souls." Once, she told him, when with the princess of Portugal, she noticed the dueñas chanting incantations "as if they were witches." Juana spoke about this for an hour ("*habló muy á proposito sin salir de la material*"). She described scenes that Borja interpreted as "illusions or malign visions" in which they mocked her, in some sort of ghastly charade, in the persons of the "count of Miranda and knight commander."

By Miranda, Juana probably meant Francisco de Zúñiga y Avellaneda, who had died in 1536 and was father of the current marchioness. Miranda had switched loyalties between Fernando and Philip in 1506, and in 1520 had opposed the admiral's moves to reinstate Juana's authority. The knight commander was Miranda's brother, Juan de Zúñiga, another former felipista, latterly Philip's *ayo*, who had died in 1546. But why Juana had these particular figures in mind is unclear.

She insisted that, once the women were removed, she would take the sacraments. Borja replied that her allegations, amounting to charges of heresy, would need to be investigated by the Holy Office. He asked if she believed in the articles of faith of the Catholic church. "How should I not believe them?" she replied. "Of course I do!" Borja felt uneasy that she was showing "desire" ("*deseo*") rather than sorrow or affliction ("*pesadumbre*)". He meant, perhaps, that Juana showed too much of an appetite for the subject. He thought that her *flaqueza de juicio* was too deep-rooted for a cure but advised Philip to keep the women away for several days to assess whether she was simply hallucinating or truly saw demons. He proposed that inquisitors might examine the women; that crosses and holy images be distributed throughout the queen's rooms; that daily masses and gospel readings be held and that the palace be aspersed with holy water. Prayers might be said in churches and monasteries and pilgrimages made and there could be a secret exorcism of the queen. Once freed of these terrible visions, she could make confession—or explain why not.

Philip rejected exorcism and inquisitorial examinations but agreed that Juana should be told that the dueñas, kept temporarily out of sight, had been placed under investigation. Thus the deceptions continued. Borja assured Juana that she was now free to "show outwardly the inward catholic soul that belongs to her" and hear mass being said in a nearby corridor. But he kept up the pressure. He raised the prospect of excommunication for her long delay in confessing and, he added, rather disingenuously, for not having mentioned that she lived with witches. "You absolved me two years ago," Juana retorted. Borja remarked on her good memory but reminded her that it had only been a "deprecatory absolution" (to ward off evil). He rose and repeated the rite, afterwards reading from the gospels of John and Mark. Throughout Juana was attentive and showed "good grace." Afterwards she asked if she should read the gospels after absolution. Yes, indeed, Borja said.[21]

Juana was subsequently visited by Luis de la Cruz, a Franciscan friar. Juana returned at once to the problem of her guards. These had returned, "and so the [royal] person cannot do what her soul requires." She had been held *chusmada*—held down and humiliated. This word she repeated over and over again. It was as if, to borrow the words of Cañizares, her frozen soul could not reach for God's hand.

Cruz expressed himself more bluntly than Borja. The emperor and prince, he said, had asked him to help relieve her of the offending dueñas, "but how can your Highness not think of helping herself by doing, for her part, what a Catholic and Christian Queen must do? How can we, her servants, help to serve and content her if she herself prevents it?" Juana's reply was dry: "You are certainly wrong, father, to insist so much on this. Do what you must and what you say the prince orders, which is to properly punish those shameless, deformed women, and for the rest, leave me to do what I must do." With this she returned to her "thousand things" and "what with me doggedly maintaining all the human and divine arguments that I could, and what with her Highness making accusations, we spent two hours."[22]

During this encounter between the queen and Cruz, she, at his insistence, dutifully recited "all the sacred mysteries of Jesus Christ our lord and of our Catholic faith." But she went on to say "so many strange things, by which her Highness showed how indisposed she was, that she horrified me (*me espanté*)." One of these stories was "extremely long" and may well have been drawn from childhood memories of the civets used at Isabel's court to produce perfume—the fierce, striped African creatures with black bands across their eyes and kept chained in cages. She spoke, for instance:

> about a civet cat who had eaten the *infantica* of Navarre and the queen Doña Isabel our lady and bitten the Catholic King our lord and many other things of this nature; and this wicked cat had been brought here by the dueñas and was even now very close by her chamber, about to inflict on her the same evil and harm they were used to doing. And her Highness took such pleasure in telling these stories that she ordered me to sit and settle myself comfortably, saying that she was very well served by my coming.[23]

Was the wicked cat a substitute for "that cruel beast and ancient serpent" to which Isabel's will refers, lurking nearby and ready to devour her? Did she remember an actual childhood incident involving her parents and the little infanta, Magdalena of Navarre, who had came to Isabel's court in 1494 as a three-year-old hostage to the peace between Castile and Navarre and whom Juana had known, but who had died when still a child?

Borja and Cruz agreed on the deep-rooted nature of Juana's illness but differed crucially on whether it rendered her incapable of judgment. Borja urged her to give outward expression to the "Catholic spirit" locked within. Cruz thought her an innocent and so far removed from being able to take the sacraments that it would be sacrilege to administer them. Juana was more to be envied, he wrote, than pitied. Yet there was something that did not quite fit with that "innocence from sin and guilt," and raised the hairs on the back of his neck. Was this because her storytelling seemed to depart so radically from the divinely providential view of the Catholic Kings? And because she who been their heir, and was their last surviving child, had told it with a certain degree of relish?

## 14.3 The Death of Juana I

Juana's last weeks were spent in agonising pain. She habitually took baths with the help of her *lavanderas de corp*, Catalina and Marina Redonda. But in mid-February, scalding water blistered her skin.

Sores developed on her back and buttocks. Lotions were applied but the agony that came with every movement made it difficult to move her and keep her clean. When, after several days, she was forcibly washed and her bedclothes changed, a spot of gangrene was noted on her left buttock. 'Egyptian ointment' was applied, but the gangrene spread. Her flesh was cauterised. Feverish, Juana refused to be bled or take medicine. She could not, or would not, move or be moved, and stopped eating.[24]

Juana of Austria went to Tordesillas with several doctors: "I asked her Highness for permission to visit her," the regent told Charles, "and, although she declined, nevertheless (seeing how much her illness had advanced) I went there and saw her. And because she seemed to feel such agitation (*pesadumbre*) at my being there, I returned, with her permission [to Valladolid], leaving the necessary surgeons and doctors …".[25]

Upset by the visit, the regent asked Borja if he would see the queen again, presumably to try to prepare her for a 'good' death. The viaticum (the sacrament of the Eucharist when administered to the dying to mitigate the punishments of purgatory) had to be received with genuine feeling. Honesty was essential. Contrition had to be real. The regent assured Charles that Borja had taken various "*buenos religiosos*" with him. Yet Borja himself did not, perhaps, feel that this was enough to ward off the demons that had troubled the queen.[26] At the last minute, he turned to one of Salamanca's greatest philosophers and most authoritative theologians, Domingo de Soto.

A disciple of the philosopher, theologian and jurist Francisco de Vitoria, the Dominican friar had been Charles' confessor and theological representative at the first sessions of the Council of Trent, particularly with regard to the Council's position on grace and original sin. He was one of the greatest pioneers in the field of international law and human rights and had presided over the famous debate in Valladolid in 1550 between Bartolomé de las Casas and Juan Ginés de Sepúlveda about the justice of conquest. In 1552, he was promoted to the Chair of Prime in theology at Salamanca, a post he retained until 1556. His book against slavery, *De Iustitia et de Jure* (*Ten Books on Justice and Law*) was published in 1557, just two years after Juana's death.

Unhappy at being asked to deal at a distance with the queen's spiritual state, Soto hurried to Tordesillas on the morning of 11 April 1555. He saw Juana first with others, then returned to talk with her alone. Afterwards, he sent a report to royal secretary Vázquez de Molina, informing him that Juana had only hours to live and was unlikely to last the night. But he was satisfied that her judgment was clear—clearer than he had been led to expect. They had spoken together "at great length" and he had been "consoled" by their conversation. She had felt unable to accept ("*no esta por*") the Eucharist, but unction might be administered, since this rite was not so demanding. They would, however, need to wait till she began to drift away, "because we fear that with the judgment she has now, because of her honesty (*por su honestidad*), she will not allow it."[27]

The viaticum was withheld, in part because the queen was vomiting, but also, perhaps, because of the "*honestidad*" that Soto mentions. That night, Borja administered extreme unction. Dr Santa Cara reports that Juana made a general confession and admission of having offended God, but this is mentioned neither by Soto nor Borja. According to a later description, possibly concerned to demonstrate the effect on the queen of Borja's saintliness, she was still alert enough to recite, or partly recite, the creed. When asked if she wished it to be read out she told Borja: "You begin to say the creed and I'll repeat it after you." When words failed her, she repeatedly struck her chest. Her eyes fixed on that central icon of contemplation, the image of the suffering Christ, the queen kissed the crucifix he held out to her.[28] Her last reported words, uttered a few hours before her death, were: "*Jesu Christo crucificado sea conmigo*" ("Jesus Christ crucified, be with me").[29] Denia, also present, gave her words as "Jesu Christ crucified, help me."[30]

The queen died between six and half past six on the morning of Good Friday, 12 April, in the presence of Soto, Borja, Santa Cara and Denia. At last, the queen's passion was over.

## 14.4 Epilogue

At court Juana's death was greeted with relief, for only this could avert the dreaded showdown between Philip and Ferdinand and close the wound that ran like a living sore through the body politic. Philip's closest confidant, Ruy Gómez de Silva, observed that "while we are saddened on a personal level, as far as other issues are concerned [her death] has guaranteed the succession in Naples and in other areas which we suspected that the King of the Romans [Maximilian] might take."[31] It also meant that funds hitherto directed towards the upkeep of her household could be released.

On the day of Juana's death, the regent, after discussing financial matters, told Charles that, to judge from Denia and Soto, the queen had shown "signs of being a Christian" and had "done more than expected." That she had died on Good Friday was significant. She had recommended herself to God and there were grounds for hope that she was on "the path of salvation."[32] This was all and it was not much. In letters to his brother and daughter, to whom he also wrote of his "*muy gran sentimiento*," Charles fretted that his mother had made no individual confession. He could only hope that, although she "did not confess," she was with God. Still, he could not disguise a certain pique with his daughter, whom he reprimanded for inadequate reports about the progress and details of Juana's illness.[33]

"One can reliably state," writes a biographer of Juana of Austria, "that from then on he would never recover from a certain existential anguish, a deep disappointment with life." His mother's "definitive absence" shook him into making life changes.[34] This view may be based on Leopold von Ranke's references to an emperor haunted by his mother's voice: "*Als seine Mutter gestorben, glaubte er zuweilen ihre Stimme zu vernehmen, die ihn rufe, nachzukommen.*"[35] Another historian, citing Ranke, asserts that certain dark stains of his life reappeared, "shadows of conscience that drew him towards an expiation."[36]

The view that Charles suffered a crisis of conscience, and that his withdrawal to the monastery of Yuste in 1557 was occasioned by filial remorse, should be treated with scepticism. At his first spectacular act of abdication, at Brussels in 1555, the emperor declared that his mother's ill health had forced him to cross the sea to recover the inheritance she could not govern herself. He had probably long convinced himself that this was so. He had been in failing health for some time, and deeply depressed as the fault lines in his empire widened. His several abdications were hardly spontaneous acts of contrition. Yet reports of the emperor's distress at his mother's death cannot be altogether dismissed. His bedchamber and office were hung with black. On the road to Yuste, he reminisced fondly about the "*longanizas a la manera de Flandes*" that his mother used to provide for him at Tordesillas.[37] This was the language of a gourmand, but also of a son, and it would be wrong to doubt the sincerity of his "very great emotion" or not to suspect that some uneasiness may have attached to it.

The absence abroad of many of Juana's relatives might explain the low-key nature of his mother's burial at Santa Clara in Tordesillas. Still, the total lack of relatives at the interment of the embalmed body of the proprietary monarch, sovereign mistress and mother and grandmother of emperors and queens, is difficult to explain. Just a small handful of notables attended the rites. They included Pedro Fernández de Velasco, constable of Castile, who, as count of Haro, had led the battle for her "liberation" in 1520; Antonio de Fonseca, president of the Royal Council; Antonio de Águila, bishop of Zamora; and the third marquis of Denia. Various chaplains and cantors were sent from Valladolid for the ceremony, during which the body, formally recognised by the *monteros de Espinosa*, was lowered into the vault.[38] This was no longer occupied by Philip's remains, which Denia, unknown to Juana, had accompanied to Granada in 1525. There they had joined those of the Catholic Kings, translated from the Alhambra to the Royal Chapel four years before.

The regent requested the holding of obsequies throughout Spain. A funeral ceremony was held at San Benito, Valladolid on 26 May. Few who heard the sermon by Father Vadillo—"*Deum timete, regem honorificate*" ("Fear God, honour the king")—would have had any personal recollection of the heated debates that took place there in the summer of 1506. Yet, just as Juana I's significance to Castile, both as person and as concept, had been instrumental in the decision to hide her away, so too it may have influenced the modesty of the obsequies that the regent organised at Valladolid.

Grander obsequies were held by Ferdinand at Augsburg and in Brussels, where Charles attended a special ceremony on 25 May. In the febrile climate of Marian London, the two-day obsequies for "Lady Jane," whom Mary may have wished to honour not only as aunt but as fellow queen regnant, assumed a special significance. They took place in "great solemnity" between 17 and 18 June, with Spanish and English nobles walking side by side behind a huge ornamental dome with a gilded canopy, and John Feckenham, dean of St Paul's, breathed fire on the congregation for their "wicked errours and heresie."[39] The main event in Brussels was postponed, at Philip's request, until he could leave England. Eventually, at two o'clock in the afternoon of 16 September, a long procession made its way from the palace on the Coudenberg to the church of St Gudula. In their midst, a pony, covered with trappings of black velvet bordered with gold, led by Italian trainers and surrounded on four sides by the heralds of Castile, León, Aragon and Sicily, bore a woman's saddle, embroidered with gold and bearing a cushion on which a magnificent crown sparkled with jewels. Philip was dressed, almost uniquely, in striking black mourning.[40]

Arrangements were made to pay, disband or re-absorb the members of Juana's household into the Castilian household of the emperor or into the households of other family members. In 1554, Juana had either renewed, or added to, her former requests for her servants and Denia had urged Philip to see to them, mentioning her extreme poverty. The marquis made another, poignant appeal to Charles in May 1555: Juana had not left a will and her servants' poverty was great.[41] Denia's letter was followed by others from Juana of Austria, who urged Charles to honour the Denias. She drew a pathetic picture of the marchioness, who had suffered so much from the queen's "illnesses and asperities (*asperezas*)," and had worked so hard, particularly during the queen's last illness, that she was still confined to bed with exhaustion a month later. The regent also reminded Charles of the services of the late marquis during the comunero uprising.[42]

An inquiry into the queen's missing treasure was opened that August. The regent took what remained of her grandmother's rosaries, songbooks and books of hours, her religious images and portraits of her mother and of Katherine. Denia received the crucifix Ferdinand had given Juana in 1550.[43] He also received, among other things, the Agnus Dei that she had used to protect them from the great storm.[44]

It is a curious fact, Zalama observes, that after Juana's death, the palace, even when still inhabited, refused to stay upright. After repeated repairs, it was demolished in 1773 under the first Bourbon monarch and new development obliterated all trace of the original site.[45] Juana's body was finally removed from Santa Clara in 1574, as part of a complex operation of intersecting funeral corteges, organised by Philip II. In snow, wind and rain, three different processions met, as it were, in a dynastic congress of the dead. The bones of the empress, her sons Fernando and Juan, and Philip's first wife, María Manuela, were transported from Granada to the royal monastery of San Lorenzo de Escorial via Yuste, where Charles's body was united with them. A second cortege brought the body of Eleanor from Mérida. A third cortege set out from Valladolid with the body of Mary of Hungary, stopping en route at Tordesillas to collect Juana's.[46]

Ferrer had once written of Juana that she "does everything by extremes." Even in death this seemed true. On 7 February, the cortege of a mother and daughter who had shared much in common temperamentally, but had never known one another, arrived at the Escorial in a ferocious storm. The tabernacle prepared for Juana's bier, in the place where the emperor's had been, was torn to shreds and "no-one dared go out for fear of losing their lives, so that much brocade was lost; and so it was said that the oaks of the Herrería sprouted flowers of brocade ...".[47] Philip had settled on the Escorial as the Habsburg pantheon, and when Juana's body took to the Granada road again two days later, it did so alone, as that of the last of the Trastámara monarchs. The cortege, met by Philip at Aranjuéz, arrived in Granada on 28 February 1574.

It had been preceded, although only after prolonged delays, by the funerary sculptures of Juana and Philip, the work of Bartolomé Ordóñez. These reached their destination in 1539 and were then stored at the Hospital Real, forgotten about until their re-discovery in a basement in 1591. By then, four fingers were missing from Philip's hands and two from Juana's, and all the points of their crowns had disappeared.[48] Possibly owing to a lingering doubt as to whether the sculptures should be placed alongside those of the Catholic Kings, it was not until 1603 that they were removed to the central transept of the Royal Chapel.

The catafalque consists of two separate sections of Carrara marble superimposed. Above these, the royal figures lie on an urn. Like Isabel's, Juana's figure, turned slightly to the left, occupies the Gospel side of the church, denoting her superior, proprietary status. But, as an art historian notes, its position also left the Catholic Kings lying on the "inferior" Epistle's side. Thus, as if "History wanted to compensate" for what it had done to her, "the funeral effigy of doña Juana, apart from being the most beautiful, occupies the most eminent position of all in that select company."[49] Perhaps the most evidently ironic fact about the effigies of Juana and Philip is their elevated position. Seen, in particular, from above, the two sets of funerary beds create the impression of a majestic seesaw that has ground to a halt with Juana's and Philip's not only occupying the 'superior' side but looming over Isabel's and Fernando's. In 1611, a report was commissioned from the master of works of the Alhambra and cathedral to look into the 'deformation'. Nothing, however, was done.

Juana, who seems suspended between sleep and a state of interior alertness, holds a sceptre as light as a lollipop. Her dress is Flemish with dalmatian sleeves. Her hair is drawn loosely back from her face. A collar of arrows and pomegranates encircles her neck. Compared with Isabel's and Fernando's, the faces of Juana and Philip are youthful and idealised, although Ordoñez followed the stipulation in the contract that Juana's face should be thinner and more aquiline than her mother's, as in life.

While Philip II gathered Habsburg bones around him at the Escorial, making of Charles the effective dynastic patriarch, Trastámaran bones remained scattered across the Castilian meseta and the royal burial site at Granada bleached and bled into the backwaters of the historical memory. Now it is on the tourist circuit. And it is clear to see that, although Philip alone bears the regnal number on the inscription at the foot of the catafalque, his position beside Juana in the overall funerary design is secondary. This was what he had most feared—to appear as a consort, his distinction as Valois prince, ruling king of Castile and founding father of the dynasty of the Spanish Habsburgs all but forgotten. To this day it is Juana's effigy that occupies the most important position and attracts the greatest curiosity and most excited comment among the visitors to the Royal Chapel.

## Notes

1. Rodríguez-Salgado (1988).
2. Ibidem.
3. Ibidem.
4. AGR, PR 42, f. 43, "Minuta del protesta que SM el Rey D. Felipe 2° hizo sobre que se quitase de la bula de la investidura del Reino de Nápoles que el Papa Julio 3° le hizo, la clausula en que se reservaba el derecho de la Reina Da. Juana su abuela" [undated].
5. Zalama (2003).
6. Girón (Sánchez Montez, ed. 1964).
7. Rodríguez Villa (1892); Carlos Morales (Martínez Millán, ed. 2000), II.
8. Álvarez Juarranz (Del Val Valdevieso/Martínez Sopena, eds. 2009), I, Gámiz to Ferdinand, 4 August 1550, 275–285.
9. Rodríguez Raso (ed. 1963), LI, Kings of Bohemia to Charles, 4 August 1550, 210.
10. Rodríguez Villa (ed. 1903), II, Salinas to Ferdinand, 16 March 1534.
11. My thanks to Isabel Aguirre for pointing out this book by Rosemarie Mulcahy (1999).
12. Venegas (Zuili, ed. 2001).
13. CSP (Queen Juana), ed. Bergenroth, 47, Denia to Charles, [October?] 1519.
14. AGS, Estado 109, f. 252, Borja to Philip, 17 May 1554.
15. Nalle (1992).
16. Ciruelo (Ebersole, ed. 1978).
17. Aram (2005), Gámiz to Ferdinand, 9 July 1550, 147.
18. AGS, Estado 109, f. 328, Denia to Charles, 20 November 1551.
19. Rodríguez Villa (1892), Denia to Philip, 9 May 1552, 385–386.

20. AGS, Estado 109, f. 327, Denia to Charles, 18 March 1553.
21. AGS, Estado 109, ff. 330–331, Borja to Philip, 10 May 1554.
22. AGS, Estado 109, f. 253, fray Luis de la Cruz to Philip, 15 May 1554.
23. Ibidem.
24. Rodríguez Villa (1892), Dr Santa Cara to Charles, 10 May 1555, 397–398.
25. Fernández Álvarez (2002), Juana of Austria to Charles, 13 April 1555, 282–283.
26. The humanist, Venegas, reassured his readers that the shadows in the room of the dying person were not necessarily demonic. Shadows cast by sunlight could enter by small holes and hollows and "this is how shadows can enter of birds in flight and cats that walk the roofs." (249). His remark seems tailor-made to comfort a queen troubled by civets.
27. AGS, Estado 109, f. 65, Soto to royal secretary Juan Vázquez de Molina, 11 April 1555.
28. Rodríguez Villa (1892), 399–402.
29. AGS, Estado 109, f. 263, Borja to Charles, 19 May 1555.
30. AGS, Estado 109, f. 245, Denia to Juan Vázquez, 12 April 1555.
31. Rodríguez-Salgado (1999), 107; and (1988), 110n.
32. Fernández Álvarez (2002), Juana of Austria to Charles, 13 April 1555, 282–283.
33. Zalama (2003), Charles to Juana of Austria, 15 May 1555, 271–272.
34. Villacorta Baños-Garcia (2005), 248.
35. Ranke (1827), 93.
36. García Simón (1995), 29.
37. In García Simón, Luis Quijada in Jarandilla to Juan Vázquez, 18 November 1556, 52.
38. Zalama (2003).
39. Duffy (2009), 146.
40. Rodríguez Villa (1892); Aram (2005); Zalama (2010).
41. Fernández Álvarez (2002), Denia to Charles, 26 May 1555, 288; second message of same date, 288–289.
42. AGS, Estado 109, f. 262, and f. 269, Juana of Austria to Charles, 31 May 1555.
43. AGS, PR, 29, f. 117, Gámiz to Ferdinand; Aram (2005).
44. Aram (2005).
45. Zalama (2003).
46. Varela (1990).
47. CODOIN, 7, 112.
48. BN Ms. 18.654.42, "Provisión para la translación de los sepulcros de Don Felipe el Hermoso y Doña Juana a la capilla de los Reyes Católicos, Granada, 16 December 1591"; "Parecer sobre la translación de los

sepulcros de Don Felipe el Hermoso y Doña Juana a la capilla de los Reyes Católicos," Granada, 27 February 1592.

49. Redonda Cantera (Zalama, ed. 2010), 214.

## References

Álvarez Juarranz, María Luisa. 2009. La Visita de Maximilian II y María de Austria, su Esposa, a su Abuela, La Reina Doña Juana I de Castilla. In *Castilla y el Mundo Feudal*, vol. I, ed. María Isabel del Val Valdivieso and Pascual Martínez Sopena. Valladolid: Universidad de Valladolid.

Aram, Bethany. 2005. *Juana the Mad: Sovereignty and Dynasty in Renaissance Europe*. Baltimore and London: John Hopkins University Press.

Bergenroth, G.A. (ed.). 1868. *Calendar of State Papers, Supplement to Vol. I and Vol. II of Letters, Despatches and State Papers Relating to Negociations Between England and Spain, Preserved in the Archives of Simancas and Elsewhere*. London: Longmans, Green, Reader and Dyer.

Carlos Morales, Carlos Javier de. 2000. Los últimos años de las Casas de Castilla y Borgoña del Emperador. In *La Corte de Carlos V*, vol. II, ed. José Martínez Millán. Madrid: Sociedad Estatal para la Conmemoración de los Centenarios de Felipe II y Carlos V.

Ciruelo, Pedro. 1978. *Reprouación de las supersticiones y hechizerías*, ed. Alva V. Ebersole. Valencia: Albatros Hispanofila.

Duffy, Eamon. 2009. *Fires of Faith: Catholic England Under Mary Tudor*. New Haven and London: Yale University Press.

Fernández Álvarez, Manuel. 2002. *Juana La Loca: La Cautiva de Tordesillas*. Madrid: Espasa Calpe.

García Simon, Augustin. 1995. *El Ocaso del Emperador: Carlos V en Yuste*. Madrid: Nerea.

Girón, Pedro. 1964. *Crónica del Emperador Carlos V*, ed. Juan Sánchez Montez. Madrid: CSIC.

Mulchahy, Rosemarie. 1999. *Juan Fernández de Navarrete el Mudo, pintor de Felipe II*. Madrid: Sociedad Estatal para la Conmemoración de los Centenarios de Felipe II y Carlos V.

Nalle, Sara T. 1992. *God in La Mancha: Religious Reform and the People of Cuenca, 1500–1650*. Baltimore and London: John Hopkins University Press.

Ranke, Leopold von. 1827. *Die Osmanen und die Spanische Monarchie im 16. Und 17. Jahrhundert*, I., vol. 25, Historische Meisterwerke. Vienna/Hamburg and Vienna/Zürich: Gutenberg Verlag.

Redondo Cantera, María José. 2010. Los sepulcros de la Capilla Real de Granada. In *Juana I en Tordesillas: su mundo, su entorno*, ed. Miguel-Ángel Zalama. Valladolid: Ayuntamiento de Tordesillas/Grupo Página.

Rodríguez Raso, Rafaela (ed.). 1963. *Maximiliano de Austria: Gobernador de Carlos V en España*. Madrid: CSIC.
Rodríguez-Salgado, María José. 1988. *The Changing Face of Empire: Charles V, Philip II and Habsburg Authority, 1551–1559*. Cambridge: Cambridge University Press.
———. 1999. Charles V and the Dynasty. In *Charles V, 1500–1558*, ed. H. Soly. Antwerp: Fonds Mercator, 26–111.
Rodríguez Villa, Antonio. 1892. *La Reina Doña Juana: Estudio histórico*. Madrid: Murillo.
———. 1903. *El Emperador Carlos V y su corte según las cartas de Don Martín de Salinas, embajador del infante Don Fernando (1522–1539)*. Madrid: Real Academía de la Historia.
Varela, Javier. 1990. *La Muerte del Rey: El ceremonial funerario de la monarquía española (1500–1885)*. Madrid: Turner.
Venegas, Alejo. 2001. *Agonía del Tránsito de la Muerte*, ed. Marc Zuili. Paris: Harmattan.
Villacorta Baños-Garcia, Antonio. 2005. *La Jesuita*. Barcelona: Ariel.
Zalama, Miguel-Ángel. 2003. *Vida cotidiana y Arte en el Palacio de la Reina Juana I en Tordesillas*. Valladolid: Universidad de Valladolid.
———. 2010. *Juana I. Arte, Poder y Cultura en torno a una Reina que no gobernó*. Madrid: Centro de Estudios Europa Hispánica.

CHAPTER 15

# Out of the Shadows

Five hundred years after the opening of the Cortes of 1506 I visited Mucientes, in the hills above Valladolid. The ruins of the castle where the queen had appeared before the procurators to ask if they recognised her as Isabel's successor, Juana I, protruded through the long grass, thistles and poppies. From the castle, the tower of the church of San Pedro Apóstol, where the procurator for Toledo, Pero López de Padilla, had argued with Cisneros and Juan Manuel, was clearly visible. But at closer inspection the church too was falling into ruin. The woman with the key told me the tower was no longer safe to climb. Nor was the pulpit. The baptistery, where she had been baptised, was out of bounds. Beside the gilt altarpiece, the giant saint, Christopher, an uprooted tree in one hand, turned a gaze full of savage curiosity to the disproportionately heavy burden of the Christ child on his back. The church is one of many of Castile's sites of the historical memory now short of funds and crumbling to bits. As the wind roared around us, the woman asked if we could pray together for its restoration.

Had Juana gone to mass at the church? Tracing a line in the air from the castle to the church door where we stood, a passer-by told me, as if he were far older than the ninety years he laid claim to, and had a personal memory of the queen: "See that path, up there? She used to walk along it from the palace on her way to mass. I say 'palace' because that was the word my grandfather and great-grandfather used. They used to say: 'Let's go and play *en palacio*' and they called it a 'palace' because doña Juana lived there …".



G. B. Fleming, *Juana I*, Queenship and Power,
https://doi.org/10.1007/978-3-319-74347-9_15

He led me down the church steps to a small town hall, then being restored, and indicated a wall covered in brown paper, at which he pulled gently, revealing a plaque. The information it contained was curiously wrong:

> La Reina Juana Primera de Castilla
> (1479–1555)
> Renuncia al Gobierno
> de la nación en Mucientes,
> Valladolid, ante el Cardenal
> Cisneros en cualidad de
> notario mayor del Reino.[1]

Mucientes is one of a number of places that tell the story of two Juanas, one visible, the other concealed. One flourishes in the warm, protective sphere of the popular memory. The man at the church of San Pedro; the taxi driver at Medina del Campo, who described a *corrida* that Juana had watched from the tower of San Antolín in Tordesillas; the bookseller in Valladolid, who regaled me with local prints after discovering my interest in the queen, each had his own view of a historical figure who they could see in their mind's eye. So too did the sombre custodian of the monastery of the Descalzas Reales in Madrid, founded by Juana's granddaughter and namesake, Juana of Austria, in 1559. Aware of my curiosity about the various royal portraits on view, he whispered conspiratorially, as if the queen, or her detractors, might yet be within earshot: "She was never mad, you know."

Alongside this public and popular Juana, willed into existence by tales passed on within families down the years, is another who belongs to a more formal, official history, as symbolised by the plaque in Mucientes town hall. This second Juana renounces, withdraws, retires or is deposed and becomes invisible, even in the very place where she took a public stand, and where the plaque that bears her name and is erroneously worded, has itself, at least temporarily, disappeared from view. Both approaches reflect the ease with which Juana's life has lent itself to popular myth and historical distortion. It has been my intention to recapture a third Juana, of crucial importance to the first decades of sixteenth-Castile, and beyond, and to consider what power she had.

Juana's life raises important questions about the meaning of success and failure and the use and abuse of power, and had far-reaching consequences. Her marriage, motherhood and contested right to rule culminated in revolutionary wars, changed Spain's relation to Europe and impacted on America. She was proud, passionate and spirited. She was also cautious and often frustrated by indecision. She had a sharp wit, a caustic tongue, a vivid grasp of language and was doubtless capable of the malice attributed to her by her adversaries. She had immense courage and formidable tenacity. Like her daughter, Mary of Hungary, she had rollercoaster moods of energy and depression and aroused suspicions with respect to her religious laxity. A biographer of Mary has rightly noted that Juana shared with her daughter (as with her sister, Katherine) a "passionate singleness of purpose" in adversity.[2]

To adopt the phrase used elsewhere of her paternal aunt, Blanca II of Navarre, there can be no doubt that Juana I was a "tremendous proprietary victim." Her father was on a mission. He had ruled her kingdoms before her and was determined to do so again-alone. Her husband, governed by others, was both weak and ambitious. Her son had an all-consuming dynastic vision that it is difficult to disassociate from greed. The ambiguous wording of Isabel's will—whether toxic residue of pain and confusion or of intense, unresolved argument—dogged Juana throughout the first and most crucial years of her reign. Her menfolk sought to use it for their own ends, resorting to a gendered language of jealousy, madness and incapability. During long imprisonment, the regal grace and gravity, the "*buona manera*" and "*buona forma*" that Querini noted and that had impressed Henry VII, yielded at times to helpless anger, self-recrimination and self-abuse. Historians have attributed Juana's complexity to a mental illness that allowed for periods of lucidity of varying length. This is a convenient device, but only begs the question as to what sanity and lucidity really mean.

This study has drawn a comparison between Enrique IV and Juana I to the degree that they were both the targets of brilliant and hostile writers. Just as Palencia portrays a failed king and fugitive within his own kingdom, inhabiting the wilderness and finding sanctuary only in its darkest parts, so Martire associates the fugitive, elusive Juana with darkness and the night. Both monarchs were said to live with demons, and Suárez, who writes elsewhere of Juana's mental instability—even dementia—believes that her melancholic uncle was unquestionably ill. Though that illness is left undefined, he declares it a decisive fact, shaping the instability of his character, even the pronounced love of music that Juana shared.[3] Neither had the driving ambition and desire for absolute control that characterise the reigns of usurpers. Both had temperamental difficulties in presenting their wishes and goals—not least a certain streak of self-deprecation, self-doubt or self-reproach. During her brief personal rule, Juana did little to shape, or put across, her message. It is as wife, mother and Habsburg auxiliary, not as independent sovereign, that Juana stands among the cast of statues at Maximilian's empty tomb, or sits beside her Habsburg relatives in Dürer's triumphal car, driven into the future with a swirling crack of the whip. Titian has left us the heroic (yet melancholic) posings of an emperor; but Charles, like Fernando before him, had no interest in perpetuating the image of the queen whose name appeared daily beside his on acts of government.

Juana's evident failings loom the larger for the perceived triumphs and successes of her immediate predecessors and successors. She seems often to have been paralysed by the thought of her mighty parents, whose dual reign bathed in a providential light. Her relations with Isabel and Fernando wavered between reverence and resentment. Isabel's order to obey Fernando "as if I were still alive" would prove anathema to a young sovereign who needed to have faith in her own considerable natural abilities, and to seize opportunities as they arose. In 1511, in the bitterness of imprisonment, she described her filial obedience—her subjection to her parents' psychic power—as a form of slavery from which, had she been able to see it at the time, her marriage to Philip might have emancipated her once and for all. At the end of her life, and in the depths of melancholy, she was haunted by the sense that evil forces had devoured, or were about to devour, what had once been glorious, or seen as glorious. Yet, to the horror of the Franciscan friar who heard her stories, this view did not seem to entirely displease her.

During her fleeting period of personal rule Juana chose the executor of, and acknowledged expert on, Isabel's will, Juan de Lazárraga, to work beside her. She showed an evident wish to fulfil at least some of her mother's desired reforms, particularly with regard to the preservation of the royal patrimony and recovery of what Ruiz-Domènec has called the "lost *bon ton*" in Castilian politics. Evidently, we cannot know for certain what would have happened had she stayed on with Isabel in 1504, but there can be little question that she made the task far more difficult by leaving Castile when she did, and by her subsequent failure to build an independent power base with which Fernando would have had to come to terms when he returned from Naples. Juana's poor relations with Cisneros, although probably inevitable, worked to her detriment. Her failure to reach Granada, and to come to a public compromise with Fernando at the crucial moment of reunion, handed the king of Aragon all the cards. Many believe that Juana's final and greatest mistake was her failure to take advantage of the freedom offered by the Junta of Tordesillas in 1520. Bergenroth observes that, although in a state of continual "rebellion," she suffered failures of nerve at crucial moments such as this. But it is a moot point whether any queen—even one with far greater resources and advantages than Juana in 1520, such as a strong negotiating team of her own choosing and a more flexible political attitude—could have risen to the challenges posed by the more radical elements of the Junta, and brought important modernising reforms to Castile and Aragon without embroiling her kingdoms in war with her imperial son.

The obverse of Juana as tremendous proprietary victim is that of Juana as lifelong personification of proprietary power and royal legitimacy whom, for this reason, many feared. She knew and cared for Castile and its institutions. She knew 'her' *grandes*. Despite her apparent abandonment of the kingdom in 1504, she became a gifted resistance fighter on Castile's behalf, endowed with the iron will characteristic of her Trastámara blood. From a daughter who defied her parents to defend her marriage, she became the wife who defied her husband to defend Castile.

We have seen that, as far back as 1502, the unmanageability of the massive legacy she inherited, and which marriage complicated and further extended, contributed to the tensions that fatally undermined her relations with Philip. Juana was adamantly opposed to the notion that Castile should be subjected to 'Flemish' or 'German' rule, on grounds not only of cultural difference and difference of interests but of the sheer impracticality of a single monarchy governing a conglomeration of territories so vast that they stretched from the "islands of the Ocean Sea" to the fringes of the Ottoman empire. When Philip ousted Fernando from Castile and tried to sideline Juana, she used the power invested within her to declare her pre-eminent right to the crown. When the Cortes showed its mettle by protecting the queen, Philip defied the Cortes, but at the risk of mounting unrest. Shortly after Philip's death, Juana emerged from mourning to reconstitute the Royal Council and ensure that his fledgling government did not survive him. If being willing and able to rule is understood as the desire and ability to choose and shape a government, influence its decisions, fight for crucial measures and bring about a reconfiguration of political forces, then Juana I, "the queen who did not govern," began to do precisely that between 1506 and 1507.

Juana's later, insistent demands for reunion with the infante suggest that, with Charles crowned emperor, and absent from Spain, she envisaged a role for her younger son in government. Although capable of harsh measures and not without streaks of his grandfather's political guile and cynicism, the infante had a mind more agile and curious than his brother's and his general approach to the problems of governance and human relations was one of moderation and flexibility. Juana's dealings with the Junta of Tordesillas in 1520, and her continuing trust in her old adviser, Ramírez de Villaescusa, suggest that her approach to governance was also one of caution and moderation. Her refusal to support the Junta by endorsing its acts of government was the consequence less of mental instability and the erratic moods from which she nonetheless clearly suffered—and knew that she suffered—than of a consistent strategy by which she withheld the charismatic weapon of her signature from those whose hostage or prisoner she considered herself to be.

Juana defended Charles from the comuneros, not because she believed in the holy imperial project but because Charles was her son and heir. She saved his political life in Spain at the expense of her own, but there is not a shred of evidence to support the view that she intended to immolate herself upon the dynastic altar. Juana was often conflicted and suffered from mood swings, but this did not extend to a wish for pious withdrawal from the world. Isabel was always her true north. As the daughter of the Catholic Kings, she too had hoped to share in government and longed to engage with political affairs, which she invariably referred to as "hers." In public protective of her father and her son, she was, in private, disillusioned, enraged and embittered. Until her death, she struggled for her freedom, understood in terms of the right to preside an independent royal household and to consult with her subjects on her own account.

Apart from the question of Juana's personal abilities and desires, a main aim of this study has been to draw attention to the long shadow that Juana cast over her kingdoms as their legitimate embodiment. While so many histories have been written in, as it were, the sunny teleological uplands, leaping from the Catholic Kings to Charles V, my central argument has been that the history of the period cannot be understood unless Juana I is restored to her place at the core of the crisis of legitimacy that broke in 1497. Between 1504 and 1526, in particular, none of the male rulers who usurped her position could feel secure. Despite repeated threats to kill herself, she did not die. Her use of negative power, or power as resistance, and the sheer importance of her status as proprietary monarch have been generally underestimated, but were real. After 1520, Juana did not re-enter public life but, in a land that remained troubled and restive, her gaolers stayed on their guard. Never legally deposed and never abdicating, her shadow lay across all who ruled in her name and "in her service." Although stripped of effective power, Juana's status meant that Charles could act only as guardian-king—not as king in his own right. This may not have mattered for much of the time, but it rendered him peculiarly vulnerable to political unrest and intra-dynastic rivalry.

The most tempestuous period of Juana's reign was marked by the discourse of tyranny, treason and legitimacy. The word 'treason' was often on Juana's lips, and with reason. Those who had sworn fealty to her but who subsequently obeyed Philip, Fernando or Charles—all of inferior status in Castile—were, technically, traitors to the crown. Treason was a common part of popular discourse and conflict sprang from the deep-rooted belief that Isabel's legacy had not been honoured and that Juana was the victim of 'traitors' and 'tyrants.' Against this, her adversaries, at least before her definitive imprisonment, exploited the concept of disordered female passion to depict her in scarcely less than apocalyptic terms as the harbinger of ruin and perdition, while arguing—often simultaneously—that the crown was a shared enterprise and that her interests and theirs were one and the same. Conscious of historical precedent and influenced by traditional concepts of female inconstancy and instability, Cisneros tried to adapt the corpus of thought on resistance to tyranny, including the notion of resistance to a shadow monarch, or *rex inutilis*, to bypass and ignore the queen's independent right to act. Again, in 1516, his role in forcing through Charles' coup can be seen within the context of a longstanding practice, continued well beyond Juana's time and kingdoms, by which the monarchs of a dying dynasty were invariably deemed unfit.

Ironically, when arguing that a Juana-led government would unleash the forces of destruction, Fernando and Cisneros opened the Spanish kingdoms to wildly unpopular foreign rule, revolutionary upheaval and successive European conflicts that bled it dry. The outbreak of the wars of the Comunidades and Germanías had complex and multitudinous political, economic and social causes that scholars will continue to address. But the melancholic consequences of Juana's captivity, her neglect and ill-treatment and the refusal to honour her legitimate right to govern lay, as the comuneros themselves asserted, at the root of Castile's problems, and created instability around a string of 'regencies,' both in Castile and of Aragon.

The comuneros saw Juana as the legitimating force for their actions. At the same time, the *Capítulos de los que ordenaban de pedir los de la Junta* repudiated the right of women to succeed to the throne in future precisely because that right, as it stood, laid Castile open to the power of foreign husbands and sons. Juana herself was unlikely to have foreseen it, nor certainly would have wished it, but her refusal to cooperate with the Junta, which had not granted her liberty as she understood it, and the emperor's consequent victory over the comuneros, dragged Spain into years of apparently endless war in the European arena, with consequent financial dislocation, unrest and near collapse. Published just a year before her death, the anonymous novel *Lazarillo de Tormes* (1554) offers a cruelly colourful vision of post-comunero Toledo and of Castile at the time of the Cortes of Toledo of 1538–1539—a Cortes about which Juana had shown much curiosity and which, as Elliott points out, destroyed "the last hopes of constitutionalism in Castile."[4] Pérez similarly observes that, at Villalar, and in its aftermath, Castile "lost part of its political elite, the most dynamic and perhaps the most enlightened."[5] The political and economic consequences have formed a part of the vigorous debate about Spanish "rise and decline" ever since.

If Castile lost the better part of itself in the mud of Villalar, the ideas on which the upheaval of the Comunidades fed, and which it promoted, were not entirely lost. Some of the Dominicans present at the great debates of 1550 on the nature and future of the peoples of the "Indias" were the intellectual descendants of the "great traitors" and "subversives" and "very bad people" who had played so important a part in the uprisings three decades before. Those who had wished to restore Juana to her people, or, failing that, had looked to the urban fabric of the kingdom, or *res publica*, as the main source of legitimacy, left their footprints in the colleges of Valladolid and Salamanca where Francisco de Vitoria, Domingo de Soto and Martín de Azpilcueta held sway, and in the developing field of international law and universal human rights. The conquest of Mexico, led by Hernán Cortés, took place in parallel to the uprisings in Castile and Aragon, and in the far flung communities of the Hispanic empire comunero ideas took root—not least, as Elliott writes, in the "conviction that the well-being of the community depended on the proper functioning of a contractual relationship between the ruler and the ruled."[6]

Ironically, not many miles from the Colegio de San Gregorio, in Valladolid, where those famous debates took place, the lawful monarch still languished in a state that she had once (and no doubt more than once) called worse than slavery. That "worse than slavery" is the last and most terrible of the stories of Juana I. Those keenest to siphon off the power she represented had placed her not in the palace-sanatorium of Maldonado's or Zurita's imaginings—still less in a royal court—but in a theatre of extraordinary cruelty and deceit, a true theatre of the absurd. The few allowed to enter found themselves in an alternative reality, in which they were obliged to participate, and in preparation for which they had to be carefully debriefed, and, as it were, decontaminated, before they entered the isolation chamber. Tier by tier, lies and deceptions were added over the years, held together by some kind of parallel logic. These elaborate processes of pretence and deception extended beyond Juana to her subjects and those who governed in her name in the distant outposts of empire. Juana's confusion (and sometimes theirs) was hardly surprising. What does surprise is the degree of sanity she managed to retain, perhaps because she channelled it into an unending struggle against the fact of her captivity.

Juana has often been portrayed as a hater of her sex.[7] This is nonsense, pure and simple. On the other hand, her hatred of the women appointed to guard her was one of the most consistent things about her. Apart from her continual demands for their replacement by "honourable" women, appropriate to her status, the only weapons with which she could pursue her campaign for liberation were targeted inwards, against her own body and soul. Especially after the end of the war of the Comunidades, and the purge of her most trusted servants, the heir and successor of the Catholic Kings put her spiritual as well as physical life at risk.

Such conduct was double-edged. Not only did she threaten to undermine the honour, reputation and even spiritual salvation of her family and its sacred pretensions, but she risked harming herself. Juana, as a prisoner, felt unable to meet the spiritual demands that her family tried to enforce upon her through the rite of penitence. That is to say, she felt unable to meet those demands with any degree of honesty. Juana was held *chusmada*. This word of hers, so often repeated, encapsulates a continuing sense of oppression, an on-going trespass against her that touched upon the whole matter of her captivity, and for that very reason could never be openly recognised or discussed. The survival of Ferrer's letter of 1511 shows that Juana felt unable to come to terms with Fernando's abandonment of her, just as she could not come to terms with her son's. All her life she struggled against the perpetrators of a systematic attempt to erase all memory of her and to liquidate her as a monarch and as a person.

And that she could not forgive.

## Notes

1. "Queen Juana I of Castile ... abdicated from the Government of the nation at Mucientes, Valladolid, in the presence of Cardinal Cisneros in his capacity as chief notary of the Kingdom."
2. Iongh (1958).
3. Suárez Fernández (2001).
4. Elliott (1990), 205.
5. Pérez (2001), 139.
6. Elliott (2006), 131.
7. The Spanish diplomat and historian, J. M. Doussinague (1944), who is among the historians of his generation to be utterly damning of Juana, attacks, *inter alia*, her "hatred of women of all social classes" (86).

## References

Doussinague, José M. 1944. *Fernando el Católico y Germana de Foix. Un matrimonio por razón de Estado*. Madrid: Espasa-Calpe.

Elliott, J.H. 1990 [reprint]. *Imperial Spain, 1469–1716*. Harmondsworth: Penguin.

———. 2006. *Empires of the Atlantic World: Britain and Spain in America, 1492–1830*. New Haven and London: Yale University Press.

Iongh, Jane de. 1958. *Mary of Hungary: Second Regent of the Netherlands*. New York: Norton.

Pérez, Joseph. 2001. *Los Comuneros*. Madrid: La Esfera de los Libros.

Suárez Fernández, Luis. 2001. *Enrique IV de Castilla. La difamación como arma política*. Barcelona: Ariel.

# Glossary

**alcaide** fortress governor
**alcalde mayor** chief magistrate
**adelantado** military governor in frontier region of Castile
**aposentador** purveyor
**asistente** official with functions similar to but not necessarily as powerful as a *corregidor*'s
**ayuda de costa** living expenses or special payments
**bandos** rival affinities or political groupings
**behetría** land in which the inhabitants have the right to choose their own lord
**besamanos** hand-kissing ritual of homage to a monarch or prince during which withdrawal of the royal hand was understood as a sign of particular favour
**camarero mayor** chief chamberlain
**capirotes** comprehensive form of headdress worn by women and covering head, shoulders and back
**cédula real** concise form of royal warrant usually bearing monarch's signature with royal secretary's counter- signature
**Chancillería** institution for the administration of justice. Originally itinerant, the *Chancillería* was subsequently based in Valladolid and judged cases north of the Tagus. A second chancery, or chancellery,



G. B. Fleming, *Juana I*, Queenship and Power,
https://doi.org/10.1007/978-3-319-74347-9

was transferred from Ciudad Real to Granada in 1505, and was responsible for the south

**ciudad de realengo** city under royal jurisdiction

**comendador mayor** knight commander of military order

**contador mayor** chief treasurer

**converso** Jew converted to Christianity

**contino** permanent servant performing a variety of duties

**corregidor** senior royal official sent to reform, judge or bring to order abuses or possible abuses in city under crown jurisdiction

**Cortes** assembly of estates or parliament with limited city representation (in Aragon: 'Corts'), dating from the latter part of the twelfth century

**Consejo Real** Royal Council, principle organ of government, established

**cuadrilla** basic unit of council militias

**grandes** high nobility (grandees)

**juramento** contractual ceremony in which monarchs and their heirs swore to uphold the rights and privileges of their subjects and in turn received their allegiance

**juros** instrument of public debt; privilege sold by the monarch to raise funds

**letrado** public administrator with legal training

**maestrazgo** mastership, or highest ranking office, of religious military order

**mercedes** awards, grants or privileges conceded by the monarch

**monteros de Espinosa** special service of guards responsible for security of royal persons

**morisco** former Muslim converted to Christianity

**órdenes militares** the three main religious military orders were those of Calatrava, Santiago and Alcántara. Their powerful resources were increasingly administered by the dual monarchy during the last years of the 'Reconquista'

**Patronato Regio/Real** royal prerogative ceded by the Holy See to the Spanish monarchs, allowing them to nominate or 'present' candidates to ecclesiastical posts on Spanish territory

**pragmática** law of a general character, in the form of a royal provision, and similar to those approved by the Cortes, but having the power to derogate laws previously approved by the Cortes. A pragmatic law had to be announced (by *pregón*) in all cities, towns and villages of Castile

**principe/principesa** title used in Castile exclusively for heir to the throne

**procurador** representative sent to Cortes by one of the eighteen cities with votes in the Cortes. The procurator was entitled to make proposals or *proposicónes* to the monarch, gathered in a *cuaderno*, in exchange for agreeing various taxes, and, at least in theory, these served as a basis for legislative action. The powers of the procurators declined during the reign of the Catholic Kings, and especially after the defeat of the Comunidades in 1521, and the *proposiciones* contained in the *cuadernos* increasingly took on the nature of complaints or *peticiones*.

**provisión real** royal provision widely issued by Royal Council in the name of the monarch but not requiring monarch's signature

**regidor** city councillor among whose duties was to elect a procurator

**renegade** a person who renounced the Christian faith, either voluntarily or by force, especially a former Christian living and professing as a Muslim

**república** the general body of residents (*vecinos*) of a city or town under crown jurisdiction

**servicio** tax in the form of a subsidy

**sobrecarta** document expedited by Royal Chancery to urge the implementation of a law

**tocas** tight-fitting under-headdress of light material

**veinticuatro** *regidor* of a municipal council in Andalucia

# Index





G. B. Fleming, *Juana I*, Queenship and Power,
https://doi.org/10.1007/978-3-319-74347-9

p14. Queens & Queenship in Medieval Europe: ed. Anne Duggan
Woodbridge, Boydell Press (2002)

Printed by Printforce, the Netherlands